# Britain
# at the Polls,
# 1979

## AEI'S AT THE POLLS STUDIES

The American Enterprise Institute
has initiated this series in order to promote
an understanding of the electoral process as it functions in
democracies around the world.  The series will include studies
of at least two national elections in each of nineteen countries
on five continents, by scholars from the United States and
abroad who are recognized as experts in their field.
More information on the titles in this series can
be found at the back of this book.

# Britain at the Polls, 1979

## A Study of the General Election

## Edited by Howard R. Penniman

American Enterprise Institute for Public Policy Research
Washington and London

**Library of Congress Cataloging in Publication Data**
Main entry under title:
Britain at the polls, 1979.

    (At the polls series) (AEI studies ; 296)
    Includes bibliographical references and index.
    1. Elections—Great Britain—Addresses, essays, lectures.
2. Great Britain. Parliament—Elections, 1979—Addresses, essays,
lectures. 3. Political parties—Great Britain—Addresses,
essays, lectures. I. Penniman, Howard Rae, 1916–
II. Series. III. Series: American Enterprise Institute for
Public Policy Research. AEI studies ; 296.
JN956.B74     324.9410857     80-27536
ISBN 0-8447-3406-3
ISBN 0-8447-3402-0 (pbk.)

AEI Studies 296

*Printed in the United States of America*

300143

# Contents

# PREFACE

*Britain at the Polls, 1979: A Study of the General Election* is another in the series of studies of elections in selected democratic countries published by the American Enterprise Institute. The first book in the series, which appeared in 1975, described the two 1974 British general elections. In the five years since then, AEI has published eighteen other election studies. A dozen more are now in progress or planned.

One of the premises of the *At the Polls* series, stated in the preface of that first British study, has been that "democratic electoral systems have enough in common that an understanding of the laws and practices of one democracy makes possible a more sophisticated analysis of the political institutions of others." This new volume on the most recent British election illustrates the validity of that assumption. Several chapters present materials of unusual interest to Americans seeking to understand their own electoral institutions and practices—either contradicting the conventional wisdom on the subject or describing British experiences that clearly parallel American ones but with somewhat different consequences. I will call attention to only two.

**The Cost of Campaigns.** Michael Pinto-Duschinsky's description of the financing of the 1979 political campaigns is at odds with the account that has so often appeared in textbooks on British government and politics. It also raises questions about the view held by many Americans that the costs of our campaigns are usually high by comparison with those of other countries.

British law rigidly regulates a candidate's constituency expenditures, but it does not recognize the national campaign—which is decisive and where most of the money is spent. British national campaign financing practices are largely unregulated, and such regulations as exist are much less demanding than American rules. Total campaign expenditures per vote in 1979, including the estimated value of government subsidies-in-kind, were considerably higher than expenditures in the 1976 American presidential contest and roughly the same as in the U.S. congressional elections the same year.

The system described in the textbooks was instituted in the 1880s and required each candidate to appoint an agent through whose hands all campaign funds would flow. The agent was required to keep careful records showing the sums received and expended, with none spent on forbidden items. Violations could result in severe penalties including the disqualification of the candidate. When these regulations were established, campaigns for the House of Commons were largely confined to the districts. Even a prime minister did not campaign outside his district until 1868. Twenty years later a party leader made occasional forays into major cities to stress campaign issues, but individual candidates and local organizations were responsible for seeing that their supporters turned out on election day. Enforcement of the new financing rules ended the flagrant corruption, including more or less open buying of votes, that had characterized some districts in earlier decades when voting was still not secret and expenditures legally unlimited.

Today local expenditures are regulated only for the three or four weeks of the official campaign. Conservative funds in most constituencies come from party members, political clubs, and businesses, while Labour depends upon central party grants, members' donations, and trade union payments. Pinto-Duschinsky estimates that companies furnish about 25 percent of a Conservative candidate's campaign's funds and trade unions put up about 50 percent of the money for the local Labour campaigns, except where a union "sponsors" a district campaign and under party rules may put up as much as 80 percent of the money. The candidate's "address" or platform—heavily cribbed from the national party manifesto—is mailed free to every voter in his district, but the cost of printing it takes up most of his limited budget. In 1979 the average candidate in a rural district could spend about £3,050 (approximately $7,290), while the urban candidate was limited to £2,725 ($5,515). The average local campaign, Pinto-Duschinsky notes, cost about one-third as much as the average local campaign in 1945.

The total costs of the 1979 campaigns, however, were the highest since the war. (If money values are held constant, the 1979 national campaign alone cost less than that of 1964.) National campaign expenditures were weighted on the side of advertising. The Conservatives' national campaign was heavily subsidized by business, and Labour depended largely on union contributions. The parties also received government subsidies-in-kind that are not available to American parties—above all, free television and radio time. All parties fielding a specified number of candidates received some free time, but the bulk of it went to the two major parties, with a smaller amount going to the Liberals. Pinto-Duschinsky has calculated that the money spent by the three largest parties, including the estimated value of public subsidies-in-kind, amounted to 49 pence ($1.05) for each Conservative vote, 47 pence ($1.01) for a Labour vote, and 61 pence ($1.31) for a Liberal vote. The subsidies-in-kind were worth roughly £8 million ($17,120,000), and the parties at both the national and constituency levels spent somewhat less than £7 million ($14,980,000). British parties, unlike those in many other countries where parties receive comparable in-kind subsidies, may not buy additional advertising time on the electronic media.

In the United States in 1976, the Democrats spent $.63 for every vote cast for Jimmy Carter while the Republicans spent $.59 for each Gerald R. Ford ballot.[1] These figures include government subsidized expenditures and money spent on behalf of the candidates by outside groups. The candidates themselves were restricted to the government subsidies. The expenditures for all members of the House of Representatives were much closer to the British figures, averaging about $1.05 per vote—though these figures include money spent during the two years beginning in January 1975, notably that used to cover the sometimes very high costs of primary election campaigns. There are no primary elections in Britain, and candidate selection (which is inexpensive in any case) is excluded from campaign estimates. Pinto-Duschinsky's figures include central party "precampaign" expenditures for one year prior to the 1979 election, but not contributions from the central office to constituency parties or expenditures for polling. Had the latter been included, Conservative expenditures would have risen by an estimated £2.5 million, or 18.3 pence $0.39 per Conservative vote.[2] The Conservatives spent a significant $2,361,000 during the precampaign period, Labour spent $674,000, and the Liberals a scanty $17,000.

Both British and American parties spend far less than parties in many other countries which are directly subsidized by their governments. German, Israeli, Swedish, and Venezuelan parties, among others, receive cash payments and free radio and television time, and in

---

[1] For U.S. campaign expenditures in 1976, see Herbert E. Alexander, *Financing Politics: Money, Elections and Political Reform* (Washington, D.C.: Congressional Quarterly Press, 1980), pp. 101 and 103.

[2] Pinto-Duschinsky gives no comparable figures for the Labour and Liberal parties, but presumably their expenditures would also have been considerably higher had the same items been included.

addition are allowed to spend any other money they can raise. The German parties in 1976 were estimated to have spent $125 million on their campaigns, excluding government television but including the government's contribution of 3.5 DM ($2.00) for each vote received by any party represented in the Bundestag. The figures are all the more striking in that total government subsidies to the parties in the years between the 1972 and 1976 elections were estimated to run as high as $200 million[3]—and the German parties have continued to raise private funds through dues and contributions from unions and corporations. The scale of government subventions is lavish, though perhaps not up to the German standard, in Sweden, Venezuela, Israel, and Italy. Total per vote expenditures—private and governmental—during the two-year campaign leading up to Venezuela's election in 1978 were much greater than those in any other country including Germany.

Both Conservative and Labour Governments in Britain have refused to subsidize the parties directly in spite of periodic pressure from public committees. Fearing that government control would follow funding, the parties have preferred to raise their own money.

**The Major Party Vote.** Together Britain's two major parties have taken a smaller share of the total in each of the past three elections than in any election since 1923. Labour, which has been hit hardest by the decline in major party support, took less than 40 percent of the vote in all three contests (though it won both 1974 elections, once with a clear majority of the seats), and its 36.9 percent of the vote in 1979 is the smallest share it has received in any election but one since 1924.

At the heart of Labour's difficulties, according to Ivor Crewe, lies a steady erosion of popular support for the party's fundamental principles. As class and party allegiance have weakened in the last twenty years, all of the parties have had to rely increasingly on the appeal of their policies to sustain their supporters' loyalty—but Labour's policies have had less and less appeal. "Since 1964," Crewe writes, "support among Labour identifiers (let alone the general public) for further nationalization, for further spending on social services, and for the amount and form of power exercised by trade unions has dramatically declined, such that each only appealed in 1979 to a one-third minority within Labour's ranks." The moderates within the party won some important battles in 1979; notably they succeeded in keeping control

---

[3] Khayyam Zev Paltiel, "The Impact of Election Expense Legislation in Canada, Western Europe and Israel," in Herbert E. Alexander, *Political Finance* (Beverly Hills: Sage Publications, 1979).

of the party's manifesto out of the hands of the left-dominated National Executive Committee. Even so, the program they put to the voters was out of line with the views of their natural constituency. "Labour lost," Crewe concludes, "through a massive hemorrhage of working-class votes. . . . It was issues, not organization or personalities, that won the election for the Conservatives."

In his chapter on the Labour party, Dick Leonard stresses the heavy approval among Labour supporters for proposals in the Conservative manifesto. "It is an open question," he writes, "how much longer those voters are prepared to stick with the party . . . unless it takes energetic steps to bring itself in line with the mass of its supporters and potential supporters." Looking to the future, Leonard says: "The postelectoral struggle for control of the party, with the majority of the Labour M.P.s and the trade union leaders fighting an increasingly rearguard action against the left-dominated National Executive Committee and assorted allies led by Tony Benn, appears a bleak enterprise indeed." Sure enough, the Labour party conference of 1980 went beyond even the 1979 conference in its divisiveness. What is more, the left gained ground, so that the party's future appears to be even bleaker than Leonard predicted.

I have chosen to pause over Labour's recent problems because they present an interesting contrast to those that faced the major American parties when minority factions gained control, first of the Republican party at the 1964 national convention, then of the Democratic party at its convention in 1972. In each case the party nominated a presidential candidate and wrote a platform that were perceived by a large majority of the American people as supporting positions out of line with their wishes.[4] Yet in both instances the losing party recovered in time to win the next presidential election.

Why does a minority drive toward the possible destruction of a major party seem to be shorter lived in the United States than in Britain, at least in the case of Labour? The answer may lie in what is often considered to be one of the major weaknesses of American parties. The very looseness of American party organization and the lack of party discipline that sometimes causes policy making to be so difficult may also be the shield that guards the party against continuing destructive leadership or struggles for party control.

Let us look briefly at the recent crises faced by the American

---

[4] For a detailed description of the differences between the attitudes of Democratic identifiers and those of the delegates at the 1972 Democratic convention who supported Senator George McGovern and who therefore played the major role in writing the Democratic platform, see Jeane J. Kirkpatrick, *The New Presidential Elite: Men and Women in National Politics* (New York: Russell Sage Foundation and the Twentieth Century Fund, 1976) pp. 281-347.

parties. The nomination of Barry Goldwater cost the Republican party the support of the independents and northern Democrats upon whom it depends for victory and sent the candidate down to the most disastrous defeat but one in the party's history. (It also opened areas in the deep South to the Republicans for the first time since Reconstruction.) Four years later the Republican candidate, Richard M. Nixon, won a narrow victory in a three-way presidential race, and in 1972 he defeated Democrat George McGovern as badly as Lyndon Johnson had beaten Goldwater. Further, he inflicted the second worst electoral college defeat suffered by any party since the uncontested election of 1820. Yet four years later, Jimmy Carter won a close election over Gerald R. Ford and returned the Democrats to the White House. During this same twelve-year period, the Democrats maintained a comfortable margin in both houses of Congress and a roughly two-to-one lead in party identification among the voters.

Several things seem obvious. First, the actions of the national convention in writing a program and choosing a presidential candidate have only marginal impact, at least in the short run, on the general welfare of the party. The presidential candidate's standing today is largely separated from the fortunes of his party. In the last twenty-eight years the Democratic party has dominated every congress but one, usually with a substantial margin of votes. During the same period, Republican presidential contenders have won five elections, Democrats three. Republican presidential candidates have garnered some 25,000,000 more popular votes than the Democratic presidential hopefuls.

It is possible that the recently reformed Democratic party rules will entrench an elite among convention delegates that will name unacceptable candidates for the White House more and more frequently. Unless and until that day comes, party disasters will probably be confined to the presidency and last no more than four or eight years. Either way, the candidate selection system used in the United States—the direct primary—ensures that the parties will remain ideologically undemanding and unable and unwilling to discipline their elected officials. The stronger, more disciplined, and more ideologically oriented parties of Britain and the rest of the democratic world may in the short run be more cohesive and more effective at passing legislation when in power, but in the long run the demand for ideological purity may be greater than the desire for party unity and may lead to the breakup of even a major party.

One French, three American, and five British scholars contribute essays to this volume. Austin Ranney describes the British political system; Anthony King sums up the economic and political developments in the years between the 1974 and 1979 elections; Dick Leonard, William S. Livingston, and Jorgen Rasmussen report on the campaigns of the Labour, Conservative, and Liberal parties; Richard Rose discusses political polling prior to the election; Michael Pinto-Duschinsky analyzes campaign financing in the three largest parties; Monica Charlot describes the role of women in British politics; and Ivor Crewe explains why the Conservatives won. In an appendix Shelley Pinto-Duschinsky supplies information on the content of the party manifestoes and the issues stressed during the campaign. Richard M. Scammon provides a breakdown of the electoral data.

HOWARD R. PENNIMAN

# 1

# British General Elections: An Introduction

*Austin Ranney*

In Great Britain there is only one kind of national election—the choice of an individual member of Parliament (M.P.). All M.P.s are elected simultaneously in a general election, and the "Government" is normally formed by the party which wins the most seats.[1] This book focuses on the general election held on Thursday, May 3, 1979—the eleventh since the surrender of Germany in 1945. The purpose of this introductory chapter is to outline the basic features of all such elections so that the particularities of 1979 may be better understood. We begin by asking, What does it matter?

## What Is at Stake in a British General Election

For the competing political parties, the stake in a British general election is nothing less than control of the entire power of British government. The reason is clear: The power to rule lies exclusively in "the Crown in Parliament," which in effect means a majority of the House of Commons. There are no American-style checks and balances to temper that power. The monarch must do whatever the prime minister advises her to do. The House of Lords has only a minimal delaying power and no veto over acts of the Commons. The courts have no power to declare an act of Parliament unconstitutional and

I am grateful to David Butler, the most distinguished student of British elections, for reading the first draft of this chapter and saving me from many errors. He is not, of course, responsible for those that remain.

[1] The British term "the Government" is roughly synonymous with the American term "the administration." It refers to the ninety-odd members of the majority party in the House of Commons and House of Lords who have been selected by the prime minister and appointed by the queen to fill the top positions (usually from three to five) in each "ministry" (executive agency). To distinguish it from "government" in the sense of the entire British governing *system*, the word is capitalized in this book.

1

thus render it null and void. Almost all of the M.P.s belonging to each party vote almost all of the time as their party's leaders direct. All the political heads of each of the ministries (executive departments) are parliamentary members of the majority party assigned by its leaders to their posts. The result of all this is that the majority party in the House has full power over what the government does and does not do during its time in power. Only under the most extraordinary circumstances does the ruling party share its power and responsibility with other parties.[2]

Thus the function of a British general election is to decide which of the competing parties shall make the government's policies and staff its top executive positions for a period of up to five years. No American election is "general" in this sense. Presidential elections come the nearest, but even they affect only a fraction of the nation's top public offices. In 1980, for example, American voters elected a president and vice-president and all 435 members of the House of Representatives, but only 34 of the 100 members of the Senate and 17 of the 50 state governors. And there is always the possibility that such an election will produce a Republican president and a Democratic congress (as in 1954–1960 and 1968–1976) or even a Democratic president and a Republican congress (as in 1946–1948). British general elections, however, are winning-party-take-all.

But aside from the relatively minor matter of which bunch of politicians holds ministerial office, do general elections really make much difference to how Britain is governed? Anthony King believes that they do. After carefully reviewing the facts relevant to the question "What do elections decide?" he concludes that, while we do not yet know enough to answer the question definitively, there is good reason to believe that governments of the left (including British Labour Governments) are readier than governments of the right (including British Conservative Governments) to use fiscal policy to combat unemployment and to narrow the distance between upper and lower income levels.[3]

---

[2] Only in the emergencies of wartime (1915-1922 and 1940-1945) and severe depression (1931-1935, 1935-1940) have multiparty coalition or "national" Governments been formed. On occasions, however, one-party Governments have remained in power with the tacit or explicit support of a third party. This was the case in 1910-1915, 1924, 1929-1931, and, most recently, in 1977-1979 when the Labour Government, though holding a minority of the seats in the House, remained in power with the support of the Liberal members. See R. M. Punnett, *British Government and Politics*, 2nd ed. (New York: W. W. Norton & Co., 1971), pp. 102-103.

[3] Anthony King, "What Do Elections Decide?" in David Butler, Howard R. Penniman, and Austin Ranney, eds., *Democracy at the Polls* (Washington, D.C.: American Enterprise Institute, forthcoming).

The 1979 general election should provide another test: the Conservative party pledged itself to a major turn away from the Labour Government's high-spending, pro-union, anti-business policies in favor of lower taxes, less regulation of business, and new measures to inhibit strikes and increase the responsibility of trade unions for their members' activities. What the Conservative Government does or fails to do in redeeming these pledges should shed additional light on the question of how much it matters who wins a general election.[4]

## The Main Features of British General Elections

**Flexible Dates and Dissolutions.** The timing of British general elections is controlled by the Parliament Act of 1911, which requires that one be held *at least* every five years. A particular parliament can by special legislation extend its term beyond five years one year at a time ("proroguing" it is called), but that has happened only in the war years of 1940–1945.

Parliament, however, may be "dissolved" and a subsequent general election held at any time prior to the expiration of the five years. The action is formally taken by the monarch, but only on the advice of the prime minister.[5] This arrangement gives the prime minister a political weapon many American presidents would like to have had: the power to initiate an election at a time that seems favorable for the governing party—for example, when wages are up and prices are down or when the Government has just successfully handled a difficult diplomatic or military problem. Sometimes, of course, prime ministers miscalculate: for example, Harold Wilson thought that his Labour Government's recovery in popularity in the winter of 1969–1970 would continue into the summer, so he called an election for June 18, 1970—and unexpectedly lost his majority to the Conserva-

---

[4] Each general election beginning with that of 1945 has been described and analyzed in great detail in a book sponsored by Nuffield College, Oxford University. Beginning with the book on the election of 1951, the sole or senior author has been David Butler, a fellow of Nuffield and an adjunct scholar of the American Enterprise Institute. This chapter leans heavily on the "Nuffield series," and any reader who wishes to pursue in depth the matters it considers should read all eleven Nuffield volumes. For my evaluation of the books' major virtues and minor deficiencies, see "Thirty Years of 'Psephology,'" *British Journal of Political Science*, vol. 6 (1976), pp. 217-230. For a useful short book on the conduct of British general elections, see R. L. Leonard, *Elections in Britain* (New York: Van Nostrand, Reinhold, 1968).

[5] Evidently the decision to ask the monarch for a dissolution and new election is one of the relatively few made by the prime minister alone rather than by the collective judgment of the cabinet. The prime minister usually consults the other party leaders, but the final decision is his or hers alone: cf. John P. Mackintosh, *The British Cabinet*, 2nd ed. (New York: Humanities Press, 1970).

## TABLE 1–1
### DURATION OF BRITISH PARLIAMENTS, 1945–1979

| Election Date | Duration of Subsequent Parliament |
|---|---|
| July 5, 1945 | 4 years, 7 months |
| February 23, 1950 | 1 year,  8 months |
| October 25, 1951 | 3 years, 7 months |
| May 26, 1955 | 4 years, 4 months |
| October 8, 1959 | 5 years, 0 months |
| October 15, 1964 | 1 year,  5 months |
| March 31, 1966 | 4 years, 3 months |
| June 18, 1970 | 3 years, 8 months |
| February 28, 1974 | 0 years, 7 months |
| October 10, 1974 | 4 years, 7 months |
| May 3, 1979 | |

Mean duration:  3 years, 3 months
Median duration:  4 years, 0 months

NOTE: Only one parliament since World War II has lasted the entire statutory maximum of five years—that governed by a Conservative majority after the election of October 8, 1959. The median duration (probably more meaningful than the mean in this context) has been four years.

SOURCE: David Butler and Anne Sloman, *British Political Facts 1900-1979*, 5th ed. (London: Macmillan), pp. 208-210.

tives. On the other hand, Wilson for Labour in 1966 and Anthony Eden for the Conservatives in 1955 calculated correctly the ebb and flow of the political tides and called elections that returned their Governments to power with increased majorities. The duration of each of the parliaments elected since the defeat of Germany in World War II is shown in table 1–1.[6]

In 1979 the sequence of events leading to the dissolution was as follows. On March 28 a vote was held in the House on a resolution "That this House has no confidence in Her Majesty's Government"; it carried, by 311 votes to 310. The next day the prime minister, James Callaghan, went to Queen Elizabeth II, and, at his request, she ordered that Parliament be dissolved on April 13 and that a general election be held on May 3. Thus there were two weeks between the announcement of the dissolution and the dissolution itself, and three more weeks between the dissolution and the election.

---

[6] In the same time period well over 300 *by-elections* were held. These are special elections held to fill vacancies in particular constituencies created by the death, resignation, or elevation to the House of Lords of their members of Parliament.

## TABLE 1–2

### BRITISH PARLIAMENTARY CONSTITUENCIES, BY AREA

| Area | Population (est. 1977) | Number of Constituencies | Average Size of Constituencies |
|------|------------------------|--------------------------|-------------------------------|
| England | 46,351,300 | 516 | 89,830 |
| Scotland | 5,195,600 | 71 | 73,180 |
| Wales | 2,768,200 | 36 | 76,890 |
| Northern Ireland | 1,537,300 | 12 | 128,100 |
| United Kingdom | 55,852,400 | 635 | 87,960 |

SOURCE: The regional population estimates are taken from *The Europa Year Book 1979* (London: Europa Publications, 1979), p. 1332; the allocation of constituencies among the four areas is taken from Howard R. Penniman, ed., *Britain at the Polls: The Parliamentary Elections of 1974* (Washington, D.C.: American Enterprise Institute, 1975), pp. 246-247.

**The Constituencies.** At the time of the 1979 general election Great Britain was divided into 635 constituencies, each of which elected one member of the House of Commons. Unlike the dreary Americans, who label their congressional districts with numbers, the British give their constituencies geographical names, some of which sound echoes for lovers of English literature (Stratford-on-Avon, The Wrekin, St. Ives), architecture (Salisbury, Wells, Winchester), and even food (Caerphilly). The number and average population of the constituencies for each of the nation's four main areas are shown in table 1–2.

As table 1–2 shows, British parliamentary constituencies are much smaller than their American counterparts: they average just under 90,000 in population compared with an average of 480,000 for U.S. congressional districts. The table also shows that Scotland and Wales have considerably more seats than their populations warrant, while England and Northern Ireland are correspondingly underrepresented.

What Americans call "reapportionment" and the British call "redistribution of seats" is conducted quite differently in the two countries.[7] In Britain both the allocation of parliamentary constituencies and the specification of their boundaries are formally promulgated by *orders in council* (the rough equivalent of what Americans call

---

[7] The British term "redistribution" includes two elements distinguished in American usage: "reapportionment," meaning redetermining the number of seats allocated to England, Wales, Scotland, and Northern Ireland; and "redistricting," meaning redrawing the boundary lines of constituencies wherever required. In practice, only the number of seats allocated to England has been altered in recent redistributions.

"executive orders") subject to revision by Parliament. On a few occasions, most recently in 1948, Parliament has chosen to amend or suspend the orders, but for the most part it accepts them. Those orders, in turn, embody the recommendations made by special *boundary commissions*. There are four such commissions, one for each of the nation's four major areas. Each commission is chaired by the Speaker of the House of Commons, and in redrawing the boundaries none are bound by any court-imposed rigid rule of "one person, one vote." A rough equality in the constituencies' populations is, to be sure, one of their goals, but there are others as well—for example, having the boundaries coincide with the boundaries of local governments, and special representation for Scotland and Wales to compensate for their lack of their own regional parliaments (Northern Ireland has a regional parliament, although it has been suspended since 1974, and its existence is said to justify the area's underrepresentation in the Westminister Parliament).[8]

The 1979 general election was structured by a redistribution developed by the boundary commissions between 1965 and 1969, set aside by the Labour Government in 1969, finally adopted by the Conservative Government in 1970, and first used for the election of February 1974. In that redistribution five new seats were added, the boundaries of 429 constituencies were changed, and only 201 were left unchanged.[9] For reasons already mentioned, the new redistribution still left wide variations in the constituencies' electorates: in 1979 the largest were Bromsgrove and Redditch (104,375) and Buckingham (103,511), while the smallest was Glasgow Central (19,826).[10] The next redistribution is scheduled for completion in 1982.

The U.S. Supreme Court would certainly not allow so great a disparity in congressional districts, but hardly any British commentators feel that a few disparities like these constitute a grave threat to the democratic character of their electoral system.

**The Electorate and the Register.** The British franchise is one of the most generous in the world. Not only are all British citizens ("subjects" is their ancient term) who are eighteen or older on election day allowed to vote, but so also are citizens of other British Common-

---

[8] See J. T. Craig, "Parliament and the Boundary Commissions," *Public Law* (1959), pp. 23-45; and Vivian Vale, "*Reynolds* v. *Sims* Abroad: A Briton Compares Apportionment Criteria," *Western Political Quarterly*, vol. 22 (March 1969), pp. 85-93.

[9] David Butler and Dennis Kavanagh, *The British General Election of February 1974* (London: Macmillan, 1974), p. 206, fn. 12.

[10] *Guardian*, May 5, 1979, pp. 7-8.

wealth nations resident in Britain at the time of the election—*and* citizens of Eire, which is most emphatically *not* a member of the Commonwealth. The only classes excluded from voting are convicted felons, certified lunatics—and members of the House of Lords.

In Great Britain, as in almost every other democratic country except the United States, the goal of the registration system is to include on the register all legally qualified persons in the nation without regard to whether they themselves take any initiative to become registered. In each constituency the electoral register is compiled by a registrations officer appointed by and responsible to the Home Office. Every October the local registration officer mails to every household in his constituency a registration form asking the head of the household to list the name of every legally eligible voter in the household. If the registration officer is not satisfied that the information provided by the returned forms is accurate and complete, he can improve it by having his representatives check door-to-door.

The register is published by February 15, and it governs the conduct of any general election or by-election that may be held until the new register is published a year later. The registers produced by this process are never absolutely perfect. Some studies have estimated that toward the end of each year the register probably contains at least a 4 percent error—that is, it includes names that should not be included and omits names that should be included.[11] But by American standards the British register is so nearly perfect that the distinction between "voting-age population" and "registered voters," which is so important in calculating turnout in American elections,[12] is all but meaningless in Great Britain.

**Turnout.** The proportions of persons on the electoral registers who have actually voted in general elections since World War II are shown in table 1–3. Since the war turnouts in Britain have ranged from a high of 84.0 percent in 1950 to a low of 72.0 percent in 1970, with an average of 77.0 percent. By contrast, the proportions of the voting-age population voting in American presidential elections from 1948 to 1976 ranged from a high of 62.8 percent in 1960 to a low of 51.1 percent in 1948, with an average of 58.4 percent.[13] Much of the discrepancy between the two countries results from their two systems of

---

[11] David Butler and Anthony King, *The British General Election of 1964* (London: Macmillan, 1965), p. 221.

[12] Cf. Austin Ranney, *Participation in American Presidential Nominations, 1976* (Washington, D.C.: American Enterprise Institute, 1977).

[13] *Statistical Abstract of the United States 1977* (Washington, D.C.: Bureau of the Census, 1977), table 813, p. 508.

## TABLE 1–3
### Turnout in British General Elections, 1945–1979

| Election Year | Percentage of Persons on Electoral Register Casting Ballots |
| --- | --- |
| 1945 | 72.7 |
| 1950 | 84.0 |
| 1951 | 82.5 |
| 1955 | 76.7 |
| 1959 | 78.8 |
| 1964 | 77.1 |
| 1966 | 75.8 |
| 1970 | 72.0 |
| February 1974 | 78.7 |
| October 1974 | 72.8 |
| 1979 | 76.0 |

Source: The figures for 1945-October 1974 are taken from David Butler and Anne Sloman, eds., *British Political Facts 1900-1975*, 4th ed. (London: Macmillan, 1975), pp. 184-186. The figure for 1979 is taken from the *Guardian*, May 5, 1979, p. 1.

voter registration, but neither country has outstandingly high turnouts. A recent study by Ivor Crewe finds that Great Britain ranks fourteenth and the United States twentieth in average voting turnout among twenty democratic countries.[14]

**The Contending Parties: Britain's Two-Plus Party System.** Many American elections, especially for the presidency, are much more contests between candidates than they are contests between parties. In Great Britain, by sharp contrast, a general election is mainly a contest among the national political parties, with the local candidates and even the national party leaders playing a much less significant role. As we shall see, in the great majority of cases each party's candidate in each constituency closely follows his national party's manifesto (platform) in his local speeches and literature. And on those rare occasions when the candidates deviate from their party's national line their vote still rises or declines at about the same rate as the votes of their nondeviating fellow partisans.[15] There is reason to believe that the parties' national leaders have become somewhat more prominent in recent

[14] Ivor Crewe, "Electoral Participation," in Butler, Penniman, and Ranney, *Democracy at the Polls.*

[15] Cf. the analysis by Michael Steed in David Butler and Michael Pinto-Duschinsky, *The British General Election of 1970* (London: Macmillan, 1971), pp. 405, 408.

elections and that there has been a modest increase in the number of voters who vote Labour more because they like Jim Callaghan or Harold Wilson than because they prefer the party; much the same is true of Margaret Thatcher and the Conservative party.[16] But the important point is that most British voters vote for a particular local candidate because they want to put a particular national party in power, not because they prefer one local candidate's personality or record or appearance over those of other local candidates. Accordingly, the following brief sketches of the contending parties may be useful for understanding what British electoral politics is about.[17]

*The Labour party.* The Labour party was founded in 1900 as a coalition between the traditional union movement and socialist intellectuals. It remained a minor party until the early 1920s, when it replaced the Liberals as the main opposition to the Conservatives. Labour formed its first Government in 1924, and the eleven general elections since 1945 have produced six Labour Governments (in 1945, 1950, 1964, 1966, February 1974, and October 1974) and five Conservative Governments (in 1951, 1955, 1959, 1970, and 1979).

In both organization and ideology the Labour party today reflects its origins. Its organization outside Parliament is a federation of trade unions and individual dues-paying members. Most of the major trade unions are directly affiliated with the party and provide most of its money; in the annual party conferences each union commands a number of votes equal to the total of its members who allow part of their union dues to be given to the party. The other part of the extraparliamentary party consists of persons who directly and individually join the party, pay its dues, and are free to participate in the organizations the party maintains in the parliamentary constituencies. The main functions of these *constituency Labour parties* are to select the party's parliamentary candidates, raise money, conduct local campaign activities, and debate policy questions. The party's extraparliamentary organization is headed by a National Executive Committee, which supervises the work of the substantial paid staff of organizers and researchers at the party headquarters in London.

Ideologically the party has perennially been split between its "socialist ideologues" and its "revisionist pragmatists." The former,

---

[16] Cf. David Butler and Donald Stokes, *Political Change in Britain,* 2nd college ed. (New York; St. Martin's Press, 1976), chap. 16.

[17] The leading works on the organization of British political parties include: Robert T. McKenzie, *British Political Parties,* 2nd ed. (London: Heinemann, 1964); S. H. Beer, *Modern British Politics* (London: Faber, 1965); and S. E. Finer, *The Changing British Party System* (Washington, D.C.: American Enterprise Institute, 1980).

now led by Anthony Wedgwood Benn, urge the party to press forward to achieve the goal, set forth in its 1918 constitution, of "the common ownership of the means of production, distribution, and exchange." The "revisionists" believe that most Britons do not believe in all-out socialism and will not vote for a party pledged to it; hence, they argue, the party should commit itself to the goal of providing every citizen with the basic conditions of the good life and should be pragmatic about the best means to achieve that goal. In the past few years their main leaders have been former Prime Minister James Callaghan and most of the members of the present "shadow cabinet." The bulk of the parliamentary Labour party are of this persuasion.

*The Conservative party.* Britain's other major party is in a sense the lineal descendant of the Tory "party" of the seventeenth and eighteenth centuries, but the modern party dates from the middle of the nineteenth century, when it emerged under the leadership of Benjamin Disraeli. Today the Conservative party outside Parliament consists entirely of dues-paying individual members. They are organized into Conservative and Unionist associations in each of the nation's parliamentary constituencies. The local associations are federated in the National Union of Conservative and Unionist Associations. The National Union conducts an annual national conference of representatives from the constituency associations, and also supervises an extensive national "central office" staff of organizers and researchers.

The Conservative party, more than its Labour opponent, is a "catchall" party in the sense that it professes no dominant, clear, and comprehensive political ideology and includes persons of several different ideologies and even different ideas about how to deal with the problems of the day. Like most catchall parties, however, the Conservatives have a programmatic center of gravity. In general, and in contrast to the Labour party, they emphasize equality of opportunity over equality of condition and the private sector over the public sector in Britain's mixed economy. The party's current leader, Prime Minister Margaret Thatcher, is identified with the party's faction that believes in removing as many shackles as possible from the operation of a free market economy.

*The Liberal party.* The Liberals were one of Britain's two major parties from the mid-nineteenth century to the early 1920s, when they were displaced by the Labour party. In general elections since World War II the party's share of the popular vote has ranged from 2.6 percent (1951) to 19.3 percent (February 1974), and has averaged 9.6 percent. Its share of the seats, however, has never exceeded 2.2 percent and has averaged 1.4 percent. It is therefore not surprising that the top priority in the Liberals' program goes to the adoption of some form of proportional representation, preferably the single-transferable-vote system now used by Eire. The party's organization is similar to that of the Conservatives. The members are all dues-paying individuals. They are formed into organizations in about two-thirds of the nation's constituencies, and the constituency organizations are federated in a national organization with a small staff and an annual conference.

Ideologically, the Liberals try to position themselves between what they regard as the excessively socialist Labour party and the excessively capitalist Conservative party. As a third alternative they propose cooperation between labor and management through profit sharing, co-ownership, and participation by workers in management. They deplore the excessive power of both the big unions and the big corporations. And they advocate devolution (that is, a greater degree of self-government) for Scotland and Wales. But so far, at least, they have not found the appeal that would return them to the major-party status they held prior to the 1920s.

*The nationalist parties.* The nationalist movements in Scotland and Wales have produced political parties (the Scottish Nationalist party and Plaid Cymru respectively) urging greater home rule for their regions. The Scottish Nationalists rose rapidly—from about 10 percent of the vote in Scotland (but no seats) in the 1960s to a peak of 30.7 percent of the votes and eleven seats (15 percent of the Scottish seats) in October 1974. In 1979, however, they declined to under 20 percent of the votes and lost nine of their eleven seats. Plaid Cymru has neither risen so high nor fallen so low: since February 1974 it has won just over 10 percent of the votes in Wales and in 1979 elected two M.P.s.

The politics of Northern Ireland are so complicated and so different from those in the rest of the United Kingdom that most analysts of British politics bypass them as much as possible. I will note here only that in 1979 candidates in Ulster were elected under six different party labels: Official Unionist (five seats), Democratic Unionist (three), Social Democratic and Labour (one), Ulster Unionist (one), United Ulster Unionist (one), and Independent (one). The party labels and divisions in Northern Ireland continue to have little to do with the labels and divisions in the rest of the United Kingdom, so we shall say no more about them.[18]

---

[18] A useful guide through the complexities of Northern Irish politics is Richard Rose, *Northern Ireland: Time of Choice* (Washington, D.C.: American Enterprise Institute, 1976).

*The National Front.* Some commentators say that the National Front has become Britain's fourth national party, although it is still far behind the Liberals. It was founded in 1967 by the amalgamation of several far-right organizations. Although there have been several internal schisms since, the National Front has consistently stood for the following main policies: ending all immigration of blacks and Asians; compulsory repatriation of all non-whites; preference for whites in jobs and housing; racial segregation in the schools; British withdrawal from the EEC and NATO; and step-by-step dismantling of the welfare state.

In a fashion similar to the nationalist movements and some elements in the Labour party, the National Front describes itself as a broad social movement seeking fundamental change, and electoral politics is only one of the tactics it uses. The movement also maintains a uniformed quasi-military organization, the Honour Guard, and publishes the propaganda tabloid *National Front News* and the magazine *Spearhead.*

The National Front has been increasingly active in electoral politics. In the 1970 general election they put up a total of ten parliamentary candidates, who won an average of 3.6 percent of the votes. In both 1974 elections they fielded more than fifty candidates, the minimum needed to qualify for free TV time. And in 1979 they put up 303 candidates, the largest total ever fielded by a fourth party. Their candidates received an average of only 1.4 percent of the votes, and it was clear that their voting support was concentrated mainly in the most depressed working-class areas of Northeast London. By most criteria, then, the National Front has become Britain's fourth national party, but its voting support is so small and so localized that it seems likely to remain a negligible factor in national elections in the 1980s.[19]

**Nomination and Candidate Selection.** Like most other Western democracies except the United States, Great Britain makes a distinction between *nomination* and *candidate selection.* Nomination is the legal process by which election authorities certify a person as a qualified candidate for an elective public office and print his or her name on the ballot. Candidate selection is the extralegal process by which a political party decides which of the persons legally eligible to hold the office will be designated on the ballot and in campaign communications as its recommended and supported candidate. In this section we shall briefly review each process.

---

[19] A useful short description of the National Front's origins, doctrines, and tactics is Martin Walker, "The National Front," in H. M. Drucker, ed., *Multi-Party Britain* (London: Macmillan, 1979), pp. 183-203.

*Eligibility.* Any British subject resident in the United Kingdom who will be at least twenty-one years of age when the new parliament convenes and who is not otherwise disqualified[20] is legally eligible to "stand" for Parliament.[21] There is no requirement that an M.P. reside in the constituency he represents and therefore none that a candidate be a local resident. We shall note some consequences of this situation in a moment.

*The nomination process.* Any eligible person may become a parliamentary candidate by filing with the constituency's *returning officer* a *nomination paper*, which states his full name, residential address, and occupation. The paper must bear the signatures of ten qualified voters registered in the constituency—one proposer, one seconder, and eight assenters. The candidate must also deposit with the returning officer the sum of £150. If he wins more than one-eighth of the votes cast in the election, the deposit is returned to him soon after the result is declared. If he wins one-eighth or less, the deposit is forfeited to the Treasury.[22]

The purpose of the deposit is, of course, to discourage frivolous candidacies, but the device is not entirely successful. In each general election from 20 to 25 percent of the candidates lose their deposits, and while some of the losses no doubt result from inflated expectations of support, many simply manifest the feeling of the candidates who forfeit their deposits that the experience of standing for Parliament, whether to advertise themselves or to advance a noble but unpopular cause, is well worth the modest cost (around $335).

*The candidate selection process.* The process by which British parliamentary candidates are selected is an important and much studied matter we can only touch on here.[23] The essentials of the process in both major parties are these: (1) Candidate selection procedures are governed entirely by party rules; no public laws apply to them. (2) The national party organizations maintain national lists of

---

[20] In 1979 as in 1974, the types of persons legally disqualified included certified lunatics, deaf-mutes, English and Scottish peers, members of the armed forces, and ordained clergymen of the Church of England, Church of Ireland, Church of Scotland, and Roman Catholic Church.

[21] Some Americans are bemused by the fact that in British terminology candidates "stand" for office, whereas in America they "run" for office. I shall resist the temptation to say whether this difference is more than merely verbal.

[22] For details of the legal nominating procedures, see A. N. Schofield, *Parliamentary Elections*, 2nd ed. (London: Shaw & Sons, 1955), pp. 78-142.

[23] The leading studies include: Peter Paterson, *The Selectorate* (London: MacGibbon & Kee, 1967); Austin Ranney, *Pathways to Parliament* (Madison: University of Wisconsin Press, 1965); and Michael Rush, *The Selection of Parliamentary Candidates* (London: Thomas Nelson and Sons, 1969).

potential candidates who have been screened and are recommended by them. (3) The candidate in each constituency is selected, almost always in secret, by the party's local organization of dues-paying members, sometimes by a mass meeting or postal vote of all the local members but usually by a committee elected by the members. (4) The local selectors choose among aspirants who are not on the nationally recommended lists as well as some who are. (5) The person selected by the local organization must be approved by a national party agency before he or she can be announced and designated on the ballot as the party's official candidate. This central veto power is rarely used by the Labour party and almost never by the Conservatives, but its continuing presence as a "gun behind the door" is a significant deterrent against the local parties' selecting candidates wholly unacceptable to the national organization and leaders.

*The candidates selected.* What kinds of persons win parliamentary candidacies in these local competitions? There are several parts to the answer.

(1) There has long been a powerful presumption in both parties that an incumbent M.P. who wishes to stand again will be reselected, usually without question or fuss. On a few occasions, detailed in the studies cited above, some local parties have "sacked" their M.P.s, usually for personal deficiencies (such as being too old, failing to participate in local party affairs, being involved in personal scandals) rather than political deviations. This presumption may become much weaker in the Labour party in the 1980s as the result of a new rule, adopted in 1979, that no sitting Labour M.P. may be automatically reselected and that before each election each M.P. must win his candidacy anew in competition with other aspirants. The rule was successfully pressed by the party's left wing, and its purpose was said to be that of facilitating the elimination of right-wing Labour M.P.s by their left-wing local parties. It remains to be seen whether that will be its effect.

(2) Where no incumbent is involved, the candidacies in the most desirable constituencies—those the party is most likely to win—are mostly captured by candidates who have had previous electoral experience. Some are former M.P.s trying to win their way back to Westminster; some are persons who have fought valiant, though losing, earlier fights in the constituency; and some are persons who have fought good fights in other, less desirable constituencies and are moving on to brighter prospects.

(3) Despite the Conservatives' upper-class image and Labour's working-class image, both parties give most of their best candidacies

14

to persons with university educations. In the election of February 1974, for example, 73 percent of the Conservative nonincumbent winning candidates had attended a university, compared with 55 percent of their Labour counterparts. Nevertheless, this educational gap was narrower than it had ever been, and should narrow even further in the years ahead.

(4) The candidates of both parties are disproportionately drawn from the nation's better-paid and more prestigious occupations. Over 60 percent of the general population hold wage-earning manual labor positions, but under 20 percent of the Labour candidates and under 5 percent of the Conservative candidates hold such positions. The occupations most favored by the Conservatives include lawyers (both barristers and solicitors), business executives, white-collar workers, and journalists.

Beyond these demographic characteristics, however, most candidates in both parties possess in good measure the personal traits highly valued by the local selectors in both parties. They are good public speakers, they mix well with the local party activists and ordinary voters, and in appearance and demeanor they are seen as well qualified to help the party put its best foot forward, both locally and nationally.

*Interconstituency movement of candidates.* Great Britain has no *legal* requirement whatever that an M.P. reside in the constituency he represents. Any otherwise qualified aspirant is legally free to stand in any constituency he wishes without regard to where he resides or earns his living.[24]

In many cases, of course, what the law allows and what the local candidate selectors demand are quite different. Some local organizations in both parties insist on local candidates over outsiders ("carpet-baggers" they are sometimes called) because they believe a local person will "nurse" the constituency more diligently and participate more actively in local party affairs. Thus about one-quarter of all Conservative nonincumbent candidates and over 40 percent of their Labour counterparts have some kind of personal connection with the constituencies in which they are selected.[25]

---

[24] This, of course, is in sharp contrast to the American constitutional requirement that a member of the U.S. House of Representatives be "an Inhabitant of that State in which he shall be chosen" (Article I, Section 1) and the extralegal but powerful rule that he must also live in the *district* he represents.

[25] Penniman, ed., *Britain at the Polls, 1974*, table 2-5, p. 53. "Personal connections" include residing in the constituency, working there, holding a local government office there, and being a member of a locally prominent family.

To American eyes, however, the striking facts are that well over half of the nonincumbent candidates do *not* have any local connections and that the absence of a local residence rule makes possible a movement of candidates from one constituency to another in successive elections that is almost unknown in the United States. Not least of its consequences is the fact that it makes it possible for a prominent party leader who loses her seat in a general election to be selected as the party's candidate in another, safer seat and win her way back to Westminster at the next election. The use of the feminine pronoun is deliberate here: in the 1979 election Labour's secretary of state for education, Shirley Williams, lost her seat at Hertford and Stevenage. Had she been an American congresswoman she would have had little option but to retire or to try again in the same district. But in Britain she could try again in the same constituency or she could become a candidate in another, safer Labour constituency. As one of the party's most popular leaders, she had very good chances of winning a candidacy elsewhere. It was not clear that she wanted to take this pathway back to Parliament, but the way was open for her.

A study of the later political careers of the losing candidates in the general elections of 1950, 1951, and 1955 uncovered some interesting patterns.[26] In those elections one Conservative and eleven Labour *frontbenchers* lost their seats. Ten of the twelve were subsequently selected as candidates in other, safer constituencies and were reelected. The *backbenchers* fared much worse. Of the ten defeated Conservative M.P.s and the seventy-five defeated Labour M.P.s, well over half were not subsequently selected in any constituency, and only seven were later reelected from constituencies other than those they had formerly held. Nevertheless this was seven more than could have won their way back in this manner in the United States.

Most first-time candidates lose for the simple reason that they are selected in seats where their party has no chance of winning. What happens to them after that? About half do not become candidates a second time, some because they do not seek second candidacies, and some because they seek but do not find. About one-fifth are reselected in the same constituencies, and about one-quarter are selected in other, more winnable constituencies.

For many M.P.s, then, the road to Parliament is long and bumpy. It is not uncommon for an ambitious young politician to secure his first candidacy in a constituency that is hopelessly unwinnable, fight

---

[26] This discussion of the movement of parliamentary candidates is drawn from Austin Ranney, "Inter-Constituency Movement of British Parliamentary Candidates, 1951-1959," *American Political Science Review*, vol. 58 (March 1964), pp. 36-45.

a good though losing fight, attract favorable notice from the selectors in other, more winnable constituencies, secure a candidacy in one of them, and finally win a seat in the second—or third or fourth—constituency in which he stands.

**The Campaigns.** We have already noted that Britain's flexible election dates mean that a general election may be held at any time and that the major parties keep up a *permanent campaign* especially by their speeches and actions in Parliament, so as to be in good combat condition when an election is formally called. Strictly speaking, however, British general election campaigns begin on the day the dissolution is announced and end on the eve of polling day—a period that averages from three to five weeks' duration.

Michael Pinto-Duschinsky makes a point we would do well to bear in mind: each general election has two quite distinct campaigns. One is official and local—official in the sense that almost all of the legal regulations apply to it, and local in that it takes place entirely in each of the 635 constituencies. The other is unofficial and national—unofficial in that almost no laws and regulations apply to it, and national in that it is directed entirely by national party leaders and conducted mainly through the national mass communications media. And of the two the national campaign is by far the more important.[27]

*The national campaign.* The national campaign of each major party is directed by an ad hoc combination of the permanent party headquarters staff and special people brought in for the election, all under the direction of the party leader. They make the same strategic and tactical decisions that all large-scale campaign organizations must make, although in Britain they are shaped to a considerable degree by decisions made in the preceding permanent campaign. Aside from the great decisions of strategy, appearances by the leader and the other frontbenchers have to be scheduled, the party's television broadcasts have to be planned, the party's polls have to be taken and analyzed, the opposition's ploys have to be countered, the leader's daily press conferences have to be arranged, and so on.

The first major event in each party's national campaign is the publication of its manifesto. This is a document of perhaps six or seven thousand words, roughly equivalent in purpose if not in length to an American party's national platform. The governing party's manifesto defends the party's record, outlines its future policies, and reminds the voters of the opposition party's past failures. The oppo-

---

[27] Michael Pinto-Duschinsky, "The Conservative Campaign: New Techniques versus Old," in Penniman, ed., *Britain at the Polls, 1974,* p. 87.

sition party's manifesto attacks the Government's failures, outlines the different policies it would introduce, and reminds the voters of its past successes in government. Unlike American platforms, British manifestoes are drawn up, at least in broad outline, a year or more in advance of the election, and a new preface is added at the last moment to fit the circumstances in which the election is held. They are usually drawn up by special committees of senior party leaders and organizers, and they are given titles dramatizing their main themes: for example, "Firm Action for a Fair Britain," "A Better Tomorrow," "Now Britain's Strong—Let's Make Her Great to Live In," and "Let Us Work Together—Labour's Way Out of the Crisis."[28] The winning party usually regards the proposals and promises in its manifesto as obligations it is bound to meet when it takes power—certainly far more than the American winning party's presidential and congressional candidates regard the planks in their party's platform as binding on them. Thus, while British party manifestoes are not read avidly by every British voter, they certainly deserve—and receive—considerably more attention than American platforms.

Otherwise a British party's national campaign consists of various activities by its leading members of Parliament, especially its leader. They include daily press conferences in London, major speeches at meetings in various parts of the country, appearances on the party's broadcasts, *walkabouts* by leaders aimed at television newscasts, and the like. Taken all in all, British national campaigns are a good deal shorter than American presidential campaigns, but while they last they are every bit as intense and they certainly overshadow the campaigns in the constituencies.

*The 634 local campaigns.* In every general election there is a campaign in each of the 635 constituencies except one, the one whose M.P. is the Speaker of the House of Commons. The British have a strong conviction that the Speaker, once elected by the House from among its members, should be politically strictly neutral. In keeping with that conviction, there has been a convention, usually but not always honored since the nineteenth century, that the Speaker should be unopposed for reelection in his constituency. Three aspects of the campaigns in the other 634 constituencies deserve special attention. The first is each local parliamentary candidate's *election address.* This is a pamphlet he prepares (often with help from national headquarters) setting forth his biographical statement and his position on the leading issues (almost always a paraphrase of the positions taken in the

---

[28] For the texts of the Conservative and Labour manifestoes in the 1959 election, see David Butler and Richard Rose, *The British General Election of 1959* (London: Macmillan, 1960), pp. 256-279.

national manifesto). He has it printed and stuffed into envelopes, which the Post Office is obligated to deliver free to all the persons on the electoral register in his constituency. This activity alone consumes about half of the expenditures the law allows him, and about half of British voters say that they have read the election addresses of one or more candidates in their constituency.[29]

Canvassing is the principal activity of the local party organizations and their candidates. It consists of going from door to door and having brief doorstep interviews with the inhabitants of each dwelling, not to make converts but to identify potential supporters. Ideally the canvass results in a complete and accurate list of all the voters favorable to the candidate, and on polling day local party *tellers* at the polls check the names as they come to vote. By mid-afternoon the local party sends representatives—in that memorable British phrase—to "knock up" the persons on the list who have not voted and urge them to vote and, if need be, provide transportation to the polling station. Public opinion polls show that around 40 percent of the voters report having been canvassed by a party. While there is some doubt about both the extent and the efficacy of canvassing, it remains the main local campaign activity, and the more thorough the canvass the better the local party organization's reputation for doing its job.

Local parties also hold some open meetings in churches and town halls at which their candidates make speeches, answer questions, and exchange insults and witticisms with the local hecklers. Attendance at these meetings has never been large, and in recent years—as more and more voters take their politics from television rather than from meetings—attendance has declined to the point where anything over fifty is considered quite a good turnout. More and more candidates rely mainly on walkabouts, in which they stroll through marketplaces and town centers shaking hands and passing out party literature. Most analysts believe, however, that these local activities make little difference in the local outcomes. Those outcomes, they believe, are determined by mainly national forces, and whatever impact campaigning has on the voters is almost entirely the result of the national campaigns.

**Campaign Finance, Regulated and Unregulated.** In Great Britain the laws regulating campaign finance apply only to the official campaigns in the constituencies, and the extralegal national campaigns have no comparable regulations. Each local candidate is restricted by law to a maximum expenditure of £1,750 plus 2 pence for every voter in

---

[29] For a detailed analysis of election addresses in one British general election, see Butler and Pinto-Duschinsky, *The British General Election of 1970*, pp. 310-311, 437-442.

county (rural) constituencies and 1½ pence for every voter in borough (urban) constituencies. This amounts to about £3,050 in the average rural constituency and £2,725 in the average urban constituency. These limits are very low by American standards, yet few candidates in fact spend as much as the law allows: in February 1974 the average candidate spent only £951, or about 59 percent of the legal maximum.[30]

The law also requires each candidate to designate someone to serve as his *agent*. The person so designated becomes legally responsible for seeing to it that the candidate complies with all aspects of the campaign finance laws, including the expenditure limits and the reporting of all contributions and expenditures. The agent usually also serves as the local campaign manager, although this is not part of his legal duties. Each national party organization maintains some full-time salaried agents to serve selected constituency parties, especially those in the marginal seats, and some local party organizations support their own full-time agents. The Conservatives have traditionally had many more full-time agents than the Labour party—in February 1974 they had a total of 363 to Labour's 135—but both parties in the 1970s had fewer agents than in the early 1960s.[31] This is at once a reflection and a cause of the increasing degree to which the national campaign overshadows local campaigns.

As we have already noted, there are no legal limits on contributions to or expenditures by the national campaigns. Even so, those expenditures are, by American standards, very modest. In February 1974, for example, the estimated total national expenditures were £290,000 ($644,000) by the Conservatives, £97,000 ($215,000) by the Liberals, and only £35,000 ($78,000) by Labour.[32] The modesty of these outlays results from several factors: the small constituencies, the short campaign, the large supply of unpaid volunteers, and above all, the fact that the parties cannot spend money on advertising by television and radio, as we shall see.

**The Media.** In Great Britain as in all other modern democratic countries, election campaigns are increasingly dominated by the mass communications media, especially television.[33] Television set-owner-

---

[30] Butler and Kavanagh, *The British General Election of February 1974*, pp. 240-242.

[31] Ibid., pp. 220-222. In 1979 the Conservatives had 346 and Labour had 70 full-time agents.

[32] Ibid., p. 113, fn. 3.

[33] Useful surveys of the role of the media in British politics include: Colin Seymour-Ure, *The Political Impact of the Mass Media* (London: Constable, 1974); J. G. Blumler and D. McQuail, *Television in Politics* (London: Faber, 1968); and the chapters on radio and television in the Nuffield series and in Penniman, ed., *Britain at the Polls, 1974*.

ship and signal-coverage are today about as extensive in Great Britain as they are in the United States, and the medium plays about the same central role in presenting and interpreting (and creating?) political reality. Since the 1950s Britain has had both public broadcasting, with the two television channels of the British Broadcasting Corporation (BBC), and commercial broadcasting, with one television channel allocated to the Independent Broadcasting Authority (IBA).

The greatest difference between Britain and the United States, however, is the fact that British parties and candidates are not allowed to purchase time from either the BBC or the IBA for broadcasting political advertisements, so the party and candidate "spot commercials" so familiar to American viewers during election campaigns are entirely absent from British airwaves.

Consequently, television and radio participate in British general election campaigns in only two ways. The first consists of the *party-controlled broadcasts*. These began in 1929 when the BBC (at that time the only broadcasting authority in the nation) offered to each of the three leading parties free radio time, leaving it up to each party to decide how to use its time. All three parties accepted with alacrity, and their broadcasts continued to be major features of the 1931, 1935, 1945, and 1950 election campaigns. The election of 1951 saw the first television election broadcasts, and there were both radio and television broadcasts in the 1955 election. In 1959 it was decided that there would be a total of twelve broadcasts on television (and eighteen on radio)—five for the Conservatives, five for Labour, and two for the Liberals, a ratio which presumably reflected the parties' relative support in the electorate.[34] This has continued to be the basic arrangement ever since, although altered in some details. In 1979 there were five ten-minute broadcasts by the Conservatives, five for Labour, three for the Liberals, one each for the Scottish Nationalists (broadcast only in Scotland) and Plaid Cymru (broadcast only in Wales), and one five-minute program for the National Front. The parties have supplemented their original "talking heads" presentations of leaders with film clips, graphics, and man-in-the-street interviews.

These are two major differences between party-controlled broadcasts in Britain and their counterparts in the United States. Perhaps the most important is the fact that in Britain the airtime for all such broadcasts is free, while in the United States it must be purchased by the parties. This, as we have seen, is one of the reasons why politics in Britain is so much less expensive than in America. The other difference is the fact that the British broadcasts focus on the *party*, its

---

[34] Butler and Rose, *The British General Election of 1959*, pp. 84-97.

collective policies, record, and some of its top leaders rather than exclusively on *the* leader, while American broadcasts focus almost entirely upon the presidential candidates, and the parties whose label they bear are all but invisible. This no doubt results from the fact that in Britain the parties control the campaigns while in the United States the ad hoc presidential candidate organizations are in charge. Whatever the cause, the results make party-controlled broadcasts in Britain quite different from anything seen in the United States.

The second feature of the campaign on television and radio is the *broadcaster-controlled broadcasts*. Quaint as it now seems, in the 1950, 1951, and 1955 general election campaigns the BBC, to ensure its complete political impartiality, "ostentatiously excluded from the air all references to politics apart from the party broadcasts. Even these were stopped five days before the poll. . . ."[35] But after 1955 the BBC faced a steep rise in the number of television viewers and sharp competition for audiences from the newly established IBA. IBA (ITA it then was) began to cover by-elections in its news broadcasts, and by the 1959 campaign both broadcasting agencies decided to cover the general election with their own programs as well as to air the party-controlled programs. They have done so ever since and have developed many different ways of covering the campaigns, many of them innovative and most of them of excellent quality. They include interview programs in which party leaders are grilled by the broadcasters' interviewers, programs in which party leaders are questioned by man-in-the-street panels or answer voters' questions sent in by postcard or telephoned, and election-night reports and analyses of the results. All in all, then, the electronic media are every bit as important in British elections as in American.

One of the respects in which Great Britain is more centralized than the United States is the presence and wide influence of a number of truly national newspapers. Moreover, their preferences for particular parties are comparatively open and consistent: the *Daily Mirror* is pro-Labour; the *Sun* is unusually pro-Labour; the *Daily Telegraph, Daily Mail,* and *Daily Express* are pro-Conservative; the *Guardian* is "floating" with a tilt toward Labour and the Liberals; and the *Times* is floating with a tilt toward the Conservatives and Liberals. There is no reason to believe, however, that Britain is an exception to the general rule that in recent years the influence of newspapers on voters' information and preferences has declined relative to the influence of television.

---

[35] Ibid., p. 75.

**Public Opinion Polls.** In the United States the principal published political polls, for example, those of the George Gallup and Louis Harris firms, are each sold to a number of newspapers. In Great Britain, by contrast, the norm is for each of several newspapers and television production firms to contract with a particular polling firm for the exclusive right to publish or broadcast the results of the firm's polls.[36] In 1979 the principal polling organizations and their outlets were as follows: The British Institute of Public Opinion, published by the *Sunday Telegraph* and *Daily Telegraph,* is loosely affiliated with the American Gallup organization, but its ownership, management, and even its polling techniques are quite different. National Opinion Polls published its results in the *Daily Mail.* The Opinion Research Centre sold its polls to the Independent Television News organization and also did a number of unpublished polls for the Conservative Central Office. Marplan's polls were broadcast by London Weekend TV and published by the *Sun.* Research Services Ltd. sold its results to the *Observer.* And busiest of all was Market and Opinion Research International (MORI), which did surveys for the *Daily Express, Evening Standard, Sunday Times,* and Thames TV.[37]

The published polls have been forecasting the distribution of popular votes in general elections since 1964, and they have usually been quite accurate. Their predictions on the average have come within three percentage points of the actual results,[38] and in 1979 the average error was only one percentage point.

The one major failure of the British polls—comparable in many ways to the American polls' debacle in 1948—came in forecasting the popular vote in the 1970 general election. In their final reports all the polls with one exception forecast a Labour victory by margins ranging from 48–46 (Louis Harris) to 50–41 (Marplan). Only the Opinion Research Centre in the *Evening Standard* forecast a narrow Conservative victory of 46.5 to 45.5. But the actual results produced a Conservative victory with 46.5 percent to Labour's 43 percent.[39] This failure touched off a round of soul-searching by the pollsters and criticism by their critics reminiscent of that in the United States after the public polls had incorrectly forecast Harry Truman's defeat

---

[36] A useful survey of opinion polling in Britain is Frank Teer and James Spence, *Political Opinion Polls* (London: Hutchinson, 1973).

[37] See Richard Rose, "Toward Normality: Public Opinion Polls in the 1979 Election," in this volume.

[38] Richard Rose, "The Polls and Election Forecasting in February 1974," in Penniman, ed., *Britain at the Polls, 1974,* table 5-4, p. 119.

[39] Butler and Pinto-Duschinsky, *The British General Election of 1970,* pp. 177-180.

in the 1948 presidential election.[40] As a result the polling firms made some changes in their research and reporting procedures, and they correctly forecast the popular-vote winners in both 1974 elections and in the 1979 election.

In the 1950s and 1960s the Conservative, Labour, and Liberal parties all commissioned a few private polls every now and then, but little use was made of their results in planning campaign strategy and tactics. In the late 1960s, however, leaders in all three parties came to believe that polls were by far the best way to acquire accurate information about their standing with the voters, information they had to have if they were to campaign effectively. In the 1970 campaign they conducted surveys for the first time on the popular images of the parties and their leaders, on what people thought were the main issues and how they felt about them, on the voters' reactions to the party broadcasts, and the like.[41] The parties have subsequently commissioned more polls and used them more extensively, and it is now common practice for both of the major parties to conduct quick telephone polls *daily* during general election campaigns. As a result, the parties' private polls now play every bit as critical a role in shaping campaign strategy and tactics as they do in the United States.

**Casting and Counting the Votes.** In a British general election the voter has only one office to vote for—the member of Parliament for his constituency. Hence there is no need for voting machines, and paper ballots continue to be used as they have been since the mid-nineteenth century. There are rarely fewer than three or more than seven candidates on a constituency's ballot, and the modal number is four.

Prior to the 1970 election the ballot carried only the name, residential address, and occupation of each candidate. It gave no indication whatever of any candidate's party affiliation or backing, and so a major objective of local campaigning had to be impressing on the voters' minds which candidate belonged to which party. In 1969 James Callaghan, then home secretary in the Labour Government, proposed that henceforth each candidate's party affiliation be printed on the ballots. His proposal, however, encountered strong objections, of which the most powerful was the argument that disputes about which candidate had the legitimate claim to a particular party's label would have to be adjudicated by the courts and that such adjudication would fundamentally alter the character of the parties. As political journalist

---

[40] Many of these commentaries are presented or summarized in Richard Rose, ed., *The Polls and the 1970 Election* (Glasgow: University of Strathclyde Survey Research Center, 1970).

[41] Butler and Pinto-Duschinsky, *The British General Election of 1970*, pp. 189-194.

R. L. Leonard put it: "The necessity of obtaining legal judgments [about who could properly use a party's label] would make party affairs justiciable, and might lead, e.g., to would-be candidates going to law about allegedly improper selection procedures."[42]

Leonard's argument may sound strange to American ears, since there is evidently no aspect of party affairs that American courts will not regulate; but it was sufficiently compelling in Britain to persuade Callaghan to abandon his proposal in favor of the milder rule that each candidate may have on the ballot under his name a description or slogan of up to six words *of his own choosing*. Most candidates simply use their party labels—"Conservative," "The Labour party candidate," and the like—though a few embellish their names with phrases like "Anti-Common Market Conservative."[43]

Thursdays are the traditional polling days, and the polling stations are open from 7 A.M. to 10 P.M. The ballots are administered by representatives of the constituency's returning officer and are marked by placing an "X" in the box beside the preferred candidate's name. Each party usually has tellers who check off the names of its known supporters as they vote. The marked ballots are folded and deposited in locked boxes until time for the count.

*Postal votes.* Great Britain has had the equivalent of American absentee ballots only since 1948. In each constituency a special register is compiled of all persons who are allowed to vote by mail in advance of the election. The registering officer places on it persons whose occupations or election duties will prevent them from voting in person (for example, seamen), persons whose physical incapacities might prevent them from doing so (the aged and chronically sick), and persons who have moved out of the constituency since the regular voting register was compiled. Persons who will merely be away on holiday on polling days are not included.

Persons who are not put on the special register can apply for it up to two weeks before the election, and the parties try to get their likely absentees to apply. Everyone on the special register is given a ballot with instructions to mark it and return it by mail. Over 80 percent usually do so, and their votes constitute an average of about 2 percent of all those cast—more than enough to tip the balance in some marginal constituencies. Secret ballot laws make it impossible to say for sure, but most observers believe that the Conservatives are

---

[42] R. L. Leonard, *Elections in Britain*, p. 218, fn. 8. See also the letter by David Butler to the *Times*, November 27, 1968, p. 11.

[43] Butler and Pinto-Duschinsky, *The British General Election of 1970*, p. 264. See also the 1979 ballot reproduced in appendix B in this volume.

more successful than the Labour party in getting their absentees to cast postal votes and that postal votes sometimes elect Conservative candidates in close races. Butler and Kavanagh estimate that in 1979 postal votes provided the winning margins for Conservative candidates in six to eight marginal constituencies.[44]

*Counting votes.* After the polls close British law requires that ballots from all the polling stations in the constituency be brought to one central location and mixed together before they are counted. The object is to make it impossible to tell how any particular area within a constituency has voted, and it works. Hence the kind of precinct-by-precinct scrutiny of election results often conducted by American analysts is unknown in Britain.

After being mixed together, the ballots are sorted into piles for each candidate, the piles are counted and recounted, and the totals are checked and verified. The returning officer, usually with all the candidates at his side, announces the total for each and declares the winner. Somewhere between 400 and 450 of the constituencies count and report right after the polls close, while the remainder wait until the next day. In a very close election, such as that of February 1974, the final results—the party that will form the next Government—are not known until upward of twenty-four hours after the polls close. But when, as in 1979, the early results show that the tide is running strongly in favor of one party or the other, the identity of the new Government is apparent within a few hours.

**The Payoff: Votes into Seats.** In Great Britain, as in all democratic countries, the final payoff in a general election is counted in terms of the proportion of the offices won, and the number of votes cast for each party is significant only as it is translated into seats won in the House of Commons. In Britain as elsewhere that translation is profoundly affected by the nature of the electoral system.[45] It is therefore appropriate to begin this concluding section by recalling that British general elections employ *single-member districts* with "first-past-the-post" decision rules. That is, the nation is divided into 635 constituencies, each of which elects one M.P.; and in each constituency the candidate who wins the most votes—even if he wins less than half of all the votes cast—is the winner. The same system is

---

[44] David Butler and Dennis Kavanagh, *The British General Election of 1979* (London: Macmillan, 1980), pp. 313-315.

[45] An illuminating analysis of how the translation is affected by the different electoral systems of modern democracies is Douglas W. Rae, *The Political Consequences of Electoral Laws*, rev. ed. (New Haven, Conn.: Yale University Press, 1971).

used for the election of a number of other legislative bodies—for example, the United States House of Representatives, the Canadian House of Commons, and the Indian Lok Sabha—and it is generally believed to give the major parties larger shares of the seats and the lesser parties smaller shares than their shares of the popular votes.

The extent to which this has been true in British general elections since the end of World War II is shown in table 1–4. The figures show, surprisingly, that in the eleven postwar British general elections no party has ever won as much as half of all the popular votes cast. Some have come close—the Conservatives with 49.7 percent in 1955 and 49.4 percent in 1959, and Labour with 48.8 percent in 1951—but no party ever has passed the 50-percent post. The leading party's vote share, indeed, has gone as low as the Conservatives' 37.9 percent in February 1974, and the average share for the leading party has been only 45.4 percent.

Yet ten of the eleven elections produced clear majorities of seats for one or the other of the major parties. To be sure, on two occasions the party with the second-largest share of the popular votes won the largest share of the seats (the Conservatives in 1951 and Labour in February 1974). But only in February 1974 did the party winning the most seats take fewer than 50 percent of them (Labour, 47.4 percent); indeed, this was the only general election since 1929 that failed to produce a majority of seats for one party.

The figures underline the fact, accepted by all analysts and party leaders, that Britain's single-member-district, first-past-the-post system plays a major role in maintaining the nation's two-party, Government-versus-Opposition politics. The most prominent victim of the system has, of course, been the Liberals: from 1950 to 1970 they limped along with vote shares ranging from 11.2 percent (1964) to 2.5 percent (1951), but never had more than 1.9 percent of the seats. In the two elections of 1974 they made a major advance, winning 19.3 percent of the votes in February and 18.3 percent in October. But their share of the seats crept up only to 2.2 percent in February and 2.1 percent in October. Apparently the Liberals are not alone in deploring this situation: the polls show that substantial majorities of the population agree that the electoral system should be changed so that each party's share of the seats fairly reflects its share of the votes.[46]

The leaders of the major parties, however, are not persuaded. They have an obvious interest in maintaining the system as it is, and

---

[46] See Richard Scammon, "The Election and the Future of British Electoral Reform," in Penniman, ed., *Britain at the Polls, 1974*, chap. 7.

## TABLE 1–4
### Votes and Seats in British General Elections, 1945–1979

| Election Year and Party | Percentage of Popular Votes | Percentage of Seats | Percentage-Point Difference |
|---|---|---|---|
| **1945** | | | |
| Labour | 47.8 | 61.4 | +13.6 |
| Conservative | 39.8 | 33.3 | −6.5 |
| Liberal | 9.0 | 1.9 | −7.1 |
| Other | 3.4 | 3.4 | 0 |
| **1950** | | | |
| Labour | 46.1 | 50.4 | +4.3 |
| Conservative | 43.5 | 47.7 | +4.2 |
| Liberal | 9.1 | 1.4 | −7.7 |
| Other | 1.3 | 0.5 | −0.8 |
| **1951** | | | |
| Labour | 48.8 | 47.2 | −1.6 |
| Conservative | 48.0 | 51.4 | +3.4 |
| Liberal | 2.5 | 0.9 | −1.6 |
| Other | 0.7 | 0.5 | −0.2 |
| **1955** | | | |
| Conservative | 49.7 | 54.8 | +5.1 |
| Labour | 46.4 | 44.0 | −2.4 |
| Liberal | 2.7 | 0.9 | −1.8 |
| Other | 1.2 | 0.3 | −0.9 |
| **1959** | | | |
| Conservative | 49.4 | 57.9 | +8.5 |
| Labour | 43.8 | 40.9 | −3.1 |
| Liberal | 5.9 | 1.0 | −4.9 |
| Other | 0.9 | 0.2 | −0.7 |
| **1964** | | | |
| Labour | 44.1 | 50.3 | +6.2 |
| Conservative | 43.4 | 48.3 | +4.9 |
| Liberal | 11.2 | 1.4 | −9.8 |
| Other | 1.3 | — | −1.3 |
| **1966** | | | |
| Labour | 47.9 | 57.8 | +9.9 |
| Conservative | 41.9 | 40.2 | −1.7 |
| Liberal | 8.5 | 1.9 | −6.6 |
| Other | 1.7 | 0.1 | −1.6 |
| **1970** | | | |
| Conservative | 46.4 | 52.3 | +5.9 |
| Labour | 43.0 | 45.7 | +2.7 |
| Liberal | 7.5 | 1.0 | −6.5 |
| Other | 3.1 | 1.0 | −2.1 |

## TABLE 1–4 (continued)

| Election Year and Party | Percentage of Popular Votes | Percentage of Seats | Percentage-Point Difference |
|---|---|---|---|
| February 1974 | | | |
| Conservative | 37.9 | 46.8 | +8.9 |
| Labour | 37.1 | 47.4 | +10.3 |
| Liberal | 19.3 | 2.2 | −17.1 |
| Other | 5.7 | 3.6 | −2.1 |
| October 1974 | | | |
| Labour | 39.2 | 50.2 | +11.0 |
| Conservative | 35.8 | 43.6 | +7.8 |
| Liberal | 18.3 | 2.1 | −16.2 |
| Other | 6.7 | 4.1 | −2.6 |
| 1979 | | | |
| Conservative | 43.9 | 53.4 | +9.5 |
| Labour | 36.9 | 42.2 | +5.3 |
| Liberal | 13.8 | 1.7 | −12.1 |
| Other | 5.4 | 2.7 | −2.7 |

Source: Butler and Sloman, *British Political Facts 1900-1975*, pp. 184-186; *Guardian*, May 5, 1979, p. 1.

they argue that the main purpose of a general election is not to be "fair" to minor parties but rather to produce Governments with enough seats to govern effectively and Oppositions with enough seats to stand forth as the official Opposition and *the* clear alternative if and when the people decide to change Governments.

The dispute continues about the relative merits of fair distribution of seats and effective single-party Governments and Oppositions. It seems highly probable that the next British general election will be conducted essentially according to the processes outlined in this chapter. But it is not inconceivable that the pressures for reform of the electoral system will become strong enough within the next decade or two to force the adoption of a more proportional system. We shall see.

# 2

# Politics, Economics, and the Trade Unions, 1974-1979

*Anthony King*

At the general elections of 1974, the three major political parties were led by Edward Heath, Harold Wilson, and Jeremy Thorpe. Five years later, at the general election of May 1979, the three major parties were led by Margaret Thatcher, James Callaghan, and David Steel. In 1974, the Conservatives were defeated because they could not cope with a national miners' strike; in 1979, the Labour Government was defeated largely because it, too, could not cope with a wave of industrial unrest. The people at the top in British politics changed; the issues, to a remarkable extent, remained the same. The purpose of this chapter is to describe the main political—and therefore economic—developments in Britain in the latter half of the 1970s. Later chapters will explore in more detail the events that culminated in the Conservatives' decisive electoral victory at the end of the decade.

## Labour and the Economy

The results of the October 1974 election came as a disappointment to the Labour party, which had hoped for a large overall majority in the House of Commons. Instead Harold Wilson, the prime minister, and his senior colleagues found themselves with a majority of only three. To be sure, if every Labour M.P. turned out to vote and voted the right way, the Government need never be defeated; and Labour's margin of seats over the Conservatives alone was a comfortable forty-three. Nevertheless, the leading figures in the Government were conscious of being at the mercy of even a tiny handful of Labour dissidents; and there seemed every chance that, as the months and years went by, Labour's overall majority would disappear as the result of losses in by-elections. In the autumn of 1974, no one could begin to predict how long the Government would survive.

Labour's legislative program was ambitious, its declared aim being to bring about a "fundamental and irreversible shift of power and wealth in favour of working people and their families."[1] The party was committed to nationalizing the shipbuilding and aircraft industries (already heavily dependent on government contracts and subsidies) and to taking a much-enlarged financial stake in the exploitation of North Sea oil and gas. It was also committed to setting up a new National Enterprise Board (NEB), to serve partly as a state holding company and partly also as the government's principal instrument of intervention in the private sector. In addition, local authorities were to be required to purchase—against the owners' wishes if need be—the great bulk of the land needed for future building development in their areas. Labour had already begun, in the short period between the two 1974 elections, to demolish the elaborate legal edifice constructed by the Conservatives for the purpose of controlling the trade unions; now it proposed to complete this work of legal demolition and at the same time to extend to inland container depots a statutory scheme reserving certain kinds of unloading work for government-registered dockers. Various initiatives were planned in the social policy field, notably a new national superannuation scheme. Not least, Labour while in opposition had committed itself to "devolution"—to giving Scotland and Wales a substantial measure of administrative and, in the case of Scotland, legislative autonomy.

Enacting the Government's full program on the basis of such a slender parliamentary majority was going to require great good luck and the exercise of considerable political skill. Even so, the main problems facing Wilson and his colleagues were not parliamentary or even political in any narrow sense; they were economic. The Government could pass more or less what legislation it liked; in the end, the electorate would judge its success or failure to a very large extent in

---

[1] *The Labour Party Manifesto 1974: Let Us Work Together: Labour's Way Out of the Crisis* (London: Labour Party, 1974), p. 15. On the 1974-1979 period generally, see David McKie, Chris Cook, and Melanie Phillips, *The Guardian/Quartet Election Guide* (London: Quartet Books, 1978), Alan Sked and Chris Cook, *Post-War Britain: A Political History* (Harmondsworth, Middx.: Penguin Books, 1979), chaps. 11-12, and Richard Clutterbuck, *Britain in Agony: The Growth of Political Violence*, rev. ed. (Harmondsworth, Middx.: Penguin Books, 1980). An indispensable source of data on economics as well as politics is David Butler and Anne Sloman, *British Political Facts 1900-1979*, 5th ed. (London: Macmillan, 1980). *The Guardian/Quartet Election Guide* somewhat belies its title, being an invaluable compendium of information on almost all aspects of the period; *Britain in Agony* does not belie its title but also, nevertheless, contains a good deal of useful information. This chapter is based partly on published sources like these and partly on the writer's own observation of British politics during the period.

economic terms.[2] And the British economy was functioning no better —if anything, rather worse—in the mid-1970s than it had been in the previous decade and a half. The Yom Kippur War and the ensuing worldwide rise in the price of oil did not hit Britain harder than other industrial countries, but they struck at an economy that was already weak. In 1974 Britain's growth rate was actually a negative quantity; gross domestic product fell substantially in the last quarter of that year. At the same time, the country was running an enormous balance-of-payments deficit, and unemployment, although lower in 1974 than it had been earlier in the decade, showed every sign of edging upward.[3]

But, grave though these problems were, they paled into insignificance beside inflation. Throughout the late 1960s and early 1970s, Britain had had a rate of domestic inflation considerably higher than that of its main industrial competitors. Now an already steep downward slope in the value of money was becoming steeper; inflation was threatening to go out of control. In the first quarter of 1974, the retail price index rose at an annual rate of 12 percent; in the last quarter, the rate of increase was more than 17 percent. Inflation was fueled partly by the worldwide explosion of oil and other commodity prices and partly by high levels of government borrowing; but it was fueled, too, by the "threshold" pay increases already agreed to by the Heath Government and, increasingly, by extraordinarily large wage settlements—settlements that bore no relationship to the real productive capacity of the economy and, as time went on, did not even bear much relationship to the current rate of inflation. In order to end the miners' strike that had brought down the Heath administration, the incoming Labour Government conceded wage increases averaging 30 percent. This figure was taken by other groups of workers as a norm, or at least as a goal to which they could reasonably aspire. By the end of 1974, the railwaymen had secured a pay increase of 30 percent, and increases of between 25 and 30 percent were commonplace in both the public and the private sector. Earnings were thus rising

---

[2] On the question of popular responses to Britain's economic difficulties, see James E. Alt, *The Politics of Economic Decline: Economic Management and Political Behaviour in Britain since 1964* (Cambridge: Cambridge University Press, 1979). For a much briefer discussion of the role played by the economy in British electoral politics, see Anthony King, "The Election that Everyone Lost," in Howard R. Penniman, ed., *Britain at the Polls: The Parliamentary Elections of 1974* (Washington, D.C.: American Enterprise Institute, 1975), pp. 25-26.

[3] These data, like most of the others in this chapter, are taken from the official publication, *Economic Trends*; but see also McKie, Cook, and Phillips, *Guardian/Quartet Election Guide*, esp. chaps. 1-3, and Butler and Sloman, *British Political Facts 1900-1979*, chap. 12.

faster than prices even though output was falling. It was as clear as anything could be that the rate of inflation, already high in 1974, was going to be much higher in 1975.

Under the circumstances, the Government might have been expected to take bold, decisive action, and some steps to deal with the problem were, of course, taken; basic foods were subsidized, some rents frozen, and a start made on reducing the scale of government borrowing. But for the most part Wilson and the other senior members of the Government behaved as though they were simply bewildered. Confronted with the crisis, they knew they should do something, but all they seemed able to do was to exhort the unions to exercise greater restraint. The Government's style was nicely captured by a spoof news item in the satirical magazine *Private Eye*:

### WAGES
#### Wilson Warns
#### *By our Political Team*

In a shock warning last night the Prime Minister Mr. Harold Wilson gave his strongest warning yet.

He warned: "Make no mistake. If wages continue to rise, people will take home more money. That is the consequence of continued wage rises."

In what was clearly intended as a warning to the Unions, Mr. Wilson warned: "You have been warned."[4]

Such exhortations went unheeded. Earnings continued to race ahead of prices. The rate of inflation rose from 19.9 percent in January 1975, to 21.7 percent in April, to 22.3 percent in July. Thirty percent inflation by the end of the year seemed a distinct possibility.

What explained the Government's extraordinary inactivity? The reasons for it were actually quite straightforward. Three avenues were open to the Government in principle; in practice, all three appeared to be closed. One way of controlling inflation would be savagely to deflate the economy, by some mixture of public expenditure cuts, greatly increased taxation, and severe monetary restraint; unemployment would rise, but with luck the rate of price increases would begin to fall. Such a course of action was not, however, available to a Labour administration. Ministers were not sure that price increases would begin to abate before unemployment had reached wholly unacceptable levels. They did not wish to achieve a reduction in inflation at the cost of high unemployment and heavy losses in industrial production. In any case, such a policy would not be accepted by the

---

[4] Quoted in Michael Stewart, *The Jekyll and Hyde Years: Politics and Economic Policy since 1964* (London: J. M. Dent, 1977), p. 204, n. 1.

parliamentary Labour party; and Labour ministers could hardly contemplate pursuing deflationary policies in the teeth of opposition from the Labour benches and on the strength of the votes of Conservative M.P.s. The Government would probably split. Even if it did not, the party undoubtedly would.

The second avenue open to Labour was, at least in principle, somewhat more acceptable. It was to introduce a statutory incomes policy—that is, to impose wage restraint by means of the law. But one difficulty with this approach was that it had just been tried by the Conservatives and failed miserably. The policy worked well enough as long as everyone was prepared to abide by the statutory guidelines; but as soon as the guidelines were challenged by a group as powerful as the miners, the whole policy collapsed. On top of this, the Labour party, with its close ties to the trade unions, was committed to the restoration of free collective bargaining. One of the first acts of the new Labour Government in the spring of 1974 had been to abolish the Conservatives' statutory controls over wages; ministers had no desire to go back on their pledges and, equally, no stomach for the kind of stand-up row with the trade unions that any attempt to reintroduce a statutory policy would certainly provoke.[5] And, again, it was not at all clear that the parliamentary Labour party could be persuaded to support such a drastic policy reversal.

The third alternative was suggested by the unacceptability of the second. If the unions would not accept statutory wage controls, perhaps they would accept a policy of voluntary restraint. After all, runaway inflation was in no one's long-term interest, not even the miners'. In hopes that this approach could be made to work, Labour's leaders during 1973 had struck a loose sort of bargain with the leaders of the trade union movement—a social contract, it was called. On the one hand, a future Labour Government would repeal the Conservatives' Industrial Relations Act, increase pensions, control prices, tax the rich and protect the poor and low-paid; on the other, the Trades Union Congress (TUC) would recommend its affiliated unions not to press for wage increases beyond those needed to keep up with increases in the cost of living.[6] "We believe," said Labour's manifesto

---

[5] On the relations between government and the trade unions in the late 1960s and 1970s, see Robert Taylor, *The Fifth Estate: Britain's Unions in the Modern World*, rev. ed. (London: Pan Books, 1980), esp. chaps. 1-5, and Gerald A. Dorfman, *Government versus Trade Unionism in British Politics since 1968* (London: Macmillan, 1979). Taylor's is much the best single-volume study of Britain's trade unions currently available.

[6] The so-called social contract is discussed by Taylor in *The Fifth Estate*, chap. 4, and by King in "The Election that Someone Won—More or Less," in Penniman, ed., *Britain at the Polls, 1974*, pp. 180-81.

for the February 1974 election, "that the action we propose on prices, together with an understanding with the TUC on the lines which we have already agreed, will create the right economic climate for money incomes to grow in line with production."[7]

If Labour's leaders really believed this, they were soon disabused. The new Government kept its side of the bargain; the unions did not keep theirs. Some unions, like the powerful Amalgamated Union of Engineering Workers, had never accepted the social contract. Others accepted it in principle but did not see why they should exercise restraint while their rivals were making a killing—claiming, and being awarded, pay increases far in excess of the increase in the cost of living. Everybody's business, as so often in human affairs, was turning out to be nobody's business. Whatever the views of the majority on the general council of the Trades Union Congress, the TUC had no power to impose its will on its member trade unions. In any case, an essential feature of the social contract was that its terms were so vague that it was almost impossible for any union to be in breach of it. Members of a union claiming pie in the sky could insist that, because they had not received their fair share of pie in the previous pay round, they now deserved to be treated as a special case and to receive an especially thick slice. Within a year of Labour's returning to office, it was clear to all but the willfully blind that the social contract was in ruins.

From the vantage point of the early 1980s, it takes an effort of will to recall the atmosphere in Britain toward the end of 1974 and in the early months of 1975. The British had never known before what it felt like to be, say, a German during the Ruhr occupation and the great inflation of the 1920s. They began to feel the ground shift, ever so slightly, under their feet, and they behaved irrationally, as people often do when they are afraid; instead of getting out of money and into goods, which is the only sensible thing to do in a time of rapidly rising prices, they began to save, as though money in the bank or the building society could secure them against an increasingly uncertain future.[8] The source of the inflation was clear enough by this time: the trade unions and their insatiable wage demands. But the Government remained paralyzed, not so much by indecision as by ignorance as to where it could possibly turn next. The British had always been

---

[7] *The Labour Party Manifesto 1974*, p. 9.

[8] Building societies have no strict American equivalent. They resemble American savings and loan associations except that they are nonprofit and specialize exclusively in home loans. To their considerable astonishment, they found during much of 1974 and 1975 that their income from investments rose sharply instead of declining—even though their rates of interest were not nearly as high as the rate of inflation.

a rather orderly people. Now they were beginning, just beginning, to become acquainted with chaos. It was all very unsettling.

Many trade union leaders, not surprisingly, were as unsettled as anybody else. They did not desire runaway inflation, nor did they seek the destruction of the existing social order; they were merely trying to look after the interests of their members. They were dismayed by the Government's paralysis, and also surprised by it: in the past, Governments faced with an economic crisis had always managed to come up with something sooner or later. Now the Government seemed incapable of action. Perhaps it was time for someone else to take the initiative. On May 17, 1975, Jack Jones, leader of the Transport and General Workers' Union, the largest union in the country, took it upon himself to put forward a practical proposal. In a speech at a rally of his union members, he suggested that for a limited period wage increases should not be allowed to exceed a very small, flat-rate amount. The amount was later set at £6 per week. No one was to receive a pay increase of more than £6; those with annual incomes of more than £8,500—not such a very large sum—were not to receive anything at all. Jones was a convinced socialist, and from his point of view the proposal had two distinct advantages. It would undoubtedly bring down the inflation rate; but it would also be egalitarian in its central thrust: it would redistribute income from the better paid to the less well paid. In a later speech, Jones added that, if the Government would take further steps to curb prices, the unions should be prepared to abandon free collective bargaining for a year.[9]

At first, Jones's proposal was somewhat cautiously received, largely because its significance was not fully appreciated. It all seemed too simple; but in fact, of course, its very simplicity was its greatest strength. The £6 proposal might be crude, but it was also unambiguous, easily understood, and relatively easy to police. It was "fair" in a rough sort of way, and it was almost certain to produce results; with earnings no longer racing ahead of prices, the rate of inflation would be bound to fall. During June and July 1975, with sterling beginning to decline precipitously on the foreign exchange markets largely as a result of the Government's failure to contain inflation, first the general council of the TUC, then (very reluctantly) the Confederation of British Industry, and finally the Government itself swung around

---

[9] On Jack Jones's initiative, see Dorfman, *Government versus Trade Unionism*, pp. 116-22. It was remarkable that the initiative should have come from Jones, who had hitherto been one of the most left-wing leaders of the trade union movement and a determined supporter of free collective bargaining. His change of heart seems to have been genuine and to have been prompted by fear of what was happening to the economy rather than by tactical considerations. His views carried weight partly because they came from such an unexpected source.

behind Jones's initiative. A Government white paper in July announced a variety of sanctions against employers who conceded pay increases in excess of the £6 limit. In August, the powerful National Union of Mineworkers accepted the policy in a pithead ballot; and at the annual TUC congress in September the majority in favor of the TUC/Government proposals was more than two to one. Jack Jones, in his speech to the congress, described the level of recent pay demands as "fantastic":

> The issues are clear. Prices are rising by 26 percent per year —26p in the £. It is estimated that our policy can reduce the rate of price increases to 10 percent or less in 12 months from 26p in the £ to 10p in the £. If we say we will not try to achieve that, we shall do terrible damage to the interests of our members.[10]

The policy was now in place. It remained to be seen whether it would be adhered to.

The period of the Government's inaction over inflation coincided with negotiations between Britain and its fellow members of the European Community aimed at improving the terms of Britain's membership. Some Labour politicians went so far as to excuse the Government's failure to deal with inflation on the grounds that nothing could really be done until the European issue was out of the way. In the end, new terms were negotiated, and on June 5, 1975, in the country's first-ever national referendum, the British people voted by a two-to-one majority to accept them and to remain in the community.[11] The European issue was somewhat tangential to the Government's main domestic preoccupations, but while it was outstanding it probably did have the effect of distracting the attention of senior ministers, including the prime minister. The referendum campaign itself increasingly took the form of a contest between the "moderates" in British politics—the Liberals, most Conservatives, and the moderate wing of the Labour party—and the "extremists," notably Labour's left wing. The moderates' overwhelming victory undoubtedly increased the self-confidence of the moderate majority within the Labour cabinet. As a bonus, it made it politically possible for Wilson to demote Tony Benn,

---

[10] *Report of the 107th Annual Trades Union Congress, Blackpool, 1975* (London: Trades Union Congress, 1976), p. 460.

[11] A good deal has been written about the referendum. See Anthony King, *Britain Says Yes: The 1975 Referendum on the Common Market* (Washington, D.C.: American Enterprise Institute, 1977), David Butler and Uwe Kitzinger, *The 1975 Referendum* (London: Macmillan, 1976), and Philip Goodhart, *Full-Hearted Consent: The Story of the Referendum Campaign—and the Campaign for the Referendum* (London: Davis-Poynter, 1976).

an ambitious left-wing, anti-European minister, whose eighteen months as secretary of state for industry had undermined business confidence but otherwise not accomplished a great deal.[12]

During its first two years, the Labour Government, despite its tiny majority in the House of Commons, encountered fewer difficulties with its legislative program than might have been expected. Most of the items in the program had been included in Labour's election manifesto and were acceptable to the party as a whole; some of the more controversial proposals were substantially modified before being placed before Parliament. The shipbuilding and aircraft industries were nationalized, the British National Oil Corporation was set up to take charge of the government's stake in North Sea oil, and a new Trade Union and Labour Relations (Amendment) Act fulfilled the Government's promise to the trade unions to restore the legal status of the closed shop to what it had been before the Conservatives' Industrial Relations Act of 1971.[13] The Community Land Act sought to effect Labour's policy for the public acquisition of development land, though it soon became clear that, because of local resistances and shortages of cash, the program was going to fall far short of its objectives.

One bill that was drastically altered before it ever reached the House of Commons was Tony Benn's Industry Bill. In its original form, the bill would have given Benn, together with the new National Enterprise Board, sweeping powers to impose "planning agreements" on companies in the private sector and even to buy them up. Many of Benn's colleagues were appalled. They did not trust him and had no idea what he proposed to do with his new powers. Moreover, they knew that the bill, if introduced in anything like its original form, would destroy what little confidence was left in the business community. Wilson subsequently described a draft of the white paper

---

12 Benn, much protesting, was moved sideways from the Department of Industry to the Department of Energy. The prime minister had clearly long wanted to move him, having a low opinion of him and being highly conscious of the effect Benn's presence in the Department of Industry was having on the morale of private business; but until the referendum Benn's popularity with some leading trade unionists and with Labour's rank and file made moving him a politically risky operation. For the prime minister's subsequent account of his transferring of Benn, see Harold Wilson, Final Term: The Labour Government 1974-76 (London: Weidenfeld and Nicolson, and Michael Joseph, 1979), pp. 143-44.

13 The 1971 Industrial Relations Act is an important landmark in the history of the postwar relationship between British Governments and the trade unions. It sought both to alter the pattern of industrial relations and to affect the relationship beween trade unions and their own members. See Michael Moran, The Politics of Industrial Relations: The Origins, Life and Death of the 1971 Industrial Relations Act (London: Macmillan, 1977).

that preceded the bill as "a sloppy and half-baked document, polemical, indeed menacing, in tone."[14] The bill, when it did eventually become law, provided the NEB with only restricted financial powers and permitted it to intervene in the affairs of a private-sector company only with the company's consent.[15] The Government's one major parliamentary defeat during its first two sessions came in November 1976 when the House of Commons, by three votes, blocked the Government's attempt to extend the dock labor scheme to inland container depots. In the crucial division, two moderate Labour M.P.s ostentatiously abstained.[16]

By the beginning of 1976, Harold Wilson had been leader of the Labour party for thirteen years. For all that an outsider could tell, he intended to remain leader for the next thirteen. But Wilson had other plans, and it seems that he had had them for some time. As early as September 1975, he informed the queen that he planned to resign in about six months' time, on or about his sixtieth birthday. True to his word, at 9:30 on the morning of March 16, 1976, shortly after his birthday, he drove to Buckingham Palace to tender his resignation to the queen, informing his cabinet colleagues in a prepared statement an hour later. The news was completely unexpected, and most members of the cabinet were flabbergasted. Rumors began to circulate that some dreadful scandal involving the prime minister was about to come to light; his political opponents accused him of running away from the sterling crisis that was already looming on the horizon. In retrospect, however, it seems clear that the reasons Wilson gave for resigning were his real ones. He had been prime minister for eight years, longer than any of his peacetime predecessors in the twentieth

---

[14] Wilson, *Final Term*, p. 33. At several points in his memoirs, Wilson makes it clear how unimpressed he was with Benn as a minister.

[15] As constituted under the 1975 Industry Act, and as it functioned under Benn's successor at the Department of Industry, the NEB did not prove to be the socialist battering-ram that its supporters hoped for and the business community feared. In the event, it acted, broadly, as a state holding company for firms like Rolls-Royce and British Leyland, which had collapsed while in the private sector, and also as a provider of capital for a limited number of high-technology firms, especially in the electronics industry. For a brief, fairly sympathetic account of the NEB's activities between 1975 and 1978, see Michael Parr, "The National Enterprise Board," *National Westminster Bank Quarterly Review* (February 1979), pp. 51-62.

[16] The two were John Mackintosh, a prominent pro-European whose apparent claims on ministerial office were never recognized by either Harold Wilson or James Callaghan and who died in 1978, and Brian Walden, another pro-European who was also denied ministerial office and who eventually quit politics altogether to become a television interviewer. The incidence of rebellion in the House of Commons increased enormously from the mid-1960s onward. On the period described in this chapter, see Philip Norton, *Dissension in the House of Commons 1974-1979* (Oxford: Clarendon Press, 1980).

century; he did not want to deny others their chance of succeeding to the premiership; he was afraid that anyone who had held office as long as he had might no longer be able to look at problems afresh.[17] It may be, too, that Wilson was influenced by his wife, Mary, who had never enjoyed political life and who would certainly have been disposed to urge him to quit while he was ahead.

The ensuing contest for the Labour leadership was a strange one. It was fought with vigor, passion, and seeming confidence by no fewer than six candidates; yet right from the start everybody seemed to know who was going to win. James Callaghan, the foreign secretary, was by no means universally popular, but he commanded far more support on the right and in the center of the party than anyone else. Even if, as seemed probable, he was not ahead on the first ballot, he was bound to pick up support on the second and third. Like Harold Wilson before him, Callaghan was hardly the stereotypical British politician. He had not attended a prestigious public school; he did not have an upper-class accent. Born in 1912, the son of a chief petty officer in the Royal Navy, he was brought up in circumstances of considerable hardship following his father's death.[18] Entering the lower echelons of the civil service straight from school, he became a full-time official in his trade union, the Inland Revenue Staff Federation, before serving in the navy—as a petty officer like his father—during World War II. He was elected to Parliament in the great Labour landslide of 1945. By the time of Wilson's resignation, he had held all of the most senior offices in the British system below the premiership: chancellor of the exchequer (1964–1967), home secretary (1967–1970), and foreign secretary (since 1974).

Callaghan's nickname was "sunny Jim." It could not have been less appropriate. Callaghan had indeed developed the knack of smiling cheerfully at the television cameras in times of crisis; but in fact he was a serious, rather insecure man with a quick temper. Few of his fellow politicians were close to him, and many over the years had felt the force of his anger. Almost always on guard, he seldom gave the impression of being completely relaxed. He looked a little like a heavyweight boxer who had once, long ago, been floored by a sudden left hook to the jaw and was determined not to repeat the experience. Compared with many of his cabinet colleagues, he was neither mentally agile nor particularly quick with words. Against all this, how-

---

17 Wilson reprints the text of his resignation statement in *Full Term*, pp. 301–04.
18 Not a great deal has been written about Callaghan. A short biography is Peter Kellner and Christopher Hitchens, *Callaghan: The Road to Number Ten* (London: Cassell, 1976). For a later assessment, see Dick Leonard, "Labour's conservative," *Economist*, April 28, 1979, pp. 37-41.

ever, Callaghan was tough, determined, and vastly experienced; indeed, by 1976 he was one of the most experienced political leaders in the Western world. Long service had brought with it a certain wisdom; he had, as the English say, "bottom." He also had an almost instinctive feel for what ordinary British people, and ordinary members of the Labour party, could and could not be made to accept. He was a truly representative figure, in a way that most of his rivals were not. Callaghan was a socialist not so much because he had been convinced of the truth of a set of abstract propositions as because he wanted ordinary working people, not just in Britain, to have a better life.

The real contest was for second place. Three other senior ministers competed with Callaghan for the votes of the center and right of the party: Denis Healey, the chancellor of the exchequer, a bluff, outspoken Yorkshireman who was widely admired but who, perhaps precisely because of his outspokenness, had never acquired more than a tiny personal following; Anthony Crosland, the secretary of state for the environment, Britain's leading socialist theorist, a competent administrator, and a man of formidable intellectual powers but not someone who ever struck others as a natural leader of men; and Roy Jenkins, the home secretary, Labour's most prominent European, a man of great capacity and total integrity who inspired intense devotion among a small circle of friends and admirers but whose very rectitude, combined with shyness and a certain grandness of manner, alienated him from many of those who should have been his natural supporters. One of the two competitors for the votes of left-wing M.P.s was Michael Foot, whose close relations with many leading trade unionists had led to his being appointed secretary of state for employment (in effect, minister of labor) in 1974. A brilliant parliamentary performer and the party's leading anti-European, Foot was the conscience of Labour's left—a seagreen incorruptible who, although a member of Parliament off and on since 1945, had always before 1974 rejected offers of ministerial office. The other left-wing candidate was Tony Benn, the former industry minister, now the secretary of state for energy. Like Foot, Benn was a darling of the constituency party activists; unlike Foot, he was evidently hungry for power and, partly for this reason, was widely distrusted.

To the considerable surprise of most observers, Michael Foot, with 90 votes, topped the poll on the first ballot, running far ahead of Tony Benn, with only 37. Second came Callaghan with 84, followed by Jenkins (56), Healey (30), and Crosland (17). Under the rules, only Crosland, the candidate with the fewest votes, was required to drop out, but Jenkins and Benn, recognizing the inevitable, also withdrew. Benn threw in his lot with Foot. On the second ballot, Callaghan, as predicted, moved into the lead with 141 votes, followed by Foot with 133 and Healey with 38. It was now Healey's turn to be eliminated, and on the third and final ballot Callaghan defeated Foot handily by 176 votes to 137.[19] Callaghan was declared leader at the parliamentary party's meeting on April 5, 1976, and later that day went to Buckingham Palace to kiss hands as prime minister. The only surprises of the election were Roy Jenkins's relatively poor showing— his supporters had hoped for 80 or 90 votes on the first ballot—and the large volume of support for Foot. Not only did Foot emerge as having a much larger following than Tony Benn on the left of the party, but it was also clear that he had picked up at least a handful of votes, perhaps a dozen, from moderates. The latter were presumably attracted by Foot's honesty and old-fashioned radicalism; they were probably also repelled by Callaghan's reputation for being something of a political operator.[20] Still, Callaghan had won decisively, and there was no chance of a challenge to his leadership before the next election.

A further point about Labour's leadership election is worth making. In the United States, those responsible for nominating presidential candidates were historically concerned above all with identifying a winner, someone who could capture the White House and whose presence at the head of the ticket would at the same time help the party's candidates for other public offices. Only in recent years has the spread of primary elections brought other, essentially nonelectoral criteria to the fore.[21] In Britain, by contrast, the criteria governing the

---

[19] The results of the election, and of all of the Labour party's previous leadership elections, can be found in Butler and Sloman, *British Political Facts 1900-1979*, pp. 135-36.

[20] Foot attracted far more votes than any previous left-wing candidate for the leadership. This was partly because the parliamentary Labour party after 1974 contained more left-wingers than in the past, but it was also partly because Foot was a man of patent integrity who was evidently not politically ambitious. Callaghan, by contrast, was universally reckoned to be ambitious, and many of his fellow Labour politicians were inclined to be cynical about his motives. Distrust had been bred in 1969 when Callaghan had semi-publicly maneuvered to block a set of proposals on industrial relations put forward by the then Labour Government of which he himself was a prominent member. On this episode, which won Callaghan some friends in the trade unions but antagonized many in the parliamentary party, see Peter Jenkins, *The Battle of Downing Street* (London: Charles Knight, 1970).

[21] It is sometimes overlooked that those who turn out in primary elections in the United States usually do so to vote for the person whom they personally would like to see elected president rather than for the person who they think would have the best chance of winning other people's votes in the general election in November. For some comments on the different criteria used in the selection of presi-

selection of a party leader have always been more numerous and more complicated. In Britain, members of Parliament choosing a new leader are not casting their ballots for some distant figure on a public platform with whom they may once upon a time have shaken hands. They are voting for someone they know well, with whom they have lived at close quarters in the House of Commons, often over a considerable period of years. They know, moreover, that they will have to go on living with him for some years to come. The election of a British party leader is more like the election of a Speaker of the House of Representatives or a Senate majority leader in the United States than like the nomination of a presidential candidate. It is an intimate election, the kind that might occur in a medium-sized private club.

British M.P.s choosing a new leader are inevitably influenced by their own personal likes and dislikes. In addition, they have to decide which of the various candidates would make the best prime minister, which would lead the party most effectively in House of Commons debates, and which would do the best job of holding together the party in the country. Not least, they are concerned to vote for a candidate who is acceptable to them on policy or ideological grounds. Particularly in the Labour party, and more in recent years than in the past, it is clear that all left-wing members have voted only for candidates of the left and that, with very few exceptions, right-wing and moderate M.P.s have voted only for right-wingers and moderates. In 1976, the fact that Michael Foot polled rather more votes than the full strength of the left-wing Tribune Group—that is, that he contrived on the final ballot to win the support of some moderate M.P.s— was a cause for considerable comment.[22]

What is striking against this background is the relatively light weight that members of Parliament appear to attach to the various candidates' abilities to win elections, to win support for the party from

dential nominees in the United States and party leaders in Britain, see Anthony King, "Executives," in Fred I. Greenstein and Nelson W. Polsby, eds., *Handbook of Political Science*, vol. 5, *Governmental Institutions and Processes* (Reading, Mass.: Addison-Wesley, 1975), pp. 184-89.

[22] See, e.g., Sked and Cook, *Post-War Britain*, p. 352. The Tribune Group, named after the left-wing weekly newspaper *Tribune*, consists of several dozen Labour M.P.s who meet regularly while Parliament is sitting to discuss policy and tactics. Their aim is to further the cause of "socialism," which they take to involve increased government intervention in industry, including public ownership, national economic planning, a more egalitarian tax structure, increased spending on the social services, drastic cuts in defense spending, and (ideally) withdrawal from the European Community. The Tribune Group constitutes, in effect, a party within the Labour party, and its members participated in a long series of revolts in Parliament against the policies of the Wilson and Callaghan Governments. On this last point, see Norton, *Dissension in the House of Commons 1974-1979*.

## TABLE 2–1

GENERAL PUBLIC'S VIEWS OF LABOUR LEADERSHIP CANDIDATES AND
M.P.s' VOTES FOR THEM ON FIRST BALLOT, APRIL 1976

| Candidate | General Public's Rank Order | General Public's Rating of Candidates[a] | M.P.s' Rank Order | Number of Votes on First Ballot |
|---|---|---|---|---|
| James Callaghan | 1 | +63 | 2 | 84 |
| Roy Jenkins | 2 | +13 | 3 | 56 |
| Denis Healey | 3 | −21 | 5 | 30 |
| Michael Foot | 4 | −26 | 1 | 90 |
| Anthony Crosland | 5 | −44 | 6 | 17 |
| Tony Benn | 6 | −50 | 4 | 37 |

[a] In percentage points. Each candidate's rating is achieved by subtracting the percentage of respondents who did not think that he would be a good leader of the Labour party and prime minister from the percentage of respondents who thought that he would be a good leader of the Labour party and prime minister. The wording of the question is given in the text.

SOURCE: *Gallup Political Index*, no. 189, April 1976, p. 12.

among the mass of the electorate. No detailed study of a British leadership election has ever been conducted, and the M.P.s of both parties cast their ballots in secret; but the pattern of M.P.s' voting is simply not consistent with the notion that most of them are greatly influenced by electoral considerations. Table 2–1 is instructive in this connection. It is based on the results of a Gallup survey conducted in the later stages of Labour's leadership election. Respondents were asked with regard to all six candidates: "Do you think that ‗‗‗‗‗‗ would or would not be a good leader of the Labour party and Prime Minister?" The scores in column 2 of the table were obtained by subtracting the proportion of respondents who did not think that each candidate would make a good leader and prime minister from the proportion who thought that he would. As can be seen, only two of the six candidates, Callaghan and Jenkins, were accorded positive ratings. Yet on the first ballot only 140 Labour M.P.s voted for these two candidates (44.6 percent of those who turned out), while 174 (55.4 percent) voted for their opponents, all of whom had negative ratings. Thirty-seven M.P.s voted for Tony Benn even though he was demonstrably one of the most unpopular individuals in the whole of Britain.[23] To be sure, many members must have backed their personal preference on the first ballot, conscious that they could switch to a more favored candidate later on. Even so, on the final ballot (not shown in the table) Michael Foot still won the support of 43.8 percent of Labour M.P.s even though he trailed far behind Callaghan in the estimation of the British people and even though there was every indication that he would be a serious liability to the Labour party at the time of the next election. That such a lack of interest in electoral considerations is not unique to the Labour party will emerge later in this chapter.[24]

The elevation of Callaghan to the premiership was not expected to lead, and did not lead, to any major changes in Government policy. At most, the new administration had a somewhat different style from the old one, less frenetic, less prone to being diverted by trivia. Wilson once said that a week is a long time in politics; Callaghan was disposed to take a longer view. The new prime minister inherited his predecessor's chief domestic preoccupation, inflation—to which now, quite suddenly, was added a sterling crisis of colossal proportions. No one to this day knows why the crisis developed as it did; the ways of markets are inscrutable. But its course is easy to chart. In January and February 1976, the pound sterling bought U.S. $2.03. This was already a decline from the pound's value at the time it had first been allowed to float, in 1972, when it had stood at $2.40; but until this point the process by which the pound lay lower and lower in the water had been fairly gradual. Then, quite unexpectedly, in the spring of 1976, the pound began to sink—rapidly. It dropped below $2 for the first time in history and then in May reached an all-time record low of $1.76. It held steady at more or less this level over the summer but then in

---

[23] For example, during the referendum campaign in 1975 Louis Harris International asked a sample of voters whether they respected and liked, or alternatively disliked and distrusted, twenty-eight prominent public figures. Of the twenty-eight, seventeen turned out to be familiar to more than 70 percent of the sample. Of the seventeen, the three who were least respected and liked, and most disliked and distrusted, were Ian Paisley, an extreme Protestant leader in Northern Ireland, Hugh Scanlon, a militant trade union leader, and Tony Benn. See "The Public Standing of Individuals and Institutions Engaged in the EEC Referendum Campaign," LHI/47509, April 1975, p. 6. Every subsequent poll along similar lines has produced similar findings.

[24] This phenomenon is not entirely easy to explain. It undoubtedly owes something to the fact that British M.P.s, unlike American convention delegates, are seldom choosing a party leader in an immediate preelection period. British M.P.s may also believe that, in the end, it is a party's policies and general image that matter, not the personality of its leader. For some evidence that they may be right, see Ivor Crewe's chapter in this volume.

the autumn began to sink even further. In October, it plumbed the depths, being worth at the end of the month a mere $1.59.[25]

Members of the Government, not unreasonably under the circumstances, were completely bewildered. Why was sterling under attack now? Of course it was the case that Britain's rate of inflation was still higher than that of most of its industrial competitors and that the country's balance of payments remained seriously in deficit. But there was nothing new in this; Britain had been suffering from both inflation and serious balance-of-payments deficits since the early 1970s, even before the Yom Kippur War and the oil crisis of 1973–1974. Why such massive pressure on sterling now? The question was particularly hard to answer because, as we shall see later, the Government was having considerable success in containing inflation with the cooperation of the trade unions, and the country's balance-of-payments deficits, though still enormous by historical standards, were actually beginning to fall.[26] The movement of sterling on the foreign exchange markets seemed to bear no relation to the real state of the British economy. Yet the decline in the value of the pound could not be ignored. A cheaper pound was of considerable assistance to British exports, but it made British imports much more expensive. There was reason to believe (or at least fear) that the price elasticity of exports was a good deal greater than that of imports, so that in the short term the higher earnings from the increased value of British exports would be more than offset by the much higher cost of imports. More than that, the increased cost of imports, by giving a further twist to the inflationary spiral, posed a major threat to the Government's still fairly fragile agreement with the unions.

Whatever the true causes of sterling's decline, one thing was clear: it was very widely attributed—in the press, on the Conservative benches in the House of Commons, in the City of London, in international financial circles—to the British Government's profligacy. Britain as a nation was widely believed to be living beyond its means, and the Government was condemned for failing to cut public expenditure and for continuing to run large, indeed increasing, budget deficits.[27] It was claimed that sterling was being sold for the simple reason

---

25 The figures are set out conveniently in McKie, Cook, and Phillips, *Guardian/Quartet Election Guide*, p. 63.

26 For example, the deficit on current account in the third quarter of 1975 was £620 million. In the fourth quarter of the same year, it was £183 million. By the first quarter of 1976, it had fallen to £90 million. The balance-of-payments figures for the period 1970-1977 are set out in McKie, Cook, and Phillips, *Guardian/Quartet Election Guide*, p. 60.

27 See Stewart, *The Jekyll and Hyde Years*, pp. 227-32. Stewart emphasizes the

that holders of sterling had lost confidence in the economic and financial policies of the Labour Government. In July the Government did introduce a package of emergency economic measures, including drastic public expenditure cuts, but the package buoyed up the sinking pound only temporarily. The Government's critics predictably condemned it as too little, too late.

Faced in the autumn of 1976 with the need to take still further emergency measures, the Labour cabinet split three ways. Arguments amongst the three factions lasted for weeks and precipitated the only serious internal crisis of the Callaghan administration. One group of ministers, led by Tony Benn, rejected the idea that the standard of living of the British people should be reduced simply because wealthy foreigners and multinational corporations happened, for some reason, to be speculating against the pound on the foreign-exchange markets. They wanted the Government not to deflate but to impose tight controls on the movement of capital and goods into and out of Britain. They were advocating, in effect, a siege economy. Another group of ministers, led by Denis Healey, the chancellor of the exchequer, took the view that substantial additional cuts in public expenditure were probably in the interests of Britain's long-term economic recovery. They also took the view that such cuts, whatever their intrinsic merits, were absolutely essential if Britain were to be able to raise an international loan massive enough to restore confidence in sterling. A siege economy, far from protecting British living standards, would seriously endanger them, by leading to foreign retaliation and to a total collapse of foreign confidence in Britain's economic future. The third group of ministers was led by Anthony Crosland, the foreign secretary, Shirley Williams, the education minister, and Peter Shore, the environment minister. This group turned out to be crucial. Crosland and his allies rejected the siege economy; but they also rejected the idea that substantial cuts were required on domestic economic grounds. Inflation and the balance of payments were already coming right, and cuts on a large scale would only drive an already depressed economy even further into recession; the agreement with the trade unions was already producing results and was based on the assumption that the Government would not resort to severe deflation. On this analysis, expenditure cuts might well be necessary to secure a

---

gap between the way Denis Healey, the chancellor of the exchequer, was behaving and the way in which his critics, both at home and abroad, thought he ought to be behaving. For a somewhat more extended account of the 1976 sterling crisis, see William Keegan and Rupert Pennant-Rea, *Who Runs the Economy?—Control and Influence in British Economic Policy* (London: Maurice Temple Smith. 1979), chap. 5.

foreign loan; but, if so, they should be kept to an absolute minimum. In the end, Callaghan gave some support to this center group of ministers, and the British Government adopted a tougher stance than might have been expected in its negotiations with foreign bankers and the International Monetary Fund. By December, Healey was able to announce in the House of Commons that, on the strength of substantial tax increases and further reductions in public expenditure amounting to some £2,500 million, he had been able to secure the necessary backing for sterling from the IMF and from the United States and West German governments.[28]

The sequel was strange. The sterling crisis ended as suddenly as it had begun, as though a cloud had passed in front of the sun. No very fundamental changes had been made in the Government's economic policy; Britain's underlying economic problems were as serious as ever. But the pound steadied at the end of 1976, then began to rise quite sharply. On the last day of 1977, it stood at $1.92; by the end of the following year, it was again hovering around the $2 mark. The British economy and the Labour Government, having been written off in one year, were both reckoned to be in rather good shape a year or two later. The ways of the foreign exchange markets remained inscrutable. The officials sent to London to keep an eye on the Government's handling of the economy following the negotiation of the IMF loan in due course went home.[29]

It was while the sterling crisis was gathering momentum in the spring of 1976 that Jeremy Thorpe resigned as leader of the Liberal party. Thorpe had been a popular leader and an electorally successful one. Under his leadership, the Liberals in February 1974 won 19.3 percent of the popular vote, much their highest total since the era of Lloyd George. In October 1974 they lost some ground, but at 18.3 percent their share of the vote was still larger than at any time since the 1920s.[30] Paradoxically, however, Thorpe's position as leader was never entirely secure. His dilettante manner and dapper clothes alienated some of the more earnest Liberals, and he never seemed to

[28] The politics of the crisis are described in Stephen Fay and Hugo Young, *The Day the £ Nearly Died* (London: Sunday Times, 1978). The account in the text is based partly on conversations with ministers.

[29] Keegan and Pennant-Rea maintain that Healey did not really want them to go home and succeeded for a time in delaying their departure. According to them, he found it useful to have another stick—in this case, the IMF—with which to beat the left-wingers within his own party, and his opponents in the cabinet. *Who Runs the Economy?*, p. 169.

[30] The Liberals obtained 23.4 percent of the vote in 1929. The relevant general election statistics are set out in Butler and Sloman, *British Political Facts 1900-1979*, pp. 207-10.

have a clear sense of political direction. In any case, the Liberals were always a wayward political movement, with an eager, disputatious, fringe-group style more than a little reminiscent of latter-day California.

Thorpe, however, was brought down not by politics but by sex. Rumors had circulated for years that he had been involved in a homosexual relationship with a somewhat hysterical male model, who was now widely believed to be blackmailing him and whose life was known to have been threatened. The story was a peculiarly sordid one, and when details of it began to surface in the press Thorpe had no choice but to go. Much later, he was tried and acquitted on a charge of conspiracy to murder.[31] His successor as Liberal leader, David Steel, was elected in July 1976. Steel's boyish manner led some of his fellow politicians to dismiss him as a lightweight; in fact, he combined personal modesty and deeply held political convictions with toughness and a cool—some said a calculating—political intelligence. As it turned out, his tactical skills were to be tested almost immediately.

By the autumn of 1976, the Government's position in the House of Commons was becoming increasingly precarious. The Conservatives had already gained one seat in a by-election, and two left-wing Scottish Labour M.P.s, dissatisfied with the Government's devolution proposals, had broken away to form the independent Scottish Labour party. Fortunately for the Government, these two M.P.s, John Robertson and Jim Sillars, could normally be relied upon to vote with their erstwhile Labour colleagues, and so could two Catholic members from Northern Ireland. All the same, the Government now had an overall majority of only one seat; and even that tiny majority disappeared on November 4, 1976, when the Conservatives captured two more hitherto Labour seats in by-elections. It seemed only a matter of time before the opposition parties would combine to defeat the Government and force a general election.[32]

The first major test of the Government's new parliamentary position came in March 1977. The Conservatives tabled a formal motion of no confidence in the Government, and all of the opposition parties, including the two breakaway Scottish Labour M.P.s, announced their

---

[31] The Thorpe affair continues to attract the attention of the prurient and the merely astonished. It also continues to attract the attention of journalists. Much the best account of it in book form is Lewis Chester, Magnus Linklater, and David May, *Jeremy Thorpe: A Secret Life* (London: Fontana Books in association with André Deutsch, 1979).

[32] A summary of by-election results during this period is given in *The Times Guide to the House of Commons May 1979* (London: Times Books, 1979), p. 244. Fuller details can be found in McKie, Cook, and Phillips, *Guardian/Quartet Election Guide*, pp. 216-23.

intention of voting for it. The Scottish and Welsh nationalists were particularly incensed by Labour's failure to carry forward its plans for devolution. It was clear that the Government would be defeated unless it could reach an understanding of some kind with one or more of the opposition parties. Moreover, the understanding would have to be for a considerable period—say, a year or two. If the Government was forced to patch together an ad hoc compromise with one or another of the opposition parties every time its House of Commons majority was threatened, it could hardly expect to survive for long, and in any case its authority would be completely undermined. In the week before the crucial vote on March 23, Callaghan and Foot first tried to do a deal with the ten Ulster Unionist M.P.s. Ministers were ready to concede that Ulster's representation in the Westminster Parliament should be increased since Northern Ireland no longer had a parliament of its own; but they balked at restoring substantial governing powers to a Northern Ireland parliament without a cast-iron guarantee that the Protestant majority would be prepared to share power with the Catholics. No such guarantee was forthcoming.[33]

In default of the Unionists, the Government turned to the Liberals. Perhaps a bargain could be struck with David Steel and his colleagues. In one sense, the Government's bargaining position was far from strong. Labour was now in a minority in the House of Commons. It followed that it could maintain itself in office and enact its legislation only with the support of at least one of the opposition parties; the opposition parties taken together had a complete veto on anything the Government might want to do. Why, therefore, should the Liberals or any other party do a deal with the Government without extracting substantial concessions from it? Some Liberals, for instance, wanted to press Labour to introduce proportional representation. In another sense, however, the Government's position was stronger than it looked. Most Liberal M.P.s preferred a Labour Government to a Conservative Government and had no desire whatever to precipitate a general election which the Conservatives would almost certainly win. David Steel was particularly anxious to demonstrate to the country at large that the Liberal party was capable of sharing in governmental power, and also that the Liberals, if they held the balance of power in the House of Commons, could exercise a valuable restraining influence on the Government of the day, whatever its political complexion; at the front of his mind was the pivotal, moderating role played by the Free Democratic party in West Germany.

---

[33] These events are described briefly by David Butler in a book edited by him, *Coalitions in British Politics* (London: Macmillan, 1978), pp. 106–07.

And there was yet another, more prosaic factor strengthening the Government's hand and weakening the Liberals'. The Liberals knew full well that, if they defeated the Government and forced an election, they themselves would probably be annihilated. They had fared badly in every by-election held so far in the parliament; their standing in the opinion polls had slumped; it seemed almost certain that in an early election they would forfeit at least five or six of their thirteen seats. Prudence suggested that, in their dealings with the Government, they should not push their luck too far.

It was against this background that the prime minister on behalf of the Government negotiated with Steel and the Liberals' deputy leader, John Pardoe, in the days leading up to the crucial vote.[34] The negotiations were not easy, and at one point it looked as though they might break down over the Government's unwillingness to commit itself to introducing proportional representation for the direct elections to the European Parliament; but a compromise was finally worked out, and during the censure debate on March 23, 1977, Callaghan was able to read out, with the cabinet's formal approval, a statement that he and Steel had prepared. Its chief features were the setting up of a joint consultative committee to consider Government policy and other issues before they came before the House of Commons and the initiation of regular meetings between the chancellor of the exchequer and the Liberal party's economics spokesman. For its part, the Government undertook to bring forward the legislation providing for elections to the European Parliament, with a free vote to be allowed on the issue of proportional representation. The Government also agreed that progress needed to be made on the legislation dealing with devolution. Neither party to the Callaghan-Steel agreement undertook to support the other in all circumstances; the joint statement contained a generous escape clause. But the clear understanding was that the Government could rely on Liberal support in the House of Commons as long as it pursued policies that the Liberal party found broadly acceptable. The agreement initially ran until the end of the 1976–1977 parliamentary session; despite mounting dissent amongst the Liberal rank and file, it was later renewed for the 1977–1978 session. In the confidence vote of March 23, 1977, the Liberal parliamentary party voted with the Government, helping to give it a comfortable majority of twenty-four.[35] Steel and most of his colleagues continued to profess

[34] The history of the negotiations is described in some detail in Alistair Michie and Simon Hoggart, *The Pact: The Inside Story of the Lib-Lab Government, 1977-78* (London: Quartet Books, 1978), chaps. 1-3.

[35] For an analysis of the voting of the minor parties in the division, see Butler, *Coalitions in British Politics*, p. 108.

themselves satisfied with the agreement; but the nature of their dilemma, given that their electoral prospects failed to improve, was well caught by a cartoon in the popular newspaper the *Sun*. It showed Callaghan and Steel sitting side by side, with Steel holding a pistol and saying, "One false move and I'll shoot!" Steel was pointing the pistol at his own head.[36]

As the result of the events of March 1977, the Callaghan Government was safe for the foreseeable future. It was just as well, since Labour continued for some time to trail well behind the Conservatives in the public opinion polls. If a general election had been held at any time before the autumn of 1977, the Government would almost certainly have lost it. As table 2–2 shows, Labour's electoral standing began to recover only toward the end of the year. Moreover, opinion poll data tended, if anything, to understate the parlousness of the Government's electoral position. In the twenty-five by-elections fought between the general election of October 1974 and the summer of 1978, Labour's share of the poll dropped in all but two, often precipitously. Labour gained no seats and lost six, all to the Conservatives, several of the losses being in seats that had never returned Conservatives before. The Tories' capture of Roy Jenkins's old seat in Birmingham was especially humiliating.[37]

The Government's immediate electoral prospects were bleak. There seemed every reason to believe, however, that in the longer term they would improve. Productivity in Britain remained low by international standards, unemployment was still edging upward, and industrial investment showed no real signs of recovery; but a number of other economic indicators suggested that, just possibly, a corner might have been turned. The country's balance-of-payments deficits had begun to diminish somewhat in size over the winter of 1975–1976; they then mounted alarmingly later in 1976 and in the first half of 1977 as the declining value of the pound pushed up the cost of essential imports; but in the second half of 1977 the pound's recovery and increases in North Sea oil production combined to produce healthy

---

36 The cartoon is reproduced in Michie and Hoggart, *The Pact*, p. 137.

37 Roy Jenkins would have liked to be appointed foreign secretary by Callaghan, but when the foreign secretaryship was not forthcoming he accepted nomination as president of the European Commission in Brussels. The parliamentary seat that he vacated, Birmingham, Stechford, had never been won by the Conservatives before. In fact, Jenkins's departure cost Labour not one seat but two, because Jenkins took with him to Brussels a well-known Labour backbencher, David Marquand. Marquand's seat, at Ashfield in Nottinghamshire, was reckoned to be one of the safest Labour seats in the country, but in 1977 it went Conservative on a swing of 20.8 percentage points. Both seats, however, reverted to Labour in 1979.

## TABLE 2–2
### Voting Intentions, 1974–1978
(percent; lead in percentage points)

| Date of Survey | Labour | Conservative | Liberal | Other | Labour Lead |
|---|---|---|---|---|---|
| **1974** | | | | | |
| December | 47 | 33 | 16½ | 3½ | 14 |
| **1975** | | | | | |
| March | 44 | 42 | 11 | 3 | 2 |
| June | 40½ | 44 | 13 | 2½ | −3½ |
| September | 41½ | 38½ | 16½ | 3½ | 3 |
| December | 41 | 40½ | 14 | 4½ | ½ |
| **1976** | | | | | |
| March | 41½ | 44 | 9½ | 5 | −2½ |
| June | 40½ | 44 | 11 | 4½ | −3½ |
| September | 42 | 42½ | 11 | 4½ | −½ |
| December | 34 | 49½ | 11½ | 5 | −15½ |
| **1977** | | | | | |
| March | 33 | 49½ | 13 | 4½ | −16½ |
| June | 37 | 47½ | 10½ | 5 | −10½ |
| September | 41 | 45½ | 8½ | 5 | −4½ |
| December | 44½ | 44 | 8 | 3½ | ½ |
| **1978** | | | | | |
| March | 41 | 48 | 8 | 3 | −7 |
| June | 45½ | 45½ | 6 | 3 | 0 |

NOTE: The initial question was worded, "If there were a general election tomorrow, which party would you support?" Respondents replying "don't know" to this question were then asked, "Which party would you be most inclined to vote for?" Responses to both questions have been merged in the table.
SOURCE: *Gallup Political Index.*

surpluses on current account.[38] At the same time, the number of industrial disputes—widely assumed by observers both in Britain and overseas to be a significant indicator of the country's general economic

[38] The balance-of-payments deficit exceeded £500 million in the third quarter of 1976 and again in the second quarter of 1977. But the third quarter of 1977 showed a surplus of £483 million and the fourth quarter a surplus of £351 million. See McKie, Cook, and Phillips, *Guardian/Quartet Election Guide,* p. 60.

## TABLE 2–3
### WORKING DAYS LOST THROUGH STOPPAGES, 1970–1978

|  | Number (in thousands) | Percentage Change since Previous Year |
|---|---|---|
| 1970 | 10,980 | +60.4 |
| 1971 | 13,351 | +23.4 |
| 1972 | 23,909 | +76.4 |
| 1973 | 7,197 | −69.9 |
| 1974 | 14,750 | +104.9 |
| 1975 | 6,012 | −59.2 |
| 1976 | 3,284 | −45.4 |
| 1977 | 10,142 | +208.8 |
| 1978 | 9,306 | −8.3 |

SOURCE: Department of Employment *Gazette; Guardian/Quartet Election Guide.*

health—was falling sharply.[39] As table 2–3 shows, the number of working days lost through stoppages was much lower between 1975 and 1978 than it had been in the first half of the decade. The Labour party's claim to be much better than the Conservatives at getting along with the trade unions seemed to have some foundation in fact.

But, above all, it was the Government's success in fighting inflation that gave Labour ministers grounds for hope that they might yet be reelected when the time came. To the skeptics' considerable astonishment, the £6 policy negotiated with the trade unions in the summer of 1975 stuck; pay settlements outside the £6 limit were exceedingly rare. More than that, the Government succeeded in obtaining two further periods of cooperation from the unions, the first, explicit, covering the year 1976–1977, the second, rather more tacit, covering 1977–1978. In April 1976, with the £6 arrangement about to expire, Denis Healey, in his annual budget speech, offered the

---

[39] It is an open question how important strikes are as an explanation of Britain's relative economic decline. The number of days lost through strikes in Britain is not significantly greater than in many other industrial countries, including the United States and Canada. It may be, however, that British strikes do more damage because so many of them are wildcat strikes that cause disruption not only in the plants and firms directly affected but in other plants and firms and even in other industries. In general, strikes in Britain are probably less important economically than the restrictive practices and overmanning that unions insist upon and managements acquiesce in. The academic research on the subject is not, on the whole, impressive. A useful introductory textbook is Charles Mulvey, *The Economic Analysis of Trade Unions* (Oxford: Martin Robertson, 1978).

unions a choice between limited tax concessions in the absence of a further year of agreement and more substantial tax cuts if they would accept a new pay ceiling of about 3 percent. The figure eventually arrived at was nearer 5 percent, but Healey reckoned that this was enough, and the larger cuts were made. A year later, in the summer of 1977, formal agreement between the Government and the TUC proved impossible; but the unions did not balk when the Government set a pay ceiling in the public sector of 10 percent, and the TUC for its part reaffirmed its decision that no union should try to negotiate more than one pay increase in any twelve-month period. The almost universal view had been that no incomes policy, whether voluntary or statutory, would be tolerated by the unions for more than two years. The Callaghan Government's policy survived for fully three years.

The results were spectacular. Together with the cuts in public spending undertaken in December 1976 and the strong measures that Healey took at the same time to limit the rate of growth of the money supply, the Government's various understandings with the unions had the effect of reducing Britain's rate of inflation from nearly 30 percent in late 1975 to under 10 percent by 1978. The rate of inflation in Britain was still considerably higher than in most other industrial countries; but in the first place it was now going down instead of up, and in the second place price rises no longer seemed in imminent danger of running out of control. The panic was over; the ground had ceased to shift under people's feet. The story told in figure 2–1 is a remarkable one. It is doubtful whether any other democratic government in history has ever succeeded in reducing a country's rate of inflation by such a large amount in so short a time. Small wonder that Labour ministers began to feel rather pleased with themselves.[40]

The general public, not surprisingly, was somewhat less enthusiastic. After all, if the rate of inflation had been brought down, it was still the case that prices were rising, taxes were high, and many people found their real incomes being squeezed; the Government itself admitted in January 1978 that between 1973 and 1977 real national disposable income had fallen by more than 2 percent and that personal

---

[40] Economists and politicians will long dispute how much of the reduction in the rate of inflation was the result of the trade unions' self-imposed restraint and how much of it was a consequence of the tighter fiscal and monetary policies that the Callaghan Government was pursuing. Labour politicians incline to credit the trade unions; most, though not all, Conservative politicians believe that the larger part of the reduction in inflation should be put down to tight money and the Government's deflationary policies generally. For what it is worth, the present writer finds it very hard to believe that, without the trade unions' restraint, the rate of inflation would have been brought down nearly so quickly.

FIGURE 2–1

INCREASE IN THE RETAIL PRICE INDEX, 1974–1979

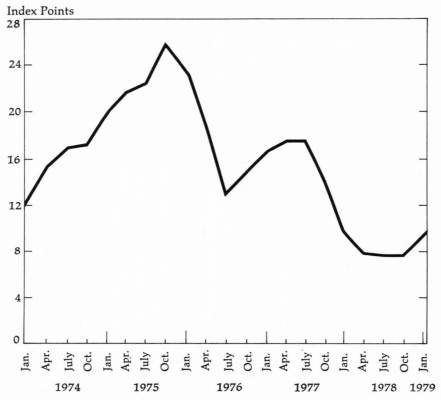

NOTE: Data show the percentage increase in the retail price index during the previous twelve months.

SOURCE: Calculated from *Economic Trends*.

consumption had also fallen during the same period.[41] Although trade unionists and others responded remarkably well to repeated Government requests to tighten their belts, they showed few signs of actually enjoying the experience. Nevertheless, the Government's success in bringing down the inflation rate, and the general impression it gave of being considerably more in control of events than in the past, did result in late 1977 and 1978 in a substantial improvement in the public standing of Callaghan and his colleagues. At the end of 1976,

---

[41] The Government's white paper which made these admissions was quoted with relish by the Conservatives' publication *The Campaign Guide, Supplement 1978* (London: Conservative Central Office, 1978), p. 37.

TABLE 2–4

RESPONSES TO THE QUESTION: "ARE YOU SATISFIED OR DISSATISFIED
WITH THE WAY THE GOVERNMENT IS RUNNING THE COUNTRY?"
(percent)

| Date of Survey | Satisfied | Dissatisfied | Don't Know |
|---|---|---|---|
| December 1974 | 44 | 38 | 18 |
| June 1975 | 28 | 60 | 12 |
| December 1975 | 25 | 63 | 12 |
| June 1976 | 22 | 63 | 15 |
| December 1976 | 22 | 68 | 10 |
| June 1977 | 25 | 62 | 13 |
| December 1977 | 40 | 47 | 13 |
| June 1978 | 38 | 50 | 12 |
| December 1978 | 40 | 45 | 16 |

SOURCE: NOP, *Political, Social, Economic Review.*

only 37 percent of voters were satisfied with Callaghan as prime minister; 44 percent were dissatisfied. A year later, fully 55 percent professed themselves satisfied; the proportion not satisfied had fallen to 33 percent.[42] Table 2–4 reports the marked improvement in the standing of the Labour Government as a whole. To be sure, the proportion of voters dissatisfied with the way in which the Government was running the country always exceeded the proportion satisfied; but, as the table shows, the Government's standing by the summer of 1978 was enormously higher than it had been two years before. Perhaps more to the point, the Labour party's standing vis-à-vis the Conservatives also improved. A glance back at table 2–2 will indicate the scale of the progress that Labour was making. In June 1977, according to the Gallup poll, Labour was trailing the Conservatives by more than ten percentage points; by June 1978, the two parties were running neck and neck. The Conservatives gained a further seat from Labour in a by-election in the spring of 1978; but the swings to the Conservatives in by-elections were tending to diminish as time went on.[43]

By the summer of 1978, Labour had been in power for nearly four years. The outlook for the Government was much better than it

[42] *Political, Economic, Social Review* (NOP), no. 9 (January 1977), p. 3; no. 13 (February 1978), p. 3.

[43] For example, at the by-election in Ashfield, Nottinghamshire, in April 1977, the swing from Labour to the Conservatives was 20.8 points (see above, n. 37). In the four by-elections held a year later, in April 1978, the largest swing against Labour and toward the Conservatives was 9.3 points. See McKie, Cook, and Phillips, *Guardian/Quartet Election Guide,* pp. 220, 222-23.

had been for some time, but it could by no means be confident of maintaining its position in the House of Commons, let alone of winning a general election. The Government's devolution proposals were arousing passionate controversy, the days of the Lib-Lab pact were numbered, and a wages explosion in the coming winter seemed possible, if not indeed probable. The prime minister was soon going to have to decide whether to dissolve Parliament and hold an election in the autumn of 1978 or try to hang on over the winter with a view to going to the country sometime in 1979. It was not going to be an easy decision to take.

## Margaret Thatcher and the Conservatives

The Conservatives after the October 1974 election were in a state of shock. Not only had they just lost two general elections in a row (and four out of the last five), but there was no escaping the fact that the Heath Government, in which such high hopes had been invested only four short years before, had been, by and large, a failure. Edward Heath had entered 10 Downing Street in June 1970 pledged to taking Britain into the European Community and to restoring the country's flagging economic fortunes. The trade unions were to be reformed; private enterprise was to be given its head; government spending was to be cut and waste eliminated. There was, in short, to be a "quiet revolution." [44]

The Heath Government had succeeded in taking Britain into Europe, but even its closest friends acknowledged that it had succeeded in little else. The 1971 Industrial Relations Act had been a total failure; it had not been accepted by the trade unions and had led to more strikes, not fewer. Private enterprise had not proved the sought-after engine of economic progress. Government spending, far from being cut back, had grown substantially; in 1974 it was nearly double

[44] The quotation is from Heath's speech to the 1970 Conservative annual conference, only a few months after the party's election victory; *Verbatim Report, 88th Conservative Conference*, Blackpool 1970 (London: Conservative Central Office, 1970). On the Heath Government, see King, "The Election that Everyone Lost," in Penniman, ed., *Britain at the Polls, 1974*, pp. 3-15; Sked and Cook, *Post-War Britain*, chap. 10; and David Butler and Dennis Kavanagh, *The British General Election of February 1974* (London: Macmillan, 1974), chap. 2. One of Heath's chief aides, Douglas Hurd, wrote a brief but interesting memoir of the period: *An End to Promises: Sketch of a Government 1970-74* (London: Collins, 1979). One of Heath's principal critics, Jock Bruce-Gardyne, analyzed the failings of the Heath administration under the appropriate title, *Whatever Happened to the Quiet Revolution?—The Story of a Brave Experiment in Government* (London: Charles Knight, 1974).

what it had been in 1970.[45] The party's defeat at the hands of the miners in February 1974 had been traumatic. Perhaps worst of all, the Heath Government had in many cases reversed the main lines of its own economic policy. It was not going to bail out private companies that got themselves into difficulties; but it bailed out Rolls Royce. It rejected utterly the philosophy of a statutory incomes policy; but it wound up introducing a particularly tough statutory incomes policy. The whole business of the Government's U-turns was undignified. Conservative M.P.s were dismayed and disoriented; the party was hurt in its pride as well as in its electoral prospects.[46] Now in late 1974 Conservatives were appalled at the thought of another five years of Labour administration. Labour's policies, they believed, were likely to do the country a great deal of damage (this was the moment when inflation seemed to be running out of control); and there was the danger that whichever party was in power in the late 1970s would be able to remain in power well into the 1980s on the strength of Britain's North Sea oil and gas resources. This last nightmare vision turned out to be nothing more than a nightmare; but no one could know that at the time.

Uppermost in the minds of most Conservatives at the end of 1974 was the problem of the party leadership. Edward Heath was something of a hero internationally; he was seen as a major European statesman and was given credit for his bravery in standing up to the miners. But he was not much of a hero at home. He had lost three elections and won only one. His Government had ended in chaos. During the nearly ten years that he and Harold Wilson were the leaders of their respective parties, Heath almost invariably trailed well behind Wilson in the opinion polls.[47] Moreover, Heath was not greatly

---

[45] Even at constant prices, the increase in public spending during the Heath years was enormous; see Alt, *Politics of Economic Decline*, chap. 2.

[46] American readers should understand that the word "U-turn," used quite frequently in the text, has become almost a technical term in British politics, referring to any abrupt changes in Government policy. The Heath Government made many such U-turns between 1970 and 1974 (see King, "The Election that Everyone Lost," in Penniman, ed., *Britain at the Polls, 1974*, pp. 10-12). After the Conservatives were returned in 1979, they announced on every possible occasion that this time there would be no U-turns. Equally, Labour politicians and journalists speculated endlessly about when the first U-turns would come and in which field they would be. One thing was clear: if the next Conservative Government was forced to make any drastic change of policy, it would deny vehemently that it was making a U-turn and find some alternative language—any alternative language—to describe what it was doing.

[47] This was true even at the time of the Conservatives' electoral victory under Heath in 1970. The data for the years 1966-1970 are neatly summarized in David Butler and Michael Pinto-Duschinsky, *The British General Election of 1970* (London: Macmillan, 1971), p. 64.

loved on the Conservative back benches in the House of Commons. His obstinate, unyielding style of political leadership alienated many Conservative M.P.s, while his stiffness of manner made most of those around him feel distinctly ill at ease.[48] In the aftermath of Labour's victory in October 1974, a large number of Conservative members, despite everything, wanted Heath to stay; they admired him, felt loyalty toward him and objected strongly to the fact that he alone was being made to carry the can for failures that rightly belonged to the Government and the party as a whole. This group included a large proportion of the ministers who had served under him. On the other side, many Conservatives were determined to get rid of Heath if they possibly could; they disliked him, regarded him as an electoral disaster, and despised him for his U-turns and his repeated failures in office. But probably most Conservative M.P.s did not have quite such strong views about Edward Heath one way or the other; they merely noted that he had not been a very successful leader. In their view, enough was enough.

The view that the party needed a new leader was widespread. Heath himself, however, showed no signs of resigning, and there were two further obstacles to his departure. The first was procedural. Back in 1965 the Conservatives had adopted a new set of rules for electing the party leader; but the 1965 rules did not provide any mechanism whereby an incumbent leader could be challenged or could submit himself for reelection, and many detailed criticisms had been made of them since they had been last used. In November 1974, under mounting pressure from his opponents in the party, Heath announced that he was prepared to submit himself for reelection. At the same time, he asked Lord Home, a former prime minister and his predecessor as leader, to undertake a review of the election procedures. Lord Home submitted his proposals in December, Heath accepted them, and it was arranged that the election should take place in February.[49]

Two features of the revised rules were thought likely to bear on the coming contest. The first was designed to ensure that the new leader, whoever he was, should not just have scraped home but should have a solid basis of support in the parliamentary party. The

---

[48] One of the consequences of Heath's style of leadership was a sharp increase in Conservative backbench rebellions in the House of Commons. See Philip Norton, *Conservative Dissidents: Dissent within the Parliamentary Conservative Party 1970-74* (London: Temple Smith, 1978).

[49] On the adoption of the new leadership election rules, see Robert Behrens, *The Conservative Party from Heath to Thatcher: Policies and Politics 1974-1979* (Farnborough, Hants.: Saxon House, 1980), pp. 29-31. Behrens's book is a useful guide to Conservative politics during the post-1974 period of opposition.

relevant provision stipulated that, in order to win on the first ballot, the leading candidate had both to gain the support of an absolute majority of all Conservative M.P.s (not only those voting) and in addition to gain 15 percent more votes than his nearest rival. Heath's supporters feared that he might win more votes than any other candidate, possibly even an absolute majority of the votes cast, yet be fatally wounded by abstentions or by the 15 percent requirement. The second significant feature of the new rules permitted candidates who had not contested the first ballot to enter the race in time for the second. To win on the second ballot, a candidate needed to win the support of a majority of all Conservative M.P.s, but the 15 percent requirement was dropped. If a third ballot proved necessary, it would be contested by the top three candidates on the second ballot, and every voter would be required to indicate both a first and a second preference. If again no candidate secured an absolute majority, second preferences would be distributed until a clear winner emerged. These provisions were complicated, but their political purpose was clear: they were designed to facilitate the emergence of compromise candidates. The maintenance of party unity, not just the election of a party leader, was the aim.

The first, procedural obstacle to Heath's departure was out of the way. He was about to stand in a leadership election; in that election, he could be defeated. The second obstacle, however, remained: who was to defeat him? Who was the next leader of the Conservative party to be? These were not easy questions to answer. In the 1970s, fate, and politics, had dealt the Conservatives a series of cruel blows. Iain Macleod, one of the party's shrewdest statesmen and most brilliant orators, had died suddenly only a few weeks after becoming chancellor of the exchequer in June 1970. Reginald Maudling, a man of immense experience who hid high intelligence and considerable firmness of purpose beneath an amiable, even indolent, exterior, had had to resign from the Heath Government in 1972 after details became known of his dealings with John Poulson, a somewhat dubious architect and financier.[50] Anthony Barber, Macleod's successor as chancellor of the exchequer, was deeply implicated in the economic failures of the Heath Government and had retired from politics in 1974. Enoch Powell, whom years before many had tipped as a future Conservative leader, had turned against his former party and now sat in the House of Commons, a largely isolated figure, on the Ulster

---

[50] Maudling defended himself in his *Memoirs* (London: Sidgwick and Jackson, 1978), chap. 14. He served briefly as shadow foreign secretary in 1975-1976 but was then sacked for reasons that are still not entirely clear. He died in 1979.

Unionist benches. As they came to elect their new leader in February 1975, most Conservatives were well aware that their range of choice was more limited than they would have liked.

The position was further complicated by the peculiar circumstances in which the election was to be held. The party leadership was not vacant. On the contrary, it was filled—by Edward Heath, who clearly had every intention of staying on if he could. It followed that anyone who declared in favor of himself was declaring against Heath. This several of his former colleagues, notably William Whitelaw and James Prior, were not prepared to do. They undoubtedly realized that, if they challenged Heath and Heath won, they would have damaged their political careers; and their own good personal relations with him could scarcely be expected to recover. But they were probably moved mainly by straightforward loyalty. They had served under Heath for many years. He had befriended and promoted them. They did not propose to be the instruments of his political destruction. William Whitelaw's position was particularly invidious. A farmer and landowner with the manner of an old-fashioned country squire, Whitelaw was in fact an astute politician, who had been a very successful Conservative chief whip. He had also been a successful minister in the Heath administration, first as leader of the House of Commons, then as Northern Ireland secretary, finally as secretary of state for employment. He had a reputation for making friends of enemies and for being adept at pouring oil on troubled waters. Cleverer than he seemed, he was in many ways Heath's obvious successor. He did not want, however, for the reasons already given, to stand against his old boss on the first ballot. At the same time, he knew full well that, if he declined to contest the first ballot and Heath lost, his refusal to stand would be put down to political cowardice and he would then find it very hard indeed to overtake the first-ballot leader, whoever that turned out to be. Whitelaw, for the moment, stood aside.

Other leading Conservatives were less inhibited. Even before the October 1974 election, Sir Keith Joseph began a series of speeches in which he questioned the actions of the Heath Government, especially after its U-turns in 1971 and 1972. Going further, he advanced the notion that the whole thrust of Conservative economic policy, at least since the end of World War II, had been misguided. Conservatives, he said, had gone much too far in compromising with socialism. They should stop apologizing for capitalism and start rejoicing in it. Conservative policy should be aimed at making the profit motive respectable again, at promoting private enterprise and competition at the expense of government spending and state handouts, at restoring the sense of individual responsibility, and, not least, at tackling inflation at its source by strictly controlling the rate of growth of the money supply. His arguments were trenchant, his phrases vivid:

> We are all monetarists now, except for a few die-hard inflationeers who cannot learn from experience or admit mistakes. . . .

> . . . the middle ground these days is a guarantee of a left-wing ratchet. . . .

> We spend more on welfare, without achieving well being, while creating dangerous levels of dependency.

> . . . decentralized ownership of wealth and decentralised decision-taking—the decentralization which is the essence of the free enterprise system—is absolutely vital to freedom.

> The pursuit of income equality will turn this country into a totalitarian slum.[51]

Joseph's views were strikingly similar to those of conservatives in the United States. He saw himself, and was seen, as a transmitter and developer of the views of Friedman and Hayek. To those who pointed out that denunciations of the policies of recent Conservative administrations came rather oddly from a man who had occupied a senior post in every Conservative cabinet since 1962, Joseph's reply was characteristically disarming. He had indeed been guilty of error in the past; but, unlike some others, he had learned from his mistakes and would not repeat them.[52]

It would be wrong to suggest that Joseph's speeches given in the period after the Conservatives lost office were universally acclaimed within the party. They were not. Many Conservatives resented their implied attacks on the record of the Heath Government, of which Joseph had been a prominent member. Others regarded Joseph's views, and his way of expressing them, as too extreme; the Conservatives had always prided themselves on being a cautious, pragmatic party, not a doctrinaire one, and Joseph was sounding increasingly doctrinaire. He was also sounding, for many tastes, too much like

[51] From a volume of his speeches: *Stranded on the Middle Ground?—Reflections on Circumstances and Policies* (London: Centre for Policy Studies, 1976), pp. 17, 19, 64, and 79. Joseph's favorable view of decentralization evidently extended to spelling: see the fourth of the five quotations above.

[52] Mea culpa is one of the themes of his speech "The Quest for Common Ground" reprinted in *Stranded on the Middle Ground?*, pp. 19-35.

an academic economist and too little like a practicing politician. After all, Milton Friedman had never had to face a miners' strike. Nevertheless, Joseph's views did sound a responsive chord in many Conservatives, among the rank and file in the country as well as in the House of Commons. Many who did not necessarily subscribe to his views in detail were delighted that someone, at last, was speaking out on behalf of the free enterprise system and carrying the war of ideas into the socialist camp. Joseph was aggressive. He did not content himself with moaning about the practical consequences of socialism; he hacked away at the very roots of the socialist system of ideas. He was a man of undoubted intellectual stature. It was good to have him on one's side.

The trouble was that Joseph never really looked like a possible leader of a major political party. He was too diffident, too emotional, too easily wounded by criticism, too intellectually honest, too insensitive to the effects that his carefully chosen words might have on others, too anxious, on a personal level, to please, to be a plausible, let alone an impressive, party leader and potential prime minister. On television he looked more like a don in his study than like a leader of men. There was too much of Brutus in him, too little of Cassius. At first, it seemed that he might nevertheless challenge Heath; in the interval between the two 1974 elections, Joseph actually put it about that he was thinking of entering the lists. But after a disastrous speech in Birmingham in October 1974, when he seemed to suggest that the working classes were having too many children and might have to be discouraged from breeding in order to protect Britain's "human stock," he quietly withdrew. He felt himself unworthy of the post.[53] Instead he threw his support behind the only other member of Heath's cabinet who had no qualms about attacking the former prime minister and his record, Margaret Thatcher.

Although they were about to become political rivals, Thatcher in many ways resembled Edward Heath.[54] Like him, she came from a relatively humble background; her father was a grocer in the provincial town of Grantham. Like him, she attended the local grammar school and then went on to Oxford. Like him, she subsequently made her own way in the world, first as a research chemist, later as a barrister specializing in tax law. Like Heath, too, she had been politically ambitious from an early age. She fought her first parliamentary

[53] Behrens, *Conservative Party from Heath to Thatcher*, p. 38.

[54] Several biographies of Thatcher have already appeared. The best, by a journalist close to her, is Patrick Cosgrave, *Margaret Thatcher: Prime Minister* (London: Arrow Books, 1979). See also Russell Lewis, *Margaret Thatcher: A Personal and Political Biography* (London: Routledge and Kegan Paul, 1976).

election when she was only twenty-four, eventually being returned for the semisuburban London constituency of Finchley in 1959 when she was just thirty-three. Her twin children were born before she entered Parliament while she was practicing at the bar. In the early 1960s, she served as a junior minister at the Ministry of Pensions and National Insurance under Harold Macmillan and then Sir Alec Douglas-Home. When the Conservatives were returned to power in 1970, Heath appointed her to the cabinet as secretary of state for education and science. This particular appointment left her somewhat outside the mainstream of events and government policy. As the only woman in the Heath cabinet, she was a visible minister, but she was not an especially prominent one. She achieved a passing fame early in the Heath administration when her decision to cease providing primary schoolchildren with free milk led to her being dubbed "Thatcher the milk snatcher."

Margaret Thatcher was a tough politician and proud of it. She wanted to reach the top in a man's world and, without ceasing to be feminine in any way, sought to do so by cultivating masculine virtues and what she saw as masculine ways of thought. She sometimes chided her male colleagues for their sentimentality and for their failure to think through problems in a sufficiently rigorous, tough-minded fashion. Like Edward Heath, she was a prodigiously hard worker. Unlike him, she was always considerate of those around her, including her junior officials; she remembered birthdays and made cups of tea at critical moments. Above all, she listened; she argued, but she also listened, at least to those in her own party. Her approach to politics comprised two distinct elements, and they were not always easy to reconcile. On the one hand, she had the lawyer's preference for solid briefs, for facts rather than speculation, and the lawyer's ability to spot at once any weaknesses in the arguments of an opponent. On the other hand, her conservatism was simple and straightforward, more like that of Ronald Reagan than Edward Heath (or, for that matter, Sir Keith Joseph). She believed in the virtues of the people among whom she had grown up: independence, self-reliance, honesty, thrift. She believed in a fair day's work for a fair day's pay. She believed that anyone who had the ability and who really wanted to could get to the top. Free enterprise was the best economic system because it produced goods efficiently, but also because it was the best way of rewarding virtue. Margaret Thatcher had a keen practical mind; she was not someone who entertained philosophical doubts.

In the months following the Conservatives' loss of office in February 1974, Thatcher drew close to Sir Keith Joseph politically.

She admired his courage and subscribed completely to his view that the Conservative party had drifted too far to the left. She expected to support him for the leadership. When, however, he withdrew from the contest shortly after his speech at Birmingham, she had no hesitation in throwing her own hat in the ring. She herself wanted to be leader; she believed that the interests of the Tory party demanded that it get rid of Heath; if no one else was prepared to challenge him, she was. Her campaign was organized by a closely knit group of friends and supporters, led by Sir Keith Joseph and a number of prominent Conservative backbenchers. To everyone who would listen, they insisted not only that it was time for Heath to go but that it was time for the Conservative party to return to its principles. The themes were free enterprise, competition, cuts in state spending, the restoration of individual incentives, and strict control of the money supply. The next Conservative Government would not be deflected from its purposes; there would be no U-turns. Thatcher and her supporters also made much of the former prime minister's failures as a political communicator. She promised not merely to lead the Tory party but to listen to it. Heath had increasingly given the impression that he regarded his political base as being somewhere in Europe, the United States, or possibly the editorial offices of the *Times*. Thatcher made it clear that, if she were elected, her political base would consist of the Conservative members of the British House of Commons.

The election campaign was bitter, at times even ugly, partly because Thatcher was seeking to oust Heath, not merely to succeed him, and partly because, as in the case of Labour's leadership election, there were so few people involved. Face-to-face politics is always likely to be more bitter than politics at a distance. Thatcher's supporters accused Heath of arrogance, insensitivity, and even "dirty tricks"; Heath's supporters accused Thatcher and Joseph of treachery (had they not been physically present in the cabinet when the Heath Government had made every one of its U-turns?), of dividing the party, and of proposing to offer to the electorate a purely class-based appeal.[55] The first ballot was held on February 4, 1975. Most Conservative M.P.s probably expected Heath to hang on. If so, they were

---

[55] The claim of Heath's supporters was that the Conservative party's electoral success depended largely on its ability to win working-class votes and that Thatcher, with her free-enterprise ideology and her appeal to middle-class values, would alienate workers and their families. Thatcher's supporters claimed that, on the contrary, Heath was an elitist and that Thatcher's views were closer to those of ordinary working people. See Behrens, *Conservative Party from Heath to Thatcher*, p. 40. The Heathite view is expressed, in somewhat strident terms, in Trevor Russel, *The Tory Party: Its Policies, Divisions and Future* (Harmondsworth, Middx.: Penguin Books, 1978).

wrong. When the results were announced, there were gasps of astonishment. Heath had 119 votes, but Thatcher had 130; another 16 went to a somewhat quixotic backbench candidate, Hugh Fraser, and 11 M.P.s abstained. In other words, Heath had won the support of only 119 Conservative members out of a total of 276—a dismal showing for a man who had been prime minister only a year before. He at once conceded defeat and resigned the leadership. At this point, no fewer than four of his former ministerial colleagues entered the race: Whitelaw, Prior, Sir Geoffrey Howe, who had drafted the 1971 Industrial Relations Act, and John Peyton, a former junior minister whose candidacy was almost as quixotic as Fraser's. Most Conservative M.P.s probably now expected a close finish between Thatcher and Whitelaw, with Whitelaw picking up most of Heath's votes and possibly a number of Thatcher's as well. If this is what they did expect, they were wrong again. In the second ballot, held a week after the first, Margaret Thatcher emerged the victor, with a clear overall majority. She had 146 votes out of the 271 that were cast. Whitelaw finished a poor second with 76 votes. Prior and Howe had 19 apiece; Peyton got only 11. Why had Thatcher won so decisively? The best single answer, and certainly the most succinct, was given a few days after the event by a young Conservative M.P. who had voted for her: "She was the one who belled the cat."[56]

Earlier in the chapter, we remarked that a striking feature of Labour's leadership election was the willingness of so many Labour M.P.s to vote for candidates who were not held in high esteem by the electorate and who were not at all likely to prove electoral assets to their party. It is worth noting that the same was true on the Conservative side. Several of the major polling organizations conducted surveys on the Conservative leadership shortly before or during the February 1975 election. They all found that most voters believed that Heath should retire; but none of them found a majority of voters, or even any very significant number, who believed that Margaret Thatcher should succeed him. It was quite clear who the voters wanted: William Whitelaw. For example, in mid-January 1975 the Gallup poll asked voters who would make the best leader of the Conservative party if Heath were to resign. Many of Gallup's respondents, fully 33 percent, had no clear view. Twenty-nine percent, however, opted for Whitelaw and 13 percent for Joseph; only 9 percent expressed a preference for Thatcher. Gallup went on to ask the

[56] Private conversation with the writer. Thatcher, in other words, was the one who rendered Heath harmless. The results of the few balloted Conservative leadership elections so far are in Butler and Sloman, *British Political Facts 1900-1979*, p. 129.

same respondents who they thought would make the next best leader. If the two sets of responses are added together, Thatcher falls even further behind. Forty percent of Gallup's sample thought that White-law would make the best or the next best leader. Only 16 percent held the same view of Thatcher, who now fell to fourth place in the electorate's estimation, not only behind Whitelaw and Joseph but also behind a former Heath minister, Robert Carr, who was not even in the race.[57] These findings and others like them received a great deal of publicity in the press and were well known to Conservative M.P.s. Yet in the end, by a substantial majority, they voted for Thatcher. It follows either that they were not greatly moved by electoral considerations or that they believed that voters would form a more positive view of the new leader when they had come to know her better.[58]

Another point is worth making in the same general connection. The opinion polls, needless to say, wanted to know not merely the electorate's views of the various individuals competing for the Conservative leadership but also whether voters thought that the party's election of a woman leader would make them more or less likely to vote for the Conservatives. The polls found that most voters claimed that they would not be influenced one way or the other. Those respondents, not a very large number, saying that the election of a woman would make them less likely to vote Tory were partially offset by those who said that the election of a woman would make them more likely to vote Tory.[59] Thus, electoral considerations, insofar as they

---

[57] *Gallup Political Index*, no. 174 (January 1975), p. 4.

[58] Indeed, within ten days of Thatcher's election there were signs that the public was responding to her favorably. The Gallup poll in mid-February asked voters, "Do you think that Mrs. Thatcher will or will not be a good leader of the Conservative Party?" Twenty-one percent had no view, but 64 percent thought she would be a good leader, against only 15 percent who thought she would not. *Gallup Political Index*, no. 175 (February 1975), p. 5.

[59] All of the opinion polls produced similar results, and this pattern still held at the time of the general election four years later. For example, in a survey conducted by the Gallup poll for the BBC on election day itself, voters were asked, "And would a woman Prime Minister be better than a man, not as good as a man, or does it make absolutely no difference?" Sixty-four percent replied that it made absolutely no difference, 25 percent said a woman would not be as good as a man, and 11 percent said that a woman would be better than a man. Predictably, women voters were somewhat more likely than men to favor a woman prime minister. Even more predictably, Conservatives were more likely than Labour supporters to favor a woman prime minister; in the great majority of cases partisan preferences were almost certainly leading voters to prefer a male or a female prime minister, rather than preferences for a male or female prime minister determining voters' choice of party. It seems doubtful whether in the end Thatcher's being a woman rather than a man influenced more than a handful of voters one way or the other. For details of the BBC Gallup survey, see chap. 9, n. 1.

weighed at all, tipped the scales against Thatcher, if only very marginally. Yet she won. More than that, the fact that she was a woman appears to have played almost no part in the Conservative leadership contest. The popular newspapers spent a great deal of time discussing whether a woman could, and should, be the leader of a major party; but Conservative M.P.s appear to have been oddly uninterested in the issue. They scarcely raised the matter in public, and published accounts of the Conservative leadership election—and there are many— make almost no reference to it.[60] It seems that, when it came to the point, the question of Margaret Thatcher's sex was simply submerged by more compelling considerations of political philosophy and party tactics. It is almost true to say that, in the end, the Conservative parliamentary party elected the first woman leader of any major political party in Europe or the English-speaking world in a fit of absent-mindedness.

Sweeping changes in Conservative policy might have been expected to result from Thatcher's election as leader. Certainly, in her election campaign, she and her supporters emphasized the profound differences of approach that they claimed separated them from Edward Heath. There was much talk of a return to the true faith. But in fact continuity rather than radical innovation marked the development of Conservative policy over the four years leading up to the 1979 election.[61] The notion that the Tory party had, in some crude way, swung to the right with the election of Thatcher was widely credited; but it was largely false, based on paying too much attention to the leader's rhetoric and too little to the details of her proposals. The major policy document of the Thatcher period in opposition, *The Right Approach,* bore a striking resemblance, not just in its title, to the equivalent documents of Heath's opposition years, *Putting Britain Right Ahead* and *Make Life Better.*[62] Moreover, in at least one im-

---

[60] See, for example, Behrens, *Conservative Party from Heath to Thatcher,* pp. 37-41, and Cosgrave, *Margaret Thatcher,* chap. 2.

[61] This is one of the themes of Behrens's *Conservative Party from Heath to Thatcher;* see esp. chap. 7. After the election, the *Economist* (May 26, 1979, p. 25) published a mock Queen's Speech in which passages from the July 1970 Queen's Speech, Heath's first, were intermingled with passages from the May 1979 Queen's Speech, Thatcher's first. Readers were invited to guess which passages belonged to which speech: "No cribbing, please. Members of Her Majesty's government may play." The present writer's score was abysmal. Members of the Government may have done better—but probably did not.

[62] *The Right Approach: A Statement of Conservative Aims* (London: Conservative Central Office, 1976). This was followed by Angus Maude, ed., *The Right Approach to the Economy: Outline of an Economic Strategy for the Next Conservative Government* (London: Conservative Central Office, 1977). *Putting Britain Right Ahead* was published shortly after Heath became party leader in 1965, *Make Life Better* in 1968.

portant field of policy, industrial relations, the Conservatives in the late 1970s were a great deal more moderate—or at least more cautious—than they had been ten years before. The Conservatives under Heath had promised a complete rewriting of British industrial relations law. In the Industrial Relations Act of 1971, they had undertaken such a revision; but it had largely failed to achieve its purposes. Instead, it had contributed to an increased level of industrial unrest and had soured relations between the trade union movement and the Government; moreover, almost all of it had been repealed by the Labour party. Whatever her instincts, Margaret Thatcher had no desire to go down that road again, and the party's industrial relations policy, as it evolved under her and her chief spokesman on the subject, James Prior, was notably restrained. In its 1979 manifesto, the party promised no more than to restrict trade unions' right to engage in secondary picketing, to modify the existing law on the closed shop, and to subsidize out of public funds voting by mail in trade union elections.[63]

The main reason for the high level of continuity from the Heath to the Thatcher eras is that the policies on which Edward Heath and his colleagues fought the 1970 election were far more "Thatcherite" than is often now remembered. The Conservatives' 1970 manifesto called for reductions in income tax, cuts in public expenditure, an end to nationalization, a reduction across the board in government intervention in industry, assistance for small businesses, the sale of council houses (public housing) to sitting tenants who wanted to buy them, urgent action to check the rise in violent crime, tighter controls on immigration, and a strengthening of the country's defenses. Margaret Thatcher had believed all this in 1970; she still believed it in 1979. So did Sir Keith Joseph. They saw no reason to change. Their complaint against the Heath Government did not arise out of its policy objectives but out of its failure to stick to them. Given the popularity of policies like these among rank-and-file Conservatives, it seems highly probable that the party would have reverted to them in opposition even if Heath had remained leader.

Another explanation for the continuity of policy lies in the continuity of personnel. An American politician on attaining high office —whether president or governor or mayor—typically brings into office with him new people, frequently people who have taken part in his

---

[63] *The Conservative Manifesto 1979* (London: Conservative Central Office, 1979), pp. 9-11. On the development of the party's industrial relations policy under Prior, see Behrens, *Conservative Party from Heath to Thatcher*, chap. 6, and Michael Moran, "The Conservative Party and the Trade Unions since 1974," *Political Studies*, vol. 27 (March 1979), pp. 38-53.

election campaign or advised him on policy questions when he was out of office. The British system is quite different. A new party leader can introduce some new faces into the top echelons of the party, of course; but for the most part he or she must live with those who have established themselves over a considerable period of years as the party's senior figures. To dismiss them and replace them by new-comers is to sacrifice their experience, to make enemies of them, and to offend against the highly collegial canons of British political life. Thatcher was thus quite tightly constrained. She could, and did, dis-miss from the shadow cabinet and the Conservative front bench a few leading "liberals" and close associates of the ousted leader; but at the same time it was inevitable that the post-1975 shadow cabinet, al-though appointed by her, would consist very largely of people who had served under Heath (and, incidentally, had probably voted for him in the leadership election).[64] Very radical departures from Heath's policies would have threatened the cohesion of this leadership group, and threats to its cohesion were tantamount to threats both to Thatcher's own position and to the Conservative party's chances of reelection. They were therefore largely avoided.

A further explanation for the continuity of policy is worth mentioning. Margaret Thatcher had not been a well-known political figure before the winter of 1974–1975; she was not even very well known within the Conservative party. She made her mark as a potential leader by being outspoken, sometimes even strident, in her advocacy of traditional values and the free market economy. Out-spokenness—the refusal to mince words, the refusal to make token gestures, the deliberate choice of language calculated to cause the maximum offense among her political opponents—continued to be the hallmark of her political style. This outspokenness was often, and quite naturally, taken for rashness, and Thatcher could indeed be rash on occasion. But caution was at least as important an aspect of her political makeup. She was cautious about not alienating the Conserva-tive parliamentary party upon whom she depended; and she was very cautious in taking on new policy commitments. The Conservative manifesto of 1970 had been long, detailed, and specific; it enunciated

---

[64] Just a few examples will make the point. Thatcher appointed Whitelaw, who had certainly voted for Heath on the first ballot, deputy leader. She appointed as shadow chancellor Sir Geoffrey Howe, who had been promoted by Heath. Another of Heath's senior ministers, Reginald Maudling, became, for the time being, sha-dow foreign affairs spokesman. The only prominent supporters of Heath to be dropped were Robert Carr and Peter Walker. Carr went to the House of Lords and largely retired from active politics; Walker later emerged as Thatcher's minister of agriculture.

a long list of specific policy pledges. This was in the Heath style. The trouble with specific pledges, however, is that if they are broken they can be seen to be broken; and, given that the world is unpredictable, some of any party's election pledges are bound to be broken. In putting her imprimatur on Conservative policy documents and finally on the manifesto for the 1979 election, Margaret Thatcher was determined not to give too many hostages to fortune.[65]

Against this general backdrop, however, one major change of policy stood out. It has already been alluded to: the Conservative party's espousal of monetarism—the belief that inflation is to be attributed solely to an over-large increase in the quantity of money and that the cure for inflation lies in tightly controlling the rate of growth of the money supply. This was not a view that had featured largely in Conservative thinking before 1970, or even before 1974, but by 1979 it was central to the party's economic thinking. The 1979 election manifesto put the point succinctly, if also fairly cautiously: "To master inflation, proper monetary discipline is essential, with publicly stated targets for the rate of growth of the money supply. At the same time, a gradual reduction in the size of the Government's borrowing requirement is also vital."[66] The Conservatives' sudden conversion to monetarism is not entirely easy to explain, but it probably had two more or less distinct sources. The first was Sir Keith Joseph's own thinking and its influence on Thatcher; Joseph became something of a disciple of Milton Friedman at an early stage, and no one did more than Joseph to popularize Friedman's ideas in Britain. The second was the Conservatives' own experience in office between 1970 and 1974. The strength of a convert's new faith often varies in direct proportion to his previous sin, and no Government in British history had ever permitted the money supply to grow more and at a faster rate than the Conservative Government of Edward Heath from 1970 onward. Much of the growth was a direct result of a vastly increased public sector borrowing requirement.[67] There was a certain

---

[65] The phrase "hostages to fortune," used in this context, is Winston Churchill's. Churchill was vehemently opposed to the idea that political parties in opposition should make policy and should commit themselves in advance to the lines of action that they would pursue when returned to office. Opposition parties, in Churchill's view, should oppose; parties in government should govern. See J. D. Hoffman, The Conservative Party in Opposition 1945-51 (London: MacGibbon and Kee, 1964).

[66] Conservative Manifesto 1979, p. 8.

[67] The graph showing the growth of the public sector borrowing requirement in Alt's Politics of Economic Decline practically runs off the printed page: p. 39. For a devastating, if largely implicit, commentary on Conservative monetary policy 1970-1974, see Alt, pp. 34-42.

irony in Thatcher's espousal of monetarism. She had sat in the Heath cabinet throughout the period when the money supply was growing at a record rate. By all accounts, she never once protested.

In the four long years of opposition between the election of Thatcher and the general election of 1979, the Conservatives' main anxiety was that Labour might yet contrive to win the coming election; but they also had another, related anxiety: party unity. Following his defeat in the leadership election, Heath announced that he intended to remain in the House of Commons and to use his new freedom to speak out on issues of national importance. He took up a conspicuous seat in the House of Commons, on the front bench below the gangway; and visitors to the gallery observed that, whenever Thatcher was being given a rough ride by the Labour benches, he did not seem wholly displeased. Privately, and not so privately, he evinced his contempt for his new leader and his deep bitterness at having been stabbed in the back. On several occasions, he took issue with Thatcher's public pronouncements in Parliament, on television, or at the Conservatives' annual conference. The most notable such occasion came in October 1978, not very long before the general election, when he declared his support for the Labour Government's incomes policy, adding that, if the policy failed, Conservatives should be the last to rejoice.

Heath was still a major public figure, and such pronouncements were bound to be damaging; as time went on, Conservatives became more and more irritated with Heath's refusal to be reconciled to the new situation. The major threat to the party's unity, however, was both more profound and more subtle, and would have existed even if Heath had retired gracefully from the political scene. The deepest division within the Conservative party was never very clearly articulated. It was not primarily an ideological division, though the strongest supporters of the free market system did tend to stand on one side of it, those readier to accept the need for government intervention on the other. Nor was it primarily a matter of personal loyalties, though, again, Margaret Thatcher's most ardent supporters tended to line up on one side of the divide, Heath's former allies on the other. Rather, the division related to different beliefs about how a country like Britain should, and could, be governed. It had to do not so much with the content of policy as with how policy should be implemented. Two different inferences could, after all, be drawn from the failure of the Heath administration. On the one hand, it could be said that the Heath Government had failed because it had not had a clear enough understanding of Britain's underlying economic problems and because, faced with opposition and changed circumstances, it had lost its way and shown itself much too willing to compromise and change its policies. On the other hand, it could be argued that the Heath Government, at least at the beginning, had grossly underestimated the complexity and intractability of Britain's economic problems, that it had similarly underestimated the need to win the consent of the people for its measures, and that the Heath Government's U-turns, however unpleasant they were to negotiate at the time, represented the beginnings of political wisdom. One group of Conservatives said, in effect, "In pursuing our objectives, we must not permit ourselves to be deflected." The other group said, in effect, "We need to be ready to compromise and to learn from our mistakes."

Members of the party and outside observers alike found it very difficult to find the right language in which to describe this division. "Right" and "left" would not do, since almost everyone in the party subscribed to broadly right-wing political views. "Thatcherite" and "Heathite" would not do either; most of the leading Heathites were loyal members of Thatcher's shadow cabinet and had long since ceased to look to their former leader for political guidance. "Economists" and "politicians" was better, because it went some way toward capturing the difference between the somewhat theoretical approach of a man like Sir Keith Joseph and the more experimental, political approach of, say, James Prior. "Hawks" and "doves" was another obvious way of making the distinction. After the 1979 election, the doves became known to their opponents in the party simply as "wets." If one had to have shorthand terms, perhaps "ideologues" and "pragmatists" were as serviceable as any.[68] The strange thing was that, however difficult people found it to articulate the differences in the party and whatever the problems about finding suitable labels, no one had any difficulty at all in deciding which leading Conservatives were on which side. One group consisted of Margaret Thatcher herself, Sir Keith Joseph, and almost every member of the party's frontbench economics team, Sir Geoffrey Howe, Michael Heseltine, John Biffen, John Nott, and Nigel Lawson; the other group included William Whitelaw, James Prior, Lord Hailsham, the former lord chancellor, Sir Ian Gilmour, one of the party's few political philosophers, and more junior figures like Norman St. John-Stevas and Mark Carlisle.[69]

---

[68] Behrens suggests "diehards" for those whose political approach was closest to Thatcher's, "ditchers" for the more accommodation-minded, but the language is opaque and has failed to catch on. See Behrens, *Conservative Party from Heath to Thatcher*, chap. 2.

[69] While Sir Keith Joseph was making (and reprinting) his speeches, a number of the pragmatists were setting out their political philosophy in book form: Ian Gilmour, *Inside Right: A Study of Conservatism* (London: Hutchinson, 1977),

This division in the party was largely latent in the period immediately following Thatcher's election as leader. It came to the surface occasionally over such issues as incomes policy and immigration; but for the most part the two groups did not find it too difficult to work together and to smooth over such policy differences as arose. Thatcher was in a dominant position, having only just been elected, and most of her colleagues were disposed to accept her lead on major issues. At the same time, her sense of the potential stresses in the party, her desire to keep the party united, her native caution, and her willingness to listen prevented her from pressing too hard for policies or forms of words that would be bound to cause difficulties. If the Conservatives after 1975 were not always a happy ship, there were few real signs of mutiny. Nevertheless, as the general election approached, there was always the fear that the latent divisions in the party could erupt into open warfare at any time. This fear was to persist after the election was over.

## "The Winter of Discontent"

Throughout the five years of its life, the Labour Government's main preoccupations were economic. There was, however, one non-economic issue which absorbed an extraordinarily large amount of its parliamentary time and involved it in tangled controversies both with several of the minor parties in the House of Commons and with a substantial section of its own supporters. That issue was devolution. It is ironic that attempts to devolve powers onto Scottish and Welsh assemblies should have played such a large part in the history of the 1974–1979 Government, because most ministers in that Government were undoubtedly bored by the whole subject and, insofar as they thought about it at all, probably had the gravest reservations about the wisdom of their own proposals.

The Labour party's reasons for taking up the cause of devolution, and persisting with it, were perfectly understandable. At the 1966 general election, the Scottish National party (SNP) won no seats in Scotland; in 1970, it won one; in February 1974, it won seven; in October 1974, it won eleven. Its share of the popular vote in Scotland, negligible in the 1960s, rose to 21.9 percent in February 1974, then to

---

Peter Walker, *The Ascent of Britain* (London: Sidgwick and Jackson, 1977), and Lord Hailsham, *The Dilemma of Democracy: Diagnosis and Prescription* (London: Collins, 1978). Perhaps surprisingly, the pragmatists were more likely to articulate their views, at least in print, than the ideologues. Perhaps it should be noted that none of the books listed in this note was ghost-written: British politicians write their own books.

30.4 percent in October, when the Conservatives were driven into third place.[70] So far most of the SNP's gains had been made at the Conservatives' expense, but in October 1974 the SNP came second in no fewer than thirty-six of Labour's forty-one Scottish seats, and Labour had every reason to believe that they would be the chief sufferers if the SNP advance continued. The threat from the Welsh nationalist party, Plaid Cymru, was always on a much smaller scale, but even Plaid Cymru increased its parliamentary representation from no seats in 1966 to three in 1974. Labour feared that, if nothing were done to try to satisfy Scottish and Welsh aspirations, not only would the Labour party lose seats, but either Scotland or Wales or both might declare themselves independent; the United Kingdom might disintegrate. Accordingly, Labour's election manifesto in October 1974 stated: "The next Labour Government will create elected assemblies in Scotland and Wales."[71]

Just over a year later, in November 1975, the Government announced its proposals in a white paper, *Our Changing Democracy*.[72] The proposals were complicated in detail, but the ideas behind them were fairly simple. Scotland was to have an elected assembly, with an executive responsible to it in the same way that the British cabinet is responsible to Parliament. The assembly and the executive between them were to have jurisdiction over virtually the entire range of Scotland's purely domestic affairs: local government, education, housing, health, transport, law and order, and so on. The Government at Westminster, however, was determined to maintain the unity of the United Kingdom, and this determination manifested itself in three ways. In the first place, the assembly was to have next to no revenue-

---

[70] For a discussion of the Scottish National party's rise based on aggregate data, see Michael Steed, "The Results Analysed," in David Butler and Dennis Kavanagh, *The British General Election of October 1974* (London: Macmillan, 1975), pp. 345-51. A more subtle, survey-based account is William L. Miller, "The Connection between SNP Voting and the Demand for Scottish Self-Government," *European Journal of Political Research*, vol. 5 (March 1977), pp. 83-102. The literature on devolution and the controversies surrounding it is vast; many books were begun when the devolution issue seemed enormously important, only to be published when interest in it had waned. Among the books of more enduring interest are Vernon Bogdanor, *Devolution* (Oxford: Oxford University Press, 1979), Anthony H. Birch, *Political Integration and Disintegration in the British Isles* (London: George Allen & Unwin, 1977), Michael Keating and David Bleiman, *Labour and Scottish Nationalism* (London: Macmillan, 1979), and Tam Dalyell, *Devolution: The End of Britain?* (London: Jonathan Cape, 1977). The last-named is by a Scottish Labour M.P. who was a vehement opponent of devolution. Indispensable for an understanding of Scottish politics is James G. Kellas, *The Scottish Political System* (Cambridge: Cambridge University Press, 1973).

[71] *The Labour Party Manifesto October 1974* (London: Labour party, 1974), p. 21.

[72] Cmnd. 6348 (London: Her Majesty's Stationery Office, 1975).

raising powers of its own; its entire expenditure was to be financed out of a block grant negotiated annually between the Scottish executive and the central government in London. Second, the Westminster Government reserved to itself all of the powers needed to manage the United Kingdom economy as a whole: not only taxation and control of the budget but also company law, industrial relations law, the whole of the social security system, counter-inflation policy, and industrial policy. Third, *Our Changing Democracy* proposed that the central government be equipped with a formidable veto power; in the person of the secretary of state for Scotland, the government at Westminster was to be able to veto any act of the Scottish assembly either on the ground that it was *ultra vires* (that is, exceeded the assembly's legal competence) or on the ground that, in the Westminster government's view, it would damage the interests of the rest of the United Kingdom. In other words, what the U.K. government gave with one hand it could take back with the other. The scheme for Wales was simply a much watered-down version of the Scottish scheme.

These proposals satisfied no one. They were criticized on almost every conceivable ground. The Conservative Opposition maintained that they gave the regional assemblies too much power and thereby threatened to break up the United Kingdom. Many Labour M.P.s agreed. Many Labour M.P.s also feared that, with such a strong regional seat of government in Edinburgh, scarce resources would be diverted to Scotland away from some of the poorer parts of England, like Tyneside and Merseyside. The Scottish National party complained that the Scottish assembly, far from having too many powers, had too few. They objected particularly to the fact that Scotland was to have no control over its own North Sea oil resources. The Liberals advocated a federal solution. They also thought it absurd that any tier of government should have such large spending powers unmatched by any ability to raise revenue. The three Plaid Cymru M.P.s insisted that "devolution" was too strong a word for what they were being offered; the Welsh assembly would be little more than a glorified county council. More disinterested observers went on to point out that, if the Government had wanted to maximize the chances of conflict between Edinburgh and Westminister, it could not have done better than to propose annual negotiations over the size of the block grant and an extensive veto power for the secretary of state.[73]

The Government, in response to criticisms like these, modified its proposals considerably over the next two years. The block grant

[73] Most of the criticisms are summarized in Dalyell, *Devolution.*

was no longer to be negotiated annually but was to be put on a fixed percentage basis; judges rather than ministers were to decide if and when the Scottish assembly was acting *ultra vires*. Even so, the passage of the relevant legislation onto the statute book was long and tortuous. In December 1976, the Government was forced to promise that referendums would be held in Scotland and Wales before the acts were brought into force. Two months later, with the debates on the Scotland and Wales Bill looking as though they would drag on forever, the Government introduced a timetabling motion—a so-called guillotine motion—only to have it defeated by 312 votes to 283 when 22 Labour backbenchers voted against it and another 25 abstained. Later, in July 1977, the Government modified its proposals still further and announced that in the next session of Parliament they would be presented in the form of two bills, one each for Scotland and Wales, instead of being combined as before. Partly as the result of these changes, and partly because the Government's dependence on the Liberals and the two nationalist parties was now much more apparent than it had been earlier in the year, the House of Commons accepted a guillotine motion on the Scotland Bill in November 1977. Still the fight was not over. In January 1978, a majority of M.P.s, at the instigation of a Labour backbencher, George Cunningham, amended the Government's bill so that it would not come into force unless the majority voting in favor of the bill in the proposed referendum totaled at least 40 percent of the eligible electorate. This provision was to be crucial some fourteen months later. Toward the end of 1978, with both bills at last safely enacted, the Government announced that the referendums in Scotland and Wales would be held on March 1, 1979.

The devolution legislation passed only because the Liberals and the nationalist parties, despite their reservations, supported it in the division lobbies[74] and made it clear to the Labour party that satisfactory progress on devolution was an essential condition of their support for the Government on other matters. Many Labour M.P.s, possibly the majority, voted for devolution not because they believed in it but only because they were convinced that it was necessary if the Government was to survive. The importance of this aspect of the matter was emphasized by the fact that, as the devolution legislation was wending its way through the two houses of Parliament, many in the Liberal party were becoming increasingly restive about the continuation of the

---

[74] The "division lobbies" in the British House of Commons are the two lobbies or antechambers—one for the "ayes" and one for the "noes"—through which members file to record their votes. There are voice votes in the House of Commons but there are no roll-call votes, nor are there voting machines.

Lib-Lab pact. The pact was having the effect of maintaining Labour in power; but, in the eyes of more and more Liberals, it did not seem to be doing their own party much good. In particular, partly because of their close association with the Government, the Liberals' performance in by-elections and in the opinion polls was appalling. In October 1974, the Liberals had secured 18.3 percent of the total vote; during the winter of 1977–1978, their standing in the Gallup poll hovered around the 6 percent mark.[75] Many Liberals, especially in the country, felt that the party should break a connection that was doing it so much electoral harm without bringing compensating advantages in terms of policy. At a special party assembly in January 1978, David Steel successfully fought off a demand that the pact be terminated at once; but he accepted that its days were numbered and on May 25, 1978, announced that it would not be renewed at the end of the current parliamentary session.[76]

The Government could no longer count on Liberal support. It was also encountering increasing difficulties with the trade unions. First the £6 pay limit proposed by Jack Jones, then the 5 percent limit negotiated between Healey and the TUC, finally the informal 10 percent norm, had had a remarkable effect, together with the Government's own deflationary policies, in bringing down the rate of inflation; but the trade unions, like the Liberals, were becoming increasingly restive. Many of their members had suffered a real decline in their standard of living; and successive rounds of pay policy had introduced more and more distorting effects into the traditional pattern of pay differentials. In any case, most trade union leaders believed in free collective bargaining and had never accepted even voluntary incomes policies as more than a temporary expedient. Ministers thus knew in 1978 that a formal agreement with the TUC would not be possible. What they hoped was that, if they made public their view about the level of pay settlements that would be in the national interest, most trade unions would adhere to it—or at least pay enough attention to it that the average level of settlements would not be too far above it. In July, the prime minister announced a proposed ceiling for the next pay round of 5 percent. The Government would seek to enforce this ceiling by using its purchasing power to impose sanctions on firms that stepped out of line; a firm awarding a pay increase of, say, 10 percent might find itself deprived of govern-

---

[75] Butler and Sloman, *British Political Facts 1900-1979*, pp. 240-41.

[76] On the later stages of the pact, see Michie and Hoggart, *The Pact*, chaps. 8-11, and Michael Steed, "The Liberal Party," in H. M. Drucker, ed., *Multi-Party Britain* (London: Macmillan, 1979), pp. 104-06.

ment contracts. But all this was too much for the majority of the trade union movement, and at its annual congress in September the TUC endorsed overwhelmingly a resolution withdrawing the unions' co-operation from the Labour Government. Its message was contained in its first two sentences:

> Congress recognises the sacrifices undertaken by union members in observing the terms of agreed pay policies but, while recognising the need to limit inflation, considers that after three years of restraint trade unions must now negotiate freely in their members' interests.
>
> Congress declares its opposition to Government policies of intervention and restraint in wage bargaining, including Government sanctions. . . .[77]

In terms of fighting inflation, the Government was back to square one.

While the Government and the TUC were making up their minds on the future of incomes policy, the time had come for the prime minister to decide whether to hold a general election in the autumn of 1978 or to defer it.[78] The dilemma that confronted the prime minister was simple in essence. On the one hand, Callaghan was acutely aware that, if the Government went to the country in late September or October 1978, it might lose. Although Labour's standing in the polls had improved out of all recognition since the previous year, the latest information suggested that the Conservatives for the moment probably enjoyed a slight lead; in August, for example, Market and Opinion Research International reported the Conservatives three percentage points ahead.[79] Callaghan was proud of his Government's achievements and did not want to put them at risk unnecessarily. On the other hand, he knew full well the risks of waiting. There might be another round of industrial disputes and a wages explosion; the Government might be deserted by the minor parties (though Michael Foot assured him that the SNP would continue to support the Government at least until after the Scottish referendum). It followed that the choice lay between holding an election now when the available evidence suggested that Labour might well lose and waiting until 1979 when Labour's position might indeed have worsened but when it might just possibly have improved. Present fears or future

---

[77] *Report of the 110th Annual Trades Union Congress*, Brighton 1978 (London: Trades Union Congress, 1979), p. 549.

[78] The thinking behind Callaghan's decision is described in detail in Dick Leonard's chapter in this volume.

[79] Butler and Sloman, *British Political Facts 1900-1979*, p. 241.

possibilities? Callaghan decided to wait. Almost any prime minister in his position would have done the same.[80]

All the same, Callaghan within weeks rather than months must have begun to wonder whether his decision had been the right one. The history of the Labour Government over the winter of 1978–1979 resembles one of those sequences of photographs that record for posterity the demolition of some famous old building. In the first frame, the building is intact; in the second, the foundations have been undermined and masonry is falling from the upper stories; in the third, the building is collapsing under its own weight; in the last frame, it has fallen. So it was with Labour from September 1978 onward.

The first blow was struck by the TUC, when it rejected any form of incomes policy. The next was struck by the Labour party's annual conference when, in October 1978, it followed the TUC's lead and, by a majority of 4,017,000 to 1,924,000, totally rejected "any wage restraint by whatever method."[81] The Government was still determined to use the sanctions weapon against employers acceding to wage claims above the 5 percent limit; but by the end of the year this policy, too, had collapsed. Workers at the Ford Motor Company struck, demanding wage increases well in excess of the Government's norm. The company at first held out, wanting to abide by the norm and fearing Government retaliation, but in the end, after the strike had lasted for nine weeks, the management capitulated and conceded pay increases averaging approximately 17 percent—more than three times what the Government maintained was a reasonable maximum. As though to rub salt in the wounds, the House of Commons just before Christmas deprived ministers of what was left of their sanctions weapon; a handful of Labour left-wingers abstained, and a Conservative motion condemning the sanctions policy was passed by 285 votes to 279. The Government, as in the days of Harold Wilson, was reduced to exhorting unions and employers and to warning them of the probable consequences of their actions.

---

[80] A former Conservative cabinet minister, Lord Boyle, once in private conversation likened the position of a prime minister deciding whether or not to hold a general election to the position of a man in a tepid bath in a cold room. On the one hand, the bath is uncomfortable, increasingly so; on the other, the thought of getting out of the bath is not at all attractive. Most people under these circumstances would stay in the bath. Callaghan did likewise. It should be added that Callaghan took the decision almost entirely by himself; he consulted fewer colleagues than most recent prime ministers have been wont to do. Cf. King, "The Election that Everyone Lost," in Penniman, ed., *Britain at the Polls, 1974*, pp. 21-22.

[81] *Report of the Seventy-Seventh Annual Conference of the Labour Party*, Blackpool 1978 (London: Labour party, 1979), pp. 214, 230.

And, as in the days of Harold Wilson, the Government's warnings went unheeded. The result was something approaching chaos, as one group of workers after another walked off the job in support of pay claims ranging from the modest to the bizarre. Some workers struck because they believed their employers could afford it, others because, in the inflation of the preceding years, their real pay had fallen further and further behind the national average, others because their wages had always been low, still others to restore differentials. Militancy was seldom politically inspired; it was often a direct response to falling living standards and a deep sense that the Government's successive incomes policies had been unfair in their results. But, whatever the strikers' motives, the results were felt in every home in the country—and seen on every television screen. Operations were postponed and hospital wards closed because National Health Service supervisory engineers and laundry staffs went on strike. The shelves in supermarkets began to empty because of a nationwide strike of lorry drivers. A strike of tanker drivers resulted in shortages of petrol in some parts of the country. Because of a strike by local authority manual workers, black plastic bags filled with garbage began to pile up in civic squares around the country; rats were seen not far from Piccadilly. One-day strikes by train drivers resulted in the disruption of intercity and suburban services. The winter of 1978–1979 was one of the worst in recent British history, but because of another strike by local authority manual workers the roads were often left unsalted and ungritted. In the northwest of England, an unofficial strike by water and sewage workers led to the water supply's becoming contaminated, with the result that drinking water had to be boiled. Also in the northwest, a strike of gravediggers left the dead unburied, with corpses stored in ever increasing numbers in temporary mortuaries. The direct impact of the various strikes and go-slows could be exaggerated; they did not all occur at the same time, nor did they affect every part of the country equally. Most people lived their lives relatively undisturbed. But the wave of industrial unrest alarmed many people and irritated many more; and above all it completely undermined the credibility of the Government's claim that it could collaborate successfully with the trade unions. As the unions became more and more unpopular, so did their Labour party allies.

The public's distaste for the scenes being enacted every night on their television screens was reflected in the opinion polls almost at once. In November 1978, two of the three major national polling organizations showed Labour in the lead. Gallup reported a Labour lead of five percentage points, National Opinion Polls (NOP) a Labour lead of one percentage point; Market and Opinion Research International (MORI) put the Conservatives ahead, but only by one point. By February 1979, only eight weeks later, the position had been transformed. The Conservatives were now ahead in all of the polls, by some of the largest margins in the history of public opinion polling in the United Kingdom. Gallup and NOP both showed the Conservatives ahead by eighteen points; the margin reported by MORI was nineteen points.[82] After the general election, a former aide to the prime minister described how one night he watched on the television news as a funeral cortege approached the entrance to a municipal cemetery. Just as the cortege reached the cemetery gates, the camera panned to a group of pickets. They were guarding the entrance, placards aloft. The cortege turned back. The prime minister's aide knew at that moment that Labour had lost.[83]

The Government's great hope in the early weeks of 1979 was that it would be able to buy time: time in which to patch up some new arrangement with the TUC, time during which the electorate's memories of the winter of discontent might fade. In the short term, it seemed reasonable to hope that the Government might be able to maintain its position in the House of Commons at least until the summer, conceivably till the autumn. There was not much joy to be had from the Liberals, who continued to vote with the Government when they agreed with it but who, now that the Lib-Lab pact had lapsed, were committed in general to the proposition that the Government had outlived its usefulness and should be forced, if at all possible, to go to the country. But the two nationalist parties had a vested interest in Labour's remaining in power for the time being. The Conservatives, having flirted with devolution in the late 1960s and early 1970s, were now firmly opposed to it, or at least to Labour's version of it. The nationalists feared that, if a general election took place before the Scottish and Welsh referendums on March 1, the Conservatives might go so far as to cancel them. Even after the referendums, there was always some danger that, if the majorities in favor of devolution had been small, the Conservatives would find some

---

[82] The results of the MORI poll published in the *Daily Express* on February 6, 1979, were particularly devastating. Not only did they show the Conservatives leading Labour by nineteen percentage points; they showed that the proportion of voters dissatisfied with Callaghan as prime minister exceeded the number satisfied by a margin of two to one: 62 percent to 31 percent. The hostility manifested toward Labour's allies, the trade unions, was profound; even among Labour voters, 85 percent were in favor of a legal ban on secondary picketing, 68 percent favored the use of troops to provide a basic service in the event of a strike in a key industry.

[83] Private conversation with the writer.

excuse to delay the implementation of the devolution statutes. The SNP had an additional reason for not wanting an early election: their standing in the polls, like the Liberals', had slumped badly since 1974. In an early election, it looked as though their ranks would be decimated. Ministers also had reason to hope that a majority of the ten Ulster Unionist M.P.s might be willing to vote with the Government or at least abstain. Most Ulster Protestants had never forgiven the previous Conservative Government for introducing direct rule in Northern Ireland, and the Unionists were also eager to see the Government fulfill its promise to increase the number of Northern Ireland M.P.s. Even after the winter of discontent, Labour still hoped it might be able to hang on.

The referendums in Scotland and Wales took place on schedule, with results deeply disappointing to both the SNP and Plaid Cymru. As table 2–5 shows, the cause of devolution in Scotland won the support of only a bare majority of those Scots who bothered to vote and nowhere near the 40 percent of the eligible electorate specified in the Cunningham amendment. Most Scots still told the opinion polls that they were in favor of some form of devolution, but the scheme proposed by the Government had few convinced supporters. The Conservative party in Scotland opposed it. Labour was split.[84] The SNP backed it, but only as a second best. In Wales, the rejection of devolution was overwhelming, with every county returning a "no" majority and scarcely one eligible voter in ten voting "yes." The Welsh had always been less enthusiastic about devolution than the Scots, and it seems that in the circumstances of 1979 many Welshmen feared that Wales, already one of the weaker parts of Britain economically, would be still further neglected if the English somehow got the idea that, since Wales had its own government, it should be allowed to look after itself.

The damage done by the referendums to the Callaghan Government's prestige and self-esteem was enormous. Ministers had devoted the better part of two parliamentary sessions to the two devolution schemes. Now one of them, the Scottish, had received only the most tepid response, while the other, the Welsh, had been rejected with contumely. Even if many in the Government were not wildly enthusiastic about devolution, they had hoped for better results than these. Still, to begin with, it seemed by no means inevitable that the events

---

84 Two Labour M.P.s, George Cunningham and Tam Dalyell—both of Scottish origin, though Cunningham represented a London constituency—led the Scottish Labour campaign against devolution. Both attracted a great deal of publicity. See Dalyell, *Devolution*, and Keating and Bleiman, *Labour and Scottish Nationalism*.

## TABLE 2–5
### Results of Devolution Referendums, March 1979

| District | "Yes" Percentage of Those Who Voted[a] | "Yes" Percentage of Electorate[b] |
|---|---|---|
| Scottish regions | | |
| Borders | 40.3 | 27.0 |
| Central | 54.7 | 36.4 |
| Dumfries and Galloway | 40.3 | 26.1 |
| Fife | 53.7 | 35.4 |
| Grampian | 48.3 | 27.9 |
| Highland | 51.0 | 33.3 |
| Lothian | 50.1 | 33.3 |
| Strathclyde | 54.0 | 34.0 |
| Tayside | 49.5 | 31.5 |
| Orkney | 27.9 | 15.2 |
| Shetland | 27.0 | 13.7 |
| Western Isles | 55.8 | 28.1 |
| Scottish total | 51.6 | 32.9 |
| Welsh counties | | |
| Clwyd | 21.6 | 11.1 |
| Dyfed | 28.1 | 18.3 |
| Gwent | 12.1 | 6.7 |
| Gwynedd | 34.4 | 22.1 |
| Mid-Glamorgan | 20.2 | 12.0 |
| Powys | 18.5 | 12.3 |
| South Glamorgan | 13.1 | 7.8 |
| West Glamorgan | 18.7 | 10.8 |
| Welsh total | 20.3 | 11.9 |

[a] The turnout in Scotland as a percentage of the registered electorate was 62.9. In Wales it was 58.3.

[b] The base for the percentages in this column includes an official adjustment to allow for the fact that, since the register was compiled several months before the referendums took place, some voters had died or otherwise become incapable of casting their ballots.

SOURCE: *Times Guide to the House of Commons May 1979*, p. 324.

of March 1 should lead to the Government's fall. After all, what good would it do the SNP, in particular, to throw Labour out? The SNP would almost certainly lose seats in an early election, and the return of a Conservative Government, which seemed the most likely outcome, would dash Scotland's hopes of home rule for at least five years, perhaps for a generation. Given that fewer than 40 percent of the Scottish electorate had voted in favor of devolution, the Cunningham amendment required the Government not to implement the Scotland Act; yet, for all that, more than half of those who had gone to the polls had supported devolution, and perhaps some compromise could be worked out between the Government and the SNP whereby the Government might somehow keep the cause of devolution alive in return for the Scots' support.

Such calculations occupied ministers' minds during the fortnight following the declaration of the referendum results; but they failed completely to reckon with the SNP's anger and frustration. The SNP was furious. The whole party, M.P.s and rank and file alike, felt it had been betrayed. There had been a deal. The eleven SNP members of Parliament would support the Labour Government, in return for which the Labour Government was supposed to deliver devolution. The SNP had kept its side of the bargain. Now it was time for the Government to keep its. The SNP did not begin to recognize the 40 percent requirement as legitimate. More than 50 percent of those who voted had supported devolution. That had been enough in the Common Market referendum four years before. It should be enough now. Callaghan and Foot probably had some sympathy with the SNP's plight, but they believed there was nothing they could do. The 40 percent requirement was clearly set out in the law, and the law could not be broken. Nor was there any real prospect of its being changed; a significant minority of Labour M.P.s was opposed root-and-branch to devolution and would resist any attempt to reintroduce it by the back door, and anyway, to keep devolution alive solely for the purpose of keeping the Government in power, despite the existing law and despite the Scottish people's evident lack of enthusiasm for it, would seem a very shabby trick indeed. Callaghan was not prepared to engage in a maneuver like that even to save his Government. Following a series of angry meetings in Scotland and discussions between Callaghan, Foot, and the SNP leaders at Westminster, the Scottish National M.P.s on March 22 tabled a motion of no confidence in the Government. The Conservatives immediately tabled their own, more generally worded no-confidence motion, which the SNP and the Liberals at once said they would support. The motion was put down for debate on March 28. The Government's fate would depend on the three Plaid Cymru M.P.s and the twelve members from Ulster.

The fall of the Government was still not a foregone conclusion. The tiny Plaid Cymru contingent much preferred a Labour to a Tory Government and after winning one minor concession from Labour—

relating to the payment of compensation to slate quarrymen suffering from respiratory diseases—announced that it would join the Labour party in the "no" lobby. Frantic efforts were made to woo the Ulster Unionists despite their irritation at the Government's failure to move toward reintroducing a measure of self-government for Northern Ireland; and in the end two Unionist members, John Carson and Harold McCusker, did support the Government. But their support was largely offset by the behavior of the two Catholic M.P.s from Northern Ireland. One of them, Frank Maguire, a dour republican from county Fermanagh, ostentatiously abstained; the other, Gerry Fitt of the Social Democratic and Labour party, from Belfast West, announced in a sorrowful speech that he had no choice but to vote against a Government that had curried favor with the Unionists and done so little for the minority community in Northern Ireland. One backbench Labour M.P., Sir Alfred Broughton, was known to be too ill to vote. Opening the debate for the Government, the prime minister was nevertheless remarkably cheerful. He was reconciled to defeat, fully realizing that, even if the Government won the division later that night, its days, under the circumstances, must be numbered. With heavy sarcasm, he scorned the unholy alliance between the SNP and the antidevolutionist Conservatives. Alluding to the electoral catastrophe that appeared about to befall both the SNP and the Liberals, he said that this was the first time in recorded history "turkeys have been known to vote for an early Christmas."[85]

After six hours of debate, the vote was taken at 10 P.M. on March 28. The result was announced a few moments later. The Government was out, by one vote. The margin was 311 votes to 310. Loud cheering immediately broke out on the Conservative benches. The prime minister announced quietly that he would go to the queen the next day and ask that Parliament be dissolved. "Now that the House of Commons has declared itself," he said, "we shall take our case to the country."[86] The next day it was announced that the election would take place on May 3.

## The Election

The ensuing campaign, like most election campaigns in Britain, was largely devoid of incident. Only the assassination of Airey Neave, a close personal friend of Margaret Thatcher and the Conservatives' spokesman on Northern Ireland, disturbed the even flow of a cam-

---

[85] *Guardian*, March 29, 1979, p. 4.
[86] Ibid., p. 1.

paign that seemed destined, from the moment the election date was announced, to lead to a predetermined outcome.[87] By the end of March and the beginning of April, the Conservatives' lead in the opinion polls had declined considerably since the heady days of February; but during the four weeks of the campaign only one of a large number of polls ever put Labour ahead, and, more to the point, after the first few days, the great majority of politicians of all parties wrote off Labour's chances.[88] Only the prime minister, proud of his Government's achievements, contemptuous of his principal opponent, still with a faith in the British electorate's good sense, apparently believed, till just before the end, that Labour might somehow pull it off.

In essence, the Labour campaign was an attempt to persuade people that Labour was the party of experience and sound judgment, that only the Labour party could be counted on to look out for the interests of ordinary working people, that Labour, despite the events of the past winter, still stood a better chance than the Conservatives of avoiding conflict with the trade unions, that Labour sought to unite the country whereas the Conservatives would inevitably divide it, that now was no time to be embarking on the kinds of rash economic experiments that the Conservative party clearly envisaged. Life under Labour had not been easy, but progress was being made; to vote Tory was to put that progress at risk. Labour's appeal was far more conservative than radical; it was an appeal not to rock the boat. Callaghan, who looked and sounded like a man who would never rock a boat, had his party's campaign largely built around him. In his final speech in Cardiff on the eve of poll, he reminded voters of the miners' strike and the three-day working week that Labour had inherited in February 1974 and pleaded with them: "Don't let them turn the clock back once again to what we endured during their term of office."[89]

---

[87] Neave was killed within the precincts of the House of Commons by a bomb planted under his car, almost certainly by an Irish terrorist. Neave had played a large part in organizing the escapes of captured allied soldiers from Germany and occupied countries on the Continent during World War II, and he was a popular figure in the House of Commons. Politicians in all parties mourned him personally and deplored the assassination, but his death could not be expected to have, and did not have, any direct bearing on either the election campaign or its outcome.

[88] An NOP survey published in the *Daily Mail* on May 1, 1979, gave Labour a small lead, 0.7 points, but almost no one believed it, and in any case it was quickly contradicted by the results of all the polls, including NOP, published during the next two days.

[89] *Daily Telegraph*, May 3, 1979, p. 1.

The Conservative campaign had three facets. One was simply to attack Labour's record and to remind voters—not that they needed much reminding—of how much they were suffering from high prices, high taxes, and high unemployment, from all the strikes, the pickets, and the trade unions' unbridled power. Thatcher starkly contrasted what was happening in Britain now with the ideals of human dignity and brotherhood of the early labor movement:

> What a world away that sort of brotherhood is from the flying pickets, the kangaroo courts, the merciless use of closed shop power, and all the other ugly apparatus which has been strapped like a harness on our people and our country, turning worker against worker, society against itself.[90]

Second, and more specifically, the Conservatives warned voters that, although Callaghan and many other leading members of the cabinet might be moderates, the Labour party was rapidly being taken over by extremists, who increasingly dominated both the selection of parliamentary candidates and the Labour party's National Executive Committee. Were Labour to be returned, Britain's drift toward socialism might become irreversible.[91] Finally, the Conservatives spoke with pride of their own policies—reductions in taxation, cuts in public expenditure, laws to curb the trade unions, help for small businesses,

---

[90] Ibid., April 17, 1979, p. 36.

[91] The Conservatives' claim that the Labour party was being taken over by the extreme left had considerable evidence to support it. From the late 1960s onward, the National Executive Committee was left-dominated for the first time in the party's history, and at the same time constituency Labour parties were showing themselves more disposed than in the past to adopt left-wing parliamentary candidates, even to deny readoption to moderates. The most spectacular case in which a moderate sitting M.P. was denied readoption was that of Reg Prentice at Newham North-East. Prentice was actually a cabinet minister when he first came under fire; he subsequently resigned first from the cabinet and then from the Labour party, standing at the 1979 election as a Conservative and finally being appointed a junior minister in the Thatcher Government. During the late 1970s, a considerable number of prominent former Labour supporters, including at least two former cabinet ministers, announced their conversion to Conservatism; the views of some of them were collected in a book: Patrick Cormack, ed., *Right Turn: Eight Men Who Changed Their Minds* (London: Leo Cooper, 1978). Reg Prentice's ordeal at Newham North-East is described by one of his supporters: Paul McCormick, *Enemies of Democracy* (London: Temple Smith, 1979). The parliamentary Labour party continued to have a solid moderate majority, though even in the House of Commons the proportion of left-wingers in the Labour ranks was tending to increase over time. The presence of so many "extremists" in the party clearly worried many voters. For example, in the Gallup BBC survey referred to earlier (n. 59), voters were asked whether, when they finally decided which way to vote, it was for one of eleven possible reasons that they were shown on a card. Only one reason was picked out by more than 10 percent of voters: 15 percent cited "Because of extremists in the Labour party."

sales of council houses, the selling off of parts of state-owned industry, higher pay for the police, more spending on the armed forces—all of which, they said, would restore freedom to the individual and make Britain safe and prosperous again. "I am a reformer," Margaret Thatcher said repeatedly, "and I am offering change. . . . The way to put Britain back into the international race is by giving new life and strength to principles which made our country the great trading nation it used to be."[92] Throughout the campaign, the Labour party hoped against hope that at some point Thatcher, who was relatively inexperienced and had never before been subjected to such continuous publicity, would crack under the strain and would make some fatal mistake. She never did.

The Liberals began their campaign handicapped by their close two-year association with the Labour Government, which the electorate was now so evidently determined to throw out. In October 1974, the opinion polls at the beginning of the campaign had given them nearly 20 percent of the vote; in April 1979, they had nearer 10 percent.[93] Undaunted, David Steel set off around the country in a converted motor coach, dubbed "the Liberal battle bus." His themes were what the party's had always been. The Liberals stood for moderation against the extremes of both major parties; they stood for a national and not a class-based approach to the problems of the day. They deplored the increasing tendency of each major party to pass extreme legislation, which their opponents then proceeded to repeal as soon as they had the chance. The Liberals sought to hold the balance of power in the new parliament so that they could act as a check on the other, overmighty parties. Steel maintained that the Lib-Lab pact had been a success, precisely in this sense. "The extremists," he said, "have had their day. Now is the time for positive national policies."[94] As the campaign went on, the opinion polls reported that the Liberals' share of the vote was edging gradually but steadily upward.

The question on May 3, especially as the early results began to come in, was not whether Thatcher and the Conservatives would have an overall majority but just how large it would be. In the end it was forty-four seats, somewhat smaller than had been expected but more than enough to maintain the party in office for a full five-year term.

---

[92] *Daily Telegraph*, April 17, 1979, pp. 1, 36.

[93] For the polls during the October 1974 election campaign, see Richard Rose, "The Polls and Public Opinion in October 1974," in Penniman, ed., *Britain at the Polls, 1974*, pp. 226-27.

[94] *Guardian*, May 2, 1979, p. 28.

The Conservatives had 43.9 percent of the popular vote compared with Labour's 36.9 percent. The Liberals had 13.8 percent, a substantial drop since 1974 but far more than had seemed even remotely possible at the nadir of the Liberals' fortunes a year before. The Scottish National party's share of the vote in Scotland was nearly halved, from 30.4 percent in October 1974 to just 17.3 percent; the party fell back in Scotland from second place to third. The fringe parties, apart from Plaid Cymru in Wales, all did badly. The national results, however, concealed significant regional disparities. Broadly, the Conservatives did better and better the further south the terrain on which they were fighting. In Scotland, they had once had half of the vote; now they had less than one-third. By contrast, in the whole of the south of England outside London, Labour's share of the vote fell to only about 30 percent. In some meaningful sense, both of the major parties were ceasing to be national parties.[95]

The swing to the Conservatives, 5.2 percentage points, was the highest to any party since World War II, and the Conservatives' lead over Labour, 7.0 percentage points, was the largest that either major party had had over the other since the Labour landslide of 1945. In terms of seats, the results were: Conservatives, 339; Labour, 268; Liberals, 11; the SNP, 2; Plaid Cymru, 2; Ulster Unionists of various kinds, 10; and Northern Ireland Catholics, 2. The Speaker made up a House of 635. The Conservatives gained 61 seats altogether, 7 from the SNP, 3 from the Liberals, the rest from Labour. Labour gained a total of 10 seats, 2 from the SNP, 2 seats that had formerly been held by the breakaway Scottish Labour party, 1 from Plaid Cymru, and 5 from the Conservatives, all but one seats that the Conservatives had gained from Labour in by-elections and were now won back. The Conservatives lost only one figure of note: Teddy Taylor, a prominent antidevolutionist Scottish member, who, had he been returned, would probably have been asked to serve in Thatcher's cabinet. The Liberals not only lost fewer votes than had been expected but also fewer seats. It had been thought that they might lose half a dozen of their 14 seats; in the event, they lost only 3. One of the losses, Jeremy Thorpe's seat in North Devon, was virtually inevitable; at the time of the election, Thorpe was awaiting trial on a charge of conspiracy to murder. But John Pardoe, the party's deputy leader, was also defeated by a Conservative in his constituency of North Cornwall. The SNP paid a heavy price for having chosen to precipitate an early election: the loss of all but 2 of the 11 seats they had won in October 1974. They had

---

[95] The election results are analyzed in Ivor Crewe, "The Voting Surveyed," in *The Times Guide to the House of Commons May 1979*, pp. 249-54.

voted, as Callaghan had said, for an early Christmas; their necks had duly been wrung. Of the leading figures on the Labour side, the only one to lose her seat was Shirley Williams, swept away by a Conservative tide that engulfed almost all of the new towns and prosperous suburbs on the outskirts of London. A prominent Labour moderate, she was one of the House of Commons's most respected members; even her political opponents were saddened by her departure.

British politics is in some ways peculiarly brusque. Polling day was May 3. The results were known by noon on May 4. That afternoon, Margaret Thatcher drove to Buckingham Palace to kiss hands as prime minister. That same afternoon, James Callaghan began to move his personal belongings out of the prime minister's residence. Margaret Thatcher, standing on the doorstep of 10 Downing Street and greeting the enthusiastic crowds, quoted St. Francis of Assisi:

> Where there is discord may we bring harmony;
> where there is error may we bring truth.
> Where there is doubt may we bring faith;
> where there is despair may we bring hope.[96]

The next afternoon, May 5, the new prime minister announced her list of cabinet appointments. Everyone noticed that one name was missing. Thatcher was unwilling to run the risk of offering a major appointment to her defeated rival. Edward Heath remained on the back benches.

## Conclusion

The results of the 1979 general election are analyzed in detail, and their significance assessed, by Ivor Crewe in the final chapter of this book. Only four points need to be emphasized here. The first is that the Conservative triumph, which looks so overwhelming at first glance, appears a good deal less so on closer inspection. The Conservatives under Margaret Thatcher gained, as we have seen, 43.9 percent of the popular vote. This was more than enough to defeat the Labour party in May 1979; but it was in fact the second-lowest percentage secured by any party winning an overall majority in the House of Commons since 1945. Only Labour won a smaller share of the vote when it scraped home in October 1974. When the Conservatives were winning their famous victories in the 1950s, their share of the vote was much higher, varying between 48.0 and 49.7 percent. Indeed, Labour, in losing its third general election in a row in 1959—a defeat

---

96 *Daily Telegraph*, May 5, 1979, p. 36.

so demoralizing that Hugh Gaitskell, the party leader, subsequently called for a radical revision of the party's constitution—in fact secured almost exactly the same share of the popular vote as the Conservatives in winning their apparently overwhelming victory of 1979.[97]

The second point is the obverse of the first. If the Conservatives appeared strong when really they were not, it was because Labour was so weak. Labour's share of the vote in 1979, 36.9 percent, was lower than that of either major political party in any of the ten general elections since the war; it was Labour's poorest vote since the party's cataclysmic defeat following the breakup of the Ramsay MacDonald Government in 1931. Labour was doing almost as well in the 1920s, when the party was still, relatively speaking, in its infancy, as it did in 1979. Moreover, the party's performance in 1979 was in no way a freak. The May 3 election was the third in succession in which Labour's share of the vote had fallen below 40 percent. The extent of Labour's long-term difficulties was concealed for some time by the party's two election "victories" in 1974; but after 1979 it could be concealed no longer. The reasons for Labour's decline are considered in chapter 9. They are of a secular rather than a cyclical nature.

The third point concerns the Liberals. The Liberals suffered something of a setback in 1979. They lost roughly a quarter of their vote compared with that of the previous general election, and only a small part of this loss can be accounted for by the fact that the Liberals fielded fewer candidates than four years before (577 instead of 619). Their loss of three seats in 1979 meant that, following the election, they had fewer seats than thirteen years before, in 1966. But in fact the downturn in 1979, however serious in itself, conceals a long-term, continuing trend in the party's favor. The Liberals' share of the vote in May 1979, 13.8 percent, although lower than at either of the previous general elections, was higher than at any other general election since 1929 and nearly double the party's vote less than a decade before, in 1970. Despite their losses, the Liberals in 1979 had cause to be quietly pleased with themselves.

The fourth point concerns all of the minor parties taken together. The British political system is still predominantly a two-party system. The two major parties between them control the great majority of seats in the House of Commons. In the 1979 election, the major parties' combined share of the popular vote recovered somewhat, having fallen sharply at both of the 1974 elections. The fact remains, however, that in the 1970s the various minor parties made considerable

---

[97] For the results of British general elections since the war, see table 1-4 in Austin Ranney's chapter.

inroads into the major parties' share of the vote; they also won more seats in the House of Commons than at any time since 1945. The minor parties' share of the popular vote in May 1979, 19.2 percent, although lower than at either 1974 election, was still nearly double that at most elections since the war; and their total of seats in 1979, twenty-seven, although, again, lower than in 1974, was still much higher than at any other postwar election. Part of the minor parties' strength was due to the resurgence of the Liberals; part of it was due to the progress of the two nationalist parties; part of it was due to the decision of the various Ulster Unionist factions to break away from the Conservatives in the early 1970s. In the case of the Liberals and the nationalist parties, much of it was undoubtedly due to a disposition on the part of a growing number of voters to turn their backs on both the Conservatives and Labour. But, whatever its specific causes, the rise of the minor parties, and their success in securing more than two dozen seats in Parliament, means that, if either of the majority parties in future is to have an overall majority of seats in the House of Commons, its margin of seats over the other major party must be considerably greater than in the past, and likewise that the chances of neither major party's having an overall majority are considerably enhanced. The postwar dominance of the two major parties could reassert itself at any time; but for the moment Britain's two-party system is visibly broken-backed.

Be that as it may, the chief significance of the 1979 election lies not in itself but in its potential consequences. In the days and weeks after May 3, Margaret Thatcher and her colleagues embarked on their great experiment, to see whether, by cutting taxes and public expenditure and by controlling the money supply, they could revive the fortunes of the ailing British economy. Ministers were well aware that the experiment was bound to be risky both economically and politically. It remained to be seen whether they had the determination to carry it through.

# 3

# The Labour Campaign

### Dick Leonard

**The Decision to Delay the Election**

In retrospect, there is no reason to doubt what few doubted at the time (with the crucial exception of James Callaghan): that October 1978 would have been the best date for the Labour party to have held the election. Indeed, so much had the inevitability of an October poll been taken for granted, that when Callaghan broadcast on September 7 and announced that there would not be one he took virtually the whole nation by surprise.

There were several reasons why the conviction of inevitability had built up. First, and underpinning all the others, was the impressive evidence that virtually all the economic indicators were likely to be more favorable to the Labour Government in October than they would be at any subsequent date in the following year (the last date on which the election could, theoretically, be held was November 15, 1979;[1] the last practical time was, effectively, October 1979).

The economic case for an October 1978 election was argued magisterially by David Blake, economics editor of the *Times*, in an article in the issue of July 20, 1978. "Short-term developments in the economy in the run-up to the election," he asserted, were "likely to be the most favourable experienced by any government since the 1966 election which produced a Labour majority of over 100." After remarking that "inflation at about 8 percent is a great deal more tolerable in the short term if wages are rising by nearly 15 percent as both are running now," Blake went on to say: "The best estimate

[1] Under section 7 of the Parliament Act 1911 the House of Commons is automatically dissolved five years after the day that it first met: an election for a new House is then held seventeen days later (excluding Sundays and public holidays).

I can make is that by the election living standards will be about 4 percent higher than they were six months previously. They will also be about 8 percent higher than they were in October 1977."

His overall conclusion was that "by luck and by judgment" the Government had "created the very model of a pre-election boom." Blake was not content to outline the economic case for an election in October 1978; he also indicated the dire consequences of delay:

> For unless there is another giveaway budget (which would risk provoking the sterling crisis which otherwise seems ruled out) living standards will fall in the first quarter of next year, by about 1½ percent. And the economic picture will also look much less favourable, with double-digit inflation very likely.[2]

Few observers had calculated the odds as closely as Blake. But the general thesis that economic indicators (especially the inflation rate) had greatly improved, but were likely to deteriorate by early in 1979, was extremely widely understood and accepted.

A second reason why an October 1978 election was expected was the choice, in mid-July, of 5 percent as the Government's projected limit for pay awards under stage four of its incomes policy. This was widely seen as an unrealistic limit but good window dressing, as it was likely to feed the expectation that inflation would fall to 5 percent or less. An October election would permit it to be put in the shop window without having to be submitted to the test of the autumn round of wage claims.

The economic indicators were largely buttressed by the opinion polls, which had seen a steady rise in Labour fortunes since the beginning of the year when Mrs. Thatcher's controversial remarks on immigration had led to a temporary Tory surge.[3] In the Gallup poll, for example, a Tory lead of nine points in February had given way by May to level-pegging between Labour and Tory, and a Labour lead of four percentage points in August.

Moreover, the parliamentary situation strongly pointed to an early dissolution. The Lib-Lab pact lapsed at the end of July with

---

[2] David Blake, "Can Mr Callaghan fly in the face of electoral history?" *Times*, July 20, 1978, p. 16.

[3] Mrs. Thatcher had suggested in a television interview on January 30, 1978, that there was widespread public concern at the prospect of the country's being "swamped" by colored immigrants, and she promised that the Conservative party would, if elected, bring in measures to restrict immigration further. The immediate effect of her broadcast was a sharp leap in Tory poll ratings; in the Gallup poll the Tories went up from level-pegging to a lead of nine percentage points, in NOP a Labour lead of two percentage points changed in two weeks to a Tory one of eleven percentage points.

Callaghan making no attempt to persuade the Liberals to renew it. Neither was any approach made to either the Scottish National party or the Ulster Unionists to conclude a similar agreement. The general feeling was that it would be too risky for the Government, which by then was in a minority of twelve seats, to carry on depending purely on ad hoc arrangements to win each parliamentary division.

A further reason for the expectation was the lack of any denial from Downing Street during July and August that an October 1978 election was planned: this was taken, perhaps uncritically, as confirmation that it would, in fact, take place, and the only uncertainty remaining, at least as far as the press was concerned, was which Thursday in October Callaghan would choose as polling day (October 5 and 12 were the hottest favorites). Callaghan was later to claim disingenuously that he had told nobody that the election would be in October: but a quiet word from his aides to selected newspaper contacts to the effect that an early election was far from certain would have gone a long way to damp the speculation down.

Far from this happening, Callaghan's team were dropping hints to the opposite effect. In particular, Tom McNally, the prime minister's political adviser, at a lunch in Rye in early August, specifically told Terry Lancaster, the political editor of the pro-Labour *Daily Mirror,* that the election would be in October. There is good reason to believe that McNally was personally authorized by Callaghan to do this. McNally even told Lancaster the probable date of the election —October 5. Journalists on other papers were given to understand that the story Lancaster subsequently wrote was authoritative.

Moreover, the top trade union leaders were overwhelmingly confident that Callaghan would use the Trades Union Congress (TUC), which met in Brighton in the first week in September, as the launching pad for Labour's election campaign. This confidence survived a private dinner party held in Sussex on the eve of the TUC, on Friday, September 1, when Callaghan met with a select group of leading trade union figures and discussed with them how the unions could help Labour's campaign. On Monday morning, September 4, the chairman of the TUC, David Basnett, opened the congress with a rousing call to fight for a Labour victory, which made no sense if a general election campaign was not imminent. On Tuesday afternoon, September 5, Callaghan himself addressed the conference, and despite his broad hint that there would be no October election, the expectation was so fervent that virtually everybody took this to be just "Jim's little joke" and assumed that he would use his broadcast on that Thursday evening to fire the starting gun.

Instead, when Callaghan met his cabinet on Thursday morning, he confounded their expectations. With the exception of Michael Foot (and perhaps also Denis Healey), ministers arrived at the meeting fully expecting that the prime minister would be asking them to rubber-stamp his decision to call an election for October 5. The only uncertainty in their minds was whether he might not have chosen instead one of two other less strongly fancied dates—September 28 or October 12. Not only did the majority of the cabinet expect an October poll: most of them—probably at least two-thirds—positively desired it. But their opinion was not asked for: Callaghan began the meeting by stating bluntly that he had decided that there would not be a general election until some time in 1979, and the remainder of the meeting was spent discussing the parliamentary and other consequences of this decision. There was no discussion of its desirability, and no minister indicated dissent.

There is little reason to doubt that Callaghan himself was reluctantly convinced when he departed for his Sussex farm at the end of July that he would, in fact, be calling an October election. By mid-August he seems to have changed his mind: this was not communicated to Labour headquarters in Transport House, which should, nevertheless, have been alerted by the prime minister's failure to take a number of decisions necessary if October were to be the chosen date.

Nor, with two exceptions, did he consult cabinet colleagues, though some of them took it upon themselves to convey to Callaghan their own thoughts on the subject. The London *Evening Standard* on August 31 carried a story headlined "The Fearful Five" which suggested that Michael Foot, Denis Healey, David Owen, Merlyn Rees, and Roy Hattersley were all urging the prime minister to delay, on the basis of their own lack of confidence in a Labour victory. The story was at least partially wrong—Hattersley had, on the contrary, written to Callaghan saying that he thought the signs encouraging for an early poll.

The two colleagues that Callaghan did consult were Denis Healey and Michael Foot—the two senior cabinet colleagues whom he invariably sounded out about difficult decisions. From Healey he sought reassurance that the inflation rate would not be substantially worse by the spring of 1979 which, with reservations, the chancellor of the exchequer was able to give. To Michael Foot he addressed the query: What are the prospects of getting through to the spring without being defeated in a confidence vote in the House of Commons?

Foot, who was in close touch with the minority parties in the House, gave Callaghan a much more optimistic assessment than that being made by most political commentators, saying in particular that he thought there was little risk of a defeat on the queen's speech.[4] There is no doubt that Foot was a strong advocate of delay and that his arguments had a powerful—probably a decisive—influence on Callaghan.

For Foot was pushing Callaghan in a direction in which he very much wanted to go. It was probably because of his fear of a parliamentary defeat that Callaghan had accepted the logic of an October 1978 poll. Once that fear was assuaged, other factors telling against an early election began to weigh more heavily on his mind, and perhaps even on his subconscious.

The most important of these was probably his own psychology. Callaghan is a deeply cautious man, given to weighing the odds with great deliberation before embarking on any risky enterprise; his natural inclination in the face of a difficult decision has always been to put it off. Moreover, he had by that time been prime minister for little over two years, and the prospect of another six months at Downing Street before he would have to put it at hazard must have been an appealing one.

Second, there were the opinion polls. These had not shown the improvement over the summer months that had been anticipated, and the poll findings published in early September were no better, from Callaghan's point of view, than those published in June.[5] Callaghan was even more depressed by a poll in marginal seats, carried out for the Labour party by Market & Opinion Research International (MORI), which showed that Labour was doing worse in the key marginal seats than in the country as a whole. He concluded from this that Labour gains were improbable. "Tell me which seats that we don't hold already we're going to win?" he asked his associates, who in the light of the MORI poll were unable to provide reassurance. Callaghan did not like minority government either in theory or in practice as he had known it throughout the greater part of his premiership, and he did not see how he could get a majority.

---

[4] The queen's speech is delivered each year at the beginning of the parliamentary session. It contains the Government's legislative proposals for the coming year. In 1978 it was scheduled for early November and was likely to be the occasion for the Tories to table a motion of no confidence. In the event, the Government survived this Tory onslaught by 312 votes to 300, with the support of the Welsh nationalists and the abstention of the Ulster Unionists.

[5] Three polls published in early June had shown an average Tory lead of just over two percentage points. The MORI poll taken at the beginning of September also showed a two-point Tory lead. Three further polls taken after Callaghan's decision not to fight an election was known showed the Tory lead increasing, on average, to six percentage points.

Because of his emphasis on where the last few necessary seats were going to come from, his advisers paid close attention to the question of the election register, and it acquired an influence out of all proportion to its importance. It was one finite fact on which they could seize when everything else was highly speculative. An October election would be held on a register which was already a year old—an election held in late February or early March 1979 would be on a new one, from which the Tories would gain less benefit than Labour. The proportion of people who had moved out of their constituencies would be lower on the new register and therefore the number of those eligible for a postal vote; as the Tories were known to be much more efficient at organizing the postal vote,[6] it was rightly assumed that the newer the register the better for Labour. The question was how much better, and it seems certain that many in the Labour camp grossly overestimated the effect. A careful calculation made by the *Economist* in September 1978 suggested that the net benefit from this source of a February 1979 election would have been six seats[7]: the prime minister's staff had earlier received from a statistically minded M.P., Edmund Marshall, an estimate of ten seats.

Callaghan seems also to have miscalculated the effect on the unions of postponing the election. He appears to have believed that this would keep them on their best behavior and that wage claims would be moderated. In fact, the postponement appears to have had precisely the opposite effect—snapping the bonds of restraint which had been straining throughout the summer.

Another reason for Callaghan's delay was his belief—often expressed to his associates—that the public had not yet realized the full benefit of the rise in living standards that had occurred in 1977-1978. "Leave them a little longer for the coins to be jangling in their pockets," the prime minister was fond of saying. He perhaps underestimated the extent to which people had become accustomed to studying the retail price index, and thereby passed up the opportunity of fighting the election at a time when the index had been falling almost continuously for sixteen months. Instead he fought the election at a time when it had been rising, albeit slowly, for five months.[8]

---

[6] The Tories benefit from the postal voting provisions because (1) eligible middle-class voters are much more likely than working-class voters spontaneously to apply for a postal vote, and (2) their better-funded organization is more able to employ professionals to build up the number of registrations of known supporters.

[7] "Six seats at stake," *Economist*, September 16, 1978, p. 26.

[8] The index had fallen from 17.7 percent in June 1977 to 7.8 percent in October 1978: it subsequently rose to 9.8 percent in March 1979, the last figure published before polling day, May 3.

The final reason was almost certainly the persuasiveness of Michael Foot. As we have seen, Foot advised that there was a good chance of Labour's getting through the winter without being defeated in key parliamentary votes, but he went well beyond this to argue with verve in favor of putting off the election. His main motivation appears to have been the strong streak of mischievousness in his character which has long been recognized as one of his more endearing qualities. "The Tories' advertising agency, Saatchi and Saatchi, has decided that polling day will be October 5th," he argued, "and are spending a great deal of money accordingly. Let's call it off and they'll be left with mud on their faces." Foot thought this a great wheeze, and recounted it to the Labour party conference a month later, as well as to numerous more private gatherings. It was a trivial, almost childish argument perhaps, but this did not prevent its receiving a very sympathetic hearing from Callaghan.

When the decision not to hold an October poll was taken, the presumption was that the election would instead be held in late February or early March 1979: to that extent, Foot's advice that the Government could probably get through the winter without being defeated in a confidence vote proved well founded. But it fairly soon became apparent that the early spring might not be a favorable time and that the Government might have to try to hold out for much longer.

## Economic Setbacks and the Referendum

The first setback to the Government's hopes was the overwhelming rejection of the Government's 5 percent policy by the Labour party conference in the first week of October, when a resolution rejecting any form of wage restraint was carried by 4,017,000 votes to 1,924,000. This led to a prolonged series of talks between ministers and trade union leaders to secure broad agreement on a modified approach to incomes policy. This almost succeeded, but the agreement that was reached in the joint discussions failed to be ratified by the general council of the TUC, largely because of the unwillingness of Moss Evans, who had recently succeeded Jack Jones as general secretary of the powerful Transport and General Workers' Union (TGWU), to commit himself.

Meanwhile the 5 percent limit was being seriously breached in wage agreements concluded in the private sector, notably the key settlement made by the Ford Motor Company with a number of unions, led by Evans's TGWU. This settlement, reached in late November, provided for wage increases averaging 17 percent. The

Government proposed to apply sanctions against Ford but was defeated in a parliamentary debate, on December 13, on the proposed sanctions, in which the Liberals, Scottish Nationalists, and Ulster Unionists all joined with the Tories, and at least four Labour M.P.s abstained.[9]

There was a strong case for the Government to declare an immediate general election, but this was not seriously considered by Callaghan. Instead, he went back to the Commons the following day and asked for a vote of confidence, which he obtained by 300 votes to 290, thanks mainly to Ulster Unionist abstentions. Looking back, it seems probable that Labour thereby lost its final opportunity of fighting an election campaign it might have won. It would have started the campaign slightly ahead in the opinion polls[10] and would have had the excellent issue of the use of sanctions, which its spokesmen could argue were essential to keep inflation down, to exploit in defending itself against Tory attack. As it was, Callaghan was still unwilling to put everything to hazard and was perhaps unduly put off by the inconveniences of a mid-winter campaign and of polling only a few weeks before the new election register would be issued. (The choice of dates for a "sanctions" election was effectively January 12 or 19; the new register came into effect on February 15.)

Instead of a January election, what Labour had to face was a series of highly damaging strikes by lorry drivers, oil tanker drivers, and, above all, local government and health service workers, which effectively destroyed its chances of winning. It was not the economic effect of the strikes that hurt the Labour party, but the psychological impact of "human interest" stories reported on television: stories of the dead remaining unburied and the sick being refused admission to hospitals. In a few short weeks one of Labour's main electoral assets —its ability to get on well with the trade unions—was cruelly mauled, and the Tory lead in the Gallup poll shot up from eight points in January to twenty points in February.

Callaghan had contributed to his own discomfiture by his response to television reporters when he was interviewed at London's Heathrow airport on his return from the Guadeloupe summit conference in early January—just after the beginning of the oil tanker drivers' and lorry drivers' strikes—and asked to comment on the crisis. He unwisely replied that no crisis existed, and the pro-Tory

9 There were two divisions, the first lost by the Government by 285-279, the second, in which there were no Labour abstainers, by 285-283.

10 The most recently published Gallup poll, in mid-November, had given Labour a five-point lead, while NOP had shown Labour two points ahead. MORI had reported a Tory lead of one percentage point.

newspapers were not slow to draw the contrast between the prime minister sunning himself on Caribbean beaches and the suffering British public.

The Government sought to recoup its position by starting urgent negotiations with the TUC leadership to get a new agreement which would restore the credibility of its claim to have a unique relationship with the unions, and on St. Valentine's Day (February 14) a so-called concordat was signed. It pledged Government and unions to work for a reduction of the inflation rate to 5 percent over three years and promised fewer strikes, less picketing, and looser closed shops. It was the best that could be obtained, in the circumstances, but only super-optimists believed it could undo the damage caused by the winter's strikes.

Not long after the ink had dried on the concordat the Government suffered another hammer blow in the results of the Welsh and Scottish devolution referendums on March 1. In Wales there was nearly a four-to-one split against devolution; in Scotland the result was almost equal (51.6 percent for, 48.4 percent against), and the "yes" vote, at 32.5 percent of the electorate, was well short of the 40 percent figure which Parliament had agreed was necessary for devolution to go ahead without further ado.

The defeat of the Welsh proposals had been widely anticipated: it was only the large margin which occasioned surprise. But the Scottish result was a grievous disappointment to ministers: up to a week or two before referendum day opinion polls had shown a consistent majority of nearly two-to-one in favor of the Government's proposals. It seems almost certain that the major reason for the failure to obtain an adequate majority in Scotland was the deep unpopularity of the Government following the January strikes. As devolution was associated in the electorate's mind with the Labour party, this had the effect of sharply diminishing the prodevolution vote: had the referendum been held in the previous December there is little doubt that a much higher positive vote (probably exceeding the 40 percent barrier) would have been obtained.

As soon as the smoke cleared after the referendum it was apparent that the Government would have a desperate struggle on its hands to survive an early confidence vote and thus preserve the priceless advantage of being able to retain control over the choice of general election date. By this time it should have been obvious that the longer the election could be deferred the better for Labour so that there would be time for memories of the distressing January strike scenes to fade. If the Nationalist parties had had a clear view of their own self-interest they too would have seen from the referendum result (and recent by-elections in Scotland) that their electoral appeal had slipped and that they might well benefit from delay, as should the Liberals whose standing in the opinion polls was pitifully low. Yet the Nationalists responded to their hurts in a self-destructive way and determined to vent their disappointment on their erstwhile Labour allies (though the Welshmen relented when offered the prospect of a parliamentary bill to pay compensation to slate quarrymen suffering from lung disease, a key issue in Plaid Cymru's North Welsh heartland). The Government was also assured of the votes of the two rebel Scottish Labour party M.P.s. As for the Liberals, they felt totally committed by an undertaking that David Steel had given the previous autumn that they would vote against the Government in any division where this would help to precipitate a general election. Probably they privately hoped that others' votes would save them from the consequences of their own.

This, effectively, meant that the Government's fate was in the hands of the twelve Northern Irish M.P.s. The two Roman Catholic M.P.s, Gerry Fitt and Frank Maguire, who had sustained the Government in previous tricky situations, had become disaffected and were calling for the resignation of the Northern Ireland secretary, Roy Mason. The most that could be expected of them was abstention. This left the ten Ulster Unionists, of whom the Government needed the votes of three or the abstentions of six (or some equivalent combination) in order to be safe. There was a great deal of toing and froing between whips and ministers and the Ulster M.P.s, and there is little doubt that sufficient support could have been obtained—at a price. Callaghan showed himself unwilling to pay the price—which was economic rather than political—and some ministers at least considered it by no means excessive. In the event, only two of the Unionists voted with the Government; the other eight went into the opposition lobby. Callaghan also vetoed the acceptance of an offer by Lady Broughton, the wife of a dying Labour M.P., Sir Alfred Broughton, to bring him to the precincts of the House of Commons in an ambulance so his vote could be counted in the crucial division.[11] (As it turned out this would have been sufficient to see the Government through, as the vote on the motion of no confidence which Mrs. Thatcher moved on March 28 was lost by the Government by a single vote—311 to 310. Sir Alfred died five days after the vote.)

---

[11] Under a procedure known as *nodding through*, an M.P. who is unwell but physically within the precincts of the House of Commons (which includes the principal car park in New Palace Yard) may participate in a parliamentary vote, the word of his party whip being accepted unquestionably by the other side.

The prevailing view among Callaghan's ministerial colleagues is that by this time Callaghan had lost the will to carry on in charge of a minority Government and that his patience had snapped. He was no longer willing to engage in constant wheeling and dealing in order to survive and was already seriously contemplating an early summer election (perhaps on June 7, to coincide with the elections for the European Parliament) rather than holding on until the autumn, which would probably have been the better option. He was not inclined to exert himself conspicuously merely for the sake of a few extra weeks in office.

## Callaghan's Campaign

Before the Labour campaign could get underway one essential preliminary still needed to be disposed of: the drafting of Labour's election manifesto. This might have been thought to be of merely symbolic significance, but Labour Governments have traditionally shown a high degree of punctilio in carrying out the specific promises made in their manifestoes, so it was widely recognized as an important element in the continuing power struggle between Labour's left and right wings. The party constitution lays down, in its Clause V, that the manifesto should be drawn up by a joint meeting of the cabinet and the National Executive Committee (NEC). This meeting, the clause says, should decide which items from the party program (which is approved by the annual conference) should be included in the manifesto.

The rule thus implied that the manifesto should be a joint enterprise. Both sides, however, the (left-dominated) national executive committee and the (right-dominated) cabinet, and in particular Callaghan, were determined to have the last word.

The NEC was effectively led by the left-wing energy minister, Tony Benn, who was chairman of its key policy-making subcommittee, the Home Policy Committee. His loyal ally was Geoff Bish, the party's research secretary, a Transport House official who was responsible for coordinating all the preparatory work which the party machine had put into preparations for the manifesto for three years preceding the general election. Bish has since recounted in a notably candid commentary how he and Benn and a majority of the members of the NEC were comprehensively outmaneuvered by Callaghan so that when the Clause V meeting was finally held on the morning of April 6, "the NEC had been set-up to agree to the very kind of Manifesto, in the very circumstances, it had always hoped to avoid."[12]

---

[12] Geoff Bish, "Drafting the Manifesto," in Ken Coates, ed., *What Went Wrong?* (Nottingham: Spokesman Books, 1979), pp. 187-206.

The result was a bland document entitled "The Labour Way is the Better Way," which strongly defended the record of the 1974–1979 Labour Government but made a minimal number of specific policy commitments for the future, none of them of a socialistic type. In particular, Callaghan, who had contrived that the draft document should be written by two of his policy advisers at 10 Downing Street, Tom McNally and David Lipsey, rather than by Bish, ensured that various controversial proposals passed by large majorities at Labour party conferences, including the abolition of the House of Lords, should be excluded. The result was a manifesto guaranteed to lose no votes by upsetting nonsocialist voters, but it was also one which aroused minimal enthusiasm amongst the party's most dedicated supporters.

It was not only the manifesto that Callaghan kept closely under his personal control: This was true of the entire Labour campaign, though it is arguable that he was merely following the precedent set by his predecessor, Sir Harold Wilson. Nominally, control of the campaign was vested in the party's Campaign Committee, presided over by the party chairman, Frank Allaun, and including eight cabinet ministers, seven other M.P.s, and seven Transport House officials. This committee met at Transport House at 8:30 A.M. every day during the campaign, though the attendance fluctuated greatly as many M.P.s were absent in their own constituencies. Yet the meetings were preceded by working breakfasts at 10 Downing Street, where Callaghan effectively took all the important decisions together with a small group of his speechwriters and personal aides. Normally present at these breakfasts were: Tom McCaffrey, the prime minister's press secretary; Derek Gladwin, a senior official of the General and Municipal Workers' Union who traveled with Callaghan as his "road manager" throughout the campaign; Roger Carroll, a journalist on secondment from the *Sun* newspaper as a speechwriter; David Lipsey, a prime ministerial aide charged with liaison with Transport House; Edward Booth-Clibburn, a public relations consultant who donated his services during the campaign to take charge of Labour's media presentation; and Bernard Donoughue and Gavyn Davies, of the policy research unit at 10 Downing Street. The breakfast table was completed by the presence of Audrey Callaghan and her son, Michael, who accompanied his father throughout the campaign.

It is the view of one of those who attended both sets of meetings that few if any ideas originated at the formal campaign committee meetings, which were completely dominated by Callaghan: only at the breakfasts was he receptive to advice. At the breakfast meeting items appearing in the morning's newspapers were discussed, the draft of Callaghan's statement for the morning press conference was considered, and ideas were exchanged for his speech the same evening. Although Callaghan's method of controlling the campaign resembled Sir Harold Wilson's in October 1974, the personnel of his advisory team was quite different: only Donoughue survived from 1974. This was part of a deliberate decision of Callaghan's to distance himself as far as possible from the Wilson inheritance: he had carefully recruited his own people, politely declining offers of help from former associates of Sir Harold.

Temperamentally, too, he was very different from his predecessor, who was always on the lookout for news events that could be quickly exploited for electoral benefit. Callaghan preferred to concentrate on a few set themes and was relatively uninterested in newspaper stories which his aides brought to his attention.

Despite the election's having come at an unexpected and unwelcome time for Labour, the party got its campaign off to an earlier and brisker start than its Tory opponents, effectively getting in an extra week's campaigning. Callaghan officially opened the campaign with a morning press conference on Monday, April 9, and daily press conferences were then held each morning (except Sundays and Good Friday, April 13) until the eve of the poll. The Tories did not start theirs until over a week later—Tuesday, April 17.

Even before this, Labour received a considerable psychological boost when London Weekend Television proposed two extended television debates between Callaghan and Thatcher. Callaghan immediately accepted, Thatcher reluctantly declined, having been persuaded by her media adviser, Gordon Reece, that she would run an unacceptable risk of being shown up as inexperienced by Callaghan. Mrs. Thatcher was strongly criticized for ducking the challenge, even in some pro-Tory newspapers, though the Labour party probably made rather less of this episode than it should have done.

Callaghan's willingness to appear—even though he was the incumbent and it is normally the challenger who is the more anxious for such face-to-face encounters—is readily explained. Labour's electoral prospects looked dreadful at the outset of the campaign: it was far behind in the polls both in voting intentions and on the issues. The only glimmer of light was Callaghan's persistent lead over Thatcher, and it clearly made every kind of sense to attempt to capitalize on this advantage. Apart from the leadership question, it was difficult for Labour to focus on specific issues at the outset of the campaign. Tony Benn made a well-publicized attempt to push the party into taking a strongly anti-EEC line in a speech in the Tory-held West London marginal seat of Kensington on April 8. He declared, "A vote for Labour in this election will be a vote against the Common Market as it now operates," and went on to list a lengthy catalogue of complaints. But Callaghan, not wishing to reopen recently healed wounds within the Labour party and mindful of his relations with other Common Market heads of government, brushed over Benn's remarks at his press conference the following morning, though he did endorse the tough line which his agriculture minister, John Silkin, was taking in negotiations in Brussels, and he said that Labour would put an end to "the nonsense" of the Common Agricultural Policy.

In the event, the EEC played only a minor part in Labour's campaign, and Tony Benn did not again emerge in a controversial light. For whatever reason—perhaps because he feared that Callaghan would drop him from the Government if Labour won or because he did not wish to risk being used as a scapegoat if they lost—Benn kept his head down, much to the Tories' disappointment.

The issue Callaghan did emphasize early in the campaign was unemployment, and in speeches in Glasgow on April 9 and Manchester on April 10 he asserted that Tory cuts in Labour's job-creation program would put 1.2 million jobs in jeopardy, one-sixth of them in Scotland.

Unemployment figured in the polls only as the second or third source of public concern, well behind inflation. This was the issue on which Callaghan would have preferred to campaign, but in the pre-Easter period he was inhibited by the fact that the retail price index for March was not due to be published until Thursday, April 12, and nobody knew on which side of the emotive 10 percent barrier it would fall. If inflation turned out to be in double digits it would ruin all Labour's boasts about having achieved single-figure inflation. To the Government's immense relief, the figure turned out to be 9.8 percent, and during the second week of its campaign Labour went onto the offensive on the prices issue, loudly trumpeting its success in halving the inflation rate over the previous three years.

Callaghan and his colleagues, particularly the prices secretary, Roy Hattersley, who was widely credited with having routed his Tory opposite-number, Sally Oppenheim, in a broadcast debate, were able to mount a sharp attack against the Tories on the prices issue, of which the bull points were the Tory intention to abolish the Price Commission, the December vote against sanctions which had deprived the Government of an essential weapon against inflationary pressures in the private sector, and the fact that inflation was now lower than when the Tories had left office in 1974.

It seems that the Labour attack was effective; the Tory lead on prices steadily declined in the polls as the campaign progressed. Yet they still remained just ahead—which shows how much Labour had lost by postponing the election from the previous October when the inflation rate was lower than 8 percent. By April it was clear to everybody that inflation was going to move into double figures again—it was merely a question of how soon—and Labour's claim to have solved rather than to have ameliorated the prices problem was looking a great deal more shaky.

But the overarching theme of Callaghan's campaign was the need for government to work in cooperation with rather than in hostility to the trade unions, with the concordat presented in the same reassuring light as the social contract had been in the two 1974 elections. The object was to cloak Mrs. Thatcher with the robes of extremism and confrontation, while Callaghan basked in the radiance of a man who preached consensus and the binding up of wounds. On at least one occasion he quoted with approval one of Churchill's more pithy remarks and said cuttingly of Thatcher, who had just made a speech highly critical of the unions in Callaghan's own Cardiff constituency, that he "marvelled at the lack of wisdom of someone who appears to prefer war-war to jaw-jaw towards people in her own country."

Yet Callaghan was obviously aware of the chink in his suit of consensus armor—public skepticism about the credibility of trade union undertakings to the Government under the concordat. At a meeting in Leicester on April 16 he spelled out at some length just what these undertakings were:

> Strikes as a last not a first resort, better protection of individuals from closed shop provisions, more arbitration, more secret ballots, a limitation on picketing powers, and "a definite commitment to enter into discussion with the government each year on the best way to achieve the target on reducing inflation to 5 percent within three years." [He went on:] "The TUC general council have given me their pledge on these matters—a pledge that will avoid a repetition of last winter. When a Labour government is elected on May 3rd I shall expect the trade unions to live up to this agreement."

By some earlier standards, Callaghan was a leisurely campaigner. Apart from his morning press conference, his daily schedule took in typically a couple of whistle-stop visits to marginal constituencies during the afternoon and a single public meeting in the evening. Nor did the media make excessive demands on the prime minister. He appeared in Labour's opening party political broadcast on April 17 and contributed the whole of the final broadcast, a straight-to-camera talk from 10 Downing Street on May 1, but he took no part in the intervening four. He did not appear on any of Labour's seven radio broadcasts, and his only other major media appearance was on Granada Television's "Granada 500" program on which the three party leaders were separately questioned by voters from Bolton.

Despite husbanding his energies, Callaghan made an extraordinarily positive impact wherever he went. Here is how I recorded my impressions immediately after hearing him speak at Birmingham on April 17:

> His stance is confident, but not overbearing. He speaks clearly and calmly. His manner exudes goodwill and reasonableness. His rapport with that 90 percent of his audience that consists of Labour stalwarts is all but total. It demands a major effort of imagination for any of his listeners not to conclude that they are listening to a man who has the election sewn up.
>
> Mr. James Callaghan is talking to an audience of 1,700 in Birmingham town hall. He looks every inch a prime minister. Nobody could doubt that here was Labour's greatest asset. On Tuesday night he was at his most assured—brushing aside Mrs. Thatcher's temerity at speaking in his Cardiff stronghold the previous evening with light-hearted mockery. So Mrs. Thatcher admired the Labour party as it was under Clement Attlee and Hugh Gaitskell, did she? He couldn't recall much praise coming their way from Tory circles when they were still around. Their "posthumous rehabilitation" smacked more of what went on in the Soviet Union than in Britain.[13]

Yet there was a limit to what one man could do. If Labour had entered the campaign only two or three points behind, Callaghan might have been able to pull the party to victory on his coattails: as it was, despite his majestic progress throughout the campaign, he was unable to do more than to diminish the scale of Labour's defeat.

Labour speakers made a determined effort to shake public confidence in the ability of the Tories to fulfill their taxation promises

---

13 "How much is Jim worth?" *Economist*, April 21, 1979, p. 22.

without unacceptable cost, concentrating on (1) the extent to which indirect taxes (notably the value-added tax) would have to be increased, and (2) the likely scale of public expenditure cuts. The Treasury was asked by ministers to make a calculation on the basis of an increase of VAT to 12.5 percent, after allowing for reducing public borrowing by £1 billion and fulfilling the specific Tory election pledge of reducing the top rate of income tax on earned income from 83 percent to 60 percent. This would leave them, Callaghan proclaimed at a meeting in Coventry on April 25, with "just enough to cut the standard rate of tax by 2p."[14] Callaghan went on to say that the Treasury calculated that only those earning more than £192 a week (against average household incomes for 1978 of £106.13) could get more back in income-tax cuts than they would pay out in higher prices.

The Tories seem to have been taken aback by this Labour counterattack and to have failed to settle in advance a line to take in responding to questions about how much value-added tax would be needed to pay for the income-tax cuts. Thatcher restricted herself to denying at one of her morning press conferences that VAT would be doubled, but Francis Pym, the shadow foreign secretary, got into very deep water when he accepted an invitation to be grilled on a BBC "Panorama" program on April 23 by two younger Labour M.P.s, Joe Ashton and Bryan Gould. He was unable to find convincing replies to their persistent questioning, and his reputation as the most likely Tory successor to Thatcher was severely bruised by the encounter. Whatever the reason, the Tory lead on the tax question steadily narrowed during the campaign, though Labour leaders were probably oversanguine in their belief that the issue had effectively been neutralized.

Any benefit which accrued from superior party organization went—as in all recent British elections—to the Tories. Virtually nothing had been done during the four and a half years since the October 1974 election to improve the run-down Labour election machine, which was able to field only some seventy full-time constituency agents (an average of only one in ten constituencies—while the Conservatives had a full-time agent in more than half the constituencies). The membership of local Labour parties had also declined to a pathetically low level—on average, about one-fifth that of local Conservative associations.[15]

---

[14] In his budget, presented to Parliament on June 12, 1979, the new Tory chancellor of the exchequer, Sir Geoffrey Howe, actually raised VAT to 15 percent and cut the standard rate of income tax by 3p.

[15] Report of the Committee on Financial Aid to Political Parties (The Houghton Committee) (London: HMSO, 1976, Cmnd. 6601), pp. 159-205.

## Assessing the Outcome

It is probably fair to conclude that the Labour party out-argued the Tories during the course of the campaign. The eventual outcome —though sufficient to give Mrs. Thatcher a comfortable parliamentary majority—fell well short of the landslide which she could have anticipated from poll findings a few weeks earlier.[16] Yet the hard truth for Labour was that, however praiseworthy a campaign it fought and however much Callaghan's image outshone Thatcher's, it was too far behind to have any realistic hope of winning a general election in May 1979. This was perceived with virtual unanimity by Labour M.P.s after the election was over, though they differed as to the reasons for the party's unpopularity.

The right—or so-called moderate—wing of the party attributed Labour's defeat to the "winter of discontent," at least implicitly putting the blame on the trade unions, and particularly public sector unions such as the National Union of Public Employees, for destroying the basis of Labour's appeal. Many—but not all—trade union leaders appeared implicitly to accept this analysis, and their public demeanor after May 3 tended to be rather shamefaced.

The left wing of the party however—together with left-wing trade unionists—put the blame squarely on Callaghan and his colleagues, claiming that it was the Labour Government's incomes policy itself—rather than the strikes which flowed from it—that was responsible for the party's defeat. According to them it was not just the choice of an unrealistic 5 percent norm that was to blame, but the whole strategy of wage restraint that had formed the centerpiece of the Government's economic policies for the previous three to four years.

This strategy, the left claimed, had been rejected by large numbers of trade unionists in the privacy of the voting booth. Moreover, they argued, the manner in which Callaghan had preempted the contents of the election manifesto had left party activists disgruntled and feeling that they lacked a cause to fight for.

Although the left case carries some conviction, there is little doubt in this writer's mind that the analysis of the Labour moderates was nearer the mark—that if the "winter of discontent" had not occurred—or if the election had taken place before its occurrence—there would have been a possibility, even perhaps a probability, of a ma-

---

16 The Conservatives led Labour by an average of 9.8 percentage points in five polls taken shortly after the confidence vote on March 28: by the time of the election this lead had been reduced to 7.2 percentage points.

jority Labour Government's being returned. Yet even if one accepts this assessment it is only part of the explanation of why Labour lost. For even without the "winter of discontent" the election would probably have been a desperately close-fought affair. There seems to have been no possibility of an easy Labour win at any time—which is remarkable for a party which has a lead of more than 2 million voters over the Tories in the long-term sympathies of the electors[17] and whose leader was so much more popular than his opponent.

The explanation for this lies in the progressive alienation of Labour voters from their chosen party. This has been charted over the past fifteen or so years by the British Election Survey, undertaken initially under the auspices of Nuffield College, Oxford, and since 1970 at Essex University.[18]

Table 3–1 shows how Labour identifiers and even "core Labour identifiers" (male, working-class trade unionists) significantly weakened in the degree of their commitment to traditional Labour objectives between 1964 and 1974. Identical questions were put to respondents in a survey carried out immediately after the 1979 general election: the detailed figures are not yet available, but the directors of the survey have indicated to me that these show a further sharp fall in the intensity of commitment by Labour identifiers.

At the same time that Labour supporters have weakened in their attachment to Labour party aims, opinion poll evidence has suggested that a high proportion of Labour voters are attracted to policy objectives shrewdly chosen by the Conservative party. A poll carried out by Research Services Ltd. for the *Observer* newspaper during the course of the election campaign showed this vividly: six out of seven objectives taken from the Tory election manifesto were assented to by a clear majority of intending Labour voters, while on the seventh there was an almost even split (see table 3–2).[19]

In the light of this evidence, there is little reason to wonder why Labour failed to win the 1979 general election. Rather it is surprising that the party polled as well as it did.

---

[17] For the evidence for this assertion see Ivor Crewe, Bo Särlvik, and James Alt, "Partisan Dealignment in Britain 1964-74," *British Journal of Political Science*, vol. 7, no. 2 (April 1977), pp. 129-190. See also "What future for Britain's two-party system?" *Economist*, March 11, 1978, pp. 22-25.

[18] The earlier findings of the British Election Survey were reported in David Butler and Donald Stokes, *Political Change in Britain* (London: Macmillan, 1969). More recent data will be presented in two forthcoming books by Ivor Crewe, Bo Särlvik, and David Robertson. Meanwhile, see the article by Crewe, Särlvik, and Alt already cited. Table 1, based on material provided by the British Election Survey, originally appeared in the *Economist*, March 11, 1978, p. 24.

[19] Anthony King, "Labour voters give Tories the nod," *Observer*, April 22, 1979, p. 4.

## TABLE 3–1

FALLING SUPPORT FOR LABOUR PRINCIPLES, 1964–1974
(percent; change in percentage points)

| Survey Response | All Labour Identifiers | | | Core Labour Identifiers | | |
|---|---|---|---|---|---|---|
| | 1964 | Feb. 1974 | Change 1964– Feb. 1974 | 1964 | Feb. 1974 | Change 1964– Feb. 1974 |
| In favor of nationalizing more industries | 57 | 50 | − 7 | 64 | 50 | −14 |
| In favor of spending more on social services | 89 | 61 | −28 | 92 | 57 | −35 |
| In favor of retaining close ties between trade unions and the Labour party | 38 | 29 | − 9 | 50 | 34 | −16 |
| Sympathies are generally with strikers | 37 | 23 | −14 | 33 | 25 | − 8 |
| Do not believe that the trade unions have "too much power" | 59 | 44 | −15 | 74 | 52 | −22 |
| Perceive "a great deal" of difference between the parties | 49 | 33 | −16 | 62 | 41 | −21 |
| Average (mean) | 55 | 40 | −15 | 63 | 43 | −20 |

NOTE: Core Labour identifiers are male working-class trade unionists.
SOURCE: *Economist*, March 11, 1978, p. 24.

It is an open question how much longer many of these voters are prepared to stick with the party. But it must be a probability that Labour will face an attrition of support—the speed of which will depend at least to some extent on the way the party comports itself—unless it takes energetic steps to bring itself more in line with the views of the mass of its supporters and potential supporters.

Against this background, the postelectoral struggle for control of the party, with the majority of Labour M.P.s and of trade union leaders fighting an increasingly desperate rear-guard action against

## TABLE 3–2
### LABOUR VOTERS' VIEWS ON TORY AIMS, APRIL 1979
(percent)

| Objective | Should the Next Government Attempt to Achieve These Objectives? | | |
| --- | --- | --- | --- |
| | Yes | No | Don't know |
| Reduce violent crime and vandalism | 95 | 3 | 2 |
| Reduce supplementary benefit for strikers, on assumption that they are getting strike pay from their unions | 63 | 30 | 7 |
| End secondary picketing by strikers | 78 | 14 | 8 |
| Reduce income tax, especially for the higher paid | 52 | 45 | 3 |
| Give council house tenants the right to buy their homes, with discounts for people who have lived in them for three years or more | 75 | 20 | 5 |
| Reduce the number of civil servants | 70 | 22 | 8 |
| Sell off parts of some state-owned companies | 40 | 49 | 11 |

SOURCE: *Observer*, April 22, 1979.

the left-dominated National Executive Committee and assorted allies led by Tony Benn, appears a bleak enterprise indeed.[20] If Benn and

[20] At the 1979 Labour party conference, held in Brighton in October 1979, the Labour left attempted to impose three changes in Labour's constitution against the wishes of Callaghan and the party's parliamentary leadership. On two of the three proposals the left was successful; on the third Callaghan succeeded in defeating the proposed amendment to the party rules. The changes approved were (1) that Labour M.P.s should henceforth be forced to submit to a periodic process of reselection by their constituency Labour party branches, and (2) that the party's election manifesto should in future be the sole responsibility of the National Executive Committee. The third (defeated) proposal was to take away from M.P.s the exclusive right of electing the party leader and give it instead to an electoral college in which local party activists would be heavily represented. Each of these proposals, as well as many others, will be reconsidered by the joint Labour party-trade union inquiry committee set up at the end of 1979 to examine Labour's constitution and organization. The crucial decisions will be taken at the 1980 Labour party conference (or more likely, now, the 1981 conference because of the delay in establishing the inquiry committee) when the report of the committee will be considered.

his supporters should triumph they will risk taking the party so far away from the aspirations of Labour voters that electoral catastrophe could well ensue at the next general election, scheduled for some time before June 1984. Yet the best chance that the moderates have of retaining control of the party is that the trade union leadership will impose its will by the weight of its block votes at the 1980 and 1981 Labour party conferences. As Labour's close tie-up with the unions is already one of the major sources of its unpopularity, the tightening of this link is unlikely to contribute to the rehabilitation of the party in the eyes of many voters.

It is a dilemma with no easy resolution in sight. It presents, perhaps, the strongest challenge in the party's eighty-year history.

# 4

# The Conservative Campaign

*William S. Livingston*

It was the Conservatives themselves who precipitated the general election. They had been pressing for it eagerly over a number of months, and they sensed that their opportunity had come. Time and the polls seemed to be running in their favor. One even heard again the old cry from 1950, "One more heave. . . ."

The Conservatives were mightily annoyed when James Callaghan decided not to hold the election in October 1978, as nearly everyone expected him to do. But he decided to soldier on, and in the event the Conservatives probably benefited from the delay more than Labour did. In October, inflation was down to 8 percent, the pound was recovering its strength, unemployment was under control, the unions were peaceful, and Callaghan was running well ahead of Mrs. Thatcher in the popularity polls. There is every reason to suppose that Callaghan would have done better in an October election than he did in the following May—indeed it is just possible that he could have won it. But he let the opportunity slip past and chose to postpone the election until the spring, or even until the following fall. It proved to be a bad mistake. The winter brought a wave of strikes which profoundly inconvenienced great portions of the population and, more important, badly damaged the Labour party's image as the only party capable of dealing with the trade unions. The strikes, moreover, affected people's daily lives more directly than ordinary industrial action. A strike by truckers produced shortages of food and other goods. When the garbage men went out, refuse clogged the sidewalks and streets. Leicester Square was piled high with great

In the preparation of this paper I have been significantly aided by Samuel Beer, David Cunningham, Lord Fraser of Kilmarock, Antony Garner, Alan Howarth, and Howard Penniman. To all of these I give grateful thanks. I alone am responsible for whatever errors remain.

bulging sacks of trash. Schools and hospitals in many cities were closed, and on occasion ambulance drivers refused to take people to hospitals, even in emergencies. The Government seemed helpless, and its touted "social contract" with the trade unions was seen to be ineffective and a sham. As the strikes were settled, Callaghan's attempt to impose a 5 percent limit on wage increases was clearly in tatters, and the Government's claim to be superior to the Conservatives in its capacity to deal with the unions was badly discredited. The two parties were thus in a very different situation from that of the previous October. The Conservatives now had better prospects and higher hopes of winning if a general election could be precipitated.

Then on March 1 came the referendums on devolution in Scotland and in Wales, the negative results of which put the Government in a difficult position. If they tried to press on with devolution, they would alienate many in their own party, and if they did not do so they would lose the support of the Scottish Nationalists. As the Government twisted and turned, trying to find a formula for evading the devolution question, the Scottish Nationalists became increasingly disaffected and finally announced that they would put down a motion of no confidence. The Liberals too decided to withdraw their support, and the Tories, seeing Callaghan's support base crumble, seized the opportunity they had been waiting for. Mrs. Thatcher introduced her own motion of no confidence, and the scene was set for a seven-hour debate on March 28. There was a great deal of scrambling on both sides for the support of the minor parties, and indeed to patch up the ranks of the major parties themselves. The issue was in doubt until the very last moment, but in the event, the House voted no confidence in the Callaghan Government—by a margin of one vote. The strikes had destroyed Labour's image; the referendums had destroyed Labour's support base; the vote destroyed Labour's entitlement to govern. And the Conservatives were quick to seize the advantage.

Both their problems and their mood were quite different from those of 1974. In February 1974, the Conservatives were in office: it was they who were buffeted by rising oil prices and striking trade unions, and the clash with the miners seemed to provide the prime minister, Edward Heath, with both an opportunity to go to the people and a cause to carry to them. There were others in the party, however, who were concerned about the difficulty of concentrating an electorate of 40 million on one issue for the whole of a three-week campaign. In any case the Conservative party is better at a broad-front prepared battle than at a snap guerrilla fight. The party was not really ready for the kind of election it had to face. Nor was the Labour party, but it was not in government.

In October 1974, the Tories had scarcely had time to adapt their attitudes and organization from the needs of governance to the needs of opposition. They knew that an election would be coming soon, but they did not know how soon. All they really knew was that Harold Wilson, not Edward Heath, would set the date. By contrast, in the spring of 1979 they were ready in both mood and organization. They had been in opposition for five years. They had been through the false start of October 1978, and, though it had cost them a great deal of money and had outraged their sense of propriety, it had left them with a good organizational structure and confidence in their ability to win. This time, though they could not be sure of the date, they knew the Government was facing a time limit that was drawing inexorably nearer. They had had plenty of time to prepare, and when Parliament was dissolved on April 7, Mrs. Thatcher reported, "My troops are ready. They have been ready for quite some time."

Indeed the troops were in high spirits. Britain had emerged from a winter of strikes and other discontents; the Opposition was in disarray; the battle on March 28 had been exhilarating; and the Conservatives expected to win. They had a new leader, and a new philosophy. A victory would produce not merely Britain's first woman prime minister; it would also produce a strong Government determined to reverse the leftward drift of British politics since 1945. In some ways, the campaign to come was simpler than those of 1974. The party had had four years in opposition to prepare its policy proposals. It pretty well knew what it wanted and where it was going. Its policies had a new and distinctive flavor, and even if they frightened a great many people on the left, they were coherent and well planned. But most important was the new leader, who had impressed her own views and preferences on both the policies and the personnel of the party.

The organization was also ready. Candidates were selected; agents were at work. Plans had been carefully made for a quick realignment of the staffs of the Research Department and Central Office. Volunteers had been recruited. Materials were ready to go. Tactical plans had been laid for concentrating the campaign on the marginal seats. And personnel had been selected to move into the key constituencies.

All three party manifestoes were published within a week of each other, which suggests that all three parties were ready for the election when it came. The Conservative document, called simply enough "The Conservative Manifesto, 1979," was issued on April 11. It was short, straightforward, and precise. It was originally drafted by Christopher Patten, then the director of the Conservative Research Department, and by now a candidate for a safe Tory seat at Bath. It was revised and edited by Angus Maude and Sir Ian Gilmour, the chairman and immediate past chairman of the Research Department. It laid out five objectives for the party and a future Conservative Government:

1. to restore the economy and control the trade unions
2. to restore economic incentives
3. to uphold Parliament and the rule of law
4. to support family life and concentrate welfare services on those in real need
5. to strengthen Britain's defenses

The bulk of the manifesto described the particular ways in which those objectives were to be achieved.

The Tories proposed to reduce income tax at both the bottom and the top of the scale and to switch the burden of taxation from direct to indirect taxes. They proposed a series of trade union reforms—prohibiting secondary picketing, discouraging the closed shop, requiring a secret ballot in union elections, permitting appeal to the courts against exclusion or expulsion from a union, and requiring unions to contribute support for workers on strike. Public expenditure was to be sharply curtailed except for police, defense, and the health service. Sharp restrictions on immigration would be enforced, although there was to be no question of compulsory repatriation. Some of the nationalized industries would be sold off to the private sector, beginning with aerospace, shipbuilding, and the national freight corporation.

Despite the Tories' state of readiness, however, the Labour party produced its manifesto five days before they did, and for all their eagerness, the Tories' campaign was a little slow in getting started. Indeed, there was a self-conscious decision at Central Office to delay the beginning of the campaign until after the long Easter weekend, April 13–16. Mrs. Thatcher withdrew to her home in Kent and made no public appearances until after the Easter holiday. In the first week, it was left to Michael Heseltine, Edward Heath, and Francis Pym to launch the campaign. But with the manifesto published and the long holiday ended, the Tories were ready to join the battle.

## Issues and Ideology

The battle took place on uneven ground. The manifesto set the tone, but unsurprisingly it by no means governed the content of the campaign. Some things in the manifesto dwindled into unimportance and were scarcely mentioned. Others that were given only slight attention—or none at all—in the manifesto exploded into major issues in the campaign. The one issue of supreme importance from the very beginning was tax reform. On that the Tories were united, and their call to action was loud and unequivocal. They made it a central issue of the campaign, and on it they seized the offensive at the beginning and never relinquished it. Indeed the *Economist* called it the "tax-cutters' election."[1]

The Conservatives' tax proposals were straightforward and concrete, but they did not answer all questions. They promised to reduce the top-level surtax on high incomes from 83 to 60 percent and to increase the exemption limit at the bottom of the scale so that fewer people at low-income levels would be paying tax. They promised, too, to cut the basic or beginning tax rate from 33 to 30 percent. This became a very popular issue, and neither the Liberals nor the Labourites had very much to say about it except to point out that it could be put into effect only by drastic cuts in government expenditure. But that didn't trouble the Tories: they were proposing to do that very thing anyway.

Taxation produced a running dispute throughout the campaign, for the parties differed sharply on the statistics of the proposed cuts. Labour insisted that the difference would have to be made up by an expansion of the value-added tax (VAT). Mrs. Thatcher was prepared to concede that, but she continued to insist that the increase in VAT would not seriously affect the standard of living of the lower-income groups, since most of the items that constituted their major expenditures were exempt from VAT anyway. The Tories were determined to balance the tax cuts by reductions in government expenditures, but they were at no time clear or precise about how large the reductions would be or which items would be reduced. Interestingly, they proposed to increase expenditures on defense and police, to maintain existing levels of spending on the health service, and to tie the pension rates to the cost of living. All of that was bound to increase costs and seemingly imperil a Conservative Government's capacity to reduce expenditures. Labour—particularly Callaghan and Shirley Williams—wanted to know where the money was coming from.

---

[1] *Economist*, April 21, 1979. The importance of the party manifestoes in the campaign is analyzed in appendix A in this volume.

Thatcher, buffeted by journalists' questions and opponents' complaints, did concede that the party would have to increase the VAT if they were going to decrease income tax. Not everyone agreed that that was the best tactic, but she came back to it time and again, at news conferences and on television. The point she made of it (and who is to say she was wrong?) was that the basic common expenditures that the housewife would have to face were immune from VAT: children's clothing, shoes, travel, rent, and food. But that was her emphasis, not something that had been decided by the strategists at Central Office. The failure to deal with the increase in VAT was probably a tactical error on the part of party strategists. Given the emphasis on income-tax cuts, and the inability to meet them by comprehensive reductions in government spending, it was obvious that VAT would have to be increased. By how much? On what? There was no prior understanding on this, or at least no settled agreement was announced and communicated to the party. This left a big gap in the Tory defenses, which Labour attacked at every turn. Healey said a Conservative Government might have to double the rate of VAT. Thatcher immediately denied it, so Callaghan promptly took her to task. "Let us assume," he said, "that it was only increased by half. That would only leave enough to cut the standard rate of tax by 2p."[2] According to Callaghan, the Treasury calculated that only those earning more than £192 a week would get more back in income-tax cuts than they would pay out in higher prices.

The problem was to fit together a complex of factors including reductions in income tax, increases in VAT, and a combination of increases and reductions in public expenditure. Sir Geoffrey Howe, the shadow chancellor, pressed to show how he could finance the government in the face of the proposed tax cuts, fell back on the somewhat disingenuous answer that he first had "to look at the books." But he surely knew what was in the books, and it was not reassuring to his hearers to be told that the Conservatives could not rationalize their proposals until they had had a chance to determine exactly what the situation was that they were addressing. There was certainly no hesitation in addressing it when it came to proposing tax reductions. For the moment, the problem of implementation was obscured by the oratory of the campaign. Cutting taxes was not only an article of Tory faith; it was good politics. It was more central to the Tory creed and to the Tory campaign than it was to Labour's. Tax reduction—and what went with it, reduced expenditures—were

---

[2] Ibid., April 28, 1979, p. 26.

not merely appeals to the cupidity of the electorate; they were at the heart of the Tories' determination to reverse the trend toward government domination of the economy, which they believed was stifling initiative and obstructing development. "Free the people's money so as to stimulate the economy, investment, production." The refrain rang loud and clear throughout the campaign.

To the Tories, the tax-reform proposals were closely tied to other policies. "We do not pretend," said the manifesto, "that every saving can be made without change or complaint." But they intended to effect important savings in government expenditure, complaints or not. They would abandon any further nationalization and reduce what had already been undertaken. They would reduce waste, bureaucracy, and "over-government." All this would hold inflation in check, encourage investment, and make Britain more productive. It would do so, however, only with the participation of the labor force, which meant that the Tories had to address themselves very directly to trade union reforms. Next to taxation, labor conditions constituted the most important element in the Tory campaign, and necessarily so, since despite the difficulties of the preceding winter, Labour campaigners still proclaimed that only the Labour party could deal effectively with trade unions.

The Tories were convinced that there were many people in the Labour movement who were disillusioned with their leaders and with the Labour party. Thus their strategy was to drive a wedge between the union leadership and the working force. But how? There were three principal emphases in the Conservative campaign: (1) There should be secret balloting in union elections at every opportunity. Indeed public funds would be provided "for postal ballots for union elections and other important issues." (2) There should be no secondary picketing of establishments not involved in the primary labor dispute. (3) The law should be changed so that it no longer encouraged the closed shop. This third point was of particular importance, and it was given great emphasis not only by Mrs. Thatcher and James Prior, but by many other speakers in the Tory campaign. The closed shop, it was said, shifted power to the union leadership and deprived the individual workman of his own right to a job. How was it to be discouraged? Not by prohibition, but by alteration of those elements of the law that encouraged it. Anyone who was excluded or expelled from a union should have the right of appeal to the courts against the union. Those who lost their jobs as a result of the closed shop were entitled to "ample compensation." No new closed-shop agreement could be established without an "overwhelm-

ing" majority vote in a secret ballot. The closed shop was to be pro-
hibited in the nonindustrial civil services.

Prior, of course, bore the principal burden of this part of the
campaign. A pleasant, avuncular man with an easy manner and a
sharp mind, he had had some experience negotiating with trade unions
and managing Conservative labor policy. He was shadow minister for
employment, and after the election was to become secretary of state
for employment.

The evidence seems to suggest that the Tory attempt to divide
the trade union leadership from the followers was at least in some
degree successful. The election saw a swing to the Conservatives of
6.5 percentage points among semiskilled and unskilled workers, 7 percentage points among trade unionists, and 11 points among skilled
workers.[3] On Sunday night before the election, the Tories held a
massive labor rally at Wembley, which produced, it was said, an
audience of some 2,300 trade unionists. There were banners, music,
and hoopla—a show-biz rally with show business people. The assembled unionists cheered and shouted her name and the Tory leader
matched their enthusiasm. "We Conservatives," she said, "do not
seek to divide or level society. We seek to unite and elevate it."[4]
Prior said this time more trade unionists would vote Conservative
than ever before in the history of the country. Possibly they did.

After taxing and spending and labor relations, the intensity of
the Tory campaign leveled off. Many other measures were offered,
protested, or promised, but none reached the level of importance
assigned to those primary matters. The European Economic Community (EEC) emerged as an issue of some importance, and on it
there was a sharp divergence of views between the Conservative
and Labour parties. Even here, however, the difference was one of
emphasis and degree rather than of sharp, straightforward disagree-
ment. The Conservatives intended to stay in the EEC, but to
renegotiate a few points on which they were dissatisfied. Labour threatened to withdraw entirely unless some drastic reforms were introduced. Each party seemed to consider the degree of difference between
them to be very considerable. But there is little evidence that the
voters were much concerned with the issue. Three Labour ministers
were sharply hostile to the Common Market—Peter Shore, Tony
Benn, and John Silkin. All were associated with the party's left wing,
but Silkin was agriculture minister and responsible for Britain's par-

---

[3] Ibid., May 12, 1979, p. 26.
[4] *Daily Telegraph*, April 30, 1979.

ticipation in the Common Agricultural Policy.[5] The Tories tended to decry Labour's inconsistency, pointing out that Wilson had strongly supported Britain's entry into Europe and now Labour's left wing sought to get out. Very little was heard during the campaign from the Tory right-wingers who had been similarly hostile to Britain's entry into the EEC. The Tory manifesto said that Britain must work "honestly and genuinely with our partners in the European community," but it also said, "There are some community policies which need to be changed." Everyone agreed that the critical problem was agriculture. As the Tories put it, "radical changes in the operation of the Common Agricultural Policy are necessary." In particular, they intended to devalue the green pound [6] within the lifetime of the coming parliament to a point that would enable British producers "to compete on level terms with those in the rest of the community." Labour responded by insisting that devaluation of the green pound would simply raise food prices in Britain.

Other issues too received repeated emphasis in the Tory campaign. Tenants in council estates and new towns were to be enabled to purchase the houses they had been renting. The party proposed to discount the market values up to half the cost and to ensure that 10 percent mortgages were available. Mrs. Thatcher returned to this theme time after time, making it a principal tenet of the Tory proposals for strengthening family life. It was left to Michael Heseltine, the environment spokesman, to defend the details of these proposals against Labour criticism that houses thus sold off would be removed from the rental market and that rural Britain would be left at a disadvantage if urban dwellers were to be given subsidized housing opportunities.

---

[5] The Common Agricultural Policy (CAP) is the EEC's effort to maintain uniform agricultural prices and support mechanisms. Decisions on farm price supports are mostly made by the Community and paid for by the Community. The major devices are a tariff on imports from outside the Community and internal support prices maintained when necessary by intervention buying. In addition the Community pays refunds to exporters when world prices are below Community prices. It was difficult for some nations such as Britain to bring existing national policies (direct payments to farmers, for example) into line with the CAP, and the CAP has continued to be one of the most controversial aspects of Britain's membership in the EEC.

[6] CAP price-support levels are set in units of account and then converted into the currencies of member states at fixed rates of exchange commonly called *green rates*—in Britain's case the *green pound*. Being fixed, the green pound preserves a stable value, while the real pound fluctuates, mostly downward. The green rate became increasingly unrealistic, and while the differential kept prices down in the shops, it depressed farm incomes. The rate was devalued by 7½ percent in January 1978, but the controversy continued into the general election.

Another major emphasis was on immigration and race relations, which in Britain tend to be much the same thing. The Conservative leaders emphasized that immigration laws would be tightened to curb the inflow of immigrants. It was understood on all sides that it was the influx of immigrants from black and brown nations of the Commonwealth that was to be restricted. Labour seized upon the opportunity and did its best to imply that under the Tories there would be forced expatriation of immigrants already legally lodged in the country. That was unequivocally contrary to Conservative policy, but the Tories had to spend a great deal of time denying the allegation. In the end, Labour seemed to succeed in painting the Conservatives as the critics of a multiracial Britain, while Labour itself, if not in favor of it, at least was able to take some advantage of the differences between the two parties on the question.

The other issues on which the Conservatives laid heavy stress were law and order and defense. There has long been a law-and-order emphasis in the Conservative party, usually associated with the right wing. Few people were surprised, therefore, when the party, now sporting a right-wing coloration, came out strongly for policies associated with that tradition. The manifesto promised "really tough sentences" for violent criminals and spoke of experiments in detention centers with a "tougher regime as a short, sharp shock for young criminals." Mrs. Thatcher spoke repeatedly about raising salaries for policemen, and her remarks about punishments and reform of the criminal law seemed to strike a fairly responsive chord. The murder of Airey Neave as the campaign opened, and the violence at Southall as it progressed, undoubtedly strengthened the Tory appeal for order and discipline in society. Even capital punishment was to be reconsidered, and both the Tory campaigners and the manifesto itself promised a review of existing law. Capital punishment is a matter of conscience, it was said, and the manifesto promised to give the new parliament an early opportunity "for a free vote on this issue."

Significant increases in defense spending were promised but not much talked about. The manifesto made clear that Britain would remain loyal to its alliances, consider SALT receptively, and give servicemen higher pay, decent living conditions, and improved equipment. It cannot be said that these proposals provoked any very strong reaction in the Labour party, and they were not much debated on the hustings. Frequently they were linked with the law-and-order theme, but it was quite clear that the Tories were serious about strengthening the forces and improving the appurtenances of servicemen.

These were not the only themes mentioned in the Tory campaign, but they were the ones stressed most frequently and most vigorously. What is equally interesting is the issues that were omitted. Despite the universal concern about inflation, prices, jobs, and the general health of the economy, there was virtually no mention in either party's campaign of North Sea oil, the Middle East, OPEC, or the energy problem. Even the devolution of power upon Scotland and Wales, which had figured so prominently in the partisan debate over the previous several years and which had been the proximate cause of the no-confidence vote on March 28, received almost no attention in the course of the campaign. It was very much a domestic-politics election, and perhaps indeed a taxcutters' election. Foreign affairs seems to have played almost no part in party contest or campaign oratory, with the one exception of the future of Britain's relations with Europe. A good bit of attention was paid to Rhodesia, although the parties seemed to differ but little on Rhodesian policy—or, more accurately, on their disinclination to state a policy. The Conservatives had sent a team to appraise the situation, and Callaghan promised to send Cledwyn Hughes to Salisbury after the election to help decide whether Britain should recognize the new regime. The only other episode that could conceivably be construed as showing an interest in foreign affairs was the universal denunciation of the American Speaker of the House, Tip O'Neill, when he remarked on a visit to Dublin that both British parties treated Ulster like a "political football." For that he was rebuffed and scorned by both parties and denounced in the British press.[7]

In some ways, the campaign was much more ideological than British campaigns have been in the recent past: the policy differences between the parties were much more clear cut. That was largely the doing of the Tories rather than of Labour, and it was above all the doing of Margaret Thatcher and her close advisers. They had had four years in opposition to prepare their platform and their proposals. And those proposals had a new and distinctive flavor. They were no more radical than Heath's had been in 1974—indeed less so on labor matters—but the presentation was different. The Tory proposals were dramatically phrased, argued with zeal, and presented with surprising panache. There was a great difference between the campaign of 1979 and those of 1974. In October 1974, one of the greatest concerns was to avoid contradicting what the party had said in February, but in 1979 there was no such need. There had been a much longer interval since the last election and the party was under new leadership.

---

[7] See, however, a more balanced appraisal in the *Economist*, April 28, 1979, pp. 17 and 18.

If the Conservative campaign was more ideological than previous ones, the same could not be said of the Labour campaign. To the extent that Labour's appeal fitted together into a coherent ideology, it did so in response to the Tory onslaught. Actually, the talk in the Labour campaign was very pragmatic—jobs, taxes, unemployment, prices, and so on. The Conservatives talked about those things too, but in their hands those mundane concerns were gathered into a noble crusade to free Britain from the stultifying restraints imposed by years of socialist rule. Nowadays, however, there was little talk of socialism from Labour. It painted itself as the party of experience, of generosity and compassion, of competence and concern. It offered itself as the calm stabilizing influence, in sharp contrast to the dramatic demands of the Conservatives.[8] Every election campaign has its small ironies. This one saw Callaghan campaigning as the spokesman of middle-ground conservatism, Thatcher as the apostle of radical change.

The paradox, if not intentional, was nonetheless the product of rational planning. The Conservatives were abetted and inspirited by a parade of intellectuals the like of which had not been seen in the party for many years. Mrs. Thatcher once remarked that she distrusted experts because they were so often wrong. But in practice she called upon them with great frequency. Most of the intellectual contribution to the election came from the Conservatives, not from Labour. This represented what Bernard Crick called "a curious reversal of roles."[9] The old intellectual tradition of the Labour party, represented in recent years by Anthony Crosland and Richard Crossman among others, had given way to a pragmatic party concerned with patching up and with bread-and-butter details. On the Tory side, not only were the intellectuals to be seen as active formulators of policy, but the policies they produced had been welded together into a coherent ideological whole. One thinks of Sir Keith Joseph with his Center for Policy Studies, Professor Douglas Hague of the Manchester University Business School, Sir Geoffrey Howe, soon to be chancellor of the exchequer, and even the Bow Group of young professionals, once a ginger group of activists within the party and now solidly in its mainstream. It was no accident that the Conservatives

---

[8] In the course of the campaign, the Tories said several times that the only reasonable policies on taxing and spending that the Labour Government had been able to produce were forced upon it by the conditions attached by the International Monetary Fund to the loan negotiated in 1976-1977. At the end of April it was reported in the press that the IMF loan had now been completely paid off. Curiously, Labour made almost no mention of the repayment at any time during the campaign.

[9] *New York Times*, April 29, 1979.

128

appeared more ideologically coherent than Labour: they were on the offensive throughout the campaign. Partly that was because it is the habit of the outs to attack; partly it was because it is easier to view with alarm than to point with pride; but partly also it was because of what they had to say and the way in which it seemed to fit together.

## Campaigning

As we have already noted, the Conservatives got off to a slow start. That was a decision prompted largely by the intrusion of the Easter weekend. The populace was distracted, and many candidates feared it might be thought improper to campaign over Easter. For the decision to wait till after the holiday Mrs. Thatcher earned the approval of no less an observer than Sir Harold Wilson: "She has paced herself very well, she was right to start when she did after Easter. And so far, she hasn't made a mistake. I can see her problem of being ahead and trying to decide 'when do I attack?' It is a good question because you can never be sure." [10] But it all made for a slow beginning. Willie Whitelaw was said to have remarked that Callaghan was going about the country "stirring up apathy." After Easter, however, everyone plunged in with zest. There were only sixteen calendar days left before the election.

Margaret Thatcher was clearly the focal point. She was a woman; she was strong in her opinions; she was vigorous in her assertion of them. She was a new and novel figure on the political stage, and her dominance of that stage was enhanced by the prominent role of television. She was the focus of interest not only in the Conservative party but in the campaign as a whole. It is not too much to say that Margaret Thatcher herself was the principal issue in the 1979 campaign. There was a conscious decision by the Central Office strategists not to use her too frequently: she was scheduled for only five major meetings throughout the entire campaign, and she refused to debate Callaghan on television. But this attempt to avoid overexposure was probably thwarted by the incessant attention given to her in the press and in the television news. Moreover, she played a central part in the daily press conferences, and she gave a number of interviews on television, so that the voters had her before them constantly throughout the three-week period.

In the Conservative, as in the other parties, the daily press conference was a continuing point of interest and a major opportunity for

---

[10] *Daily Mail*, April 27, 1979.

policy statements throughout the campaign. The Tory conference was held in a large square room on the ground floor at Central Office, crowded and hot, capable of accommodating perhaps a hundred visitors. One corner contained a stage raised three feet off the floor and large enough to accommodate four or five seated notables with microphones in front of them. In the opposite corner of the room was a large raised platform filled with cameras, microphones, consoles, cables, and technicians. The space in between contained auditorium seating for reporters, visitors, and dignitaries. After the crowd was gathered, the four or five key figures who were to participate in the conference would appear from behind a curtain and take their seats. More often than not, Mrs. Thatcher was in the group and presided. She or someone else would read an opening statement and then invite questions from the floor. The questions might be addressed to her or to one of her colleagues, though even those addressed to her were sometimes handed on to someone else. Traveling microphones on the floor were carried quickly to the reporters seeking to ask questions. The exchange went on for thirty or forty minutes and then the meeting was adjourned, when Mrs. Thatcher or whoever was presiding would stand up, thank the group, and leave.

In times past, the Tories and the Labourites have held their conferences an hour apart so that reporters could easily move from one to the other. That made for some interesting questions, especially at the second conference where spokesmen could be asked to comment on what their opponents had said a few minutes earlier. In 1979, for reasons never publicly explained, both parties insisted on having their conference at 9:30 A.M. There was, therefore, a twenty-four-hour gap before anyone could be pressed to comment on the other side's remarks. The press didn't much like this new arrangement, but the Liberals liked it very much. They promptly set their press conference for 10:30 A.M. and wound up entertaining a great many of the press who otherwise might not have bothered to come.

Seats and space at the press conferences were always difficult to come by and had to be arranged for in advance. Curiously enough, the Labour party was more grudging of its space than the Conservatives, although my personal impression—it is no more than that—is that there was rather more clamor for accommodation at the Conservative conferences.

The team to go on stage at the press conference each day was briefed early in the morning by a rather shadowy group of varied composition which included Lord Thorneycroft, the party chairman, Adam Ridley, director of the Research Department during the campaign, representatives from the Private Office, and sometimes specialists on particular subjects from the Research Department. The conferences were well planned and, in the words of the *Economist*, "were run with some flair for publicity." [11]

The politicians know the journalists and the journalists know the politicians, and each group knows what to expect of the other. Most newspapers were committed to one side or the other well before the campaign began. Until the last week, among the London dailies only the *Mirror* and the *Guardian* had come out for Labour. All other national newspapers had declared for the Conservatives—the *Express*, both daily and Sunday, the *Daily Mail*, the *Financial Times*, the *Daily Telegraph*, and others. The *Times* and the *Sunday Times* were, of course, on strike. On Saturday, April 28, the *Economist* came out for Mrs. Thatcher, hoping that "her intensely practical side will, even more in office than in opposition, outweigh her intensely visceral (but mostly undogmatic) one." The *Economist* concluded that she should be "given her chance." [12] On April 29, just four days before the election, the *Observer* came out in support of Callaghan—principally on the grounds that there was less likelihood of a confrontation between the Government and the trade unions with Callaghan rather than Thatcher in office.[13] In the *Daily Telegraph*, Peregrine Worsthorne produced a lead article on the same date commenting at length on the two candidates and concluding that the election was no big thing after all. He urged voters to give Margaret a chance: it was only "a British election," he said, "not a Wagnerian climacteric."

One reason for the difficulty in gaining casual access to the press conferences was the heightened concern for security that permeated all kinds of events during the campaign, not merely at the parties' head offices but in the constituencies and at public meetings as well. Britain had been facing intermittent threats of terrorist attacks by Irish groups for some time, but what really precipitated the new security consciousness was the assassination on March 30 of Airey Neave, the Conservative frontbench spokesman on Irish affairs. A bomb which had been placed in his automobile exploded as he was driving up the exit ramp from the House of Commons parking facility. The fact that he was a frontbench spokesman, the fact that he was a specialist on Irish matters, the fact that the murder took place on the premises of Parliament itself—all of these things produced in Britons of all parties a sense of outrage and an awareness of the need for in-

---

[11] *Economist*, April 28, 1979, p. 22.

[12] Ibid., pp. 16 and 17.

[13] *Observer*, April 29, 1979, p. 10.

creased security measures. All parties put guards at the doors of their headquarters and were given additional police protection. Whenever a party notable spoke at a meeting outside of headquarters, the police were there, sometimes in impressive numbers. Premises were searched in advance of meetings, tickets were sometimes required for admission, and identification was required for the issuance of tickets. The Conservatives searched all cars that went into their parking lot beneath the Central Office, metropolitan police were on duty outside, and special security police were on duty inside the front door. Persons seeking admission were asked to identify themselves and to state whom they wanted to see. Someone from the appropriate office then came down to accredit the visitor. Only then was the visitor given an identification tag—in effect a permit to enter the building.

The Conservatives were a good deal more sensitive about these security measures than either of the other two parties. Special security guards, tickets for admission to political rallies, special passes—these were seen only at Central Office. But both Labour and the Liberals had guards at the gate and special police available.[14]

The use of the metropolitan police was considerably increased after the riot at Southall on April 23 when violence broke out between the supporters of the National Front who were holding a rally and the supporters of the Anti-Nazi League who sought to prevent it. In the melee that followed, several thousand police were involved and one member of the league was killed. Thereafter, the police were present at all National Front rallies and at any other meeting where any kind of protest or abuse was expected. They were not always clearly in evidence, but one could frequently find thirty or forty policemen in a bus around the corner waiting to be called into action. Even if no violence was expected, several constables would be near the door and in the hall if the speaker was of some prominence.

The grand old habit of heckling at British political rallies almost seemed to have disappeared. Many meetings were carefully screened in advance so that only supporters were admitted, although in some instances space was reserved for members of different groups on the theory that public meetings should be open to the public. On one occasion when the National Front had scheduled a meeting, the Anti-Nazis tried to get there early and occupy all the seats. The police did not permit that, but did allow them to retain a substantial portion of the space available. The consequence was an ill-humored meeting

14 The tight security measures were mostly evident in London. On the road or in the provinces security was much more relaxed, being provided, according to R. W. Apple, Jr., "by a few harassed, unarmed local policemen, who seldom ask for credentials." *New York Times*, April 22, 1979.

fraught with unpleasantness and threatening at any moment to get out of hand. The point to be made is that the good humor was gone. The heckling that took place was malevolent and unpleasant. There were very few opportunities for the good-natured badinage and witty exchange that used to mark a British political meeting. Groups of Irish men and women followed Callaghan about and interrupted him with shouts of, "What about Ireland?" and "What about torture in the Irish jails?" Occasionally Callaghan would respond to the gibes, and now and then he would agree to speak for a few minutes on Irish policy; there was little good feeling on either side, though there was a great deal more patience on his than on theirs. Mrs. Thatcher was rarely subjected to that kind of abuse, though at her eve-of-poll meeting in Finchley she did encounter some hostile critics from the Workers' Revolutionary party. There was no difficulty getting into Callaghan's meetings, however, or into David Steel's, and no ticketing or prearrangement was necessary.

The tightened security also affected the candidates' informal campaigning in the constituencies. In this campaign when the candidates went on walkabouts they did not announce the itinerary in advance. The consequence was that crowds were predictably smaller. Indeed, on most days only one or two of the morning papers would supply a tiny notice announcing the main speakers of the day, listing two or three for each party and noting times and places. When any of the party leaders showed up with press and television crews in tow, a crowd was likely to gather quickly. But when Roy Mason, the minister for Northern Ireland, undertook a walkabout in his own constituency a week before the election, he found no one there to talk to except his own police escort.

On the whole it was a rather solemn campaign and there were few occasions for old-fashioned fun. From time to time, however, the traditional Tory humor did break through. For all their occasional stiffness, Tories can mobilize a wit that Labour seldom attempts. Labour stickers and posters tend to be somber and straightforward. "The Labour Way Is the Better Way" or "A Labour Government Is Good for *You*." Some Conservative signs were equally dull, but not all of them. One of the most widely used in 1979 was a billboard (hoarding) showing a long line of people waiting to get into an employment exchange, the caption reading "Labour Isn't Working. Vote Conservative." Another, more recondite, featured a large date "1984" and in smaller letters, "What Would Britain Be like after Another 5 Years of Labour Government?" Another said simply, "Cheer Up! The Conservatives Are Coming." The bookstore at Central Office was selling a small decal saying, "If Labour's the Answer, It Must Have Been a Silly Question" and a T-shirt with the message, "I Thought 'On the Rocks' Was a Drink 'Til I Discovered Labour Government." Not real knee-slappers, perhaps, but cheerful and light-hearted.

The truth is, however, that not many posters, stickers, or billboards were in evidence during the campaign, and in this respect it was certainly different from other campaigns. Except for the newspapers and television, one would scarcely have known there was a campaign in progress. Part of the explanation seems to have been that both major parties had spent much of their money on such things in the summer and fall of 1978, expecting an October election. When activists at the two major headquarters were asked about the paucity of posters, they seemed a bit surprised at the question, but all admitted that in other campaigns posters had been more numerous and had gone up much earlier. The explanations ran in all directions. One is entitled to some doubt that the supply had really been exhausted in 1978 and had never been replenished. Some said that the posters would not last more than a few days anyway since people would cover them up or tear them down. They were waiting until the end of the campaign when they would have more effect. Both parties insisted that a good many more posters and billboards would be seen in the last week of the contest, but one could drive all over London without seeing anything of the sort.

On the weekend before the election, I took an hour's bus trip from Paddington out to Wembley, just to see what I could find. On the way I saw three or four Tory billboards, one on the 1984 theme and one on the theme that Labour wasn't working. I saw eight or ten Labour posters, smaller in size, perhaps four by six feet. The top half was occupied by a picture of Callaghan and the bottom half by the slogan "The Labour Way Is the Better Way." This was the only Labour poster visible in London, and the only examples were on walls or hoardings, not in shop windows, grocery stores, or on fences. Why they were so little used by either party is still something of a mystery. One official at the Conservative Central Office suggested that since the election was unexpected, hoardings available for rent could not be found in time. Another suggested that many people feared that if they put a placard in a shop window they might be rewarded by vandalism. The memory of Airey Neave's murder was still very fresh, and people feared to be blown up. Perhaps the explanation lies in some combination of these considerations, but the result was a rather curious campaign in which the customary placards, posters, billboards, and handouts were much less obvious than in the past. At least that was true in London: it has been suggested to me that they were more extensively used outside the metropolitan area.

Sometime about the middle of the campaign, a curious reversal of ancient reputations began to take place. The Tories began to speak with fondness and nostalgia of former Labour leaders like Clement Attlee, Ernest Bevin, and Hugh Gaitskell. At the same time, Labour leaders became sentimental about Benjamin Disraeli and Winston Churchill. On each side, the trick was to compare, as odiously as possible, the responsible and statesmanlike moderation of the other party's leadership of yesteryear with the extravagance of the current bunch of raving extremists. What was interesting was that both parties were doing the same thing.

The treatment did not extend to the very recent leadership. Callaghan could not bring himself to say anything nice about Edward Heath, nor did Mrs. Thatcher say anything nice about Sir Harold Wilson. Perhaps those leaders were too recent, and each was a candidate in the current election. Callaghan pointed with great glee to Disraeli's thesis about the "two nations" and insisted that Tory policies would take the country right back to the distinction between rich and poor that Disraeli had deplored. He also quoted occasionally and approvingly from Churchill, especially the early Churchill, and at one time he even had a good word to say for Harold Macmillan.

It is rather too bad that Mrs. Thatcher could not find something generous to say about Sir Harold Wilson, for Sir Harold was reported by the *Daily Mail* as thinking that Mrs. Thatcher might have the right blend to make her a winner. In a lengthy interview in mid-campaign he astonished many observers by remarking that the Conservative leader's appeal and charisma as a woman might lead Mrs. Wilson to change her mind and vote Conservative. Thatcher, he thought, was "good, very good. I can't remember a time when Tory policies had such a bite . . . Margaret may be a lawyer, but she was born a politician." [15]

Wilson was not the only Labourite to have a kind word for the Tories. Indeed, Wilson's remarks concerned Mrs. Thatcher, not the Conservative party, and they were counterbalanced by a strong commendation of Callaghan and the Labour party. But there were others who came out in direct support of the Conservatives and urged the election of Mrs. Thatcher. Lord Chalfont, Hugh Thomas, Alan Day, Lord Wilson, Lord Robens, and Sir Richard Marsh, all one-time

---

[15] *Daily Mail*, April 27, 1979.

staunch Labourites, came out for the Conservatives.[16] Still more remarkable was George Brown, formerly deputy leader of the Labour party under Harold Wilson and now a life peer under the curious title Lord George-Brown, who urged his friends to vote against Labour Perhaps the most noteworthy convert of all was Reg Prentice, a former member of the Wilson cabinet who had lost a bloody fight with the left-wingers in his constituency party at Newham and in the previous parliament had renounced his party and crossed the floor. He managed to find a fairly safe Tory seat and was elected as a Conservative and appointed to a ministerial post in the Thatcher Government. It may have been the first successful switch of its kind since Winston Churchill managed it.

Not everything went so swimmingly, however, and not all the luck was on the Tory side. There was the noteworthy case of the Collingwood letter. A Mrs. Evelyn Collingwood wrote a note to Mrs. Thatcher "to let her know what ordinary people were thinking" about Tory plans to sell council houses. "Some of us have never been in a position to buy our houses," she said. No doubt the letter never reached Thatcher, but Mrs. Collingwood got an answer from the leader's private office written by the Tory candidate for Derbyshire West, which said, "It may well be that your Council accommodation is unsatisfactory, but considering the fact that you have been unable to buy your own accommodation, you are lucky to have been given something, which the rest of us are paying for out of our taxes." The Labour party was quickly apprised of the letter and made haste to reprint it on a campaign flier. Half a million copies were ordered. It was much discussed in the press, and even the Tories had a chuckle out of it here and there—especially when the printed fliers were delivered to Transport House one evening about 10 P.M. The security-conscious policeman came out to the van and demanded to know what was in it. The first consignment of the Thatcher letter, the driver told him. "Oh no, mate, you've got it wrong," the policeman explained, "Thatcher's lot are over there on the other side of the Square." The driver dutifully drove the few yards over to Tory headquarters and delivered the fliers. The officials at Central Office returned them with

---

[16] Lord Chalfont, minister of state at the Foreign Office in the Labour Government of 1964-1970, had resigned from the Labour party in 1974. Professor Hugh Thomas, a distinguished historian and one-time Labour candidate, had joined the Conservatives in 1976. Alan Day was professor of economics at the London School of Economics and a long-time Labour supporter. Lord Wilson of Langside had been lord advocate in the 1966-1970 Labour Government. Alf Robens has been a powerful leader of the trade union movement and was now a life peer. Sir Richard Marsh had been minister of power and later minister of transport in the Labour Government of 1964-1970.

great glee to Transport House the next morning—proving that not all sporting instinct had yet been extinguished by the heat of battle.[17]

Shortly before the election, the Tories launched a coordinated campaign, in which a number of speakers participated, suggesting that if he were elected Callaghan would last only a year or so. He was then sixty-seven years of age, and he would be replaced, according to the Tories, by some hard-line extremist of the left. All through the campaign the Conservatives had emphasized the extremism of the Labour party. Sometimes they characterized the whole party as extremist, sometimes only the leftist faction. On April 10 the voters were told that a Labour victory would result in a blank check for nationalization. On April 11, the Tories pointed out the similarities between the Labour and the Communist manifestoes. On April 12, the Conservatives leaped upon a publication by the Social Democratic Alliance of a list of forty-three Labour M.P.s who were said to have "overtly associated themselves variously with extreme Marxist-Leninist activities." [18] And now in the waning days of the campaign, the suggestion was made on many sides that the modest and moderate Callaghan would soon be replaced by some ardent left-winger. The most frequently mentioned candidate was Tony Benn. Whitelaw spoke of the "silent legions of the left," waiting to seize power on Callaghan's passing. Callaghan countered that he expected to stick it out through the entire five years of the new Labour Government. When asked if he expected to fight the election beyond that, he said, "Some people have spoken of me as Moses, but I am certainly not Methuselah."

One of the biggest boosts given to the Tories during the campaign was a poll by Research Services Ltd., reported by Anthony King in the *Observer* for April 22.[19] It inquired about the general acceptability of Conservative objectives and Labour objectives among the voters and showed that the Conservatives' purposes and proposals were much more popular than Labour's among the voters who responded. The poll also reported opinions on whether a Conservative or a Labour Government would be more successful in achieving its objectives. On this count, too, the Conservatives came out far better than Labour. Indeed, there was hardly an issue on which Labour's chances of succeeding in doing what it was promising were rated highly. What was

---

[17] The tale was reported in detail by David Leigh in his "Election Diary" in the *Manchester Guardian* over several days. The letter was originally published in the *Daily Mirror* for March 30, 1979.

[18] *Daily Notes*, no. 2, April 12, 1979, p. 32.

[19] Table 3-2 in the chapter by Dick Leonard in this volume gives the findings of this survey.

still more interesting (and deadly) was the report of Labour voters' opinions about the Conservative objectives. The Labour voters approved seven out of the eight Tory objectives mentioned in the questionnaire, often by substantial margins. The only exception was the Tory proposal to sell off parts of some state-owned companies.

The results of all this were devastating. Voters generally were more favorable to Conservative objectives than to Labour objectives, and by a considerable margin they felt that the Conservatives would succeed in achieving their objectives whereas Labour might not. Labour voters thought that the Tories would try harder than Labour to carry out their pledges and that the Tories would succeed in doing so more effectively than Labour could. As King remarked, "Seldom can a major party have penetrated so deeply into the political thinking of the other side's staunchest supporters."[20]

At the same time, every poll showed that Callaghan was more popular than Thatcher, and some polls indicated that Steel was still more popular than Callaghan, which suggested all the more sharply that one of the key issues in the campaign was Thatcher herself. In the polls the party's objectives ran ahead of the party, and the party ran ahead of its leader.

### Mrs. Thatcher as Campaigner

The key to interpreting the 1979 election is the confluence of Margaret Thatcher's personality and ideology with the movement of opinion and the circumstances of the times. It was a fortunate match of time, place, and person. Above all, her comparative lack of top-level experience was more an advantage than a handicap for campaign purposes. She was not encumbered with a past. She was quite new to the spotlight, and a woman besides. She was the right person in the right place at the right time. In Britain as in several other countries there was visible in 1979 a movement of opinion to the right. Margaret Thatcher was part of that movement and she rode it to success.

Thatcher had been a member of Ted Heath's Government in 1970–1974. She had fought the election with him on a platform committed to the reduction of income tax and government expenditures, to the restoration of free enterprise, and to the deregulation of industry. As a member of the Heath cabinet, however, she found herself in command of one of the principal spending departments, namely education and science, and she played the part of a money-spending minister with vigor and success. That is to say, she fought tooth and

---

[20] *Observer*, April 22, 1979.

nail with her cabinet colleagues for a greater share of governmental resources for her own department and her own programs. She was proud of the battles she won and pointed with pride to "the highest sum ever to be allocated in one year solely for the betterment of our schools."[21] The Heath Government did make some strong moves toward tax reform and reducing government expenditure, and Thatcher did her best to play along. Ironically, she is better remembered for ending free milk in the schools and imposing admission charges on museums[22]—a total saving that was absurdly small compared with the increased expenditures for school buildings, the expense of raising the school-leaving age, and the costs of the new Open University.[23]

Three years after its election, the Heath Government had abandoned some of its earlier positions and embraced an incomes policy, support for industry, and, tragically, a sharp increase in government expenditures. It cannot be claimed that Thatcher opposed those changes, for she remained a member of the Government throughout; but it can be suggested that she learned a lesson. So far as she was concerned, the lesson was that political leadership requires firmness and will—especially when it comes to reducing expenditure. Even the smallest cuts bring howls of despair from the civil service, from pressure groups, and from members of Parliament. After she replaced Heath, she was determined not to be misled by his example. Hers was an unblinking determination to restore a free market economy, end arbitrary and futile controls, reduce government spending, liberate funds for incentive and investment, and thus create a new Britain—free, productive, patriotic, and proud.

Thatcher seemed to have learned a great deal from her experience in the years 1970–1974, and she persuaded her colleagues that her view of that experience was correct. It cannot be said that she emerged from it intellectually consistent. Her response was pragmatic and political. She inherited—and subsequently modified—a set of principles from her forebears in the party, and she thinks principle is important. Simon Jenkins in the *Economist* commented that she was

---

[21] *Economist*, April 21, 1979, p. 41.

[22] I think this is true enough, but it is a bit unfair: it was Lord Eccles, not Mrs. Thatcher, who imposed the museum charges.

[23] The Open University, inaugurated in 1971, offers degree programs through a combination of radio and television broadcasts, correspondence courses, and summer schools. It has no campus. It has no formal entrance requirements, being "open" to all; but its degree standards are similar to those of other universities. By 1979 some 82,000 students were taking courses and more than 5,000 degrees had been awarded. *Britain 1980: An Official Handbook* (London: HMSO, 1980), p. 159.

"a politician not so much of principle as of will."[24] It may be more accurate to say that she is a politician of both. Clearly one of her principles is that a politician must have principles, and she is also convinced that only by force of will can a party leader put principles into effect. Her intention was to move quickly once in office and demonstrate by shock tactics if necessary that she and her Government were intent on putting their principles into practice. During the campaign, she neither hesitated nor equivocated about her intentions. She sought not to build a consensus, but to convey her conviction, and indeed she herself has said that she is a conviction politician, not a consensus politician.

The combination of her ideology, her determination, and her conviction, together with the special qualities of her personality, produced a campaigner with some flair and no little stridency. She was clear, forceful, quick to respond, impatient, volatile, and abrasive—qualities which at their best gave the impression of firmness, confidence, and strength, but at their worst made her sound shrill, scolding, and intolerant. People were fascinated by her and by what she had to say. Partly it was that she was a woman, but partly it was the way she handled herself and dealt with the issues that came before her. She was a fast learner but she could never quite shed the abrasiveness that now and then emanated from her conviction and impatience. She was given to lecturing her listeners. She was ill at ease on television in the give-and-take of question and answer. Her attempts to deal with broad policy sometimes came through in obscure metaphor. Both Labour and the Liberals went out of their way to stress the imprecision and exaggeration that often characterized her policy statements. When she talked about law and order, she spoke of re-creating a strong and vigorous police, giving sharp shocks to miscreants, and erecting in the streets a steel barrier against crime. Nobody knew just what she meant by all that and many libertarians were frightened at the prospect. Her responses were frequently general rather than specific, and they tended toward broad-ranging analogies rather than careful statements of her views.

A great many people liked what they believed she stood for—or at least were tired of what she decried—but they were uncertain whether she was properly fitted by character and personality to accomplish the objectives she proclaimed. In consequence, though the Conservatives consistently led Labour in the polls,[25] Mrs. Thatcher

---

[24] *Economist*, April 21, 1979.

[25] The one exception was the NOP survey reported in the *Daily Mail* on May 1, which showed the only Labour lead of the entire campaign. The margin was 0.7 percentage point. Two days later the same poll reversed itself and showed the Conservatives ahead by 6 percentage points.

consistently trailed behind Callaghan in personal popularity all the way through the campaign. When the question was who would make the best prime minister, Callaghan came out ahead. When respondents were asked which party they favored and which candidate for prime minister, the responses always gave a higher percentage to the party than to Mrs. Thatcher personally. Pollsters and canvassers—in both parties—found significant opposition to her personally, and they insisted that it was not because she was a woman. The pollsters made a point of studying that issue, and frequently the polls showing Thatcher trailing Callaghan in personal popularity also showed that the reason was not that she was a woman but that people were put off by the harshness of her public image. Even more devastating was one MORI poll that compared her unfavorably with Ted Heath. When the interviewers asked how people would vote if Heath were Tory leader instead of Thatcher, the Tory lead shot up from five points to eighteen.[26]

Late in the campaign, Thatcher's abrasiveness seemed to diminish and the stridency of her early appearances gave way to a calmer, less intense mood. It was clear that she was gaining confidence, and if an occasional poll showed the Tory lead sagging, the next day's results were likely to restore it. No doubt the qualms that must have been engendered by her own poor showing in the polls were outweighed by the consistent reports of a likely Tory victory. In any case, Thatcher abandoned the harsh dogmatism of the early days, especially on economic policy. At her press conference on April 30, on the morning after the big rally of trade unionists at Wembley, she beamed with confidence and wit, a quality that she frequently displays in the House and in private but which she kept under tight rein during the campaign itself. In the last week, she was more responsive, less urgent, and a great deal more relaxed both at the press conference and on television.

Mrs. Thatcher's own strategy throughout the campaign was to appeal not only to convinced Conservatives but to wavering Labourites. Her audiences were full of cheering and cheerful supporters, but her words were often aimed over their heads to traditional Labour voters who might be persuaded to join the crusade. At Cardiff on April 16, she gave the first of her five major campaign addresses. There was no concealing her right-wing views and no attempt to paint them with any other color. Her belief that there was a deep frustration in the country certainly extended to members of the Labour party, whom she urged to take up their courage and break with their own tradition.

---

[26] *Economist*, April 28, 1979, p. 23.

Consensus politics, she said, was a breach of faith, and she called to those outside the fold, "If you believe it too, then come with me." In a phrase reminiscent of Goldwater in 1964, she said to the Labour faithful: "You know in your hearts that Britain must take a different road."[27]

The Cardiff speech was portrayed in a curious light. Even the friendly press described it as a message from the radical right. Some papers said Thatcher had abandoned the middle ground to Labour, although she herself felt that she was reaching out to the middle ground and trying to induce voters out there to come into her camp. The prime minister immediately welcomed the speech, saying he thought it a gesture of despair and proclaiming himself the middle-of-the-road candidate who appealed to the vast center of the electorate. The stories in the newspapers differed according to the paper's perspective; the *Guardian* and the *Telegraph,* for example, reported it quite differently. But that particular speech is worth examining because it illuminates not only the strong right-wing ideological commitment of the party leader but also her technique of appealing to Labour voters. Both were to continue throughout the campaign.

Mrs. Thatcher's speeches fell into three categories, differing in length, preparation, and presentation. First came the big set speeches delivered to large and carefully planned audiences. There were five of these, beginning at Cardiff and ending the night before the election at Finchley. Each speech was delivered from a manuscript, of which copies were distributed to the press. Speeches in the second group were briefer, delivered before smaller and sometimes more specialized audiences. They were well planned but no manuscripts were prepared. Thatcher would speak from notes, and the press would be given a summary rather than a complete text. The third group consisted of impromptu remarks to small groups on street corners, at factory gates, or in grocery stores. For these the press had to do the best it could do without briefings or handouts.

The Conservatives made a tactical decision before the campaign began that may have had more significance than was intended. Callaghan had challenged Thatcher to a three-part debate on television. When she refused—wisely, most people thought—her opponents chided her harshly for her lack of courage. She suspected Callaghan might get the better of such a debate and she could see no advantage in her participation. Later on she may have regretted that decision. She found she could deal with hostile questioners, and she disappointed many people by refusing to make disastrous blunders. In

---

[27] Ibid., April 21, 1979, p. 21.

view of her strengthened confidence and softened tone during the last week or so, it is quite possible that she would have emerged the victor in the exchange. We shall never know.

There was another reason, however, why she refused to debate. With her principal advisers—mainly her publicity director, Gordon Reece—she decided that she should fight the campaign on different lines. Some said American lines. She would limit her television appearances to "exhibition bouts with selected sparring partners"[28] and special coverage of her walkabouts and whistle-stop personal appearances. The press responded with enthusiasm, and from the very first her movement about the country was dogged (and plagued) by an overwhelming number of television cameras, reporters, technicians, and hangers-on. The coverage was unprecedented. She moved about the country in a caravan, her staff in one bus and up to ninety (accredited) press representatives following in two more. When she moved by air, the size of the group was reduced so that all could be accommodated in her airplane, a BAC 111.

The media event—that is to say, a campaign stunt performed because it will attract attention in newspapers and on television, and not because it has any connection with the issues of the campaign—became a principal element in the Thatcher campaign. A firm of commercial television packagers called Saatchi and Saatchi was employed to handle the posters, the advertising, and the party political broadcasts. Mrs. Thatcher's appearances were carefully orchestrated and designed to encourage the maximum possible television coverage. Before the campaign began she got advice on her voice, her movements, her timing, and her facial expression.[29]

Some of these careful plans worked out very well. But situations were not always easy to control, and some of them turned out to be faintly ridiculous. Thatcher was much photographed wielding a new broom at one factory in the West Country with an obvious intent at symbolism. In Suffolk, she inspected cattle. On several occasions, she was photographed in a shop looking with dismay at prices and comparing them with those of a year or so ago. "I do my own shopping," she often said, always shocked at what Labour had done to the housewife. In East Anglia, near Willisham, she picked up a twelve-hour-old calf and, smiling, showed it to the cameraman. What that did, either to her image or to her immaculate houndstooth suit, went

---

[28] *Guardian*, April 30, 1979.

[29] The *Observer* and the *Guardian* reported that after each appearance special opinion surveys were commissioned for the purpose of appraising and improving her performance. but this was denied by officials at Central Office. See the *Guardian*, April 30, 1979.

unrecorded.[30] On the following day there occurred what may have been the most bizarre media event of the entire campaign. The Thatcher party, followed by two buses full of press and cameramen, arrived at the Cadbury chocolate factory at Bournville outside Birmingham. The whole crowd had to put on long white coats and little paper hats. The workers were wearing identical clothing and it was difficult to tell one player from another. Mrs. Thatcher wound up giving a hard-sell pitch to an American journalist. She helped stuff boxes with chocolates, watched creme eggs being wrapped in foil, and fought her way to brief conversations with women on the production line. The cameramen swarmed all over one another, climbing on the machinery, battering one another's equipment, and getting in the way. There was no talk of campaign issues. "You have more temptations than most of us," Mrs. Thatcher called to a woman stacking chocolate trays. "We never eat them," she replied.

Mrs. Thatcher was rather good at this kind of thing. She was able to establish an immediate sense of intimacy with the barest minimum of remarks. She had a good store of small talk and an instinct for the interesting comment. And of course the whole scene was dutifully reproduced that evening on television sets throughout the nation.[31]

When Mrs. Thatcher rejected the invitation to debate Callaghan on television, she proclaimed loftily that this was not a presidential election—the country was choosing a Government and not a prime minister.[32] But the resort to television and the extended use of the substantively irrelevant media event raised in many people's minds the question whether the British campaign was undergoing a significant change, and throughout the campaign one found people asking themselves and foreign visitors whether the 1979 campaign was not much more like an American presidential campaign than campaigns used to be.

Yes and no. To most people the query meant one of two quite different things. First, was it true that the contest focused on the two party leaders and was in effect an election of the prime minister? The answer was surely yes, but that was nothing new. The voter in Britain actually casts his vote for his local M.P. rather than for the prime minister, but the character and quality of the local candidate, except in a few unusual cases, have but little influence on the outcome

---

[30] The event was widely reported; see, for example, the photograph on the front page of the *Daily Telegraph*, April 19, 1979.

[31] There is a very readable account of the Cadbury visit by R. W. Apple in the *New York Times* for April 22, 1979.

[32] *Guardian*, April 30, 1979.

of the election. The voter tends to vote for a party, and if he has anyone in mind when he goes to the polls, it is far more likely to be the
party leader than the local candidate.

But the question was also whether the expanded use of television
and the development of the media event had produced campaign tactics much more like those used in American presidential races. Here
again, the answer was clearly yes, and that *was* new. Television is not
newly come to British politics, but the deliberate use of television the
way it was used with Mrs. Thatcher had few precedents.

Still, the differences between British and American campaigns
seem more significant than the similarities. There was practically
nothing about foreign policy in the campaign. The hoopla and enter-
tainments of an American campaign were only rarely in evidence in
Britain. The exigencies of the campaign in the United States require
the candidate to cover tremendous distances, and though the Liberal
and Conservative bus caravans covered a great deal of territory, they
faced nothing like the itineraries of an American campaign. Mrs.
Thatcher covered about 3,000 miles in the whole campaign. American
presidential candidates may well do that in a day.

More important, however, is the length of the campaign. The
contest for the American presidency may span fourteen or fifteen
months, and even the official period from the first primary to the
general election may be ten months. The official British campaign is
seventeen days plus bank holidays, which works out usually to be
almost exactly three weeks; during that period the campaigning is
intense. Of course, that is not the whole story. Political campaigning
in Britain is more continuous—at a low level of intensity—than in
America. When an election is in the offing there is a surge in campaign activity well before the date of the dissolution, and that was
true in 1978–1979. But, to quote again from R. W. Apple, Jr., "British
party leaders exert, but unlike their American counterparts, do not
exhaust themselves."[33] Mrs. Thatcher spent about nine days on the
road, making about six stops each day; the rest of the time she was
in London. Indeed, when she was on tour, she frequently returned to
London at night in order to participate in the press conference the
next morning. But the point is that American presidential nominees
make an astonishing number of personal appearances over a period of
a year or more.

Ultimately and most significantly, the British campaign differs
from the American in the cogency and responsibility of its political
argument. If there is less hoopla there is also less irrelevance. The

---

[33] *New York Times*, April 22, 1979.

media event notwithstanding, debate is searching, the response is usually constructive, and people are held accountable for what they say. And in the 1979 campaign, if there was little considered argument on energy or on foreign affairs, there was no lack of serious and constructive debate on economic policy and fiscal matters. The British campaign has become like a presidential campaign, but only in part.

## The Party Headquarters during the Campaign

The roots of the Conservative party lie deep in the past, but in modern times the party has been made up of three components: first, and preeminent, the parliamentary party in both houses, Lords and Commons; second, the National Union of Conservative and Unionist Associations, founded in 1866, which is the federation of the constituency associations and their area organizations; and third, the party headquarters, consisting of the Conservative Central Office in Smith Square, Westminster, and the Conservative Research Department in Old Queen Street nearby.

The Central Office was created by Disraeli in 1870—to match, complement, and work with the National Union. From the beginning it has served as "the link between the party in Parliament and the party in the country."[34] Since early in this century Central Office has been under the general control of a party chairman, appointed by the leader of the party. The Conservative Research Department was created in 1929, primarily to serve the party leadership and the parliamentary party by providing them with policy research and briefings, but also since the war to help the departments of Central Office and the organs of the party throughout the country.[35] For the 1979 campaign the party chairman was Lord Thorneycroft, and the deputy chairmen were Lady Young and Angus Maude, who was also at that time chairman of the Research Department.

Although in "peacetime" the party headquarters has a whole range of departments—Organization, Communications, Women's Organization, Community Affairs, Local Government, International, and the Conservative Political Center—during a general election, the basic and really important departments are Organization and Communications at Smith Square and the Conservative Research Department, which until after the 1979 election, was in Old Queen Street. The

---

[34] Richard Rose, The Problem of Party Government (New York: Macmillan, 1974), p. 138.

[35] A most useful overview of the recent evolution of Central Office and the Research Department can be found in David Butler and Dennis Kavanagh, The British General Election of October 1974 (London: Macmillan, 1975), pp. 38-41.

three must work together, and, though their physical separation caused occasional inconvenience, there were compensating advantages. Their collaboration was close and effective during this campaign.

The Communications Department, headed in 1979 by Gordon Reece, mounted a seven-days-a-week operation all though the campaign. The department regularly distributes a series of publications—*Conservative News, Briefing Notes, Politics Today,* and *Speakers' Notes*—which continued to appear during the campaign. The department is responsible for all manner of relations with the press corps, for the distribution of posters, brochures, leaflets, and similar materials, and, most important of all, for the preparation of the party political broadcasts on radio and television. In April 1978, the firm of Saatchi and Saatchi Garland-Compton was engaged as the party's advertising agent, and preparations were set in motion for an advertising campaign during the run-up to the general election. Saatchi and Saatchi were responsible for developing the posters and billboard signs and aided in the preparation of the party political broadcasts. Those broadcasts were intended for an autumn 1978 election, but they were still on hand in May 1979, and some were used without significant alteration, which many observers thought rendered them less effective than they might have been.

The largest department by far was the Organization Department, whose director in 1979 was Antony Garner. It was responsible, first, for communication with the area organizations and constituency associations. It was continuously in touch with the local agents, local candidates, and the local associations in order to help them in any way possible and to keep them working at full speed. Second, it had to make sure that the materials to be supplied to local candidates were prepared, duplicated, and distributed with dispatch. Third, the department played an important part in the management of the national campaign, not so much in the constituencies but in the country as a whole. That involved it in organizing press conferences, managing tours of party notables, managing the schedules of a hundred or so leading figures in the party, and making sure that speakers were available for radio and television broadcasts when needed.

The task of maintaining communication with candidates and others concerned with policy was crucial, for policy changed from time to time in emphasis and content. The Conservative plan had to respond to Labour charges, to unforeseen events, to the reactions of the press, and to newly perceived opportunities. The campaign changed almost from day to day, and the shifts of emphasis can be traced in the pages of the *Daily Notes,* issued by the combined forces of the Research Department and the Organization Department.[36] The *Daily Notes*—a feature of every Conservative campaign since the war—were issued to all campaign activists for the purpose of keeping them alert to the latest emphases and opportunities. If something new came up, such as the Anti-Nazi riots against the National Front, or if a Labour leader made a statement that the Conservatives found particularly wrong or offensive, the party was likely to come out the next day with advice on how local candidates should respond. The *Notes* also included summaries of stated party policy, analyses of Labour proposals, quotations from notables on the issues, comment on what Labour would do if it got into office, reasons for not voting Liberal, questions that Callaghan *must* answer, and anecdotes of various sorts, principally ones that could be used to embarrass the other team. The *Notes* were elaborate, comprehensive, detailed, and directly responsive to the events of the preceding twenty-four to forty-eight hours. The staff of the Research Department was always in a desperate rush to keep abreast of events and to make sure that the *Daily Notes* were of maximum use to candidates, agents, and other party activists.

Supplementing the *Notes* were the confidential policy-guidance memoranda, a series called "Questions of Policy." These were distributed daily to candidates throughout the campaign. Like the *Daily Notes*, the "Questions of Policy" had been employed in previous campaigns.

In addition to supplying policy information to candidates and others with a policy orientation, the Organization Department was responsible for communications with area and constituency agents and for supplying them with a continuing flow of information, advice, and instructions. All of this was gathered in a numbered series of documents entitled *General Election Memorandum*.[37] In them, the Organization Department provided advice, help, admonitions, reminders, and so on. They advised the agent when to send out his election addresses, how to fill out the proper forms, when to rent committee rooms, how to organize canvassers, how to make sure that the nomination papers were filed in good order, and on and on. Changes in the law, changes in rulings from the Home Office, what to include in the allowable election expenses—all of these were proper subjects for

---

[36] The *Daily Notes* were not quite daily; there were three or four each week, thirteen all together. They were numbered as well as dated, the first appearing on April 11 and the last on May 1.

[37] The memoranda were numbered and dated. They were issued at intervals of three or four days throughout the campaign. In 1979, there were ten in all, the first dated March 30 and the last April 30. Number 10 contained a comprehensive index.

the *Memorandum*. The *Memorandum* provided help on campaign procedures just as the *Notes* and the "Questions of Policy" provided help on campaign substance.

The Research Department, like Organization and Communications, was subjected to increased pressures during the campaign. In 1979 the chairman of the department was Angus Maude, M.P., who was also a joint deputy chairman of the party. The acting director was Adam Ridley (replacing Chris Patten, now fighting for a seat at Bath) and the deputy director (and day-to-day operations officer) was Dermot Gleeson.[38] The organization of the department, like that of other Central Office Departments, has varied a great deal. By 1979 there was a clear understanding that a desk officer was to be assigned to virtually every functional subject over which a minister might preside. The desk officers are very important people in the department, and many of them played key roles in the development of policy materials in the 1979 campaign. In peacetime if the party is in opposition, the desk officer works very closely with the appropriate shadow minister and sometimes becomes something like a personal assistant to him; when the party is in power, of course, shadow ministers will have become ministers with their own staffs. When the election campaign started, the shadow ministers tended to use the desk officers less rather than more, since most of them had to go off and fight in their own constituencies. This meant that the desk officers were left to do their own jobs in the Research Department. During the campaign, a desk officer for every functional subject had daily responsibilities for collecting, collating, analyzing, and preparing materials on any topic within his field.

These three—Research, Organization, Communications—are the major departments during a campaign. As we have seen, in 1979 their functions expanded and their work tempo quickened; but the character of their work was intensified rather than altered. The same was true of the Community Affairs Department, in which the ordinary peacetime tasks are of such a character as to fit easily into campaign requirements. Directed during the campaign by Andrew Rowe, the department is responsible for programs aimed at students, young

---

[38] Shortly after the election, Lord Thorneycroft appointed Alan Howarth, his personal assistant, to be the new director of the Research Department. The director was now to report to the chairman, though he was also to have direct access to the leader. The department also was to be moved out of its office in Old Queen Street and incorporated into Central Office in Smith Square. The move engendered some controversy, the first tentative (and incomplete) reports of which can be examined in the *Economist* for May 26, 1979, pp. 14-15, and in a brief article by Arnold Beichman, "The Conservative Research Department in Controversy," in the *British Politics Group Newsletter*, no. 17 (Summer 1979), pp. 7-9.

Conservatives, small businessmen, trade unions, and community and ethnic groups. All these were key targets in the campaign, and the department could point to several successes in mobilizing particular groups' support.

Other departments for the most part found themselves reduced to an ancillary role and many of their customary functions put in abeyance for the duration of the campaign. Personnel were regularly shifted to the more election-related departments. Winning the election became the prime concern of every person and every department, and all else gave way to that overriding objective. The Women's Organization, the International Department, the Conservative Political Center—all found themselves with diminished functions and reduced staffs. The only real exception was the Local Government Department which had continuing responsibilities arising from the fact that local government elections were being held in many places simultaneously with the general election. Even so, the director of the department, Joan Varley, was coopted to serve as secretary of the "working lunch," a planning and discussion group that met daily throughout the campaign.

Another change in the character of life at Central Office during the campaign was that the staff was not only realigned but considerably augmented by volunteer help from many quarters. Most of these volunteers were long-time party workers, constituency activists, friends of people on the headquarters staff, and so on. They were identified and arranged for in advance as being available for this kind of service, and most of them worked without pay. There was no sense of resentment or ill will against the newcomers. On the contrary, their help was much appreciated, for they were all friends and co-workers. As one assistant director remarked, "If somebody had turned out to be incompatible or offensive he simply wouldn't have been asked to join in."

Still another change at Central Office had to do with Mrs. Thatcher's personal role in the campaign. As leader of the Opposition she maintained a Private Office at the House of Commons, but since she was no longer a member of the House after the dissolution, she was no longer entitled to office space there. Consequently, her Private Office, including the director, Richard Ryder, and three or four staff people, was shifted to Smith Square, although a staff of secretaries remained in the House of Commons handling ordinary correspondence. The same thing had happened in previous campaigns when the party was in opposition. For election purposes it was a good arrangement, permitting closer cooperation between the Private Office and the Central Office staff. Ryder continued, of course, to report to the leader, and after the election the office moved to Downing Street.

One should not overemphasize the formal structure of the organization at party headquarters. During the campaign period the needs of the election displaced all other concerns. Formal organization gave way to informal collaboration and flexibility. The decision-making system itself reflected this same spirit of informality and cooperation. The group centrally involved was an ill-defined aggregation of directors, division heads, and specialists who met twice a day for a discussion of events and tactics. The group varied from time to time depending on the leadership's perception of the problems that required discussion. Lord Thorneycroft was nearly always in the chair, and the heads of the principal departments—Antony Garner, Gordon Reece, Adam Ridley, Andrew Rowe, Angela Hooper, and others—would be joined by some of the deputies or specialists such as Keith Britto from the Research Department or John Lindsey, the television specialist. The deputy chairmen, Angus Maude and Lady Young, were usually part of the group when they were available; but Lady Young more often than not was on tour with Mrs. Thatcher and thus attended only rarely. A shadow minister might well take part if the subject of the day was appropriate to his concern. The same was also true of the appropriate desk officer from the Research Department.

The group met twice a day at 10:30 in the morning and again in the evening. It had no formal name, no formal powers, and indeed no formal existence. But it was not without structure or plan. It had a secretary in the person of Alan Howarth, personal assistant to Lord Thorneycroft. It was his job to gather information and suggestions, to brief the chairmen before the meetings, and to coordinate and chase progress between meetings. Thus the meeting had an agenda even if it was not always made explicit. The group discussed the most recent polls, the issues that seemed to claim attention, and the manner in which they should be handled. What had Labour done that required a response? What should be the subject of the next day's press conference? Who would be available? What new theme should be introduced and what old ones reemphasized? At the evening meetings, reports were brought in by Antony Garner and Alan Howarth from the eleven areas, and the area agents when available were asked to report on the progress of the campaign in their territories.

It was never presumed, however, that the committee (as it was often called) was a formal decision-making body. Votes were never taken. The discussion took place in Lord Thorneycroft's presence and it was construed as advice to him which would be conveyed to Mrs. Thatcher. The tactical decisions of the campaign were ultimately made by Thorneycroft with the leader's sanction.

Some of the tactical decisions arrived at through this process were prompted by actions of the Labour party, others by the defection of key Labour figures, still others by particular events such as the Southall riot. The timing of the announcements, though not necessarily the contents, was orchestrated at these meetings. For example, the Labour party argued that the tax cuts would help the rich, not the poor, and that cutting expenditure would raise the cost of living. How to respond to this contention was a topic much discussed among the Tory planners, and the countermeasures were very carefully considered at the morning and evening committee meetings. Or to take another example, the plan for the party political broadcasts on television had been made well in advance of the campaign. At the beginning it was fairly rigid; the details had been worked out and much of the filming had been completed in advance of the campaign itself. Then about halfway through the three-week period, the group meetings decided to shift some of the emphases and introduce new elements into some of the broadcasts, clearly in response to new perceptions of campaign exigencies. On one occasion Gleeson, Reece, and Lindsey were called in midafternoon to help restructure a broadcast scheduled for that very evening in which Mrs. Thatcher had decided that she herself should play a role. A new recording had to be executed and substituted for some of the material already on the tape.

These group meetings occasionally had an indirect influence on the development of Mrs. Thatcher's principal speeches. Ordinarily first drafts were prepared in the Private Office, drawing on materials assembled by the Research Department; then Mrs. Thatcher, working closely with Lord Thorneycroft and her Private Office advisers, would settle on the final version. That final version was very much a reflection of Thatcher's own opinions and preferences. As the campaign went on, however, and new demands and responses were required, the content of her speeches became a subject of discussion in the committee. Mrs. Thatcher herself was not present at those discussions, but their substance was conveyed to her through Lord Thorneycroft.

The same sort of observations might be made about her itinerary and to a lesser extent the itineraries of other frontbench notables. The plan was worked out well before the election, but details were added and alterations introduced as the campaign progressed. And those changes of plan were always subject to discussion in the committee.

What is interesting here is the flexibility of the campaign plan and the capacity of the party to adapt that plan to changing circumstances and changing perceptions of the progress of the campaign.

In addition to the morning and evening gatherings of the committee, another group assembled daily at what was called a working lunch. This was a larger group of perhaps twenty-five or thirty people that included most of the regular committee plus officers of the next rank as well. If anything, it was even more informal than the morning and evening meetings but it did have a secretary in the person of Joan Varley. The working lunch dated back to at least the 1966 campaign, when it had included no more than ten or twelve people and had been devoted to a serious discussion of tactics. By 1979 it had grown in size and had become more of an information meeting and a pep rally. Many matters were discussed and reported on; opinions were solicited and offered; the day's events and the next day's plans were surveyed. But there was no suggestion that decisions were being taken: that was more nearly the function of the twice-a-day committee.

As stated earlier, the Conservatives, through the National Union, divide the country into eleven areas, Scotland making twelve. The headquarters for the southeastern area (Kent, Surrey, and Sussex) was itself located in Central Office. (It was moved to Old Queen Street after the election.) Its area agent was John Lacy, an experienced and adroit campaigner. Lacy had a good territory. Many of the southeastern constituencies were safely Tory, and on the eve of the election the Tories held thirty-seven of the forty seats. Lacy was determined to do what he could to win those three extra seats, and he developed a very elaborate system of what was called mutual aid in an effort to do just that. The scheme was worked out to the most minute detail. Every constituency had a mutual-aid officer. Each constituency was assigned a particular role in the campaign. Those with the safest seats were mobilized to assist those that needed help. The three Labour-held seats (Dartford, Rochester, and Gravesend) got most of the help, but marginal Tory seats were given assistance as well. The assistance took the form of personnel assigned in advance and prepared to move at the appropriate time during the campaign. Lacy thus could shift his troops like a regimental commander, moving them from the strong areas to buttress the weak. Each constituency knew which other constituency it was to help or from which other constituencies help would be forthcoming; in one or two instances, the constituency was left to its own devices, neither receiving support nor asked to supply it. The mutual-aid plan was not unique to the southeastern area but it was prepared with great care and executed with great vigor—and it paid off: the Tories won all forty seats.

It was quite clear that the Tories were very proud of their campaign. One of the activists at Central Office remarked that it was the best coordinated campaign they had ever had, with more cooperation forthcoming from every quarter. The widespread opinion was that a great deal of the credit was due to Lord Thorneycroft; indeed the *Economist* reported the behind-the-scenes comment "Lord Thorneycroft has operated the Tory Party machine at a level of efficiency not seen since the days of Lord Woolton." [39] He worked comfortably within the formal structure of Central Office but equally well within the informal networks that permeate the entire Conservative structure. One of Thorneycroft's great strengths was that he was very good at handling Mrs. Thatcher, who tended to be a bit edgy and often quite impatient. But he was very effective with other campaigners as well. One reason for the change in tempo and character during the 1979 campaign was Thorneycroft's own personality. He was well liked and respected, he was on top of his job, and he was accepted by both the leader and the staffs at Smith Square.

## Conclusion

At last the 1979 campaign came to an end—long planned for, hurriedly precipitated, and intensely fought. The participants were pretty well exhausted—candidates, leaders, bureaucrats, activists, and not least the journalists who covered it all.

The night before the election is usually something special. Most candidates try to hold one final rally in their own constituency, and very few notables are present to lend a hand since they are all in their own constituencies playing the same game. Margaret Thatcher was no exception. She held a large eve-of-poll rally in a school building in her constituency of Finchley in North London. It was the fifth and last of her major meetings but the first one she had held in her own constituency. Security was heavy and comprehensive. Protests and demonstrations were expected, and they materialized. As at her other meetings, admission was by ticket only, and tickets were not readily available to those outside the circle of known Conservative supporters.

At the door, the ticketholder ran a small gauntlet of police and other officials and was admitted to the hall. Outside was a growing line of the less fortunate who could only hope to get a ticket at the last minute. They were all disappointed. Nearby was a busload of about fifty policemen waiting to be summoned if needed. As the time

[39] *Economist*, April 28, 1979, p. 22.

grew nearer, a group of thirty or forty women assembled outside the hall waiting for Mrs. Thatcher's arrival. They carried signs saying "Thatcher out—let's have a real woman" or "We want women's rights, not a right-wing woman." The group was said to have been organized by the Workers' Revolutionary party. They caused very little difficulty, in part because there was a line of policemen keeping them out of the hall. When Mrs. Thatcher arrived the women set up a chant, "We want women's rights, not a right-wing woman!" By that time the hall was completely full and many people were standing outside listening to the proceedings over a public-address system.

Mrs. Thatcher arrived pretty well on time, a little breathless and seemingly disconcerted by the demonstration outside. On the stage were three people: the candidate, her husband Denis, and the chairman of the constituency association. The chairman took five minutes to introduce her and she talked for about fifty-five minutes, which seemed (and perhaps was intended) to belie the charges that she was exhausted and that her voice had now collapsed. Her voice was not perfect, but it was in good shape and she clearly could have gone on even longer. Just why she spoke at such length is not clear. At one point she remarked that she wanted to cover as many topics as she could because she had been able to spend so little time with her friends in the constituency.

Her speech ranged over all the issues of the campaign—taxes, expenditures, prices, council houses, immigration, Rhodesia, law and order, defense, patriotism, and the future of Britain. She was in good spirits and good form, and quite obviously she was exhilarated by the likelihood of victory, which the polls were still predicting by a margin of some seven percentage points. By the time she was finished, the demonstration outside had subsided, although a small group stuck through to the end. She took no questions on that final evening, but as she moved out of the hall she paused frequently to greet friends and acquaintances. A car was waiting outside the door to speed her and Denis off into the night. The campaign was over and the waiting would now begin.

The polls in Britain do not close until 10:00 P.M. and the vote counting is seldom completed before 1:00 A.M. or later. The 1979 count was protracted by the fact that in many constituencies local elections were being held simultaneously, and the ballots for local elections had to be separated from the parliamentary ballots before the counting could begin. By 1:30 or 2:00 A.M., however, the trend toward the Conservatives was clear, and as the night wore on the measure of the victory increased.

Central Office was busy and well lighted that night, and the mood was light-hearted and confident, in contrast to the gloom at Transport House across the square. A mixed troop of stalwarts, activists, and officials watched television sets, greeted the returns happily, ate, drank, and were merry. Many of the Central Office staff were there, and a stream of visitors came and went, including prominent politicians, officials giving reports and advice, Sir Charles Johnston, the chairman of the Executive Committee of the National Union, Lord and Lady Fraser, the Duke of Rutland, Lord Thorneycroft, and finally the Thatchers themselves. It was a long vigil but a happy one, and it became happier by the minute as the returns showed an increasingly impressive Conservative victory. By 4:30 the next afternoon, the Thatchers had moved into Downing Street.

The voting patterns were analyzed immediately after the election in a survey sponsored by the BBC, designed by Ivor Crewe of the University of Essex and conducted by the Gallup organization.[40] The survey showed that 11 percent of those who had voted Labour in October 1974 voted Tory this time, while the Tories lost only 4 percent to Labour. About half the Liberal vote from October 1974 defected, splitting three to one in favor of the Conservatives. At the same time, the Liberals attracted 10 percent of those who had voted Labour the last time and only 4 percent of those who had voted Conservative. The Conservatives also carried the preponderance of new voters and lost but little to Labour in nonvoting. The number of abstainers was about equal in the two major parties. Labour also suffered a mass defection of working-class voters. The swing to the Conservatives was 6.5 percentage points among unskilled and semiskilled workers, 7 points among trade unionists, and 11 points among skilled workers.

Was there a male chauvinist opposition to Margaret Thatcher? Some people thought there was and thought it was much greater in the North and the Northwest than in the South or Southeast. The feeling was that the London metropolitan area was rather more cosmopolitan and less likely to be put off by a woman candidate. On the other hand, the Tories simply did better in the South and Southeast and the swing was greater there than it was in the North. So the evidence would seem to suggest pro-Toryism as much as willingness to accept a woman. A better judgment might be that if there was a chauvinist vote against a woman prime minister, there was also a feminist vote in her favor. Most analysts considered that the two balanced each other out and that the key issue was not whether the

---

[40] The poll is reported in detail in the *Economist* for May 12, 1979, pp. 25-26. See also Ivor Crewe's chapter in this volume.

candidate was a woman but whether one approved of her. Successive polls had demonstrated (insofar as they can be said to demonstrate such matters) that people who opposed Margaret Thatcher opposed her because they disliked her personality. The Ivor Crewe study suggested that there was no surge of male chauvinism even at the last minute. On the contrary, it suggested that men swung much more strongly to the Conservatives (nine points) than did women (three points).

It is not the purpose of this chapter to provide a detailed analysis of the results. But there are one or two aspects that seem particularly germane to the Conservative campaign. In areas where there were substantial numbers of Asian immigrants, Mrs. Thatcher's presumed threat to their status seems to have worked to Labour's benefit. Bradford West and Leicester South, both Conservative before 1974 and now containing large concentrations of immigrants, both swung to Labour and have seemingly become safe Labour seats. The greatest Tory strength was shown to be in the South and Southeast where the swing was highest. It was less high in the Midlands and scarcely visible in the North and in Scotland.

And so Margaret Thatcher became Britain's first woman prime minister, committed to the restoration of the free market and the capitalist economic system, determined to reduce taxes, reduce unemployment, reduce government spending, and reduce the power of the unions. In the end, a great number of people responded to her appeal. They found in her what they had long wanted and thought they recognized—a leader of conviction and integrity, representing something sharply different from what had gone before, and committed to restoring Britain to health and self-respect. Nothing had seemed to work. Even the Labour party could not deal with the trade unions. There had to be some way out, and here was Margaret Thatcher saying, "Follow me." Britain followed. Now the question was what would come next.

The appointment of her cabinet, which was the first step in her administration, seemed to betoken a calm, rational, and conciliatory approach. It was a well-balanced cabinet, comprising young and old, experience and verve, Heath men and Thatcher men (no women), and if it did not include Heath himself, it included such close former colleagues as Whitelaw, Prior, Peter Walker, and Lord Carrington. Indeed, of the twenty-two members of the cabinet, sixteen had been in office under Heath.

Fortified by a strong cabinet, the new prime minister could face the future with eager confidence. The question is whether her will is adequate to overcoming the obstacles that confront her. And that is still to be determined. A postelection budget did reduce taxes and government expenditures, but making reductions stick is extraordinarily difficult, and budget proposals are not the only factors that go into it. Labour has bequeathed to the Conservative Government a series of commitments and ongoing expenditures that cannot be avoided, and as the spending departments begin to bring pressure upon the Thatcher ministers, the will to cut spending may well be overborne by the political instinct to improve one's department, one's program, and one's budget. By its campaign commitments and by its own ideological orientation, the Thatcher Government is committed to a risky and uncertain course. Prime Minister Heath, too, came to office pledged to cut spending, cut taxes, curb the unions, and restore a capitalist economy. But after three years in office he had to abandon much of that program under the same kinds of pressures that will plague Mrs. Thatcher. She is clearly a politician of conviction. What is yet to be seen is whether she is also a politician of will.

# 5

# David Steel's Liberals: Too Old to Cry, Too Hurt to Laugh

*Jorgen Rasmussen*

The Liberals are so perpetually optimistic that to say they entered the 1979 campaign with high hopes seems uninformative. Optimism was hardly to be expected even from them, however, considering the reverses the party had suffered during the two years prior to the election.

## The Liberals' Situation in the Late 1970s

The year 1974 was the Year of Jubilee for the Liberals. True, they had elected only fourteen members of the House of Commons in February, but they had gained 19.3 percent of the popular vote.[1] They had finished second in 144 constituencies, having managed to shove either the Conservatives or Labour into third place. As for that measure of electoral futility always associated with the Liberals—the lost deposit—they had forfeited two fewer than had the Labour party. The general election that followed only a few months later in October brought a slight check to their advance—thirteen seats, 18.3 percent of the vote, 102 second places. Nonetheless, the Promised Land was in sight. When by-election defeats and resignations made Labour a minority Government in 1976, the Liberals' years of wandering in the wilderness—which had exceeded forty some time ago—seemed ended. Liberal Leader David Steel reached an accord with Prime Minister Callaghan in March 1977 to support the Labour Government in Parliament in exchange for regular consultations between the Government and the Liberals which seemed to offer the Liberals some par-

---

[1] Because the total electorate earlier in the twentieth century was much smaller than it is now, it also was true that never—even in the days when the Liberals had a majority of seats in the House of Commons—had as many people voted Liberal as did so in February 1974.

ticipation in policy formation. From that point on, however, it was all downhill for the Liberals.

Those Liberal supporters who were more sympathetic to the Conservatives than to Labour were alienated by the agreement to keep Labour in power, especially since the Liberal M.P.s had great difficulty citing any examples of important policies for which they had been responsible.[2] The eventual ending of the pact in the summer of 1978 did nothing to reclaim the loyalty of those who had abandoned the party.

Then there was the Thorpe trauma, which had started even before the Lib-Lab pact had been arranged. Jeremy Thorpe, perhaps the most effective leader the party has had in the twentieth century, had been forced to resign his position (although he remained a member of Parliament) in May 1976 because of public allegations that he was a homosexual. While the party managed to weather this storm, the affair returned as a more threatening thundercloud in the latter half of 1978. In August Thorpe was formally charged with incitement to and conspiracy to murder a man who claimed to have had a relationship with him. When Thorpe was brought into court in November to ascertain whether he should stand trial, the press was filled with sordid allegations day after day, and the court, deciding that there was a valid charge to be answered, scheduled him for trial early in 1979.

While no one could guess whether the Thorpe affair would alienate still more supporters, it hardly could benefit the party. Many Liberals wanted Thorpe to resign from Parliament or, at the very least, not to be a candidate when the next election occurred. When it became clear that he did not intend to do either, the party tried to keep as much distance from him as possible. During the 1979 campaign there was an obvious reluctance at Liberal headquarters to discuss Thorpe even in private.

In 1977, following the pact, support for the Liberals dropped below 10 percent, and throughout 1978 most of the polls showed them having only 5 to 8 percent of the electorate—considerably less than half of what they had polled in 1974. Evidence of a decline in popularity was not confined to the polls. In twenty of the twenty-nine by-elections which the party fought during the 1974–1979 parliament, it lost its deposit and twice even obtained fewer votes than the National Front.

Nonetheless, the Liberals were optimistic at the start of the 1979 campaign, and this optimism was better grounded in reality than it

---

[2] While preventing the gasoline tax from going up 5½ pence per gallon was welcome to most people, it was not exactly world shaking.

had been most times in the past. First of all, no intelligent political observer believed that the election results would correspond to the partisan strengths the opinion polls were showing early in 1979— the Conservatives, with well over 50 percent of the electorate, ahead of Labour by nearly twenty percentage points. Since Labour seemed unlikely to regain much popularity, any decline in Conservative support was likely to mean increased strength for the Liberals. Furthermore, conditions seemed ideal for encouraging widespread tactical voting. Since Labour had no prospect of winning the election, Labour supporters' only hope of preventing the Conservatives from winning a majority of the seats was to vote Liberal in those constituencies where the Liberal was well placed. Of the 102 constituencies where the Liberals had come second in October 1974, 92 were held by the Conservatives. In 18 cases the Liberals could defeat the Conservative M.P. with a swing of 5 percent or less.

All this, of course, was speculation; what seemed to make the dreams reality was the by-election that occurred the day after the Labour Government's defeat on a motion of no confidence forced calling an election. Labour had won Liverpool Edge Hill in October 1974 with 13,000 votes. The Liberals had been second, but more than 6,000 behind. In the by-election the Liberals' David Alton gained almost 13,000 votes, while Labour fell below 5,000. (The Conservative candidate lost his deposit.) The swing to the Liberals was a gigantic 32.4 percent.[3] The Liberals concluded that their vision of twenty seats was now a certainty and that up to fifty was possible. The public seemed to agree. A Market and Opinion Research International (MORI) poll a couple of days after the dramatic victory in Edge Hill found that half of the respondents expected the Liberals to have more seats in the new parliament and only 18 percent thought they would have fewer.[4]

## The Liberal Campaign

**Strategy.** Paradoxically the Liberals expected their parliamentary strength to increase even though they conceded that both their total

---

[3] As always with Liberal victories, special local circumstances were involved. The Labour M.P. in Edge Hill had been under fire from his constituency party for some time prior to his death. Thus the local Labour party was split between those who thought that they were well rid of their former M.P. and those who felt that the left-wing militants had hounded the member to his death. As for the Liberals, their local organization in Liverpool may well be their best in the entire United Kingdom. They have been a power on the Liverpool city council for some years and David Alton himself had gained considerable visibility as chairman of the city council's housing committee.

[4] MORI, *British Public Opinion: General Election 1979, Week 1*, p. 19.

161

vote and their share of the electorate would be lower than in 1974. Recognition of this decline in support forced the Liberals to adopt a strategy that might seem counterproductive: to run as many candidates as they had done in 1974. With the total Liberal vote certain to decline, not to reduce the number of candidates meant spreading the Liberal vote more thinly, with the result that the party would suffer the embarrassment of losing a large number of electoral deposits, a result which had made the party a virtual laughingstock in 1950.[5] But cutting back to contest only those seats where the party could make a creditable showing would have been even more injurious. The Liberals' decline in popularity from 1974 would reduce their total vote considerably; reducing the number of candidates would only cut it further. For the Liberals the size of their popular vote was almost as important as the size of their parliamentary representation. Only by polling a few million votes could they hope to convince anyone that an electoral system that converted so many votes into only one or two dozen seats in the Commons was fundamentally unjust. The Liberals' hope of eventually converting Britain to electoral reform depended upon maintaining a great disparity between their popular vote and their parliamentary strength. Thus a substantial increase in lost deposits was the price that had to be paid to maintain a sizable vote. The Liberals withdrew from only 44 of the 619 constituencies which they had contested in October 1974 and offered 577 candidates.[6] Except for the October 1974 election, this total was the largest the Liberals had offered at any election in the twentieth century, including even those prior to World War I, when they were one of the two main parties.

**The Liberal Appeal.** Granted, then, that in almost all constituencies in Britain a voter would have a chance to vote for a Liberal, why should he or she do so? At this point a detailed summary of Liberal policy as contained in the party's manifesto might seem in order, especially since, according to the *Economist*, "The Liberals . . . [had] once again

---

[5] In 1950, 319 of the Liberals' 475 candidates failed to gain the 12.5 percent of the vote necessary to save their electoral deposit. As the results were read on the radio during election night it seemed as though the final words for every constituency were, "and the Liberal lost his deposit." For a discussion of the debate over electoral strategy which racked the party as a result of the 1950 debacle see Jorgen Rasmussen, *The Liberal Party: A Study of Retrenchment and Revival* (London: Constable, 1965), pp. 93–102.

[6] The Liberals intervened in two seats which they had not contested in the previous election, one in Scotland and the other Lincoln, where they had not stood in 1974 so as not to hamper the efforts of Labour rebel Dick Taverne to retain his seat in Parliament against the official Labour candidate.

produced strikingly the best party manifesto."[7] To believe, however, that most people who vote Liberal do so because an objective analysis of party manifestoes has convinced them that the Liberal one is best would be naive.

The basic Liberal appeal remains what it has been for the last decade or even quarter of a century. The Liberals charge that both major parties are beholden to limited segments of society, so that neither of them can govern in the general interest. Rather than seeking the common good, they spend most of their time trying to score trivial points in an ideological battle irrelevant to Britain's problems. Only a party free from special interests—the Liberals—can break out of this morass and restore good, effective government.

The best popular presentation of this argument was the Liberal poster that showed David Steel in front of Jim Callaghan and Margaret Thatcher, flintlock pistols in hand and back-to-back, squaring off for a duel. The caption, which was the Liberal theme for the campaign, was "The Real Fight is for Britain." The clear message was that Steel wanted to work on improving British life, while the main party leaders continued to insist on using outdated methods to settle a personal squabble. Similarly, one of the Liberals' newspaper ads showed Callaghan and Thatcher as Punch and Judy battling on behalf of the unions and the big business bosses. What Britain needs, the ad explained, is "more co-operation and less conflict. Only the Liberal party offers this to Britain."

The need for a middle, balancing party was the theme of the Liberal TV program telecast a week before election day. The telecast opened with a series of people explaining why they were voting Liberal, including a managing director who had been a life-long Conservative. Then Cyril Smith, the party's gargantuan plebeian M.P., put it in simple terms. All one needed to get things right was common sense. The other parties wanted to fight ideological battles rather than peoples' battles. Those who were in the other parties were nice people, but they were caught up in the system.

As these comments suggest, the Liberal stance is one that all too easily can become sanctimonious; it certainly has the capacity to incense those active in the two main parties. One Conservative M.P. called the Liberals' claim that their M.P.s were the only ones who acted disinterestedly in the Commons a libel on the great bulk of the members. Nonetheless, the image the Liberals project of being above the squalid, special-interest bickering of the main parties clearly does have appeal for some voters. An unpublished analysis of survey data

---

[7] *Economist*, April 28, 1979, p. 15.

from the 1960s and 1970s suggests that many of those voters who defected from the main parties to the Liberals did so because they disliked the class biases of the main parties.[8]

Even were a voter willing to grant that the Liberals were more pure in heart than Labour or the Conservatives, what practical difference did this make? As we have seen, even the Liberals themselves at their most optimistic talked of winning no more than fifty seats, well short of enough to form the new Government. The Liberal goal was to deny either main party a working majority in Parliament so that the Liberals would hold the balance of power.[9] Such a situation has come to be referred to in Britain as a "hung parliament." But since that term seems to have a negative ring to it, the Liberals talked of seeking a "people's Parliament." In his final television broadcast of the campaign David Steel appealed for a big wedge of Liberal M.P.s to curb the extremists in whichever party gained the most seats so that moderates and Liberals could work to implement a national program. The real question, he said, was not who would reside in 10 Downing Street, but what kind of society Britain would be in 1984.

Whether even people who favor Liberal policies approve of a parliament, by whatever name, in which no party has a majority is unclear. MORI polls in September 1978 and during the campaign found only 14 to 20 percent agreed that it would be good for the country "if no party achieves an overall majority."[10] Even among those who planned to vote Liberal, considerably more people thought this would be bad than thought it would be good. On the other hand, a Research Services Ltd. poll during the campaign which presented respondents with five different alternative party combinations in Parliament found that nearly half thought that either a three-party coalition or a major party needing Liberal support "would be best for the country."[11]

**Additional Liberal Assets.** Beyond the attractiveness to some voters of the Liberals' independent, apolitical image, an additional Liberal asset was the party leader, David Steel. The Liberals have been blessed throughout the television era with leaders able to communicate well on television. Jo Grimond, Jeremy Thorpe, and David Steel all

---

[8] Analysis by Bruce Cain of data from surveys carried out by the University of Essex.

[9] David Steel explained the Liberals' goal and its necessity in an article for the *Observer* on April 22, 1979, entitled "Dictatorship by election."

[10] Report of MORI survey 3720, p. 16 and MORI, *British Public Opinion: General Election 1979, Week 3*, p. 10.

[11] Reported in the *Observer*, April 29, 1979.

have made very favorable impressions on the electorate with their telecasts. In fact it is difficult to think of any Labour or Conservative Leader who has been the equal of any of these three. Their main talent has been to be able to convince the viewers that they were the voice of reason and moderation.[12] (Whether such favorable impressions can be transformed into Liberal votes is, of course, another matter.) Straightforwardness and sincerity were the keynotes of Steel's final TV broadcast. He opened by saying that he knew that the viewers did not want slick public relations—a fairly obvious reference to the PR "packaging" and media events that had characterized Mrs. Thatcher's campaign. Instead, he asserted, he was going to talk to them straight. Although the rest of the broadcast did not introduce any new themes, it did contain one rather courageous comment. Steel noted that although everyone was looking for scapegoats to blame for the decline in the quality of British life, they must recognize that "We have failed as a nation."

Even before this final television appearance Steel had had a considerable impact upon the electorate. Of those who had seen him on television—and three-fourths recalled having done so—45 percent said that they were "impressed." For Callaghan and Thatcher the figures were 41 and 37 percent, with all other politicians trailing behind.[13] A poll taken on the two days after Steel's final TV appearance found that 22 percent of the respondents thought he would make the best prime minister.[14] Not only was that 8.5 percentage points greater than the proportion of respondents planning to vote Liberal, but it was only 3 percentage points fewer than the proportion of respondents that thought Mrs. Thatcher would make the best prime minister.

Also of some aid to the Liberal campaign was the fact that although their television coverage was not the equal of the main parties' in either frequency or length, it was greater than that which the party received between elections. A television panel of political journalists discussing the campaign toward its close all agreed that the Liberals had received remarkable attention.

---

[12] For example, a MORI poll in April 1978 found that a slightly larger percentage of respondents regarded Steel as honest and in touch with ordinary people than so regarded Margaret Thatcher. MORI report 3311, pp. 16, 18.

[13] MORI poll reported in the *Daily Express* on April 28, 1979.

[14] Gallup poll reported in the *Daily Telegraph* on May 3, 1979. A National Opinion Poll (NOP) survey taken at about the same time as the Gallup one did find that Callaghan was the leader who had favorably impressed the most people in the campaign—37 percent chose him—but that Steel had done better than Thatcher—28 percent to 23 percent. Reported in the *Daily Mail* on May 1, 1979.

**Impediments to Success.** Even though more people were being made aware of the Liberals during the campaign, the party still had to contend with the belief that has become deeply rooted among the electorate over the past quarter of a century—the Liberals are irrelevant. This argument was made explicit by a Conservative poster in the 1950 election, which showed a ballot marked Liberal torn in half and carried the caption "A Vote for the Liberals Is a Vote Wasted." Try as they might over the years, the Liberals never have been able to rid themselves of the wasted-vote argument. Thus David Steel felt that in his final TV broadcast he had to tell the voters, "A vote for the major failed parties is the real wasted vote."

Similarly, while the media did give the Liberals extensive coverage, at times they did not seem to take the party seriously. For example, one newscast closed with a series of short quotations from various politicians' speeches. While for the others serious comments were selected, for the Liberals Cyril Smith was shown saying: "Everyone's very bored with the election. I know that I am." One had the impression that the Liberals had been included to provide light relief.

Additional evidence of some slighting by the media was the fact that Liberal press conferences tended to be less well attended than were those of either of the main parties even though times did not conflict, as those of the main parties did, and the Liberals easily had the most spacious room in which to hold conferences. Also, while many reporters traveled around with Callaghan and Thatcher, only two regularly accompanied Steel in the bus which he used to journey around the country to various constituencies.

Even more of a problem was the concerted effort of some newspapers to obliterate the Liberals. Typical of the efforts of the *Daily Express* was a cartoon that appeared on election day. Three ballot boxes were shown nested one inside another. As a voter dropped a ballot marked for the Liberals through the slot in the first box—the mouth of David Steel—the ballot fell through the slot of the second box—the mouth of Jim Callaghan—into the third box, marked with a hammer and sickle, which was being held by a wild-eyed Tony Benn wearing a large sign saying "Left." The *Sun* used what appeared to be a more objective, scientific approach. Its front page the Thursday before the election was dominated by the headline "Disaster Looms for Libs." The story reported the results of opinion polls in twelve of the thirteen constituencies which the Liberals had won in October 1974. The polls were supposed to have found a 10 percent swing from Liberal to Conservative in these seats, with the result that the Liberals would be lucky to have five or six M.P.s left in the Commons

Cummings

VOTE LIBERAL HERE

LIB X

LIB X

LEFT

LIB X

LONG LIVE THE LIB-LAB PACT!

DAILY EXPRESS Thursday May 3 1978

167

after the election. The story glossed over the fact that 21 percent of the respondents in these constituencies had not decided how to vote and that the average number of people sampled in each constituency was only sixty, nor did it mention what prospects the Liberals might have of winning new seats elsewhere.

On the other hand, on the same morning as the *Sun* story the *Daily Telegraph,* a staunch Conservative paper, carried a front-page story with a decidedly different headline—"Tories Fear Liberal Upsurge." The story explained the Conservatives' concern that the Liberal vote seemed to be holding up better than most observers had anticipated and that some Liberal supporters might vote tactically for Labour in some constituencies to keep the Conservative party out and thereby produce the Liberals' goal of a hung parliament. Clearly the Liberals had become what they had not been at the start of the campaign—a credible influence upon the results. Attempting to chart how this change occurred is interesting.

**The Swing to the Liberals.** Given the margin of error in British political polling—95 percent of the time the ascertained level of support for a party will be within plus or minus three percentage points of the true level—discussing shifts in partisan preferences during the short British electoral campaign is difficult. When a trend can be identified in the results obtained by several polling agencies, however, shifts can be discussed with some confidence. The level of Liberal support found by the five main polling organizations during the campaign is shown in figure 5–1.[15] In summary, these figures suggest that from the time of Labour's defeat in the Commons on the motion of censure until two weeks prior to election day, the Liberal vote stagnated at 9 percent plus or minus one percentage point. Then a swing appears to have begun. Thus, during the last full week prior to election day Liberal support had risen to 11 percent plus or minus one percentage point. The trend accelerated during the last half-week prior to election day as the Liberals increased their strength to 13.5 percent plus or minus one percentage point. The actual share of the vote the Liberals gained in the election proved to be 13.8 percent.[16]

[15] Fractions greater or less than 0.5 usually are rounded off by the polling agencies before the results are reported. Since surveys normally are carried out over two or more days, the results in this graph are reported as falling at the midpoint of each period of fieldwork. The graph does not include the results of panel studies or of surveys that focused on only a portion of the electorate, such as Marplan's survey of 100 English marginal constituencies.

[16] The polls understated Liberal strength a bit more than these figures suggest. Since no polling is done in Northern Ireland, party percentages need to be calculated on the basis of the total national vote minus votes cast in Northern Ireland. On this basis the Liberals received 14.2 percent of the vote.

## FIGURE 5–1

### LIBERAL SUPPORT IN OPINION POLLS, MARCH 29–MAY 1, 1979

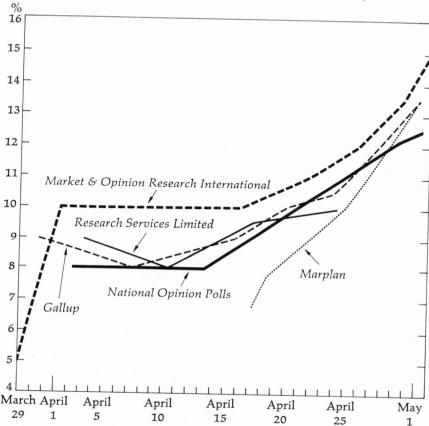

Since no major event, scare, or blunder occurred during the 1979 campaign, it is not possible to identify any occurrence that produced this shift to the Liberals.[17] Simply to speculate, however, it may be relevant to note that Mrs. Thatcher did not really become active in the campaign until after Easter. She entered the campaign at the start of the week toward the close of which the shift to the Liberals

---

[17] The shift to the Liberals was not unanticipated even among those who were not supporters of the party. Peter Jenkins told readers of his column in the *Guardian* of April 16 that one of the developments to look for in the campaign was an increase in Liberal strength. By April 24 the head of one of the major polling agencies was saying in private that the squeeze was on the Conservatives and that the Liberals would get 12 percent of the vote.

seems to have begun, with a combative speech proclaiming that consensus was not the goal of a conviction politician like herself. This was followed a few days later by the celebrated incident of Mrs. Thatcher hugging a newborn calf and lying down with lambs in the field during her visit to a farm—all for the benefit of media camerapeople.[18] It is not inconceivable that events such as these helped to convince some people that the Liberals had a useful role to play in the new parliament.[19]

While Mrs. Thatcher's campaigning may have driven voters to the Liberals, one should not conclude that the Liberal vote was strengthened because the party became a refuge for male chauvinists. The results of a panel study that interviewed respondents three times during the campaign and once immediately after polling day indicated that the Liberals' gains were confined almost entirely to women. Only 0.5 percent of the male respondents were converted to voting Liberal during the campaign, while 7 percent of the women shifted from their voting intention at the start of the campaign to cast a vote for the Liberals.[20]

## The Results

Had it not been for the success they had enjoyed in both general elections in 1974, the 1979 results would have looked pretty good to the Liberals. Between February and October 1974 the Liberals had lost 0.7 million votes and between October 1974 and May 1979 they lost another 1 million. Nonetheless, the Liberal vote in 1979—4.3 million —was about 40 percent larger than that which they had received in any other general election in the last half century except those of 1974. The price for this sizable vote, however, was, as anticipated, a major increase in lost deposits. Over half (53 percent) of all Liberal candidates failed to obtain the 12.5 percent of the vote necessary to save their deposit; in this respect for the Liberals, it was the fifth worst of the eleven post–World War II elections.[21]

---

[18] For a scathing description of the "packaging" of Mrs. Thatcher see Peter Jenkins's column in the *Guardian*, April 19, 1979.

[19] Note that John Cole and Adam Raphael writing in the *Observer* on April 29 characterized the week of April 22-28 as the "week of the wobble," "the week in which Margaret Thatcher was rattled." This was the week that clearly showed that a swing to the Liberals was occurring.

[20] Peter Kellner, "Not a defeat: a disaster," *New Statesman*, May 18, 1979, discussing the results of the MORI panel study which had been intended for the *Sunday Times*.

[21] In 1950, 67 percent of the Liberal candidates lost their deposit and in 1951 61 percent did. In both 1955 and 1970 the figure was 55 percent, only slightly higher than in 1979. At the other six general elections the figure never was greater than 33 percent and in February 1974 it was only 4 percent.

The total number of votes cast for the Liberals was remarkable, yet it provided evidence, as did the Conservative victory, that British politics have not yet become "presidential." Just as a number of people voted Conservative despite not caring for Margaret Thatcher, so, obviously, many who believed that David Steel would make a good prime minister refused to vote Liberal. Steel doubtless was a factor, however, in the importance of television in swelling the Liberal vote. "Almost a third of all Liberals, and over half the last-minute Liberals, mentioned a television broadcast as a factor."[22]

**The Changing Composition of Liberal Support.** The Liberal vote showed considerable turnover since the last general election. Only half of those who had voted Liberal in October 1974 did so again in 1979.[23] For the Conservatives the figure was 87 percent and for Labour 75 percent. Low as this level of Liberal loyalty was, it improved upon past patterns. Only 44 percent of the 1959 Liberal voters remained loyal to the party in 1964, and support was no more stable during the shorter interval between the 1964 and 1966 elections.[24] Furthermore, only 38 percent of those who voted Liberal in 1966 did so again in 1970.

Those 1974 Liberal voters who defected helped the Conservatives much more than Labour—almost one-third of the 1974 Liberal vote went to the Conservatives in 1979 and only one-tenth went to Labour. Nor do the gross figures provide any evidence that the Liberals benefited from tactical voting. Those October 1974 voters who defected from one or the other of the main parties did not move disproportionately to the Liberals: 4 percent of former Conservative voters defected to Labour and 6 percent switched to Liberal, while 11 percent of former Labour supporters voted Conservative this time and 10 percent voted Liberal. Furthermore, the Liberals were unable to do as well—

---

[22] *Economist*, May 12, 1979, p. 26. MORI's panel study found that Liberal voters were more likely than either Conservative or Labour supporters to have voted for the party of their choice because they liked its leader(s). Nonetheless, a larger share of the Liberal voters—fourteen percentage points more—gave their preference for Liberal policies as the reason for their vote. MORI, *British Public Opinion: General Election 1979*, p. 52.

[23] This and the following figures, except where otherwise noted, are from the results of a Gallup survey designed by Ivor Crewe of the University of Essex, portions of which were reported in the *Economist*, May 12, 1979, pp. 25–26. The source for figures for the 1974 comparisons is NOP surveys.

[24] Figures for past instability in the Liberal vote have been calculated from the information presented by David Butler and Donald Stokes in *Political Change in Britain*, 2nd college ed. (New York: St. Martin's Press, 1976), pp. 179–85. These calculations were made after excluding that part of the electorate that had died since the last election.

even relative to their proportion of the total vote—as the main parties in mobilizing support from young, first-time voters or from former abstainers. Both the Conservatives and Labour got over four times as many of the October 1974 abstainers as did the Liberals and almost three times as many of those who had been too young to vote in October 1974.

The relative instability of the Liberal vote produced a considerable change in the social composition of the party's electoral support. The proportion of skilled manual workers supporting the Liberals was halved to 10 percent, while Liberal strength among the professional and managerial class was cut by a third. On the other hand, office and clerical workers remained steadfast: 20 percent voted Liberal. It was among this social class that the Liberals enjoyed their greatest support. Thus while in October 1974 the Liberals got about the same proportion of support in each of the three social classes mentioned, in 1979 they received one-third more support among office and clerical workers than among managerial and professional types and twice as much support among the former as among skilled manual workers. Also, while in 1974 the Liberals had almost twice as much support among the professional and managerial class as Labour, now the Liberals have the smallest share of any of the three leading parties in every social class.

**Winning and Losing M.P.s.** Sociological analysis of the Liberal vote provides interesting information about the nature of the party's appeal, yet in the case of the Liberals, more so than for the two main parties, electoral success is likely to turn upon particularistic, local factors.[25] A summary of how each of the Liberal M.P.s elected in October 1974 fared in 1979 appears in table 5–1. Contrary to what the *Sun*'s survey had foretold, only three Liberal M.P.s were defeated.

Each of these defeats was in one way or another something of a shock. The Welsh seat which Emlyn Hooson lost had been held by the Liberal party for a century and no one had thought that it was in any danger of changing hands in 1979. No satisfactory explanation has been offered for this defeat except, perhaps, that Hooson, assuming that his victory was certain, failed to campaign actively enough. While Jeremy Thorpe's defeat, given his personal problems discussed at the start of this chapter, hardly could be called unanticipated, the

---

[25] MORI's panel study suggests that this statement should perhaps be qualified. Its respondents who voted Liberal were no more likely than were those who had voted Conservative or Labour to mention the attractiveness of the party's local candidate as a reason for their vote. MORI, *British Public Opinion: General Election 1979*, p. 52.

## TABLE 5-1
### ELECTORAL EXPERIENCE OF LIBERAL M.P.s

| M.P. | 1979 Vote | Gain or Loss from October 1974 | October 1974 Margin of Victory | 1979 Margin of Victory[a] | Gain or Loss in Margin |
|------|-----------|-------------------|------------------|------------------|-------------------|
| Alton | 12,701 | 5,849 | −6,171[b] | 4,248 | 10,419 |
| Beith | 19,351 | 4,667 | 73 | 5,688 | 5,615 |
| Hooson | 10,158 | −1,122 | 3,859 | −1,593 | −5,452 |
| Freud | 26,397 | 4,357 | 2,685 | 3,330 | 645 |
| Grimond | 10,950 | 1,073 | 6,852 | 6,810 | −42 |
| Howells | 13,227 | −1,385 | 2,410 | 2,194 | −216 |
| Johnston | 15,716 | 2,588 | 1,134 | 4,157 | 3,023 |
| Pardoe | 20,742 | −626 | 3,856 | −3,747 | −7,603 |
| Penhaligon | 33,571 | 11,022 | 464 | 8,708 | 8,244 |
| Ross | 35,889 | 6,192 | 2,040 | 352 | −1,688 |
| Smith | 22,172 | 2,080 | 2,753 | 5,294 | 2,541 |
| Steel | 25,993 | 5,987 | 7,475 | 10,690 | 3,215 |
| Thorpe | 23,338 | −4,871 | 6,721 | −8,473 | −15,194 |
| Wainwright | 20,151 | −1,846 | 1,666 | 2,352 | 686 |

[a] A minus sign in the 1979 victory margin column indicates that the M.P. was defeated in 1979.

[b] Alton was second in October 1974. In a 1979 by-election he received 12,945 votes, winning by 8,133 votes.

SOURCE: For 1979, *Guardian*, May 5, 1979, pp. 7-11. For 1974, *The Times Guide to the House of Commons, October 1974* (London: Times Books, 1974).

size of his rebuff was a shock, especially given past evidence of his personal support in North Devon.[26] John Pardoe had had a premonition of his defeat; since his 1974 majority was one of the larger Liberal ones, however, and since he was, in effect, the Liberals' deputy leader, he seemed to have a good chance of victory. Again, perhaps the most surprising thing was that he was defeated as easily as he was. Two factors may have contributed to this. Although the Labour vote in Pardoe's constituency had gone up by 1,000 votes in October 1974, at only 6.4 percent of the vote it did not provide much of a reserve that the Liberals could squeeze for additional support by encouraging Labour tactical voting. Thus any defection of Liberal supporters from Pardoe to the Conservatives was likely to make him

---

[26] Since the date originally scheduled for Thorpe's trial would have fallen during the election campaign, it was changed to shortly after the election. In mid-June Thorpe and the other three defendants were found not guilty on all charges.

vulnerable. And such defection was an obvious danger since Pardoe's constituency bordered on Thorpe's, and Pardoe, refusing to turn his back on Thorpe during his personal difficulties, had campaigned for him in Thorpe's constituency. Thus, limited scope for tactical voting plus the Thorpe affair may well account for Pardoe's defeat.

On the other hand, personal factors apparently worked in the Liberals' favor in the case of Alan Beith and David Penhaligon, both of whom were extremely vulnerable and yet managed to retain their seats with relative ease. Penhaligon even had to contend with the fact that his constituency was the next one down the coast from Pardoe's and, thus, not all that far from Thorpe's. Although he had had the second-smallest Liberal margin of victory in October 1974, Penhaligon's personal appeal as a true Cornishman gained him far and away the largest increases in vote of any Liberal M.P. in 1979. The Liberal M.P. polling the most votes in 1979, however, was Stephen Ross, who, paradoxically, now has the narrowest Liberal margin of victory. Despite his great success in expanding his vote, Ross saw his majority cut considerably; a significant enlargement of the electorate and the collapse of the Labour vote in the constituency helped his Conservative opponent more than they benefited him.

In addition to losing three seats, David Steel had to deal with the disappointment of the Liberals' failure to win a single one of the several seats that appeared to offer some chance of expanding Liberal strength in the Commons. While the Liberals increased their vote in twelve of the eighteen seats where they had been within ten percentage points or less of the Conservatives in October 1974, in every instance the Conservatives increased their vote by more than the Liberals did. As a result, in every one of the eighteen seats which had been the Liberals' best prospects for gains, they were farther from victory in 1979 than they had been in 1974. The trend to the Conservatives had been too strong for the Liberals to buck even where they were serious challengers.

The Liberal parliamentary party did have one relatively new recruit, however, to make its total eleven M.P.s. David Alton, winner of the startling Liverpool by-election at the very end of the old parliament, managed to retain this seat in the general election even though his total vote declined and his victory margin was cut almost in half. Despite this reduction, Alton's victory margin was larger than that of five of the other ten Liberal M.P.s.

Perhaps of greater significance for the Liberal party than the changing sociological composition of its vote is the changing geographical distribution of its M.P.s. As the party declined into third-party status in the first half of the twentieth century, it increasingly became a party of the Celtic Fringe—Scotland, Wales, Devon, and Cornwall. Thus, geographically, as well as in terms of power, it seemed to be on the periphery of British politics. In every general election since the war—including even the resurgence of 1974—more than half of the Liberal M.P.s represented seats in the Celtic Fringe. In 1964 the proportion reached 89 percent; only one of the nine Liberal M.P.s was not from the Celtic Fringe. In total, 71 percent of the Liberals' ninety-two general election victories from 1945 through October 1974 occurred in the Celtic Fringe. In 1979, however, only five of the eleven Liberal M.P.s were returned from Celtic Fringe constituencies— three in Scotland, one in Wales, and one in the English West Country. If the Liberals ever are to return to the heart of British politics, this trend must continue.

**Implications for the Future.** In five-sixths of the constituencies which the Liberals contested both times, they received fewer votes in 1979 than they had in 1974. Of the ninety-three seats where the Liberals did increase their vote, 41 percent were in Scotland. This means that what limited advance the Liberals made in 1979 often occurred where they had been particularly weak before. In October 1974 the Liberals had lost more deposits in Scotland than in England, despite having more than seven-and-a-half times as many candidates in England. While only 10 percent of the Liberal candidates fighting English seats in 1974 had lost their deposits, 85 percent of those fighting Scottish seats had. The growth in support for the Scottish Nationalists in the early 1970s had made considerable inroads into Liberal strength in Scotland. Of the electoral collapse of the SNP in 1979 the Liberals were a beneficiary, although certainly not the major one. In the great majority—84 percent—of the Scottish seats where the Liberal vote increased in 1979, the Liberals, even with their gains, ran third or worse.

In 1979 the Liberals came second in eighty-two constituencies. As is the case for so many other aspects of the party's achievements, this is the best post-World War II result ever obtained except in 1974. The political situation in these eighty-two constituencies might seem to offer some prospect for Liberal gains in the near future. Past experience indicates that by the time a Government is two or three years into a parliament the electorate regards the honeymoon as over and is ready to turn against the Government in by-elections. The Liberals will be looking forward to this because in every constituency, save two, where they now are the challenger the Conservatives were the winning party in 1979.

The Liberals would do well, however, not to be too expectant. In fifty-four of the eighty-two constituencies where they were second in 1979 the Liberals polled fewer votes than they had in October 1974. As a result, in only three constituencies are they now within 3,000 votes of winning, and one of these is a seat that they had won in October 1974 but lost in 1979. Thus, when disillusionment with Mrs. Thatcher's Government sets in, by-elections doubtless will begin to swing to the Liberals. There will have to be an extraordinarily sizable swing, however, for the Liberals' strength in Parliament to show any significant increase. Victories like that of David Alton in Liverpool Edge Hill do occur and help to put the troops in good heart, but they don't happen frequently enough to alter the fundamental realities of political power in Britain.[27]

---

[27] In the Southend East by-election in March 1980, for example, the Conservatives just barely retained a seat that they had won easily in 1979; their share of the vote dropped by nineteen percentage points. The Liberals, with an increase of twelve percentage points, nearly doubled their share of the vote, while Labour expanded its share by only seven percentage points. Despite this, the Liberals were third in the by-election, about 4,200 votes short of victory.

# 6

# Toward Normality: Public Opinion Polls in the 1979 Election

*Richard Rose*

Politicians and the general public approach every British general election with an idea of what a normal outcome would be. First of all, public opinion would positively favor one of the two major parties, and this would be translated into individual voting decisions. Second, the electoral system would give an absolute majority of seats in the House of Commons to the party winning the largest share of the popular vote. Third, public opinion polls would forecast correctly which party would win the election.

The 1979 general election was the first since 1966 that approached this idea of a normal election.[1] In October 1974, Labour won a bare parliamentary majority, as forecast by the polls, but it did so with less than 40 percent of the vote and subsequently lost its parliamentary majority. In February 1974, the electoral system got the result wrong: as the polls forecast, the Conservatives won a larger share of the popular vote than Labour, but Labour won more seats and formed a minority Government. In 1970, the electorate and the electoral system worked normally, but the polls failed, and failed spectacularly: four out of five picked the wrong party to win.

The outcome of the 1979 general election was a move *toward* normality, for none of the three cardinal requirements of a normal election outcome was violated. But one more-or-less normal election

---

[1] This chapter is the latest in a series of papers by the author evaluating the role of public opinion polls in British elections. See Richard Rose, *The Polls and the 1970 Election* (Glasgow: Strathclyde Survey Research Centre Occasional Paper No. 7, 1970); Richard Rose, "The Polls and Election Forecasting in February, 1974," and "The Polls and Public Opinion in October 1974," in Howard R. Penniman, ed., *Britain at the Polls: The Parliamentary Elections of 1974* (Washington, D.C.: American Enterprise Institute, 1975), pp. 109-130, and 223-239; and for a summary and overview, "Opinion Polls and Election Results," in Richard Rose, ed., *Studies in British Politics*, 3rd ed. (London: Macmillan, 1976), pp. 305-322.

after three cuckoos does not provide a solid basis for generalization. The purpose of this chapter is to examine carefully the role of public opinion in the 1979 election in order to assess to what extent this seemingly normal event may be regarded as a pattern for the future, or whether this move toward normality may itself be regarded as abnormal.

## The Run-Up to the Campaign

In the mind of an inveterate campaigner such as Harold Wilson, every general election campaign begins the day after the last one is over. This was inevitably the case in March 1974, for the Labour Government found itself in office without a majority, and the October 1974 election left Labour with a very insecure parliamentary majority.

The political events of 1974 produced a greater reaction against the established party and electoral system than any for nearly half a century. A campaign *against* the electoral system began under the auspices of a newly formed cross-party National Committee for Electoral Reform. It advocated proportional representation to allocate seats in the House of Commons in proportion to votes. Critics of the traditional British system of "adversary politics" attacked the first-past-the-post electoral system for alternating 100 percent power in government between parties that won less than half (and in 1974, less than 40 percent) of the popular vote. Proportional representation was recommended by such academics as S. E. Finer as a method for producing moderation in British politics.[2] A 1978 Opinion Research Survey reported 64 percent endorsing the election of M.P.s in proportion to the vote for their party.[3]

Parliament accepted that the system used to elect Westminster M.P.s was not ideal for all circumstances, mandating proportional representation in Northern Ireland for the 1973 assembly and local government elections, for the 1975 Northern Ireland Constitutional Convention election, and again for the 1979 election of Ulster members of the European Parliament. But the Commons remained ada-

---

[2] See Samuel E. Finer, ed., *Adversary Politics and Electoral Reform* (London: Anthony Wigram, 1975). Popular attitudes toward political parties were generally more favorable than those expressed by academics and journalists; compare the survey reported in Lord Houghton, chairman, *Report of the Committee on Financial Aid to Political Parties* (London: HMSO, Cmnd. 6601, 1976).

[3] See "The Majority in Favour of Electoral Reform," *Economist*, May 13, 1978, and more generally, publications of the National Committee for Electoral Reform. The NCER differed from the long-established Electoral Reform Society in many ways, including the specific type of proportional representation it tended to favor. See Lord Blake, *The Report of the Hansard Society Commission on Election Reform* (London: Hansard Society, 1976).

mantly opposed to any use of proportional representation in Great Britain itself. When legislation was put forward for devolved assemblies in Scotland and Wales and for the European elections, parliamentary votes were forced on proportional representation. The divisions showed the satisfaction of most Conservative and Labour M.P.s with the system that had elected them.

Much of the story of the 1974–1979 parliament was a history of the Government's seeking to avoid an election because both by-election results and public opinion polls showed the Conservatives running far ahead of the Labour Government. There is nothing unusual in a governing party running behind the Opposition in opinion polls between elections. In eight of ten parliaments since 1945 the Government has more often than not been behind the opposition party in the monthly Gallup poll. In three of the seven cases at hand as of 1977—1950, 1955, and 1959—the subsequent general election was nonetheless won by the Government.

Normally a prime minister can seek to engineer an election date when his party will be ahead—if only momentarily—in popular favor. But in the 1974–1979 parliament it was always possible that an election would be forced on the Government because it lacked a majority in the Commons. Once Jim Callaghan negotiated a pact with the Liberals in March 1977 (at a time when the Gallup poll showed the Conservatives 16½ percentage points ahead of Labour), the prime minister could think about a strategy to win the next election. By October 1977, the Labour party had pulled even with the Conservatives on the Gallup poll.

The ambiguity of opinion poll evidence for election strategy was made evident when the prime minister faced the prospect of calling a general election for October 1978. In the twelve months preceding Callaghan's early September announcement that there would *not* be an autumn election, opinion polls had shown the gap between the parties closed. Labour was ahead or tied with the Conservatives in six of the preceding twelve monthly Gallup polls. The August 1978 Gallup poll showed Labour four percentage points ahead of the Conservatives. During the course of an election campaign, the prime minister's personality could give the party a margin of victory. Equally important, economic indicators and the industrial relations calendar suggested that the six months from October 1978 would be increasingly difficult for the Government.[4]

---

[4] See Richard Rose, "Marking the card at No. 10," *Daily Telegraph*, August 11, 1978. Cf. Peter Kellner, "Why it's got to be October 12," *Sunday Times*, May 7, 1978.

But public opinion polls could also be interpreted as evidence against an immediate ballot. The Tuesday before the prime minister announced he would not call an autumn ballot, the *Express* published a survey by MORI (Market and Opinion Research International), also the Labour party's private pollster, showing the Conservatives two percentage points ahead, a swing of three points from the Government, enough to lose its office if repeated on election day.[5] Moreover, the Conservative lead was greater in England and in marginal seats; only in Scotland did MORI show Labour ahead. There was in the Labour cabinet—as there is in any Government threatened with suddenly losing office—a group actively urging the prime minister not to call a general election in October 1978. In the event, the prime minister decided the certainty of months more in office was preferable to the uncertainties of an election test, and did not call a 1978 ballot. Later, the former prime minister was quoted as telling the parliamentary Labour party that an October election could have given Labour an extremely small majority or left Labour a minority Government, an outcome that he rationalized as unsatisfactory—though the dozens of Labour M.P.s and ministers ousted in May 1979 might have viewed matters differently.[6]

In the seven-month period after the announcement that there would be no autumn election, opinion polls consistently showed Labour's position deteriorating. Gallup placed Labour ahead in October and November 1978, and the Conservatives moving ahead thereafter, with a lead of 20 points over Labour in mid-February, and 14½ points in mid-March. MORI showed the Conservative lead as high as 19 points in February 1979, and it averaged nearly ten percentage points in four MORI polls.

Referendums in Scotland and Wales on March 1, 1979, provided a test of public opinion—and of public opinion polls—immediately prior to the general election campaign. In Wales, the result was clear-cut. Nine polls taken in Wales from December 1975 until a week before the vote all showed the opponents of devolution outnumbering its supporters. Marplan's final referendum survey indicated 75 percent against devolution; a final Abacus survey the same; and a survey by Research and Marketing Wales, 73 percent voting against. In the event, the "no" vote was 80 percent of the total cast. The average error of the three polls in forecasting the Welsh result was six points.[7]

---

[5] See "Tories Keep Ahead," *Daily Express*, September 5, 1979, and Peter Jenkins, "On the brink, the Foot faction still votes for spring," *Guardian*, September 7, 1978, and "Mr. Callaghan reacts sharply to opinion research," *Times*, September 9, 1978.

[6] "Thatcher gets a boost from Benn," *Daily Telegraph*, May 17, 1979.

[7] For details, see Richard Rose and Ian McAllister, *United Kingdom Facts* (Lon-

In Scotland, opinion poll data had been used tactically in 1974 to demonstrate to unenthusiastic Labour party supporters in Scotland that there was a strong popular demand for devolution and that this was crucial for Labour's electoral survival. The key question asked by MORI gave only three alternatives—"a completely independent Scottish Parliament," "a Scottish Parliament as part of Britain but with substantial powers," and "no change." It found upward of 60 percent of Scots favoring the middle way. But surveys offering Scottish voters five options produced a different result. Opinion Research Centre normally found about one-fifth favoring devolution, with a third or more wanting no change or only nominal change, and a third or more wanting federalism or independence.[8]

The final Scottish referendum forecasts of six opinion polls were reasonably accurate; the average error was only three percentage ponits, with a 52 percent "yes" vote for Scottish devolution.[9] But the referendum campaign produced reminders of the difficulty of forecasting, for opinion moved very quickly against devolution during the campaign. At the beginning of 1979 a public opinion poll conducted by System Three Scotland showed 64 percent in favor of devolution, compared with its correct forecast of 52 percent in favor only nine weeks later. A decline in Scottish Nationalist party support and a crystallization of Conservative opinion against devolution were the chief causes of the shift. Moreover, the referendum rules produced an ambiguous outcome. A majority of Scots voting favored devolution, as the polls forecast. But this majority fell seven points short of 40 percent of Scots eligible to vote, and thus did not meet the "more than majority" requirement laid down by Parliament for automatic approval. The referendum failed to provide the clear-cut statement of opinion that the Labour Government had wished.

When the general election was announced, pollsters as well as the media sponsors and consumers of polls were relatively cautious. The day after the Government fell, the Conservatives' substantial lead was confirmed by a MORI survey undertaken on March 29, showing the Conservatives nine points ahead. But such figures tended to be discounted by many journalists and politicians. Writing in the *Observer*, Adam Raphael noted, "the polls often get it wrong," that is, they had

---

don: Macmillan, forthcoming), chap. 5, and J. Barry Jones and R. A. Wilford, *The Welsh Veto—the Politics of the Devolution Campaign in Wales* (Glasgow: University of Strathclyde Studies in Public Policy No. 39, 1979).

[8] See Rose and McAllister, *United Kingdom Facts*, chap. 5.

[9] The forecast percentage of "yes" votes in final preelection polls were: MORI, 50 percent; System Three Scotland, 52 percent; NOP and the Gallup Poll, 55 percent each; and 57 percent each by Marplan and the election-day polling station survey by Opinion Research Centre for ITN.

failed to forecast the 1970 result correctly.[10]  At the other extreme of confidence, Paul Whiteley, a politics lecturer at Bristol University, declared that by applying complex statistics to a precampaign series of polls, it was possible to predict a general election outcome to within an average error of 1.6 percentage points for each party at each general election from 1950 through October 1974.[11]

The *Economist* raised a specter disturbing for both voters and pollsters, namely the possibility that published polls influence results. Of the two alternative theories—that polls produce a bandwagon effect helping the leader, and that they produce a backlash effect helping the underdog—the *Economist* plumped for the latter.  In the context of 1979, the *Economist* was implying that Labour stood a far better chance of winning the election than appeared on the surface, precisely *because* the party was running behind.[12]  In a "belt and braces" statement, Lord Thorneycroft, chairman of the Conservative party, cautioned his supporters against complacency in the face of a large poll lead, and against despair if polls showed the Conservative lead narrowing.

## What Was Done

A general election provides millions of pounds of publicity—some of it unfavorable—for survey research firms.  But it does not provide an equivalent amount of revenue.  The money spent on polls by the media and the political parties during an election campaign is much less than one percent of the £65 million spent annually on market research in Britain.  The best-known organization, the Gallup poll, estimates that only 7 percent of its annual election-year turnover comes from opinion polls.  The company with the largest degree of dependence on polls—MORI—reckoned that less than one-fifth of its business came from political polling in an election year.  Some major British market research firms do not even undertake public opinion polls because they believe the extra effort required and the inevitable public criticism are not worthwhile.  Even some firms that do publish

---

10 "Jim's ray of election hope," *Observer*, March 25, 1979.

11 "Election Forecasting from Poll Data: The British Case," *British Journal of Political Science*, vol. 9, no. 2 (1979), p. 231.  The average excludes the 1951 general election, which the Conservatives won with fewer votes and more seats. For a summer 1978 election, Whiteley's model (p. 236) forecast a narrow Conservative plurality of votes, and a plurality or wafer-thin majority of seats.

12 Cf. "Do polls change votes?" *Economist*, June 10, 1978, and a letter from Robert J. Wybrow, Gallup poll, printed July 1, 1978.  For another example of criticism, see "Polls watcher wanted," *Economist*, January 13, 1979.

polls reckon that they may lose business goodwill because of the suspicion with which polls are sometimes regarded.[13]

Notwithstanding the large reservoir of media skepticism about public opinion polls, the 1979 campaign produced more public opinion polls than any previous British general election. There were twenty-eight Britain-wide polls during the campaign, and seven panel surveys. This total of thirty-five surveys was an average of one a day between the announcement of the general election and May 3 (see table 6–1). Given sampling fluctuations, more frequent polling meant that there were sure to be more occasions when polls published on the same day or within twenty-four hours of each other produced different statements about the state of the parties, even if no change had actually occurred in the electorate. The confusion would be compounded by the tendency of the press to headline small or insignificant shifts in opinion.

Of the national daily papers, four each sponsored a poll. The Gallup poll continued with the *Daily Telegraph* and *Sunday Telegraph* and National Opinion Polls (NOP) with the *Daily Mail*. The *Sun* published four nationwide polls by Marplan in 1979, plus additional surveys of special groups of voters. The *Daily Express* turned to Market and Opinion Research International for surveys. Among the mass circulation papers, only the *Mirror* did not sponsor a poll. The *Guardian* continued to abstain from spending money on polls, and the nonpublication of the *Times* because of an industrial dispute meant it did not consider a poll. Among the Sunday press, the *Sunday Telegraph* carried Gallup poll findings, the *Observer* employed Research Services Ltd., and the *Sunday Times*, anticipating a return to publication before election day, sponsored a major panel survey in the marginal constituencies by MORI. In addition, special constituency surveys and samples of subgroups of voters appeared during the campaign; only Scottish and Welsh surveys can be considered here (see tables 6–7 and 6–8). In short, whatever journalists jealously wrote against the polls, editors thought that it was worth paying substantial sums—approximately £3,000 per survey—to have their own opinion poll story.

The bulk of polling undertaken in 1979 was done by fully experienced organizations, but developments in the market research business caused some changes in survey work in the 1979 general election. Opinion Research Centre, the firm that correctly forecast the 1970 election outcome and polled for the *Times* and *Evening Standard* in the 1974 elections, did not publish any Britain-wide polls during

---

[13] For details on revenue, see Barrie Clement, "Are opinion polls worth the time?" *Sunday Telegraph*, April 22, 1979.

## TABLE 6–1

NATIONWIDE POLLS DURING THE 1979 GENERAL ELECTION CAMPAIGN

| Firm | Year Began Political Polling | Place of Publication/ Client | Number of Surveys | Range of Sample Size |
|------|------|------|------|------|
| Gallup Poll | 1938 | Daily & Sunday Telegraph, BBC | 7 | 970–2,435 |
| National Opinion Polls (NOP) | 1959 | Daily Mail | 4 | 1,036–1,089 |
| Opinion Research Centre (ORC) | 1965 | ITN; Conservative Central Office | 1 very frequent | 4,328 average to small |
| Marplan | 1963 | Sun; London Weekend TV | 4 4 | 1,189–1,973 1,000–1,192 |
| Market and Opinion Research International (MORI) | 1970 | Daily Express; Thames TV; Evening Standard; Sunday Times[a]; Labour party | 6 1 1 3 very frequent | 974–1,099 1,075 1,089 896–1,087 approx. 700 |
| Research Services Ltd. | 1979[b] | Observer | 4 | 1,181–1,199 |

[a] Because of the nonpublication of the Sunday Times during the campaign, the most accessible record of MORI results is a series of New Statesman articles, April 27, May 11, and May 18, 1979. The fullest details are in MORI, British Public Opinion: General Election 1979 (London: MORI Final Report), which includes one postelection panel survey not tabulated here.

[b] While the name remained the same, Research Services Ltd. had changed ownership and personnel since the retirement of Mark Abrams, who had directed its political polls until 1970.

the campaign. It concentrated upon unpublished surveys for the Conservative Central Office plus surveys for the Scotsman and election-day interviews for Independent Television News. ORC's affiliate, Louis Harris International, a firm founded in the United States to do public opinion surveys, also did not undertake any election-time polls in 1979. The other nonstarter was Business Decisions Ltd., which had worked for the Observer in October 1974 but normally did not do political surveys. The most prominent polling was done by MORI, under the energetic direction of Robert Worcester, an American who had been doing unpublished polls for the Labour party since 1970. In 1979, MORI published more nationwide poll results than any other firm. It worked for five different media clients, as well as for Transport House. Marplan was also especially active, doing nineteen nationwide and special-sample surveys for the *Sun*, the *Birmingham Mail*, London Weekend Television, and Capitol Radio.

Through the years, public opinion polling organizations have progressively abandoned the textbook-approved method of random sampling in favor of quota sampling.[14] The rising cost of fieldwork has meant that random-sample polls have been priced out of the market; they are also slower to conduct since interviewers must return again and again to the same address in hopes of finding a respondent at home. There is no empirical evidence in the published final forecasts or from the more detailed unpublished analyses of quota sample returns that quota methods are unsatisfactory, as sampling purists assert to be the case on a priori grounds. Given time constraints and the declining quality of the electoral register, quota surveys are normally suitable for the purposes of election interviewing.

The pressures of journalism—plus a desire to interview as close to publication and to election day as possible—makes speed a major concern in public opinion polls. Fieldwork for three-quarters of the surveys was completed in two days, and seven were done in one day. Normally, two days is the minimum time between the completion of a survey and its publication in a morning newspaper. This effectively allows only one day for the final tabulation of the results and delivery to a newspaper office by six o'clock the evening *before* the date of publication, when papers begin printing. In 1979, most daily newspaper surveys were processed in this minimum time, notwithstanding the obstacles created by increasing delays in the mails, especially in London, where all the polls have their offices. Increasingly, the telephone was relied upon to transmit survey results from the field; the price paid for greater speed tends to be a reduction in the amount of information reported for analysis. As only half the electorate—and a skewed portion—have telephones, interviewing must still normally be done face-to-face.

Economic pressures led most polls to reduce the average number of interviews in their samples by comparison with 1974. Most polls

---

[14] For a spirited defense of quota sampling by a practitioner, see Norman Webb, "Opinion Polling Viewed by a Late Starter," ESOMAR/WAPOR Congress, 1975. For an academic appreciation, see J. P. Bluff, *"British Opinion Polling before the 1970 General Election"* (M.Sc. dissertation in politics, University of Strathclyde, Glasgow, 1971).

based results upon samples of 1,000 to 1,200 respondents; Gallup was distinctive in setting a target of 2,000 interviews for each of its campaign surveys. Given the increasing heterogeneity of the electorate—with Liberals often challenging the Conservatives in England, as well as multiparty competition outside England—sampling points should in theory have been increased. In fact, this was not done. The typical 1,000-interview survey involved one sampling point in each of 100 constituencies.

Technically, a panel survey is most appropriate for an election campaign. It provides more accurate information about changes in electoral opinion, because a panel requires that the same voters be reinterviewed at different points in time. Thus the changes reported are real changes (that is, differences between what the same respondents said at different times) rather than aggregate changes (differences between what different respondents said at different times). Panel surveys are more expensive and slower to undertake because of the need to locate the same individuals repeatedly in successive weeks. There can also be an interview effect on members of the panel. The 1979 MORI panel survey found that 92 percent of those questioned in its postelection call-back said that they had voted.

Two polling firms—MORI and Marplan—undertook panel interviews during the general election, but both tended to be ignored by the media because of the way their findings were reported. The Marplan survey, conducted in 100 English marginals, was broadcast at lunchtime Sundays by London Weekend Television's "Weekend World" program. To study its findings, a sophisticated viewer needed to copy down the numbers as they were flashed upon the screen, for there was usually only a cursory reference to the results in the press the next morning. MORI ran panel interviews for the *Sunday Times,* but it could not publish the results because of a failure to settle its industrial problems. The MORI panel findings were analyzed extensively in *New Statesman* articles before and after the election. Because neither panel survey was published on election day, they are not evaluated as election forecasts, but they are particularly useful as a guide to opinion trends.

The polls read most closely during the campaign were not the published polls, but the private polls sponsored by the Labour party National Executive Committee and the Conservative Central Office. They were not so much forecasts of the results as a means of finding out how to influence the results. On both sides of Smith Square, party organizations were working with familiar firms. Opinion Research Centre was undertaking its fifth election with the Conservatives, MORI its fourth election with Labour. The budgetary squeeze at Central Office brought the Conservatives closer to parity with Labour in survey work. All in all, Transport House spent upward of £30,000 for surveys and the Conservatives twice that. Both parties also commissioned special studies in Scotland.

Both party headquarters used their polls for tactical purposes in responding to immediate problems, such as the issues to publicize at a morning press conference or an evening party political broadcast, or how to handle an issue where the party might be losing rather than winning votes. The immediacy of campaigners' concerns was summed up by the comment of one party official who said, "Within twenty-four hours everything is dead. We have to start afresh each day to face each day's problems." To meet the Labour party's needs, MORI concentrated upon ten samples of about 720 respondents, interviewed in one- or two-day "quickie" surveys intended to give prompt feedback on a small number of questions. Results from quickie surveys were presented to early morning meetings of the campaign committee by Robert Worcester. MORI also drew upon a backlog of information from its published media polls, as well as on a panel study done for the Labour party before the start of the 1979 campaign.

Opinion Research Centre conducted major weekend surveys confined to England and Wales for the Conservative party throughout the campaign; separate surveys were undertaken in Scotland. ORC also did an average of two daily surveys a week during the campaign; and it did quickie surveys of reactions to party political broadcasts of the Conservative, Labour, and Liberal parties. The Conservatives scrutinized breakdowns of polling data to see whether their lead was holding up in English regions crucial for parliamentary victory and also monitored their strength among different social and opinion groups. John Hanvey, managing director of ORC, met daily during the campaign at 7 A.M. with Adam Ridley, acting director of the Conservative Research Department, and Keith Britto, its opinion poll expert. The Research Department staff communicated conclusions of these discussions to relevant party groups, and Hanvey attended some campaign planning meetings.

MORI and Opinion Research Centre differed more in style than in their effective political role. Robert Worcester, the director of MORI, was frequently quoted in the media about his published polls; their findings during the 1979 campaign were usually unfavorable for Labour. Opinion Research Centre kept a low profile during the campaign. It did not publicize its relationships with the Conservative party, nor were its results leaked by its clients, as sometimes happened with MORI reports to Transport House. In an interview well before the campaign commenced, Worcester defined his role as "to communicate public opinion to a relatively unlistening client, who is much more at home talking than listening." As far as influence was concerned, Worcester declared:

> I characterize the responsibility I have as one of bringing witness to the ripples, the waves and the tides. If the Labour Party leadership wants to swim against the tide of public opinion that is their responsibility. I see my role as telling them which way the tide is running and how strongly, and then I stop.[15]

Because of the common technology of professional polling, each party's poll will tend to come up with the same findings if it asks the same questions. During the campaign the unpublished polls, like the published polls, showed the Conservatives clearly ahead. This produced a chastened (and at times, almost resigned) mood among Labour campaigners, and cautious optimism among Conservatives.

## Public Opinion in the Campaign

Public opinion is both an active and a passive element in a general election campaign. It is active in that the priorities and wishes of the voters influence what party leaders talk about—and what they avoid mentioning. It is passive insofar as the public is subject to partisan influence about party images, personalities, and issues. Polls provide the means by which the opinions of the voters can be systematically assessed, in order to influence the public or the behavior of party headquarters.

In addition to asking about voting intentions, opinion surveys in Britain concentrate upon two broad sets of questions concerning political personalities and political issues. Nearly every opinion poll asks some questions about party leaders; the exceptions occur in Scotland, Wales, and Northern Ireland, where the party systems and leadership are less clearly defined. The Gallup poll first asked systematically about the prime minister and leader of the Opposition's popularity in 1958, more than a decade after Gallup started asking voters to assess the government and opposition parties. The questions start from a journalistic interest in personalities; names make news, and a leader who is a woman is doubly news. Politically, they imply that a general election campaign is like a presidential campaign—or

---

15 Both quotations from "Rasmussen interview with Robert Worcester," *British Politics Group Newsletter*, no. 8 (Spring 1977), p. 10. See also, Humphrey Taylor, "The Use of Survey Research in Britain by Political Parties and the Government," *Policy Analysis* (Winter 1977).

even more, like a presidential *primary* campaign—in which party labels are of no account; a voter is assumed to choose solely or primarily on the basis of personality.

The British record shows that the party with the most popular leader is far from certain of winning an election. This is true even though there is a natural tendency for the popularity of a party's record to rub off on the party leader, and vice versa, thus producing a self-fulfilling prophecy. Harold Wilson dominated the popularity sweepstakes from his election as Labour leader in opposition in 1963 until his retirement in 1976. But in that period, he fought and won one election conclusively (1966), lost another conclusively (1970), and three times emerged with the barest of majorities (1964 and the two 1974 ballots). Notwithstanding relative personal popularity, Wilson was never able to use his coattails to produce a steady lead for his party in monthly opinion polls. From 1966 to 1970, for example, Wilson led Heath in forty of forty-nine Gallup polls, but the Conservatives led Labour in thirty-eight of the same forty-nine monthly surveys.[16]

When the general election campaign started, politicians in both parties agreed on one thing—the prime minister was far more popular than the leader of the Opposition. Jim Callaghan had led Margaret Thatcher by an average of six percentage points, and in twenty-six of the thirty-six monthly Gallup polls, since his election as party leader in 1976. There were two sets of reasons to explain this lead. The first was Callaghan's undoubtedly greater political experience. He was, after all, a veteran of thirty-four years in the House of Commons and had won his post by a "survival of the shrewdest" test against a number of heavyweight frontbench competitors. By comparison, Mrs. Thatcher was a novice, having reached the cabinet only in 1970 and won the leadership by the default of Edward Heath.

Another cause of Mrs. Thatcher's unpopularity was sometimes said to be her sex. But surveys indicate that this cut two ways, for Thatcher was relatively more popular with women (the complement of being less popular with men). The Conservative vote is disproportionately female, and as women outnumber men in the British electorate, it is by no means clear that being a woman is an electoral liabilty. In the harsh words of one observer, Mrs. Thatcher's prin-

[16] For basic data on attitudes toward leaders, see monthly Gallup poll reports and the cumulative historical record in Gallup poll, *Election 70: Pre-Election Handbook* (London: 1970), p. 72-77. Note also, David Butler and Donald Stokes, *Political Change in Britain*, 2nd ed. (London: Macmillan, 1974), chap. 17, and Richard Rose, "British Government—the View from the Top," in *Presidents and Prime Ministers*, ed. by Richard Rose and Ezra Suleiman (Washington, D.C.: American Enterprise Institute, 1980), table 4.

cipal handicap was being Mrs. Thatcher: her aggressive and pointed promotion of issues from a strong Conservative point of view alienated many people who were not already committed Tories. Surveys showed Thatcher rating as high as or higher than Jim Callaghan on such presumed masculine traits as toughness and determination.[17]

Both Callaghan and Thatcher showed their sensitivity to public opinion in their reactions to proposals from London Weekend Television for a television confrontation during the campaign. Both parties knew that Callaghan's popularity stood higher with the electorate than Thatcher's. The same logic that led the Labour leader to accept the TV confrontation led the Conservative leader to reject it. The decision was undoubtedly tactically wise on the part of each; the upshot was that there was no face-to-face confrontation between the two personalities during the campaign.

The two party leaders inevitably remained the central figures in the campaigns of their respective parties. It was thus not difficult for media editors to contrive a "Maggie and Jim" show, and there is always a tendency for journalists, especially in a popular press increasingly devoid of political content, to portray a campaign in these terms. Journalists watch, question, and interrogate party leaders; the tools of their trade do not equip them to come to grips with issues or with abstractions such as mass public opinion.

In rejecting a television confrontation between party leaders, Conservative Central Office said that it wished the campaign to be about policies rather than personalities.[18] There was shrewd self-interest behind this platitudinous alliteration. The Conservatives consistently led Labour on Gallup poll questions asking which party could best handle the most important problem facing the country, just as Callaghan consistently led Thatcher when the same voters were asked whether they approved of the two party leaders.

Whereas the manifestoes catalogued pledges dealing with dozens of issues, most of these issues were of little salience to the ordinary British voter. During the election campaign, public opinion polls were used by party headquarters to identify, from the multitude of topics interesting frontbench politicians, the issues most important to voters.

Before, during, and after the election as well, polls consistently showed a handful of issues to be of primary concern to the electorate.[19]

---

17 See "It's not because she's a woman," *Economist*, April 28, 1979, a report of a MORI/*Sunday Times* survey of personalities.

18 See "Thatcher hedges on TV confrontation," *Financial Times*, April 4, 1979.

19 Almost every survey asked some questions about issues during the campaign, and answers tended to be consistently similar for similar questions. The figures cited here come from the *Gallup Political Index*, no. 225 (May, 1979), p. 18.

Gallup found six issues mentioned as first or second in importance by at least 10 percent of the electorate. Four were variations on the familiar theme of the economy: the cost of living (48 percent), unemployment (38 percent), labor relations (22 percent), and a hodgepodge of other economic issues such as productivity (11 percent). Law and order was mentioned by 11 percent of the electorate, and taxation ranked sixth with mentions by 8 percent.

The polls also provided ample evidence of issues that did *not* concern the electorate much. There was limited interest in bread-and-butter welfare state policies; only 5 percent ranked housing as one of the top two issues, and pensions and education received even fewer mentions. Many politicians in both parties were glad to see that the status of colored immigrants was of little electoral interest, for in 1979, unlike previous elections, there were reckoned to be a significant number of black and brown votes to be won (or lost). Among the important ignored issues was foreign policy, once of major concern to voters and politicians alike, and Britain's membership in the European Economic Community, a matter of hot debate within the Labour party. (The direct election to the European Parliament on June 7 confirmed Britain's lack of interest; the turnout of 32.7 percent was by far the lowest among the nine member nations of the EEC.) Northern Ireland was another nonissue in Great Britain, though still the one issue dividing Ulster voters.

The same cluster of economic issues concerned Conservative, Labour, and Liberal voters. Supporters of all three parties agreed completely in the selection of the six most important issues, though differing slightly in the relative emphasis given them.

In facing up to the issues, each party suffered from a different handicap. The Labour party's primary handicap was that it had been governing the country since 1974. During that period the cost of living had doubled and unemployment greatly increased. Labour could not run on its record without explaining (or explaining away) a great deal that had happened in its five years of office. Vulnerability on the issues was a major reason why the Labour campaign stressed Callaghan's personality.

Labour also had a second option—to emphasize the necessarily unknown quality of the Conservatives' alternative policies. An implicit premise of Labour's appeal was: However bad it has been, things will be worse under the Conservatives. Labour politicians, led by Jim Callaghan, also hammered away at Labour's special relationship with the trade unions (a less convincing asset after a winter of industrial unrest) and the industrial uncertainties that a new Conservative Government would bring. Labour talk about "confrontation not cooperation" was a barbed reminder of the circumstances in which Mrs. Thatcher's predecessor as Conservative leader had left Downing Street in March 1974.

The effect of the debate about issues can be measured by the MORI *Sunday Times* panel survey. During the campaign, voters were asked which party had the best policies for a cluster of five issues rated important. Since MORI reinterviewed the same group of voters each week, the panel can show to what extent individual voters' views changed under the pressure of campaign propaganda.

Overall, the Conservatives led the Labour party on the issues at all times from August 1978 until election day. But the lead was not steady. In August 1978, when the prime minister was contemplating an autumn election, the Labour party was ahead on two major economic issues—industrial relations and inflation. The aggregate Conservative advantage of two percentage points was derived from its greater lead on the relatively less important issue of law and order. By February 1979, however, the Conservatives had pulled well ahead on all the major economic issues and enjoyed an average advantage of thirteen points over Labour (see table 6–2).

The election campaign showed the Conservatives continuing to lead Labour by substantial margins, though their aggregate lead owed most to their popularity on the relatively less high-ranking issues of law and order and taxation. On the issue of industrial relations, Labour was ahead in popular confidence during the campaign, and it was almost even with the Conservatives in its perceived ability to handle inflation.

During the election campaign, both parties saw the electorate's confidence in their handling of the issues increase. At the beginning of the campaign, on average 28 percent did not know which party had the best policy on the five major issues listed in table 6–2. By election day, the don't knows had declined to 15 percent. The partisan nature of the campaign tended to polarize opinions, giving those inclined toward a party more confidence in what they were voting for.

Overall, public opinion rejected the proposition that the new Conservative Government had a vote of confidence from the electorate for all its major policies. A majority of the electorate expressed positive support for the Conservatives' handling of law and order and taxation. The Conservatives had plurality support on two issues, but on industrial relations a plurality favored Labour's presumed approach. A cautious interpretation is that voters were more inclined to believe the Conservatives would succeed than Labour, without themselves being familiar with the detailed arguments about the best way to achieve these goals.

## TABLE 6–2

### TRENDS IN VOTERS' ATTITUDES TOWARD MAJOR ISSUES, AUGUST 1978–MAY 1979

(percent; change and advantage in percentage points)

| Issue Rated "Impor- tant"[a] | Issue and Party Rated Best | Campaign Panel | | | | Change | |
|---|---|---|---|---|---|---|---|
| | | Aug. 78 | Aug. 79 | Apr. 4-6 | May 4-6 | Long- term[b] | Cam- paign[c] |
| 63 | Industrial relations, strikes | | | | | | |
| | Conservative | 32 | 39 | 35 | 39 | +7 | +4 |
| | Labour | 41 | 26 | 36 | 41 | 0 | +5 |
| | Conservative advantage | −9 | +13 | −1 | −2 | +7 | −1 |
| 59 | Prices, inflation | | | | | | |
| | Conservative | 31 | 39 | 36 | 44 | +13 | +8 |
| | Labour | 40 | 27 | 33 | 39 | −1 | +6 |
| | Conservative advantage | −9 | +12 | +3 | +5 | +14 | +2 |
| 50 | Unemployment | | | | | | |
| | Conservative | 36 | 39 | 37 | 42 | +6 | +5 |
| | Labour | 29 | 24 | 28 | 36 | +7 | +8 |
| | Conservative advantage | +7 | +15 | +9 | +6 | −1 | −3 |
| 31 | Law and Order | | | | | | |
| | Conservative | 42 | NA | 49 | 58 | +16 | +9 |
| | Labour | 24 | NA | 19 | 19 | −5 | 0 |
| | Conservative advantage | +18 | NA | +30 | +39 | +21 | +9 |
| 30 | Taxation | | | | | | |
| | Conservative | NA | NA | 48 | 54 | NA | +6 |
| | Labour | NA | NA | 24 | 28 | NA | +4 |
| | Conservative advantage | NA | NA | 24 | 26 | NA | +2 |
| | Average Conservative advantage | +2 | +13 | +13 | +15 | +10 | +2 |

[a] Percentages of respondents rating the issue "important" as of April 4-6, 1979, the start of the election campaign.

[b] Long-term change, August 1978 to May 1979.

[c] Campaign change, April 4-6 to May 4-6, 1979.

SOURCE: Calculated from Market and Opinion Research International, *British Public Opinion* (London: MORI, 1979), pp. 57-58, 77.

TABLE 6–3

DIVISIONS IN PUBLIC OPINION ABOUT THE WELFARE STATE, MAY 1979
(percent)

QUESTION:

People have different views about whether it is important to reduce taxes or keep up government spending. How about you? Which of these statements comes closest to your own view?

| | |
|---|---|
| 1. Taxes being cut, even if it means some reduction in government services, such as health, education, and welfare. | 34 |
| 2. Things should be left as they are. | 25 |
| 3. Government services such as health, education, and welfare should be extended, even if it means some increases in taxes. | 34 |

SOURCE: *Gallup Political Index*, no. 225 (May 1979), p. 7.

Divisions within public opinion emerged even more clearly when choices were posed about the costs people were prepared to pay to achieve a given benefit. The Gallup poll summarized persisting trade-offs in the costs and benefits of the welfare state by facing voters with a forced choice between three alternative approaches to the welfare state. The answers in table 6–3 show the public evenly divided: 34 percent wanted more benefits and were prepared to pay more taxes for them, but an equal proportion wished lower taxes and reduced benefits. The median voter wished welfare state policies left as they were.

## The Polls and the Result

"Twice bit, next time still shy." This was the attitude of many campaigners in 1979 toward the electoral system. In 1970, a last-minute swing away from the Government meant that even though twenty-seven polls had shown Labour ahead, only the last poll, published on the afternoon of election day, had the winner right. In February 1974, the electoral system gave Labour the most seats, even though it trailed the Conservatives in the popular vote. In 1979, there was a further complication: it was easier for Labour to lose its parliamentary majority than for the Conservatives to win control of the Government. Any swing away from Labour would cost it dominance of the Commons. But for the Conservatives to win an absolute majority, they required upward of a 3.5 percentage-point swing (that is, a lead of about 3.5 points in Britain-wide polls). The uncertainties of the Liberal vote and of party competition in Scotland further complicated the task of turning a British opinion survey into a correct forecast of seats in 1979.

During the election campaign, the polls tended to show the gap between the two parties narrowing, but the Conservatives' lead did not disappear (see table 6–4). The biggest campaign shift was reported by Gallup; its forecast Conservative lead declined by 8.5 points during the campaign. The two panel-surveys showed very little change in the party preferences of voters during the campaign (see table 6–5). Marplan's survey for London Weekend Television registered a 2 percentage-point reduction in the Conservative lead during the campaign. The MORI *Sunday Times* panel showed a 5-point reduction in the Conservative party lead. Only NOP showed the Conservative lead widening, and that by but 1 percentage point. Only once during the campaign—in an NOP survey reported in the *Daily Mail* on May 1 —was Labour shown ahead. Given the timing, it was a pointed reminder of the possibility that a last-minute swing might once again produce an upset result—especially when other polls were similarly showing a narrowing of a very large Conservative lead.

One series of surveys—the Research Services poll published in the *Observer*—was consistently out of line with all other surveys during the campaign. Its first published result on April 8 showed a 21 point Conservative lead, 15 points bigger than that shown by an NOP survey conducted at almost the same time. Anthony King, who wrote the analysis, described it as a "staggering" lead which "could be a fluke." Successive weekly surveys showed fluctuations, the lead going down to 16 points, back to 20 points, and the Sunday before the ballot, 11½ points. In his write-ups, King walked a fine line between pointing out reasons why they might be right and admitting reasons why there might be "a slight pro-Tory bias."[20] Research Services forecasts on average showed a nine percentage point greater Conservative lead than other polls taken on the same or overlapping dates. Research Services itself was so nervous about its unprecedented Conservative lead that a week before election day it called a meeting with other pollsters to seek reasons why its forecasts were so out of line with theirs. Because Research Services was not an established political polling organization, its competitors could dismiss its findings as the result of inexperience. But in advance of the election, there was no way of being sure that Research Services was wrong:

---

[20] "Poll Shows Tories with 21% Lead," *Observer*, April 8, 1979, and "How to Solve the Riddle of the Polls," *Observer*, April 29, 1979.

## TABLE 6–4

### PUBLIC OPINION POLLS DURING THE 1979 GENERAL ELECTION CAMPAIGN

(percent; lead in percentage points)

| Dates of Fieldwork | Poll | Con. | Lab. | Lib. | Nationalist, Other | Con. Lead | Sample Type, Size[a] | Date, Place of Publication |
|---|---|---|---|---|---|---|---|---|
| March 28–April 2 | Gallup | 49 | 38.5 | 9 | 3.5 | 10.5 | Q 970 | April 5 Telegraph |
| March 29 | MORI | 51 | 42 | 5 | 2 | 9 | Q 1,075 | March 29 Thames TV |
| April 1–2 | MORI | 51 | 38 | 10 | 1 | 13 | Q 1,041 | April 4 Express |
| April 2–3 | NOP | 48 | 42 | 8 | 2 | 6 | Q 1,036 | April 6 Mail |
| April 3–4 | Research Services | 54.5 | 33.5 | 9 | 3 | 21 | Q 1,188 | April 8 Observer |
| April 6–9 | Gallup | 50 | 40 | 8 | 2 | 10 | Q 1,855 | April 12 Telegraph |
| April 8–9 | MORI | 49 | 39 | 10 | 2 | 10 | Q 1,054 | April 12 Express |
| April 10–11 | Research Services | 53 | 37 | 8 | 2 | 16 | Q 1,181 | April 15 Observer |

| Date | Pollster | | | | | | Sample | Published |
|---|---|---|---|---|---|---|---|---|
| April 13–14 | NOP | 48 | 42 | 8 | 2 | 6 | Q 1,076 | April 17 *Mail* |
| April 14–18 | Gallup | 47.5 | 42 | 9 | 1.5 | 5.5 | Q 1,977 | April 22 *Sunday Telegraph* |
| April 17 | MORI | 50 | 38 | 10 | 2 | 12 | Q 1,032 | April 19 *Express* |
| April 17–18 | Research Services | 54 | 34 | 9.5 | 2.5 | 20 | Q 1,199 | April 22 *Observer* |
| April 17–18 | Marplan | 51 | 41 | 6 | 1 | 10 | Q 1,189 | April 20 *Sun* |
| April 18–19 | Marplan | 51 | 39 | 7 | 3 | 12 | Q 1,264 | April 23 *Sun* |
| April 19–21 | Gallup | 46.5 | 41.5 | 10 | 2 | 5 | Q 2,036 | April 25 *Telegraph* |
| April 21–23 | MORI | 47 | 40 | 11 | 3 | 7 | Q 1,099 | April 25 *Express* |
| April 23–25 | Gallup | 48 | 40 | 10.5 | 1.5 | 8 | Q 2,144 | April 29 *Sunday Telegraph* |
| April 24–25 | Research Services | 49.5 | 38 | 10 | 2.5 | 11.5 | Q 1,185 | April 29 *Observer* |
| April 25 | Marplan | 48 | 40 | 10 | 2 | 8 | Q 1,247 | April 27 *Sun* |
| April 26 | MORI | 44 | 41 | 12 | 2 | 3 | Q 1,061 | April 28 *Express* |

*(Table continues on next page)*

## TABLE 6-4 (continued)

| Dates of Fieldwork | Poll | Con. | Lab. | Lib. | Nation-alist, Other | Con. Lead | Sample Type, Size[a] | Date, Place of Publication |
|---|---|---|---|---|---|---|---|---|
| April 29–30 | NOP | 42.4 | 43.4 | 12.2 | 2.3 | –1 | Q 1,080 | May 1 Mail |
| April 29–May 1 | MORI | 44.4 | 38.8 | 13.5 | 3.3 | 5.6 | Rein 947 | May 3 Express |
| May 1 | Marplan | 45 | 38.5 | 13.5 | 3 | 6.5 | Q 1,973 | May 3 Sun |
| May 1–2 | NOP | 46 | 39 | 12.5 | 2.5 | 7 | Q 1,069 | May 3 Mail |
| April 30–May 1 | Gallup | 43 | 41 | 13.5 | 2.5 | 2 | Q 2,348 | May 3 Telegraph |
| May 2 | MORI | 45 | 37 | 15 | 3 | 8 | Q 1,089 | May 3 Evening Standard |
| May 2–3 | Gallup | 45.6 | 37.9 | 13.5 | 2.3 | 7.6 | Q 2,435 | May 4 BBC |
| May 3 | ORC | 44 | 38 | 14 | 4 | 6 | R 3,702 | May 3 ITN |
| Actual Great Britain | | 44.9 | 37.7 | 14.1 | 3.3 | 7.2 | | |

NOTE: Marginal-seat, Scottish, Welsh, and single-constituency surveys are excluded. For the first three groups, see tables 6-5, 6-7, and 6-8.

[a] Q = quota sample; R = random sample; Rein = reinterview of panel sample.

TABLE 6–5

THE TREND DURING THE CAMPAIGN: PANEL SURVEY EVIDENCE

(percent; lead and change in percentage points)

| Fieldwork | Con. | Lab. | Lib. | Con. Lead | Weekly Change in Lead | Sample Size |
|-----------|------|------|------|-----------|----------------------|-------------|
| MORI/Sunday Times Panel | | | | | | |
| April 4-6 | 50 | 40 | 10 | 10 | — | 1,087 |
| April 17-19 | 49 | 40 | 9 | 9 | −1 | 928 |
| April 24-26 | 47 | 42 | 9 | 5 | −4 | 896 |
| Marplan/London Weekend TV Panel | | | | | | |
| March 30-31 | 55 | 40 | 4 | 15 | +14[a] | 1,192 |
| April 6-7 | 54 | 41 | 5 | 13 | −2 | 1,035 |
| April 20-21 | 53 | 41 | 6 | 12 | −1 | 1,005 |
| April 27-28 | 53 | 40 | 7 | 13[b] | +1 | 1,000 |

[a] Change from October 1974 actual vote.

[b] The final Marplan marginal-seat survey forecast a six-point swing to the Conservatives; in the event, there was an average swing to the Conservatives of five points in these seats.

1970 had shown that a "poll of polls," averaging the findings from all reputable surveys, could produce a wrong forecast.

A rise in Liberal support was the most important campaign trend registered in the polls. Whereas Liberal support was between 5 and 10 percent in polls conducted from March 28 to April 19, it subsequently rose to between 10 and 15 percent. An upward trend in Liberal support during a campaign is a common occurrence, as a campaign gives the Liberals far greater political visibility than they normally have. A Marplan survey, conducted in twelve Liberal seats on April 23 and published three days later in the *Sun*, showed at that time a ten-point swing to the Conservatives, but this did not occur on election day. Necessarily the rise in Liberal support meant a decline in support for the two major parties; and the Conservatives declined more than Labour.

On election day, four of the five polls published forecast a clear win for Mrs. Thatcher, and their press reports unambiguously supported this interpretation (see table 6–6). MORI, Marplan, and NOP differed only in estimating the size of Mrs. Thatcher's absolute majority. The Gallup poll in the *Daily Telegraph* showed a Conservative lead of only two points. Given that in 1979 the Conservatives were handicapped in turning votes into seats, Gallup said a small Conserva-

TABLE 6–6

THE MARGIN OF ERROR IN FINAL POLL FORECASTS, 1979

(in percentage points)

| Fieldwork Dates | | Margin of Error | | | Con. Lead | Average Error, Three Parties |
|---|---|---|---|---|---|---|
| | | Con. | Lab. | Lib. | | |
| Actual Result, Great Britain[a] | | 44.9% | 37.7% | 14.1% | 7.2 | — |
| May 1-2 | NOP, Daily Mail | +1.1 | +1.3 | −1.6 | −0.2 | 1.3 |
| May 1 | Marplan, Sun | +0.1 | +0.8 | −0.6 | −0.7 | 0.5 |
| May 2 | MORI, Evening Standard | +0.1 | −0.7 | +0.9 | +0.8 | 0.6 |
| April 29-May 1 | MORI, Express | −0.5 | +1.1 | −0.6 | −1.6 | 0.7 |
| April 30-May 1 | Gallup, Telegraph | −1.9 | +3.3 | −0.6 | −5.2 | 1.9 |
| Average | | 0.7 | 1.4 | 0.9 | 1.7 | 1.0 |

[a] Northern Ireland is excluded as none of the polls sampled there.

tive lead meant that "Mrs. Thatcher [might] not achieve an overall majority."

In the event, the election produced a result that the polls could be proud of. All five of the polls completed immediately before the election correctly forecast the Conservative victory.[21] In predicting the size of the Conservative lead, four of the five polls were far more accurate than sampling error might suggest, forecasting the gap between the two parties to within 1.4 points of the final figure for Britain.[22] NOP was within 0.2 points of the final gap between the parties; it achieved this precision by overestimating the vote for both

[21] The Research Services survey is not included in these calculations because, as Anthony King noted in the Observer, May 6, 1979, "No one will ever know how accurate the Observer's poll was, since Research Services Ltd. conducted its final interviews on 25 April, eight days before polling."

[22] Technically, it is not possible to calculate sampling error for a quota sample. In practice, such figures are quoted by the polls and the press and usually claim a higher degree of accuracy than statisticians would expect in a random sample. By overclaiming the accuracy of their sampling techniques, the polls give themselves less leeway for explaining away inaccurate forecasts. For margins of error in 1979, see NOP, Political, Social, Economic Review, no. 19 (June 1979), p. 9.

the Conservative and Labour parties. Since both estimates erred in the same direction, the gap between the parties was hardly affected. By contrast, the Gallup poll was least accurate, because it underestimated Conservative support and overestimated Labour's strength; its two sampling errors thus were compounded. Marplan and MORI's *Evening Standard* polls were also accurate in measuring the gap to within 1.0 percentage point. These two polls, along with MORI's *Express* survey, had an average error of less than 1.0 point in forecasting the average level of support for the Conservatives, Labour, and Liberals separately (see table 6–6).

Overall, the 1979 campaign polls support the following generalizations:

1. *The Government's vote is usually overestimated by the polls.* In every general election since 1964, polls have consistently overestimated the vote for the governing party of the day. This pattern was repeated in 1979 by four of the five final polls; the average overestimate was 1.4 percentage points.

2. *The gap between the parties tends to close during the campaign.* This pattern was shown by three of the four polling organizations conducting nationwide samples throughout the campaign: MORI, Gallup, and Marplan; NOP showed a one point increase in the Conservative lead. Gallup's forecast of a narrowed lead reduced its accuracy, for it underestimated the eventual Conservative margin of victory.

3. *Conservatives are more likely to express a readiness to vote.* MORI, Gallup, and NOP gave the Conservatives a bigger lead among those definitely committed to voting. But this difference may have reflected higher morale among the winners, rather than a greater middle-class propensity to vote.

4. *There is no anti-Labour bias in the polls.* Four of the five polls erred by overestimating Labour's share of the vote and did so by a larger margin than similar errors favoring the Conservatives.

5. *There is no pro-Conservative bias in the polls.* Two of the five polls underestimated Conservative support. On average, the five final forecasts underestimated the Conservative vote by 0.2 percentage points.

6. *The Liberal vote tends to be underestimated.* The extent of underestimation of the Liberal vote was small, averaging 0.9 points, but Liberal strength was reported much lower at the beginning of the campaign. It is not unreasonable to argue that early in a campaign Liberal support *is* low, then rises thanks to campaign publicity, and that this rise is noted by the polls. In 1974, however, the polls consistently overestimated Liberal support.

7. *Late polls are not invariably the most accurate polls.* Election-day surveys conducted for the two television networks were not significantly more accurate than those concluded earlier. Gallup's poll for the BBC showing a 7.6 point Conservative lead was within 0.4 points of the final figure. But ORC's forecast for ITN of a 6.0 point Conservative advantage was not one of the most accurate forecasts of the 1979 campaign. Among newspaper surveys, the three most accurate were those concentrating interviews in the two days before the election (see table 6–6).

8. *Britain-wide polls are normally more accurate than samples in parts of Britain.* In 1979, Scotland presented a treble problem to British polls: its party system was different, with the Scottish National party ranking second in votes in the October 1974 election; its electorate was unusually volatile; and the pattern of party competition varied greatly within Scotland. Because Labour appeared to be regaining ground from the SNP in Scotland, Labour strategists were particularly (and rightly) worried that a Britain-wide survey would exaggerate their overall strength. In the event, the Conservatives enjoyed a 10.5 point lead in the popular vote in England, as against Labour's 10.1 point lead in Scotland.

The three Scottish surveys conducted during the final week of the campaign attained a high level of overall accuracy, when compared with previous surveys in Scotland or, for that matter, with polls throughout Britain in 1974.[23] The average error in forecasting the Labour lead over the Conservatives was 2.3 points, and the average error in forecasting each of the four parties' share of the vote was 1.5 points; the SNP vote was the most accurately forecast (see table 6–7). The Scottish surveys were pipped by the extraordinary accuracy of the Britain-wide polls. The 1979 Scottish surveys, however, were more accurate than British polls at previous elections back to 1964 (see table 6–9).

In Wales, two local firms—Abacus Research Associates (working for the BBC) and Research and Marketing Ltd. (working for the *Western Mail*)—made a poor showing with their constituency surveys. The average error of Research and Marketing in forecasting the winners' lead was 6.7 percentage points, the average error of Abacus was 13.0 points. Moreover, in two of the nine constituency surveys (Brecon and Radner, and Pembroke), Abacus predicted the wrong winner; and in two more, Research and Marketing Ltd. was more than 12 points off in forecasting the winner's margin. The degree of inac-

---

[23] See the chapters by Richard Rose in Penniman, ed., *Britain at the Polls, 1974*, especially table 10-3.

## TABLE 6–7

### SCOTTISH PUBLIC OPINION POLLS, 1979 GENERAL ELECTION CAMPAIGN

(percent; lead and error in percentage points)

| Dates of Fieldwork | Poll | Con. | Lab. | Lib. | Nat. | Labour Lead | Sample Type, Size[a] | Date, Place of Publication |
|---|---|---|---|---|---|---|---|---|
| March 26–April 2 | System Three | 29 | 45 | 6 | 19 | +16 | Q 1,003 | April 4, Glasgow Herald |
| March 31–April 2 | MORI | 34 | 46 | 4 | 15 | +12 | Q 1,000 | April 5, Scottish Daily Express |
| April 10–12 | System Three | 27 | 49 | 6 | 17 | +22 | Q 1,079 | April 17, Glasgow Herald |
| April 20–23 | ORC | 33 | 42 | 9 | 16 | +9 | Q 1,015 | April 25, Scotsman |
| April 23–25 | NOP | 33 | 44 | 6 | 16 | +11 | Q 806 | April 30, Daily Mail |
| April 27–29[b] | ORC | 34 | 42 | 8 | 15 | +8 | Q 1,016 | April 30, Scotsman |
| April 28–29[b] | System Three | 30 | 41 | 11 | 17 | +11 | Q 1,091 | May 1, Glasgow Herald |
| April 31–May 1[b] | MORI | 30 | 44 | 6 | 18 | +14 | Q 1,025 | May 3, Scottish Daily Express |
| | Actual Result | 31.4 | 41.5 | 9.0 | 17.3 | +10.1 | | |
| | Average Error | 1.8 | 1.2 | 2.0 | 1.1 | 2.3 | | |

[a] Q = quota sample.
[b] Final forecasts.

203

## TABLE 6–8

### WELSH CONSTITUENCY POLLS AND ELECTION RETURNS, 1979 GENERAL ELECTION CAMPAIGN

(percent; error and lead in percentage points)

| Place and Date of Poll | Con. | Lab. | Lib. | Plaid Cymru | Error in Estimating Lead | Sample Size[a] | Date of Publication |
|---|---|---|---|---|---|---|---|
| *Research and Marketing Ltd./Western Mail* | | | | | | | |
| Carmarthen, April 28, 1979 | 23 | 35 | 11 | 31 | +0.2 | Q 523 | April 24–25 |
| *Actual result* | *23.6* | *35.8* | *8.1* | *32.0* | | | |
| Cardigan, April 26, 1979 | 27 | 25 | 28 | 19 | −12.4 | Q 503 | April 23–24 |
| *Actual result* | *29.7* | *20.2* | *35.6* | *14.5* | | | |
| Cardiff, SE, April 25, 1979 | 37 | 55 | 5 | 2 | −3.6 | Q 540 | April 21–23 |
| *Actual result* | *37.7* | *59.3* | *—* | *1.5* | | | |
| Pembroke, April 27, 1979 | 51 | 37 | 10 | 1 | −1.9 | Q 513 | April 23–24 |
| *Actual result* | *49.2* | *37.1* | *10.1* | *2.5* | | | |
| Swansea West, May 2, 1979 | 38 | 54 | 6 | 2 | +15.2 | Q 500 | April 24–26 |
| *Actual result* | *45.3* | *46.1* | *6.0* | *1.9* | | | |
| Overall average error in estimating lead | | | | | 6.6 | | |

*Abacus Research Associates/BBC*

| | | | | | | | |
|---|---|---|---|---|---|---|---|
| Brecon and Radnor | 31.5 | 54.5 | 10.3 | 3.4 | +29.3 | Q 390 | April 24–26 |
| *Actual result* | *47.2* | *40.9* | *9.7* | *2.1* | | | |
| Pembroke | 45.2 | 46.2 | 4.9 | 2.2 | +13.0 | Q 450 | April 24–26 |
| *Actual result* | *49.1* | *37.1* | *10.1* | *2.5* | | | |
| Carmarthen | 28.6 | 36.7 | 7.1 | 23.6 | +9.3 | Q 455 | April 24–26 |
| *Actual result* | *23.5* | *35.8* | *8.0* | *32.0* | | | |
| Cardigan | 27.2 | 19.2 | 33.6 | 18.8 | +0.5 | Q 371 | April 24–26 |
| *Actual result* | *29.7* | *20.2* | *35.6* | *14.5* | | | |
| Overall average error in estimating lead | | | | 13.0 | | | |

[a] Q = quota sample.

## TABLE 6–9

ACCURACY OF OPINION POLL ELECTION FORECASTS, 1964–1979

(percentage points)

| Year | Mean Error in Estimating Gap | Average Error per Party | Number of Polls |
|---|---|---|---|
| 1964 | 1.8 | 1.3 | 4 |
| 1966 | 3.9 | 1.7 | 4 |
| 1970 | 6.7 | 2.6 | 5 |
| 1974 February | 2.5 | 2.2 | 6 |
| 1974 October | 4.2 | 1.6 | 4 |
| 1979 | 1.7 | 1.0 | 5 |

SOURCE: See Richard Rose, "Opinion Polls and Election Results," in Richard Rose, ed., *Studies in British Politics*, 3rd ed. (London: Macmillan, 1976), table 2, and supra, table 6-6.

curacy can easily be explained by the small samples used. For BBC Wales, Abacus produced four constituency forecasts with a total number of interviews suitable for only a single Welsh forecast. Research and Marketing Ltd. used samples of 500 to predict a four-way division of constituency votes (see table 6–8).

The varying degree of accuracy of polls taken under varying circumstances confirms fundamental sampling principles. The Britain-wide samples were conducted with far higher technical standards than the Welsh surveys—and produced far more accurate results. Similarly, the Britain-wide samples, inevitably devoting nearly five-sixths of their interviews to the relatively uncomplicated English electorate, were even more accurate than similarly sized Scottish samples, taken in politically more complex circumstances. Overall, opinion polls are like the press—some are more reliable and valid than others. They differ from the press in that their standards of conduct are based upon statistical principles, and the polls are far more open in explaining how they secure their information. Moreover, opinion polls do not "adjust" their facts to make a better story, as is the wont of some of the British media today.

In the 1979 election campaign the opinion polls also compared favorably with the Stock Exchange and those who play it in the City of London. During the campaign, the City was swept repeatedly by rumors of results of public opinion polls that did not exist. For the price of a phone call, City speculators could have ascertained that a given organization was not about to release a poll showing a purported swing to Labour, which would depress share prices. The City also propagated rumors about the purported findings of polls actually in process, typically before the polling organizations had themselves finished their tabulations. Pollsters were concerned about City speculators' using these rumors to manipulate prices on the Stock Exchange to their personal profit. They were also shocked that the City could see big sums of money change hands on evidence that the most junior staff of polling organizations would reject. Robert Worcester of MORI wrote the Stock Exchange chairman asking for an investigation "in the interests of the good name of the Stock Exchange." The chairman replied that this would serve no purpose since "a securities market is among the most sensitive to guess-work and rumour." His letter, dated May 9, 1979, read as follows:

Dear Mr. Worcester,

Thank you for your letter of 3rd May. There is of course no way in which anyone can stop rumours spreading in any walk of life. The preoccupation of the press generally with opinion polls at election times and the often uninformed guessing that goes on in the media encourages rumour.

I am not one of those who thinks that opinion polls should not be published during an election campaign. I do however think that they are bound to add to uncertainty both at home and abroad. The users of the securities markets do not have a monopoly on rumour, but I agree that a securities market is among the most sensitive to guess-work and rumour.

It is usually quite impractical to attempt to pin point the source of any particular piece of guess-work. I have tried it in the past without much success with much more specific subjects than the one you mention in your letter. I would obviously be grateful for any information you can give me either on this occasion or on occasions in the future.

Yours sincerely,
Nicholas Goodison

## Conclusion

Overall, the polls' record for accuracy in 1979 was better than at any general election in many years. The five polls in the field were on average accurate to within 1.0 percentage point per party, and their average error in estimating the gap was 1.7 percentage points—in both cases the best record since 1964, the first year for which meaningful averages can be compiled (see table 6–9). Robert Worcester of MORI triumphantly interpreted the result as "a poke in the ear with a sharp stick for all those journalists who always complain when the polls get things wrong and are so quiet when we get things right."[24]

The success of the polls in 1979 is not, however, a guarantee that they will be equally successful in the next general election. There is no trend toward increasing accuracy in the polls; they scored their best record prior to 1979 in 1964. By any normal statistical standard, the accuracy of the polls in 1979 was very high, but by the same token it is a record vulnerable to random fluctuations of sampling error. Polls that were most accurate in 1979 cannot be sure of being equally accurate at the next election; the Gallup poll had the highest degree of accuracy at both 1974 elections, but in 1979 its *Telegraph* survey was farthest off—while its BBC election-day survey was virtually spot on. The procedures of the long-established Gallup organization were relatively constant; normal sampling fluctuations accounted for its variable accuracy.

Election forecasting appeared easy in 1979 because the election outcome was normal: the party leading when the election was called won, and won by a big margin. An election campaign that starts as a very close race or, even more, ends as a close race, threatens the reputation of the polls by demanding a superhuman degree of accuracy or a modicum of luck in erring on the winning side. This was not necessary in 1979. The polls, the voters, and the electoral system all produced the same result.

The electoral system produced a clear-cut political outcome—a Conservative Government with an absolute parliamentary majority—from an electorate whose opinions were more divided than the outcome suggested. During the campaign, opinion polls showed that public confidence in the Conservatives was not unreserved. The Conservatives were "on balance" favored on the major policy issues of the day, but there was always a substantial group that preferred Labour on a given issue. The Gallup poll found that more Conservative voters gave a strong dislike of the Labour party (44 percent) rather than a strong liking for the Conservatives (41 percent) as their chief reason for voting as they did.[25]

The judgment of the electorate on May 3 was a judgment expressed on one day, but its effects will last for the life of a parliament. Within six weeks of entering office, the Conservatives found how

---

[24] "Sharp stick," *Evening Standard*, May 8, 1979.
[25] See *Gallup Political Index*, no. 226 (June 1979), p. 7.

fickle voters can be. After a June 12 budget raising some taxes as well as cutting others, Labour moved 1.5 points ahead of the Conservatives in the Gallup poll.[26] The long-term security of both major parties is less than it was a decade or more past. The proportion identifying themselves as either Conservative or Labour in 1979 was 75 percent—the same as in February 1974, but 7 points lower than in 1970.[27] Public opinion thus is less firmly anchored to the choice of a Conservative or Labour Government than might be inferred from the results produced by a general election. In a long-term perspective, the swing back to the two major parties in 1979, following the rise in "third force" voting in 1974, has increased the proportion of the electorate fickle enough to swing to *or* from the two major parties, as well as between them.

The electoral system is only an instrument for recording preferences at one point in a four- or five-year cycle. By comparison with a general election, opinion polls have two great advantages. They can measure party popularity at any time. Equally, they can produce information for the asking about popular attitudes toward any issue that concerns their sponsors. Even though referendums were invoked twice in the 1974–1979 parliament, Britain's politicians do not want the voters to intervene in making (or rejecting) public policies. Politicians do not wish to allow the expression of public opinion to substitute for their own authoritative determination of what measures are best for governing Britain. Nevertheless, only by asking the views of the voters—at the ballot box if not in doorstep interviews—can politicians continue to claim the right to govern Britain today.

---

[26] "Labour lead 1½ p.c. as Budget proves unpopular," *Daily Telegraph*, June 22, 1979, and subsequent monthly Gallup poll reports on Labour's lead.

[27] Cf. *Gallup Political Index*, no. 226, p. 9, and Ivor Crewe, Bo Särlvik, and James Alt, "Partisan Dealignment in Britain, 1964-1974," *British Journal of Political Science*, vol. 7, no. 2 (1977), p. 143.

# 7

# Financing the British General Election of 1979

*Michael Pinto-Duschinsky*

The financial condition of British political parties has been keenly debated in recent years. Yet there has been a lack of reliable information. Even the Houghton Report of 1976, which gave the results of an important official investigation into party funds, was riddled with gaps and inaccuracies. In 1978 and 1979, there was some very wild speculation about the cost of the Conservative party's political advertising. As in some previous elections, it was suggested that professional advertising agents were being paid to sell the party to the voters like the proverbial can of beans.

This chapter is probably the first detailed examination of party finance in any British election. It attempts to answer the following questions:

- What was the total cost of the Conservative, Labour, and Liberal campaigns?

I wish to express my appreciation for the help I have received in preparing this chapter. It would not have been possible to write it without the cooperation of the three national party organizations. In particular, I want to thank, at the Conservative Central Office, Alistair MacAlpine and Leslie Corp; at Transport House, John Pittaway and Ron Hayward; and, at the Liberal Party Organization, Hugh Jones and Dee Doocey. I also would like to thank George Carlyle, formerly of the Conservative Central Office. The analysis of spending by parliamentary candidates has been largely taken, with the kind permission of the authors, from work prepared by David Butler and Leslie Seidle for David Butler and Dennis Kavanagh, *The British General Election of 1979* (London: Macmillan, 1980).

Useful information was received from Labour regional organizers, Larry Whitty (General and Municipal Workers' Union), Lord Chitnis and Lois Jefferson (Joseph Rowntree Social Service Trust Ltd.), David Miller (Scottish Liberal party), Bill Fagg (Oxford City Labour party), Sheila Chaplin (City of Oxford Conservative Association), the editor and circulation manager of the *Oxford Star*, Norma Percy (Granada Television), Mrs. Chambers (Home Office), and Michael Steed (Manchester University). Finally, I particularly wish to acknowledge help received from Shelley Pinto-Duschinsky.

- What were the main categories of expenditure?
- What were the most important sources of party funds?
- How did spending in 1979 compare with earlier British general elections?
- Was the Conservative victory to any extent a consequence of the party's superior financial resources? In particular, did Margaret Thatcher become prime minister because her party had a larger advertising budget than Labour and the Liberals?

Before answering these questions, it will be useful to put the 1979 campaign into its institutional context by giving an outline of the pattern of party organization and of political finance in Britain.[1]

## The Pattern of Party Finance

**National Organization and Constituency Organization.** A British general election is the occasion for two different campaigns, which are almost entirely separate. On the one hand, there is the official, legally recognized campaign. This takes place in each of the 635 constituencies where candidates compete for seats in the House of Commons. On the other hand, there is the national campaign: informal, unrecognized by election law, but nevertheless decisive. The only votes actually cast in a general election are for individual candidates for the House of Commons. Unlike American voters, who are faced with a long ballot for a multitude of national and local offices, the British voter puts only one cross on his ballot—for his choice as the local member of Parliament.

In practice, general elections determine not only individual constituency results but which party will form the new Government. The leader of the party that wins most seats in the House of Commons becomes prime minister. As countless voting studies have shown, British voting choices are determined far more by national considera-

---

[1] See, for example, Richard Rose, *The Problem of Party Government* (London: Macmillan, 1974), especially chapters 9 and 10; Dick Leonard, *Paying For Party Politics*, Broadsheet, vol. 41, no. 555 (London: Political and Economic Planning, 1975); Dick Leonard, "Contrasts in Selected Western Democracies: Germany, Sweden, Britain," in Herbert E. Alexander, ed., *Political Finance* (Beverly Hills: Sage Publications, 1979); Michael Pinto-Duschinsky, "Britain: The Problem of Non-Campaign Finance" (Paper presented to the Conference on Political Finance, University of Southern California, December 1977); and Michael Pinto-Duschinsky, "Britain's General Election: Labour Funds Are Catching Up," *Economist*, November 11, 1978. Patterns of party funding from the nineteenth century to the 1970s are analyzed in the author's forthcoming book, *British Political Finance* (Washington, D.C.: American Enterprise Institute). See also Committee on Financial Aid to Political Parties, *Report*, Cmnd. 6601, London, Her Majesty's Stationery Office, 1976. (This is usually referred to as the Houghton Report.)

tions than by local issues or by the popularity of parliamentary candidates. Consequently, every party runs a full national campaign largely designed to bolster party loyalties in general rather than to achieve particular results in individual constituencies.

The distinction between the national campaign and the 635 local contests is crucial. Only the constituency fights are subject to legal restrictions on spending. The national campaigns are not subject to similar limits unless it can be shown that particular expenditures by the party centrally have been directed toward the election of particular candidates. In 1979, the spending limits for parliamentary candidates were as follows: county (rural) constituencies, £1,750 plus 2 pence per elector; borough (urban) constituencies, £1,750 plus 1½ pence per elector. This amounted to £3,050 for an average county constituency and £2,725 for a borough constituency. These restrictions determine the nature of local campaigning. Normally the lion's share of the permitted budget is spent on printing an "election address," a pamphlet that is delivered free of charge by the Post Office to every registered elector. The spending limits severely restrict newspaper and poster advertising on behalf of particular candidates.

The practical distinction between the constituencies and the center applies not only to the campaign period but also to routine party organization between elections (although in electoral peacetime, constituency as well as central party organizations are free from legal restrictions on spending).

**The Variable Election Date.** The prime minister may normally call for a new election at any time within the five-year term of a parliament. This affects party organization and political finance in two important ways. First of all, the fact that there might be a sudden election makes it necessary for parties to maintain permanent organizations nationally and locally during the entire period between elections so that the framework of a campaign organization will already exist when the date of the poll is announced. Second, the uncertain date of the election means that a British election campaign (particularly at the national level) divides into two phases: a preliminary phase of indefinite duration toward the end of a parliament when it is expected that an election is in the offing, and the short span (usually about four weeks) between the prime minister's announcement of the impending dissolution of the House of Commons and the date of the poll. If an election is called unexpectedly early (as in 1970 and February 1974), the precampaign period is relatively short—or absent altogether. In this case, expenditure, especially on national preelection advertising,

## TABLE 7–1
### THE PATTERN OF BRITISH POLITICAL PARTY EXPENDITURE

| Type of Expenditure | Central Expenditures (by national party organizations) | Local Expenditures (by constituency organizations) |
|---|---|---|
| Routine | Maintaining<br>—permanent party HQ<br>—regional offices<br>—parliamentary party secretariat<br>—leader's office | Maintaining a constituency office<br>Employing a full-time constituency agent |
| Precampaign | Poster and newspaper advertising<br>Private opinion polling<br>Preparing broadcasts and publicity materials | Employing temporary staff |
| Campaign | Advertising<br>Grants to constituencies<br>Subsidizing party literature<br>Extra administrative costs<br>Private opinion polling<br>Producing election broadcasts | Printing election addresses, handbills, and leaflets<br>Election agent's fee |

SOURCE: Author.

is small. If a campaign is called unexpectedly late (as in 1964) the precampaign period is protracted and expenditures are likely to be heavier.

These institutional factors make it convenient to distinguish between (1) local and central finance and (2) routine, precampaign, and strictly campaign finance. This means that there are six main categories; the main expenditures in each are shown in table 7–1.

Having distinguished between local and central finance and between routine, precampaign, and campaign finance, we must set out some of the ambiguities and limitations of these categories. First of all, a simple distinction between constituency and national organization conceals the fact that each main party has several different national organizations. The most important unit of a modern British central party is the extraparliamentary headquarters in London. In addition, there are offices in the regions, in Scotland, and in Wales. The party leader and the party's members of Parliament also need services of their own. The published accounts of the Conservative,

Labour, and Liberal parties all include the routine costs of their extra-parliamentary headquarters, but they vary sharply in their procedures for reporting the finances of other central (that is, nonconstituency) organizations such as the party leader's office or the regional organizations.

In general, the published accounts of the Conservative party are most inclusive and those of the Liberals least inclusive. These differences mean that it is not possible to make appropriate comparisons between the raw accounts published by the three parties. It is essential to make adjustments for those elements of organization which are included by one party but excluded by another. A guide to the published central party accounts is given in the postscript to this chapter. For the purposes of this chapter, adjustments have been made to the statistics issued by the central party organizations to include all aspects of nonconstituency organization under the category of central finance.

The division between routine, precampaign, and campaign costs also raises problems. The main parties incur extra expenditures in fighting general elections. There is no clear-cut boundary between "routine" and "campaign" phases of certain activities. And here again, accounting conventions vary between parties. To give one example, the Conservative election accounts for 1979 include the costs of producing party political broadcasts during the entire year ending March 31, 1979, as an election item (although some of the costs might reasonably be regarded as routine). But private opinion polling in the same period is listed as a routine cost. It appears that accounting for the Conservative campaign in 1970 was somewhat different. The private polling undertaken in the precampaign period of 1969–1970 was included as a campaign cost.[2] Theoretically, an activity ought to be classified as routine if it would have been undertaken had there been no election. In practice, this is often not possible to determine precisely. When it comes to assessing the main sources of party income, the distinction between routine and campaign can be even more artificial. Money collected for electioneering is often used for routine purposes, or vice versa.

In spite of these problems, this chapter uses these categories. It concentrates on the campaign and precampaign finances of the three main parties in the period leading up to the poll on May 3, 1979. Routine party finance in the parliamentary cycle 1974–1979 is not considered except where it relates to the 1979 election. The precampaign period lasted from the summer of 1978, when the parties were

---

2 See Michael Pinto-Duschinsky, "Central Office and 'Power' in the Conservative Party," *Political Studies*, vol. 20, no. 1 (March 1972), p. 3.

preparing for an election in the autumn, until the end of March 1979, when the prime minister finally announced the date of the election. The campaign period lasted from the end of March until polling day. (For accounting purposes, the campaign is reckoned as beginning on April 1, 1979.) The cost of the three main election campaigns and the main sources of income will be estimated in three parts: central expenditure and income, constituency expenditure and income, and the estimated value of subsidies-in-kind.

## Central Campaign Finances

**Conservative.** The Conservatives' preparations for the general election campaign started in earnest in April 1978 when Saatchi and Saatchi Garland-Compton were appointed the party's advertising agents. A major poster, press, and cinema advertising drive was launched in the late summer of 1978. Over £0.5 million was spent in August-October 1978 in anticipation of an announcement of an autumn election. When James Callaghan announced that the Labour Government intended to soldier on, the rate of Conservative preelection spending fell until the spring of 1979. During the campaign itself, political advertising was, once again, by far the largest item of expenditure.

The Conservative party's central expenditures for the general election are itemized in table 7–2.[3] The published Conservative party accounts do not distinguish between routine and campaign costs. The figures in table 7–2 are based on breakdowns provided by the Conservative Central Office for the purposes of this study.

It can be argued that some further expenditures ought to be included in the preelection category. For example, some direct payments to constituency organizations and opinion researchers in the 1978–1979 period possibly ought to be regarded as preelection rather than routine items. If these were included, the total cost of the Conservative campaign would rise to about £2.5 million. By contrast, it can be argued that the campaign total ought to be reduced—that a portion of the cost of television production in the year before April 1979 should be categorized as routine. For our purposes, however, the figures given in table 7–2 will be used.

It is not possible to describe the party's sources of campaign funds or the amount raised with the same precision as its campaign spending. This is partly because there is no formal distinction be-

---

[3] In view of the large and frequent fluctuations in exchange rates during 1978 and 1979, all figures in this chapter are given in pounds sterling. The rate of sterling against the United States dollar fluctuated around the level of two dollars to the pound during the precampaign and campaign months.

TABLE 7–2

CONSERVATIVE PARTY CENTRAL PRECAMPAIGN AND CAMPAIGN
EXPENDITURES, 1978–1979
(in thousands of pounds)

| Item | Precampaign | Campaign | Total |
|---|---|---|---|
| Grants to constituencies | 0 | 42 | 42 |
| Advertising | | | |
|     Posters | (380) | (211) | (591) |
|     Press | (267) | (499) | (766) |
|     Cinema | (111) | ( 33) | (144) |
|     Total | 758 | 743 | 1,501 |
| Political broadcasts | 276[a] | 149 | 425 |
| Opinion research | 0 | 70 | 70 |
| Party publications (net of receipts) | 0 | 113 | 113 |
| Leaders' tours[b] and meetings | 0 | 13 | 13 |
| Staff[c] and administration costs | 0 | 169 | 169 |
| Total | 1,034 | 1,299 | 2,333 |

[a] Includes expenditures for April 1978–March 1979.
[b] Mrs. Thatcher's tour cost an estimated £10,000 net of receipts from journalists
for seats in the campaign airplane.
[c] Cost of additional staff and overtime payments for routine staff.
SOURCE: Director of finance and resources, Conservative Central Office.

tween fundraising for elections and for routine purposes. In addition,
the Conservative party has never released details of the amounts given
by individual contributors. Since the passage of the Companies Act of
1967, companies have been obliged to declare all political donations of
over £50 in their annual reports. This provides useful information
about some major sources of Conservative funds.[4] But most annual
reports for 1979 will only be published during 1980 and were not
available while this chapter was being prepared.

Nevertheless, it is possible to give a general picture of the party's
campaign fundraising on the basis of interviews and of analyses of
published total expenditures during recent years. Almost three-fifths
of the central Conservative income for routine purposes seems to
have come from companies during the 1970s. The proportion of con-

---

[4] Lists of company donations to the Conservative party and to organizations such
as British United Industrialists, which raise funds for Conservative party purposes, are collected and published by the Labour party's Research Department
(see, for example, "Company Donations To The Tory Party And Other Political
Organisations," Information Paper no. 17, September 1979). Company donations
are also listed, on the basis of company reports, by the Labour Research Department (a separate organization).

tributions for election purposes coming from companies appears to have been about four-fifths; most of the rest probably came from individual supporters.

An analysis of the overall pattern of Conservative income in the period 1974–1975 to 1977–1978 suggests that 56 percent came from contributions by companies and other institutions, 14 percent from donations and bequests by individuals, 21 percent from constituency associations, 2 percent from interest payments, and 6 percent from the Conservative share of the state grant for parliamentary services for opposition parties.[5] It appears that the extra costs of an election campaign are generally borne by companies or by individual donations. This is indicated by the fact that constituency payments to the Central Office have in past years been only marginally higher in election than in nonelection years. Also, bequests, a useful supplementary source of routine funds, do not grow to meet the sudden needs of an election, nor does the state make grants to the party while it is in opposition.

A normal feature of fundraising by the Conservative Central Office during a general election is that the sum collected not only covers central election costs but leaves a surplus for use in the leaner years of electoral peacetime. This did not happen in 1974–1975 but certainly appears to have been the case in 1979. At the opening of the campaign, late in March, the party's central reserves were exhausted.[6] The party treasurer subsequently reported that when the election was over, the Central Office had paid all the bills for the campaign (including outstanding debts from the preelection months) but also had a reserve sufficient to cover several months of routine spending by the Central Office. Besides making the usual approaches to companies, the Conservatives made a special appeal to about 3,000 landowners.

**Labour.** As the 1979 election approached, the reserves of the political levy funds of some of the major trade unions stood at record levels.[7]

---

[5] Based on calculations for Pinto-Duschinsky, *British Political Finance.*

[6] On March 31, 1978, the central cash and invested reserves of the party totaled £726,000 (Conservative and Unionist Central Office, *Annual Report, 1977/1978,* London, 1978, p. 1). During the financial year April 1, 1978, to March 31, 1979, the party's expenditures, including campaign items, exceeded central income by £1,373,000. (*Annual Report, 1978/1979,* p. 3). The deficit during 1978-1979 was therefore far larger than the total in reserve at the start of the year. The inflow of funds during the campaign period was sufficient to meet bills outstanding from the previous year, to pay for the new expenses incurred during April 1979, and to leave what was reportedly a healthy reserve.

[7] See, for example, Michael Pinto-Duschinsky, "No Handouts Needed," *Times,* November 9, 1978.

## TABLE 7–3

PRECAMPAIGN AND CAMPAIGN EXPENDITURE OF THE LABOUR PARTY
NATIONAL EXECUTIVE COMMITTEE, 1978–1979
(in thousands of pounds)

| Item | Precampaign | Campaign | Total |
|---|---|---|---|
| Grants to constituencies | 0 | 213 | 213 |
| Advertising | | | |
| Posters[a] | (224) | (130) | (354) |
| Press | (0) | (260) | (260) |
| Total | 224 | 390 | 614 |
| Political broadcasts | 2[b] | 71 | 72 |
| Opinion research | 48[b] | 39 | 87 |
| Party publications[a] | 40 | 54 | 95 |
| Leaders' tours and meetings | 0 | 45 | 45 |
| Staff and administrative costs | 0 | 190 | 190 |
| Miscellaneous | 1 | 48 | 48 |
| Total | 315 | 1,050 | 1,366 |

[a] There may be marginal errors in assigning spending in these categories to the precampaign and campaign phases.
[b] These particular figures are not readily comparable with those for the Conservative party as the two parties used different definitions of "precampaign" expenditure for these categories. The Conservatives included all broadcasting production costs during the year before the election as "precampaign" while Labour did not; for opinion research the difference was the other way around.
SOURCE: Finance officer of the Labour party.

The problem faced by Labour's National Executive Committee was how to persuade union leaders to dig into these reserves. Also, there were disagreements about whether to direct money toward political advertising in an attempt to match Conservative efforts, or whether to use the political resources of the Labour movement to meet the future routine running costs of the party's headquarters.

In line with party tradition, the Labour managers adopted a fairly cautious policy on campaign spending. The Labour party's advertising started in 1978 and continued during the campaign. Its efforts were on a smaller scale than those of the Conservatives, especially in the precampaign period. In total, Labour's central election spending was about two-thirds that of the Conservatives.

The breakdown of Labour's general election spending in table 7–3 is based on statistics prepared by the party's finance office. The figures are those of the National Executive Committee. They correspond largely, but not completely, with those of the Conservative Central Office. The main difference is that the Conservative accounts include all funds raised at the regional (area) level whereas Labour's do not.

In order to assess Labour's total central spending, it is necessary to add to the figures in table 7–3 an estimate of the sums raised and spent by the regional councils of the Labour party. The annual reports issued by regional councils after the elections of 1974 indicate that they raised and spent a total of about £150,000 in that year—that is, about 15 percent of the National Executive Committee's election budget. A preliminary check on some regional general election funds in 1979 suggests that the ratio of regional to NEC funds remained the same. If so, the regions spent approximately £200,000 in addition to the £1,366,000 spent by the NEC. Most regional money was collected from trade unions, and approximately three-quarters of it was devoted to grants to constituencies. Table 7–4 gives total Labour central campaign spending, including estimated spending by regional councils. The figures in this table are comparable to the Conservative party totals given in table 7–2.

In addition to the total estimated in table 7–4, Labour's central effort was supplemented by a special election committee spearheaded by the General and Municipal Workers' Union. This committee, Trade Unions Campaign for a Labour Victory (TULV), paid £41,000 for extra advertising in the regional press and £38,000 for pamphlets and leaflets for distribution to trade unionists. If one includes the expenses of this committee, Labour's central election expenditure probably amounted to over £1.6 million. However, the TULV's spending has not been included in the tables in this chapter as the committee was not part of the regular central Labour organization.

Labour's National Executive Committee relies almost entirely for its routine income upon trade union affiliation fees. This dependence upon trade unions increases with the financial demands of a general election. At the beginning of 1978, the party had a reserve of £338,000 in its special General Election Fund. During 1978, £287,000 was paid into the fund, and in 1979 a further £916,000. The party received a windfall donation of £80,000 from the League Against Cruel Sports. This payment was apparently arranged, much to the annoyance of the Conservative Central Office, by the veteran Labour politician Lord Houghton. Apart from this donation, all but £25,000 came from donations by trade unions. A feature of union donations was that a large proportion of the total came from the handful of largest unions. This contrasts with gifts given to the Conservatives by companies, which come in smaller sums from a larger number of sources. The main

## TABLE 7–4

ESTIMATED CENTRAL LABOUR PARTY PRECAMPAIGN AND CAMPAIGN
EXPENDITURE, INCLUDING SPENDING BY REGIONAL COUNCILS, 1978–1979
(in thousands of pounds)

| Item | Precampaign | Campaign | Total |
|---|---|---|---|
| Grants to constituencies | 0 | 363 | 363 |
| Advertising | | | |
|   Posters | (224) | (130) | (354) |
|   Press | (0) | (265) | (265) |
|   Total | 224 | 395 | 619 |
| Political broadcasts | 2 | 71 | 72 |
| Opinion research | 48 | 39 | 87 |
| Party publications | 40 | 79 | 120 |
| Leaders' tours and meetings | 0 | 50 | 50 |
| Staff and administrative costs | 0 | 200 | 200 |
| Miscellaneous | 1 | 54 | 55 |
| Total | 315 | 1,251 | 1,566 |

NOTE: In addition to the figures for NEC spending given in table 7-3, it has been assumed that £200,000 was spent by regional councils, divided as follows: grants to constituencies, £150,000; publications, £25,000; administrative costs, £10,000; speakers and meetings, £5,000; press advertising, £5,000; miscellaneous, £5,000. These are crude estimates, subject to revision.

SOURCE: NEC spending, finance officer of the Labour party; regional spending, estimates by regional organizers together with regional election accounts for 1974.

contributions to the NEC's General Election Fund are set out in table 7–5.

The sums in table 7–5 give only part of the trade union contribution to Labour's election effort. In addition to their contributions to the NEC's General Election Fund, major unions helped in four ways: by making donations to the Trade Unions Campaign for a Labour Victory; by contributing money at the regional level; by sponsoring specific parliamentary candidates; and by making payments to the election appeals of many constituency Labour parties.

**Liberal.** Although the amounts involved in Liberal central finances are very small in relation to those of the two principal parties, they are worth describing in some detail because the control of central funds, especially in recent years, has been a crucial element in Liberal internal power struggles.

The annual publication of accounts by the Liberal Party Organization (LPO), the extraparliamentary headquarters, has merely di-

TABLE 7–5

ESTIMATED MAJOR CONTRIBUTIONS TO THE GENERAL ELECTION FUND
OF THE LABOUR PARTY NATIONAL EXECUTIVE COMMITTEE, 1978–1979

| Source | Contribution (in £1,000s) | Percentage of Total |
|---|---|---|
| Trade union donations | | |
| Transport Workers (TGWU) | (150) | (12) |
| Municipal Workers (GMWU) | (150) | (12) |
| Electrical Workers (AEUW) | (102) | (8) |
| Miners (NUM) | (100) | (8) |
| Technicians (ASTMS) | (50) | (4) |
| Public Employees (NUPE) | (50) | (4) |
| Other union donations | (496) | (41) |
| Total, union donations | 1,098 | 91 |
| League Against Cruel Sports | 80 | 7 |
| Other nonunion donations | 25 | 2 |
| Total | 1,203 | 100 |

NOTE: These figures may underestimate the totals given by some of the major unions to the NEC General Election Fund. Although individual unions eventually publish their political fund accounts, and although the Labour party is, in theory, in favor of the publication of individual donations to its funds, there was on this occasion reluctance both by some individual unions and by the Labour party to reveal the totals donated by the major unions. The figures in the table are therefore based on estimates in *The British General Election of 1979*. (The Conservative and Liberal organizations also refuse to give details of individual donations.) Columns may not add to totals because of rounding.

SOURCE: Finance officer of the Labour party and David Butler and Dennis Kavanagh, *The British General Election of 1979* (London: Macmillan, 1980).

verted attention from the fact that several other funds have remained undisclosed. Secret funds have multiplied because each section of the central party has wished to guard its own sources of money. In particular, the leader of the Liberal members of Parliament has traditionally insisted on maintaining an independent cache of his own. The existence of "special" funds has caused controversy within the party from time to time. The matter came to a head after the 1974 elections amid revelations and speculation about the Norman Scott affair.[8] There was intense publicity about funds which had been pri-

---

[8] For the Norman Scott affair and the attendant speculation about Liberal party funds, see Barrie Penrose and Roger Courtiour, *The Pencourt File* (London: Secker and Warburg, 1978); Peter Chippindale and David Leigh, *The Thorpe Committal: The Full Story of the Minehead Proceedings* (London: Arrow Books, 1979); Lewis Chester, Magnus Linklater, and David May, *Jeremy Thorpe: A Secret Life* (London: Fontana, 1979).

vately collected by Jeremy Thorpe, the party leader from 1967 until 1976. It was suggested before and during Thorpe's trial in 1979 that £20,000 of secret money had been diverted to finance a murder conspiracy. The charge was not proved. Thorpe and his codefendants were found not guilty, and later the mysterious £20,000 was returned to its donor. Nevertheless, the aura of scandal led to a widely expressed determination to end the existence of separate, unpublished Liberal funds.

However, the new Liberal leader, David Steel, and his colleagues in the parliamentary Liberal party appear to have been reluctant to place control of the party's central finances completely in the hands of the Liberal Party Organization. Indeed, there was grave criticism after the 1974 elections of the LPO's alleged ineffectiveness. A report commissioned by the party's National Executive Committee suggested in 1975 that the LPO should be abolished altogether and that the party should make do without any headquarters bureaucracy. The LPO survived, but arrangements continued to channel some important donations and sources of money directly to the party's M.P.s and to the leader, bypassing the LPO. The accounts of the LPO, both for the preelection phase and for the campaign itself, therefore represent only one ingredient of the Liberal party's central campaign finances.

In the struggle over Liberal funds before the 1979 campaign, a vital, though low-key, part was played by the Joseph Rowntree Social Service Trust Ltd. This is one of several major foundations established by the Rowntrees, a family of leading businessmen and social reformers with Liberal party leanings. The trust, as it has operated in recent years, could in some respects be described as an alternative Liberal headquarters. Its executive director, Lord Chitnis, is a former head of the Liberal Party Organization. The trustees include Jo Grimond, an ex-leader of the party, and Richard Wainwright, a Liberal M.P. In the two years before the 1979 election, the Rowntree Trust seems to have made its Liberal donations with two aims. First of all, it distrusted what it regarded as the bureaucratic tendencies of the LPO.[9] Second, it wished to encourage alliances between Liberals and moderates in the two main parties. Accordingly, the trustees were strong supporters of the Lib-Lab pact of 1977, and, around the time it was made, gave a grant of £55,000 to David Steel and the parliamen-

---

[9] Detailed figures kindly supplied by the trust indicate that untied donations to the LPO fell from £92,400 in the four years 1971-1974 to £3,500 in the four years 1975-1978. During 1975-1978, the trust gave a total of £161,769 for various Liberal projects apart from the LPO's general funds. By May 1979, this total had risen to about £250,000. This pattern of grants was intentional. According to a letter from the trust secretary, "a decision was made to make Trust funds available only for special and particular projects outside the Party Headquarters."

## TABLE 7–6

ESTIMATED LIBERAL PARTY ORGANIZATION PRECAMPAIGN AND
CAMPAIGN EXPENDITURE, 1978–1979

(in thousands of pounds)

| Item | Precampaign | Campaign | Total |
|------|-------------|----------|-------|
| Grants and guarantees to constituencies | 0 | 50 | 50 |
| Advertising | | | |
|    Posters | (0) | (0) | (0) |
|    Press | (0) | (26) | (26) |
|     Total | 0 | 26 | 26 |
| Political broadcasts | 0 | 1.5 | 1.5 |
| Opinion research | 0 | 0 | 0 |
| Literature (including manifesto)[a] | 4.5 | 2 | 6.5 |
| Tours and travel | 1.5 | 13.5 | 15 |
| Central operating expenses[b] | 1 | 31 | 32 |
| Miscellaneous | 1 | 5 | 6 |
| Total | 8 | 129 | 137 |

[a] This item consists mainly of free copies of the manifesto and leaflets.

[b] This item includes the cost of renting accommodation for press conferences since the Liberals, unlike the Conservatives and Labour, did not have sufficient room on their own premises. Other significant items included in this category are grants to regions and recognized units, postage, telephone, printing and stationery, security, and hire of equipment.

SOURCE: Secretary general of the Liberal Party Organization.

tary Liberal party. A further £45,000 was allocated to David Steel at the rate of £5,000 a month between September 1978 and May 1979. These two grants gave the Liberal leader considerable financial independence from his party organization. It is estimated that about £50,000 from these two grants was used on what can reasonably be regarded as preelection expenditure and almost all the rest on routine political activities. In addition to these grants and to other important donations for specific Liberal projects, the Rowntree Trust gave £60,500 for the LPO's general election campaign. It insisted that none of the money be used for the operating expenses of the headquarters. In order to ensure this, the election donation to the LPO was placed into a separate LPO general election account, Account No. 2.

LPO campaign spending, as estimated for this study by the LPO, is set out in table 7–6. It excludes (1) election expenditure out of the grants allocated by the Rowntree Trust to David Steel, (2) precampaign and campaign spending by the Scottish, Welsh, and regional units of the party, and (3) precampaign and campaign spending by "recognized units" of the party.

The elements of central Liberal spending not included in the LPO's election accounts have been estimated. The most important additions are (1) about £50,000 spent by Steel out of the Rowntree grants for campaign purposes, (2) approximately £10,000 spent by the Scottish Liberals, and (3) campaign spending by the Welsh Liberals and by regional federations and recognized units. The amounts involved are reported to have been very small—hundreds rather than thousands of pounds per unit. It is assumed that these separate bodies spent £15,000 combined. According to these estimates, the total Liberal central election expenditure comes to about £213,000. A breakdown into categories of spending is given in table 7–7. The figures are only approximate because precise information on the spending of regional federations and recognized units has not been collected.[10]

The LPO raised about £150,000 for the election. Apart from the Rowntree Trust's tied donation of £60,500, some £45,000 was reported raised by the normal Liberal election appeal to the party's traditional supporters, and the rest came from larger donors. The LPO had set up a committee in 1977 to solicit money from business corporations. It apparently met with little success.

If account is taken of other units of Liberal central organization, an overall total of at least £230,000 appears to be a reasonable estimate of the Liberal election effort. Almost half of this came from the Rowntree Trust (that is, £60,500 to the LPO and £50,000 for election purposes out of the £100,000 granted to David Steel). Most of the rest came from individual donations.

**Some Comparisons.** Strong contrasts between the central election finances of the three parties emerge.

---

[10] Since this chapter went to press, the secretary general of the Liberal Party Organization has expressed the view that the overall total of £213,000 given in table 7-7 is too high. (1) The LPO does not have figures for election spending by the Welsh Liberals and by the party's regional organizations in England, but their total expenditure is estimated at £3,000 (rather than £15,000). (2) It is further argued that campaign spending out of the Rowntree grants to David Steel amounted to only £18,000, not £50,000 as indicated in this chapter.

The discrepancy between estimates of spending by regions results from the fact that no solid information has been collected. However, this is a relatively small item in comparison with the overall total. The lower estimate would reduce total central Liberal spending from £213,000 to £201,000. The important discrepancy, about spending out of the Rowntree grants, reflects a difference in interpretation of what constituted "campaign" rather than "routine" uses of these grants. The estimate in this chapter that £50,000 out of the £100,000 granted to David Steel was used for campaign purposes is based on detailed information provided by the Rowntree Trust and on a definition of the precampaign period similar to that used for the Conservative and Labour parties.

TABLE 7–7

ESTIMATED LIBERAL PARTY CENTRAL PRECAMPAIGN AND CAMPAIGN
EXPENDITURE, 1978–1979, INCLUDING SPENDING BY THE
LEADER'S OFFICE, REGIONAL FEDERATIONS, AND OTHER
CENTRAL ORGANIZATIONS

(in thousands of pounds)

| Item | Precampaign | Campaign | Total |
|---|---|---|---|
| Grants and guarantees to constituencies | 30 | 54 | 84 |
| Advertising | | | |
|   Posters | (9) | (0) | (9) |
|   Press | (0) | (26) | (26) |
|   Total | 9 | 26 | 35 |
| Producing political broadcasts | 0 | 1.5 | 1.5 |
| Opinion research | 0 | 0 | 0 |
| Literature (including manifesto) | 8.5 | 7 | 15.5 |
| Tours and travel | 1.5 | 16.5 | 18 |
| Central operating expenses | 9 | 44 | 53 |
| Miscellaneous | 1 | 5 | 6 |
| Total | 59 | 154 | 213 |

SOURCE: The Liberal Party Organization, the Scottish Liberal party, and the Joseph Rowntree Social Service Trust Ltd.

• At the center, Labour spent about seven times as much as the Liberals, and the Conservatives about eleven times as much.

• Grants to local party organizations and candidates constituted a small part of the Conservative budget but much larger portions of the Labour and Liberal budgets.

• The Conservatives spent little on meetings and tours. This resulted from the fact that the cost of Mrs. Thatcher's campaign airplane was almost entirely met by the journalists to whom seats were sold. The aircraft, with about 100 seats, seems to have cost no more than the Liberal leader's "battlebus."

• The Conservatives greatly outmatched their opponents in two areas: in their preparation of material for party political broadcasts (on which they spent six times as much as Labour) and in their advertising. The Conservative outlay on advertising was two-and-a-half times that of Labour. (This was much less, however, than the ten-to-one margin claimed by Labour.)[11] One reason why the Tories were

---

[11] Labour party, *Report of the National Executive Committee, 1978–79*, London, 1979, p. 5.

## TABLE 7–8

PATTERNS OF CENTRAL ELECTION SPENDING, BY PARTY, 1978–1979

| | Percentage of Total Central Spending | | |
|---|---|---|---|
| Item | Conservative | Labour | Liberal |
| Grants to constituencies | 2 | 23 | 39 |
| Advertising | 64 | 40 | 16 |
| Political broadcasts | 18 | 5 | 1 |
| Opinion research | 3 | 6 | 0 |
| Party publications | 5 | 8 | 7 |
| Tours and meetings | 1 | 3 | 8 |
| Administrative costs | 7 | 13 | 25 |
| Miscellaneous | 0 | 4 | 3 |
| Total | 100 | 100 | 100 |

NOTE: Percentages may not add to totals because of rounding.
SOURCE: Official party sources cited in tables 7-2, 7-4, and 7-7.

able to devote more to national advertising was that, unlike Labour, they were relieved of the need to prop up local party organizations.

• The proportion of the Conservative total spent in the precampaign period was larger than that of the other two parties—a result of Conservative expenditure in this phase on advertising.

• It is worth noting that, as a broad approximation, the Conservative election budget was equivalent to slightly more than a half-year's routine expenditure at the Conservative Central Office. The equivalent for Labour was two-thirds of a year's routine spending and, for the Liberals, about a year's routine spending.

The pattern of central spending of the three main parties is given in table 7–8. Since the categories used by the parties are not exactly comparable, the statistics need to be interpreted with caution.

### Constituency Campaign Finances

Parliamentary candidates are required by law to make itemized public declarations of their campaign expenditures. Although these accounts are subject to a degree of manipulation, they nevertheless give a fairly accurate record of constituency electioneering during the campaign period. By contrast, it is difficult to gather reliable information about local expenses which might be categorized as precampaign. Also, there is a shortage of precise information about the sources of election income (as distinct from routine income) in the constituencies.

## TABLE 7–9
### PARLIAMENTARY CANDIDATES' ELECTION EXPENSES, 1979

|  | Conservative | Labour | Liberal |
|---|---|---|---|
| Number of candidates | 622 | 622 | 576 |
| Average expenses | £2,190 | £1,897 | £1,013 |
| Total expenses | £1,362,000 | £1,180,000 | £583,000 |
| Number of lost deposits | 3 | 22 | 304 |
| Cost of lost deposits | £450 | £3,300 | £45,600 |
| Total expenses, including lost deposits | £1,363,000 | £1,183,000 | £629,000 |

NOTE: These figures, which are derived from Home Office returns of declared expenditures by candidates, exclude candidates' personal expenses.

SOURCE: David Butler and Dennis Kavanagh, *The British General Election of 1979*, (London: Macmillan, 1980).

The average amounts spent in the 1979 campaign by parliamentary candidates are given in table 7–9. The statistics are quoted directly from David Butler and Dennis Kavanagh's book *The British General Election of 1979*, which takes them from the officially declared election expenses of candidates collected by the Home Office. Table 7–9 also shows the cost to each party of lost deposits. Each candidate must upon nomination deposit £150. This is forfeited to the government if the candidate fails to obtain 12.5 percent of the votes cast in his constituency.

**Categories of Constituency Campaign Spending.** Home Office statistics are available showing the totals spent in 1979 by parliamentary candidates on several categories of activity. By far the costliest item was printing. This accounted for 80 percent of total spending by all candidates (including minor parties). Other categories were: agents, 5 percent; hire of committee rooms, 3 percent; clerks and messengers, 2 percent; hire of rooms for meetings, 2 percent; miscellaneous, 8 percent. Breakdowns by party are not available.

**Sources of Constituency Campaign Funds.** According to election law, the candidate (or his agent) is responsible for his own election expenses. In practice, candidates of all three parties do not normally pay out of their own pockets (as was common before the Second World War) but receive the money from their local party organizations. Conservative and Labour candidates are strictly limited by party rules in the amounts they are permitted to contribute toward their

## TABLE 7–10

### Sources of Conservative and Labour Party Campaign Funds in a Marginal Constituency (Oxford), 1979

| | Percentage of Total Raised | |
|---|---|---|
| Source | Conservative | Labour |
| Collections at meetings | 3 | 2 |
| Grants from central party | 0 | 25 |
| Donations (members and supporters) | 45[a] | 18 |
| Donations (political clubs)[b] | 29 | 3 |
| Company payments | 23[c] | 0 |
| Trade union payments | 0 | 52 |
| Total | 100 | 100 |
| Amount raised | £5,216 | £3,261 |
| Total election expenses | £2,941 | £2,881 |

[a] The constituency party received 305 separate donations.
[b] Political clubs are mainly social bodies affiliated to political parties. The financial contribution of Conservative clubs in Oxford is considerably above average.
[c] The party received 23 separate donations from businesses.
SOURCE: Returning officer, City of Oxford; agent of the City of Oxford Conservative Association; hon. treasurer of the Oxford City Labour party.

own campaigns. Liberal candidates occasionally contribute substantially to their election expenses and are not subject to a formal limit by party rules.

Conservative constituency associations are in general stronger than those of Labour or the Liberals. They have four to five times as many individual members as those of either of the other parties. For a local Conservative organization, with an average routine income of some £10,000 a year, the £2,000 needed for the normal constituency campaign is easy to collect. Local Conservatives raise funds from their lists of members and subscribers through an election "fighting fund." The short notice at which elections are called means that there is no time to arrange social fundraising events—a typical way of collecting money between elections. The election fighting fund usually comes from small and medium-sized contributions from individuals and small businessmen. If the fund collects more than necessary for the campaign—as frequently happens—the balance is put toward the routine activities of the local party association. The main sources of Conservative and Labour campaign funds in 1979 in the Oxford constituency are shown in table 7–10.

Constituency Labour parties find it considerably more difficult to raise money for election expenses from their members. Individual

Labour membership fell to some 300,000 in the late 1960s and has remained around that level ever since. Consequently, many Labour candidates rely on grants from London (or from the regional office of the party) or on donations from trade unions. According to the estimates in table 7–4, national and regional grants to Labour candidates probably amounted to over £350,000—about 30 percent of total constituency election expenses. Most are supplied out of money given to the central organs of the Labour party by trade unions. In 1979, some of the funds for constituency grants came from the £80,000 donation from the League Against Cruel Sports, much of which was directed toward candidates who included statements opposing hunting in their election addresses.[12]

Trade unions contributed to constituency election expenses in other ways. Candidates in 191 constituencies were directly sponsored by a particular trade union or by the Co-operative party.[13] Unions concentrated these financial efforts in safely held Labour seats: 150 out of the 191 union-sponsored candidates were elected. According to party rules, sponsoring organizations were permitted to meet up to 80 percent of the election expenses of their candidates. Some indication of the amounts contributed by sponsoring unions is given by *Transport Review*, the magazine of the National Union of Railwaymen.[14] It predicted during the campaign that sponsoring thirteen candidates would cost £25,000, that is, nearly £2,000 a candidate. This is probably above the average figure. Even £1,000 per sponsored candidate still gives a hefty total for all sponsored candidates of about £200,000.

Three points about union sponsorship should be noted. First, the limits on the percentage of total expenses which a union is permitted to donate applies only to the sponsoring union. The subsidy may be supplemented by other trade unions. Thus the total percentage of election expenses coming from all union sources may be in excess of 80 percent. Second, the fact that union-sponsored candidates are normally in safe Labour constituencies permits the national party organization to direct its grants to marginal seats or to areas of Conservative strength. Third, the practice of sponsorship has grown in

---

[12] Ibid., p. 12: "The League Against Cruel Sports gave financial help in appreciation of the section of the party manifesto with regard to cruel sports and the welfare of animals. There was consultation on the allocation of grants to selected marginal constituencies."

[13] The Co-operative party is the political organ of the Co-operative Union, to which are affiliated retail stores' "Co-operative Societies," which are "owned" by their consumers along Owenite principles. The Co-operative party sponsors Labour candidates on the same basis as unions.

[14] April 20, 1979.

FINANCING THE GENERAL ELECTION

recent elections. More union-sponsored M.P.s were elected in 1979 than in any election in the party's history with the exception of 1966. (In 1966, there were also 150 union-sponsored M.P.s. The total of Labour M.P.s was much greater than in 1979, however, and the percentage of those sponsored by unions was therefore much lower.)

Besides sponsoring particular candidates, unions gave further financial aid. Local branches of trade unions were among the most generous subscribers to the campaign appeals of constituency Labour parties. An impression of the sums involved is given by the figures for the Oxford City Labour party in table 7–10. Over half the money collected for the constituency campaign came from trade union branches.

If trade union funds from all sources are added together—those channeled through the NEC and regional Labour councils, and those paid directly to sponsored candidates and constituency Labour parties—it would appear that well over half (possibly two-thirds) of the election expenses of all Labour candidates came from unions and Co-operative societies. This contrasts with the Conservative party, where a far smaller proportion of candidates' expenses come from large and medium-sized businesses.

In the Liberal party, candidates depend largely on the response to financial appeals at their adoption meetings and to appeals to their traditional local individual subscribers. The party benefited from the fact that it had almost as many individual members as Labour, though, of course, far fewer than the Conservatives.

A comparison of the three main parties' spending on constituency campaigns shows that the gap was smaller locally than at the national level. This was largely the consequence of the strict legal limits on spending by parliamentary candidates. Conservatives spent only 15 percent more than their Labour counterparts. Candidates of the two major parties spent on average about twice as much as Liberal candidates. This gap reflected low Liberal spending in hopeless seats. According to an analysis for *The British General Election of 1979*, Liberals spent 91 percent of the maximum permitted sum in their thirty best constituencies. In the sixty-two most marginal Conservative/Labour contests, Conservatives spent 91 percent of the maximum and Labour 87 percent.

## The Value of Subsidies-in-Kind

This chapter has so far considered the amounts actually raised and spent by the parties nationally and locally. But the overall cost of the 1979 campaigns cannot realistically be calculated without taking into account the estimated value of subsidies-in-kind. Three subsidies-in-kind will be considered: (1) free postal deliveries to electors on behalf of parliamentary candidates, (2) free television and radio broadcasts by the parties nationally, and (3) free hire of halls.[15]

**Free Postal Deliveries.** A parliamentary candidate is entitled to send one item of mail to each elector in his constituency, which is delivered free of charge by the Post Office. After the general election of October 1974, the Post Office received £2.1 from the Treasury to cover the cost of delivering 75 million communications. Official figures for the 1979 election are not yet available. Considering the sharp rise in postal rates, the total paid by the Treasury to the Post Office is likely to exceed £5 million—some £2,000 per candidate. However, this grossly overstates the commercial cost of a door-to-door delivery and also the usefulness of this facility to candidates. Information from a commercial firm indicates that the charge for door-to-door delivery throughout an urban constituency would be about £400. In rural areas costs would be higher. A national average of £500 per constituency is therefore used as the basis for calculation. The free postal delivery is probably of most practical use to Labour and Liberal candidates since the Conservatives, with their reserves of voluntary help, could more easily deliver election addresses themselves. On the basis of £500 per candidate, the value of the free postal delivery in 1979 was £311,000 each for the Conservative and Labour parties and £288,000 for the Liberals.

**Party Political Broadcasts.** It is hard to overstate the importance of the regulations affecting political broadcasting. On the one hand, political parties are not permitted to purchase advertising time on television or radio. This means that the most powerful advertising medium is not available for purchase. On the other hand, the parties are given free allocations of time to present party political broadcasts on radio and on all three television channels. Broadcasting time is given to the parties between elections and during campaigns.

The time allotted to each party is decided by informal but tough bargaining in a committee including representatives of the broadcasting authorities and the main political parties. The exact allocations to each party have varied over time. The pattern has been consistent:

---

[15] Local government authorities in Britain are responsible for all aspects of voter registration. According to the Houghton Committee, local authorities (excluding Northern Ireland) spent a net total of £6,025,000 on this service in 1973-1974 (Houghton Report, p. 2). This could be considered a fourth major subsidy-in-kind since it eliminates the need for parties to pay for expensive publicity drives to encourage voter registration.

the Conservative and Labour parties have received equal time; the Liberals have been given less time than the two major parties but more than that to which they would be entitled on a per-vote basis. Over the past twenty years, the Liberals have received about twice the time to which they would have been entitled if allocations had been based on the number of votes received in general elections.

During the 1979 campaign, the Conservative and Labour parties had five free broadcasts of ten minutes each and the Liberals three. Most broadcasts were shown simultaneously on all three television channels, a device to deny politically apathetic viewers the option of avoiding the parties' messages by switching to another channel. It is impossible to give a definitive estimate of the value of these broadcasts since they have no commercial counterpart. One must bear this in mind in interpreting the statistics given below.

- In 1979, advertising time on Independent Television network cost about £40,000 a minute.
- Since the two BBC channels combined have the same total audience as ITV, the cost of a minute's advertising on all three channels was a notional £80,000 a minute. The notional cost of ten minutes—the length of a party political broadcast—was £800,000.
- The cost of five broadcasts of ten minutes each for Conservative and Labour was about £4 million; the cost of the three Liberal television broadcasts about £2.4 million.
- There are party political broadcasts between elections as well as during campaigns. The party political broadcasts in the eight months before the campaign will be treated as precampaign—four ten-minute broadcasts each for the Conservative and Labour parties and two for the Liberals. This gives a total notional cost, including the precampaign period, of £7.2 million each for Conservative and Labour and £4 million for the Liberals.
- In view of the crude nature of these estimates, no separate estimate is being made for radio time.
- So far, the notional *cost* of broadcasting time has been calculated.

However, the *value* to the parties of the time available was undoubtedly reduced by the fact that they were obliged to take it in clumsy ten-minute slices. The value of ten minutes together is less than the value of ten separate minutes. Research in Europe has apparently shown that the most effective length for a political broadcast is four minutes. It is therefore reasonable to calculate that the value of each party political broadcast was one-third to one-half the value of the number of minutes allotted. Each ten-minute party political broadcast, then, will be valued at £300,000.

TABLE 7–11

ESTIMATED VALUE OF SUBSIDIES-IN-KIND, 1978–1979

(in thousands of pounds)

| Party | Free Postage | Free Broadcasting | Free Hire of Halls | Total |
|-------|--------------|-------------------|--------------------|-------|
| Conservative | 311 | 2,700 | 62 | 3,073 |
| Labour | 311 | 2,700 | 62 | 3,073 |
| Liberal | 288 | 1,500 | 58 | 1,846 |

SOURCE: The basis of these figures is described in the text.

The calculated value of free broadcasts was £1.5 million to the Liberals and £2.7 million each to the Conservatives and Labour. That these are not fanciful figures is indicated by the sums the two main parties invested in producing their broadcasts. Over £400,000 of the Conservative election budget was devoted to this task, and some of the party's press advertising during the campaign consisted of a simple reminder to newspaper readers to watch a forthcoming party political broadcast.

These media estimates clearly show two things: (1) the value placed on party political broadcasts in comparison with central party spending on press, poster, and cinema advertising, and (2) the fact that the system of free broadcasts is biased toward the Liberals helps to compensate for that party's inability to raise funds to pay for large-scale press and poster publicity.

**Free Hire of Halls.** During a parliamentary election campaign a candidate is entitled to hold meetings in schools situated in his or an adjoining constituency or in any rooms available for public meetings that are maintained wholly or mainly out of public funds. The candidate is not required to pay for the hire of the room, but has to pay any heating, lighting, and cleaning costs. Public meetings have gradually declined in importance in constituency campaigns. The average candidate holds six to eight public meetings. The value of the free hire of public halls in 1979 was possibly about £100 per candidate, or a total of £62,000 each for the Conservative and Labour parties and £58,000 for the Liberals.

## Analysis

**How Much Did the 1979 Campaigns Cost?** Using the estimates for central campaign expenditure, local expenditure, and the value of

## TABLE 7–12

### Estimated Total Conservative, Labour, and Liberal Campaign Spending, 1978–1979

(in thousands of pounds unless otherwise indicated)

|  | Conservative | Labour | Liberal |
|---|---|---|---|
| Central campaign expenditures | 2,291 | 1,203 | 159 |
| Local campaign expenditures | 1,363 | 1,183 | 629 |
| Total campaign expenditures | 3,654 | 2,386 | 788 |
| Value of subsidies-in-kind | 3,073 | 3,073 | 1,846 |
| Total campaign costs including subsidies-in-kind | 6,727 | 5,459 | 2,634 |
| Votes received (in millions) | 13.7 | 11.5 | 4.3 |
| Expenditures per vote[a] | 27p | 21p | 18p |
| Total cost per vote[b] | 49p | 47p | 61p |

[a] Excludes subsidies-in-kind.
[b] Includes subsidies-in-kind.
Source: Official party sources and author's calculations in text.

subsidies-in-kind, we can calculate the total cost of the 1979 campaign for each of the three main parties. In order to avoid double counting, grants by central party organizations toward constituency election expenses will be subtracted from the totals for central spending given in tables 7–2, 7–4, and 7–7.

Table 7–12 indicates that the Conservative spending advantage was greater at the central than at the local level. This superiority was almost entirely in the area of political advertising. Yet, it is precisely in this area that the two other parties, and particularly the Liberals, benefited from subsidies-in-kind. Expressed in terms of costs-per-vote, and including subsidies-in-kind, the Conservative and Labour parties spent 49p and 47p respectively. The Liberals spent most heavily— 61p per vote. This unexpected result is an effect of the Liberals' disproportionately large allocation of free broadcasting.

*What were the main sources of campaign income?* The subsidies-in-kind received by the three main parties were worth a total of nearly £8 million, compared with under £7 million spent by the parties themselves for all purposes before and during the election campaign. Apart from the subsidies-in-kind, which benefited all the parties, the sources of the parties' income differed widely. The Conservative and Labour parties both relied heavily on institutional sources for their central funds—the Conservatives on companies and Labour on unions. Companies probably gave slightly over £2 million to the Conservative campaign at all levels and trade unions a total of some £2 million for the Labour effort. However, there were strong differences between business and union donations. To those perturbed about the consequences of political payments by institutions, union money gave more ground for concern than contributions from companies, for several reasons. (1) Whereas company contributions went almost exclusively to the Conservative Central Office, trade union money dominated at both the national and the constituency levels of the Labour party. Because Labour raised less, the proportion of its total campaign spending that came from institutional backers was considerably greater. (2) Although most companies have not yet published their annual accounts for 1979, it is clear from annual reports since 1968 that the largest single donations to the Tories from companies have been far smaller than the payments made to the Labour party by the half-dozen largest unions. The concentration of financial power over the Labour party in the hands of a few union chiefs has no counterpart in the Conservative party. (3) The Labour party's constitution gives contributing unions specific rights—votes at the annual party conference, sponsorship of parliamentary candidates, and so on. Companies that contribute to the Conservative party receive nothing specific in return.

As far as donations from individuals are concerned, the Conservatives seem to have raised at least £1.5 million, the Liberals over £600,000, and Labour about £0.5 million.

*What were the main categories of expenditure?* The breakdown of spending at the center is given in table 7–8. If estimates for central spending, local spending, and the value of subsidies-in-kind are combined, the overall pattern shown in table 7–13 emerges: most expenditure was devoted to two major categories, advertising (which was almost entirely a central cost) and printing (which was largely a constituency cost).

*How did spending in 1979 compare with earlier general elections?* A comparison of the officially declared expenses by parliamentary candidates at successive general elections indicates that, in real terms, the level of local campaign spending has fallen dramatically over the last hundred years. The long-term trend toward lower spending has continued since World War II, as shown in table 7–14.

The trend of campaign spending at the center has been more complex and irregular. The 1979 campaign was among the more costly since the war. The two main parties spent more heavily in real terms than in 1951, 1955, 1966, February 1974, and October 1974. The 1979 campaign, however, was far cheaper than that of 1964. If the

## TABLE 7–13
### MAIN CATEGORIES OF ELECTION EXPENDITURE, 1978–1979, INCLUDING ESTIMATED VALUE OF SUBSIDIES-IN-KIND
(percent)

| Category of Expenditure | Conservative | Labour | Liberal | All Three Parties |
|---|---|---|---|---|
| Advertising | 69 | 62 | 60 | 65 |
| Party literature[a] | 23 | 25 | 30 | 25 |
| Other | 8 | 13 | 10 | 10 |
| Total | 100 | 100 | 100 | 100 |

[a] It is assumed that the proportions of total constituency expenditure devoted to printing were the same for candidates of each party.
SOURCE: Derived from tables in this chapter and from Home Office statistics about categories of spending by parliamentary candidates.

central budgets of the Conservative and Labour parties are combined, 1979 cost roughly the same as the elections of 1959 and 1970.[16]

The length of the preelection period has been important in determining the cost of central campaigning. The less costly postwar campaigns have been those called suddenly or after short parliaments. The elections of 1951, 1955, 1966, February 1974, and October 1974 all fall into this category. The parliament of 1974–1979 was the longest since that of 1959–1964. Therefore, it is significant that central spending in 1979 was much lower than in 1964 (particularly on the Conservative side).

If the comparison is extended to the prewar years, two main trends emerge. First, the gap between the Conservatives and Labour has narrowed since the elections of the 1920s and 1930s. Second, Conservative central campaign spending was higher in several general elections before World War II than in most postwar campaigns. There has certainly been no sign in British elections of the sharp rises in campaign costs witnessed in countries like the United States. Indeed, despite the comments in 1979 about the Conservatives' use of "modern" media techniques, the party spent no more, in real terms, on centrally funded publicity than it had half a century earlier in 1929.[17]

---

[16] Trends in election spending are discussed more fully in Pinto-Duschinsky, *British Political Finance*.

[17] Robert Rhodes James, *Memoirs of a Conservative: J. C. C. Davidson's Memoirs and Papers, 1910-37* (London: Weidenfeld and Nicolson, 1969), p. 303.

### TABLE 7–14
#### THE FALLING COST OF CONSTITUENCY ELECTIONEERING, 1945–1979
(in April 1979 pounds)

| Election | Average Declared Expenditure per Candidate | | | |
|---|---|---|---|---|
| | Conservative | Labour | Liberal | All candidates[a] |
| 1945 | 6,427 | 4,903 | 4,384 | 5,257 |
| 1959 | 3,668 | 3,398 | 2,564 | 3,297 |
| 1970 | 3,027 | 2,641 | 1,675 | 2,428 |
| October 1974 | 2,410 | 2,198 | 1,370 | 1,820 |
| 1979 | 2,190 | 1,897 | 1,013 | 1,394 |
| 1979 spending as share of 1945 spending | 34% | 39% | 23% | 27% |

[a] Minor parties included.

SOURCE: Derived from David Butler and Anne Sloman, *British Political Facts 1900-1979*, 5th ed. (London: Macmillan, 1980), p. 223.

*Was the Conservative victory a result of the party's financial superiority?* It is beyond the scope of this chapter to attempt any assessment of the effectiveness of the Conservative advertising campaign, which is the only large item on which the party spent significantly more than its opponents. However, it appears most unlikely that the Conservatives owed their success to the size of their election budget.

At the local level, the Conservatives' financial advantage over Labour was slight. It was negligible in the marginal seats, where it mattered most. Centrally, Conservative spending on publicity was considerably smaller than suggested by the party's opponents during the campaign. The £1.5 million devoted to central advertising was probably less than half the amount spent in the 1964 election. Moreover, the publicity for which the Conservatives paid had roughly half the value of the free advertising which the party received on television and radio—a facility also available to the party's political opponents. To put it simply, it is difficult for a British party to win an election by purchasing additional forms of advertising, since the most potent medium of communication is not for sale and is equally available to the two main parties.

## Postscript: A Guide to Published Central Party Accounts

The Conservatives started to publish annual accounts of their central income and expenditure in 1968. The Labour and Liberal parties had already done so for many years. However, the accounts of all three parties are incomplete and potentially misleading. They cannot be compared with each other unless important adjustments are made, and extra, normally unpublished, information is obtained.

**Routine Spending and Campaign Spending.** In the past none of the accounts have distinguished clearly or consistently between routine and campaign income and expenditure.

*Conservative.* The published Conservative accounts make no distinction between routine and campaign items. Campaign spending is contained within the overall total spending for the relevant year. Estimates in this chapter of election expenditure in 1979 and in several earlier postwar elections are based on unpublished information supplied by the Conservative Central Office.

*Labour.* The National Executive Committee of the Labour party has maintained a General Election Fund since before World War II. The total yearly income and expenditure from this fund are shown in the published accounts. However, these figures do not reliably show spending for election purposes. Money from the General Election Fund has sometimes been used for routine purposes and at other times money from the General Fund appears to have been used for campaign purposes. Moreover, the published figures do not regularly specify how much money has been paid into the General Election Fund by trade unions, constituency Labour parties, and other sources (information which is given for the General Fund). Nor has there been any published breakdown of categories of election expenditure (though it is apparently intended to include this information for the 1979 election in the accounts to be issued in the autumn of 1980). Finally, when two elections have occurred in one year (as in 1974), no distinction has been drawn in the accounts between the spending for the two campaigns. As with the statistics for the Conservative and Liberal parties, the breakdown of Labour's central income and spending in the 1979 campaign was provided for use in this chapter by party officials.

*Liberal.* For several elections before those of 1974, the accounts of the Liberal Party Organization simply omitted election income and spending, a fact that seems curiously to have escaped the notice of

238

TABLE 7–15

INCLUSIVENESS OF THE MAJOR PARTIES' PUBLISHED ACCOUNTS

| | Included in the Party's Central Accounts Published Annually | | |
| Unit of Organization | Conservative | Labour | Liberal |
| --- | --- | --- | --- |
| Extraparliamentary HQ | Yes | Yes | Yes |
| Scottish HQ | Yes[a] | Partly[b] | No[c] |
| Welsh HQ | Yes | Partly[b] | No[c] |
| Regional organizations | Yes | Partly[b] | No[c d] |
| Parliamentary secretariat | Yes | Partly[b] | No[e] |
| Party leader's office | Yes | Partly[b] | No |
| Special units of national organization (women, youth, local government, and so on) | Yes | Yes | No[c] |
| State grant to opposition parties in the House of Commons | Yes | NA[f] | No[g] |

[a] Only since 1977-1978.

[b] Sums paid by the NEC to these units are included in the central accounts. Extra funds raised independently by the units concerned are not included.

[c] However, ad hoc subsidies to these units by the LPO are included.

[d] In the late 1960s the costs of regional federations were largely included in the LPO accounts.

[e] These costs have normally been borne by a separate unit of national organization called the Liberal Central Association (LCA).

[f] In 1975, when this grant was introduced, Labour was in office and the party therefore did not benefit until after losing the election of 1979. Whether Labour's share of the grant received after May 1979 is included in the NEC's balance sheet will become apparent when the accounts for 1979 are issued in the autumn of 1980.

[g] The Liberal share of the grant is not included in the accounts of the LPO but in those of the LCA. The LCA accounts, previously secret, were first published, as a separate item, in the LPO's annual report of 1979.

SOURCE: Published party accounts and interviews with party officials.

some academic researchers and also of the Houghton Committee. The LPO annual report for 1974 included a brief account, separate from the routine income and expenditure account, for each of the elections of that year. However, these election accounts excluded the activities of the Direct Aid Committee and did not give a breakdown of the main headings of expenditure. The fact that the Liberal party was later, in the wake of the Norman Scott affair, obliged to set up a special committee to examine important undisclosed aspects of election finance in the 1974 elections indicated how misleading the published accounts for those elections had been.

**What is Included in the Central Party Accounts?** The central accounts of the three main parties differ in their definitions of what constitutes "central party organization." The checklist in table 7–15 gives a guide to what appears to be included and excluded by each party.

*Conservative.* (1) The Conservative Central Office accounts do not list the costs of fundraising, which have already been deducted from the totals shown as donations. The total received as donations is thus larger than the figure shown. (2) Since the amount reportedly received from constituencies includes notional "quota credits," the sum actually paid to the center by the local parties is slightly less than the published figure and the amount received in the form of central donations is slightly larger. (3) The catchall category "donations" includes contributions from companies, professional partnerships, individual gifts, and bequests. As no distinction is made between these sources, it is not possible to tell from the accounts how much has been contributed by companies.

*Labour.* (1) The NEC accounts are divided into a number of separate funds. The most important of these is the General Fund. For purposes of comparison with the other parties, however, it is also necessary to include the annual income and expenditure of the special funds. In 1978, the special funds were the Development Fund, General Election Fund, By-Election Fund, Deposit Insurance Fund, and Party Headquarters Fund. (2) The accounts show the payments into the General Fund by trade unions, constituency Labour parties, and so on. But similar information is not regularly shown for the special funds. Therefore it is not possible to tell from the published figures the total annual contributions by trade unions to the NEC.

# 8

# Women and Elections in Britain

*Monica Charlot*

Women's suffrage was first mooted in Britain in 1792 by Mary Woll-stonecraft in her book *Vindication of the Rights of Women*. It was a subject of concern throughout the nineteenth century. In 1830 came the first organized campaign to promote it, that of the Chartists; and in 1832 the first debate on the subject in the House of Commons, on Mrs. Hunt's petition that every unmarried female possessing the necessary pecuniary qualifications be allowed to vote. In 1867 the first suffrage society was set up, in Manchester. But by the end of the century the vote was no nearer than it had been at the beginning.

In the early twentieth century the battle intensified. Peaceful meetings and public speeches gave way to provocative demonstrations. As the movement became more revolutionary it lost its moderate members and violence increased. Militant women chained themselves to railings, picketed, went on hunger strikes, smashed windows, threw bombs, and the escalation of feminist action continued until the First World War. The government's reaction was essentially repression. No political party as such supported women's suffrage.

Historians are divided as to whether the war accelerated the granting of the right to vote to women. Some claim that women would have obtained the vote before the war had they not resorted to violence, others that their war efforts earned them the right to vote. What the war did undoubtedly ensure was that when it was finally given to women in 1918 the vote was not subject to a property or other class qualification. The age qualification, on the other hand, was more restrictive for women than for men: only those over thirty could vote, while the voting age for men was twenty-one. The argument was that owing to the war the men would be swamped by the women if the latter were granted the vote on equal terms. Although successive Governments were continually harried and heckled, they played for time, and it was not until March 1928 that the Government brought forward the Representation of the People (Equal Franchise) Bill which gave women the vote on the same terms as men. It is thus just over half a century since women were first able to sit in, stand for, and help elect the House of Commons.

The doors of the other place however remained firmly shut. No peeresses could sit in the House of Lords. After the Second World War the problem was taken up again, but opposition was still strong. Gladstone's famous claim that if peeresses came into the Lords "the majority of peers would die of shock and the peeresses would die of boredom," was quoted with relish. The first change in favor of women came, ironically, in April 1958 with the law permitting the creation of life peers, who could be women. A few months later, in January 1959, a motion was carried to admit peeresses in their own right. But although the motion was carried, the Government ignored it until four years later when a law finally enabled peeresses to claim their right to a seat, place, and voice in the upper house.

The 1979 election saw for the first time a woman elected prime minister in Britain. Does this mean that women are now in Parliament on equal terms with men? As we look successively at the woman voter, the woman candidate, the woman M.P., and the first Government of a woman premier we shall see that there is little cause for the feminists to hang out the flag.

## The Woman Voter

Many—among both its advocates and its opponents—believed that women's suffrage would substantially change the nature of politics. Dicey writing on women's suffrage in 1909 remarked, "A revolution of such boundless significance cannot be attempted without the greatest peril to England."[1] This fear was based essentially on numbers. From the day they first got the vote on an equal footing with men, women have constituted an absolute majority of the electorate. In 1979 they made up 52 percent of potential voters.

Since 1929 fourteen general elections have come and gone but very little in the way of systematic research has been done on the way women vote. This has not prevented generalizations—usually unfavorable to women. Let us look at some of them and see to what extent they are borne out by what we know of voting in the 1979 election.

The data for this article were collected within the framework of a study on the voting behavior of women in France, Britain, and Sweden, financed by the Délégation Générale à la Recherche Scientifique et Technique (DGRST), Paris.
[1] *Quarterly Review*, 1909, p. 277.

TABLE 8–1

VOTING DECISION, BY SEX, 1979 CAMPAIGN

(percent)

|  | Men | Women |
|---|---|---|
| Undecided | 2 | 4 |
| Nonvoter | 9 | 6 |
| Decided long ago | 67 | 63 |
| Decided during campaign | 14 | 13 |
| Decided in last few days | 8 | 14 |
| Total | 100 | 100 |
| N | (1,162) | (1,275) |

SOURCE: BBC Gallup survey designed by Ivor Crewe, May 1979.

**Volatility.** Women, it is said, are less interested in politics than men, less likely to be committed, and therefore less likely to vote. The 1979 election showed, however, that declared nonvoting was in fact rarer among women than among men (see table 8–1).

The notion that women were more faithful to former allegiances than their male counterparts was also scotched. In 1959 Trenaman and McQuail working on television and the political image in Britain wrote:

> The explanation of Labour's support amongst women, and of the slight movements measured by the Gallup Poll, may be a greater solidarity among women supporters, a reluctance to abandon a former allegiance, rather than a positive pro-Labour movement. In a time of movement away from the left, women's traditional conservatism may in fact not operate in favour of the conservative party.[2]

This stereotype did not match reality in 1979. The volatility of the electorate certainly transcended the sex variable, as table 8–1 shows: women were in fact less committed to a particular party from an early date and more influenced by the campaign itself, especially in its final stages. A Gallup poll on April 1–2 substantiated the claim that women cast their votes less automatically than men in favor of a given party.[3] At that stage 20 percent of women had not made up their minds how they would vote as against 16 percent of men. The

[2] Joseph Trenaman and Denis McQuail, *Television and the Political Image, A Study of the Impact of Television on the 1959 General Election* (London: Methuen, 1961), p. 140.

[3] *Economist*, May 12, 1979.

TABLE 8–2

PARTY LOYALTY, BY SEX, 1979

(percent)

| | Men | Women |
|---|---|---|
| Conservative or Labour loyalists | 48 | 48.3 |
| Conservative or Labour recruits | 18.4 | 17.3 |
| Conservative or Labour defectors | 11.6 | 11.7 |
| N | (1,162) | (1,275) |

SOURCE: BBC Gallup survey.

most undecided (28 percent) were women in the twenty-five to thirty-four age group. Loyal supporters of the two major parties constituted only just under half of the electorate for both sexes (see table 8–2).

**Conservatism.** Women, it is claimed, are more conservative than men and therefore vote more to the right. It is true that men favored Labour in nine out of the ten elections held between 1945 and 1974, while women favored the Conservatives in seven out of ten. In 1945, 1966, and February 1974, however, more women voted Labour than Conservative. Figure 8–1 shows that in the 1970s the gap between men and women has greatly diminished. In 1970 the same proportion of men as women voted Conservative, and in 1979 the voting patterns for the left and for the right were identical for the two sexes.

Butler and Stokes refined the notion of conservatism, claiming that "conservatism of established tendencies" rather than Conservative party identification increases with age.[4] This would imply that the Conservative advantage among women is partly a function of their longevity—older people having had a more limited chance of being socialized in favor of what was, in their youths, a very new Labour party.

In 1979 women made up 67.7 percent of the over sixty-fives, and given the fact that in this election as in preceeding elections the voting behavior of the over sixty-fives was clearly more conservative than that of the electorate as a whole (plus four percentage points), one may well hypothesize that the younger women voted less to the right than the younger men, since for all ages combined the pattern of voting for men and women was virtually identical.

---

[4] David Butler and Donald Stokes, *Political Change in Britain* (London: Macmillan, 1969), p. 83.

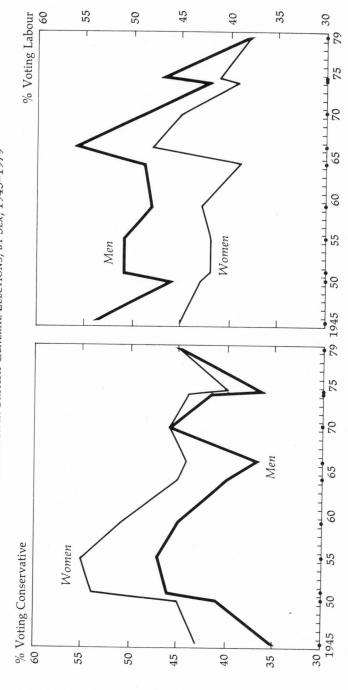

FIGURE 8–1

Voting Behavior in British General Elections, by Sex, 1945–1979

% Voting Conservative

% Voting Labour

Note: Data indicate the percentage of each sex voting for the stated party.
Source: Gallup Poll Election Studies.

**Dominance.** Women are presumed to be apolitical and passive, following their fathers' and husbands' voting decisions. Way back in 1797 Charles James Fox declared that the law of nations and the law of nature had made "that sex dependent on ours" and that therefore "their voices would be governed by the relations in which they stand to society."[5] If women were given the vote, Fox believed, they would use it as directed by males. A century and a half later political scientists continued to harp on the same theme. Nordlinger, studying working-class Tories, only questioned men, for "in many instances the women's political attitudes are simply those of their husbands as reflected in a female mirror."[6]

Yet a study of women voters in February 1974 carried out by NOP (National Opinion Polls) showed that only 54 percent of the sample had discussed how they would vote in the election with their husbands or boyfriends.[7] Only a quarter said their husbands or boyfriends had either "a great deal" or "quite a bit" of influence over their choice.

In order to examine more closely the dependence of one sex on the other I undertook a study of married couples in the June 1979 election, hypothesizing that constant living together would accentuate any dependence of one sex on the other.[8] The preliminary results showed that, within couples, interest in the election was almost as widespread among women as among men but that among men it was more intense (see table 8–3). Roughly the same proportions of men and women were not at all interested in the election, and a slightly larger proportion of women (14 percent) than of men (10 percent) were not very interested in the election. The overwhelming majority of both husbands and wives were interested in the campaign. Even so, only a third of the respondents discussed politics frequently with their spouses (see table 8–4). Significantly, the frequency of political discussions declined with social class (see table 8–5). The figures show clearly that there is little difference between the way women and men view the problem. Lazarsfeld stressed some ten years ago that there was a marked discrepancy between husbands and wives when they reported discussions: "45 of the women," he reported, "stated that they had talked the election over with their husbands, but . . . only 4 [men] reported discussions with their

---

[5] L. Reid, *Charles James Fox* (London: Longman, 1969), p. 209.

[6] Eric Nordlinger, *The Working Class Tories* (London: MacGibbon and Kee, 1967).

[7] *Daily Mail*, February 18, 1974.

[8] The survey was carried out by Survey Research Archives and designed by Monica Charlot. National sample of 430 couples.

## TABLE 8–3
### SURVEY OF COUPLES: INTEREST IN THE ELECTION
(percent)

| Degree of Interest | Husbands | Wives |
|---|---|---|
| Very interested | 52 | 40 |
| Fairly interested | 34 | 41 |
| Not very interested | 10 | 14 |
| Not at all interested | 4 | 4 |
| Total | 100 | 100 |

NOTE: Columns may not add to totals because of rounding.
SOURCE: National survey of 430 couples designed by the author and carried out by Survey Research Archives (SRA), May 1979.

## TABLE 8–4
### SURVEY OF COUPLES: DISCUSSION OF POLITICS WITH SPOUSE
(percent)

| Discuss Politics | Husband | Wife |
|---|---|---|
| Often | 35 | 36 |
| Rarely | 50 | 49 |
| Never | 15 | 15 |
| Total | 100 | 100 |

SOURCE: SRA survey, May 1979.

wives." Lazarsfeld concluded that "Only the wives are aware of the political opinions of their husbands. Men do not feel that they are discussing politics with their wives; they feel they are telling them."[9] This is certainly not the case in Britain today. Both husbands and wives are clearly aware of what constitutes "discussion." Although discussion was not necessarily frequent, the vast majority of couples (80 percent) did discuss the election with each other. Discussion tended to be more frequent among those voting Liberal and Conservative than among those voting Labour, but this can probably be accounted for by the class factor.

The vast majority of both men and women declared that they had no influence on how their spouses voted. The number was higher for women (94 percent) than for men (85 percent). When the ques-

[9] Paul Lazarsfeld, Bernard Berelson, and Hazel Gaudet, *The People's Choice*, 3rd ed. (New York: Columbia University Press, 1968), p. 141.

TABLE 8–5

SURVEY OF COUPLES: DISCUSSION OF POLITICS WITH SPOUSE,
BY SOCIAL CLASS
(percent)

| | Discuss Politics Frequently with Spouse | |
|---|---|---|
| Social Class | Men | Women |
| Intermediate and professional occupations (AB) | 51 | 52 |
| Routine nonmanual occupations (C$_1$) | 41 | 42 |
| Skilled manual occupations (C$_2$) | 33 | 30 |
| Semiskilled and unskilled manual occupations (DE) | 20 | 29 |

SOURCE: SRA survey, May 1979.

tion was put the other way around and the respondent was asked whether his/her spouse had influenced his/her voting behavior, 95 percent of the men and 90 percent of the women replied in the negative. The overall picture was thus clearly one of conjugal independence. This might be thought to reflect simply a desire for autonomy and not necessarily real freedom of action, but it becomes more significant when we note that 20 percent of the male respondents and 21 percent of the women considered that it was their parents who had had the most influence on their voting behavior. Socialization if it is an important variable is equally important for both sexes—a finding that is not consistent with the Duverger model of the male, whether husband, fiancé, or lover, as mediator.[10]

Lazarsfeld postulated "almost perfect agreement between husband and wife" in the field of politics and claimed it came about "as a result of male dominance in political situations."[11] Our survey shows the agreement to be certainly less than perfect. Roughly a quarter of the respondents did not identify their spouse's vote correctly—with once again very similar proportions of ignorant wives and ignorant husbands (see table 8–6). As far as actual voting is concerned, in almost two cases out of five husband and wife did not have similar voting intentions (see table 8–7). There seems little doubt that in contemporary Britain men's dominance in politics does not extend to commanding the vote of their spouses.

[10] Maurice Duverger, The Political Role of Women (Paris: Unesco, 1955), p. 129.
[11] Lazarsfeld, Berelson, and Gaudet, People's Choice, p. 141.

## TABLE 8–6
### SURVEY OF COUPLES: IDENTIFICATION OF SPOUSE'S VOTE
(percent)

| Voting Intention of Spouse | Husband Identified Wife's Voting Intention Correctly | Wife Identified Husband's Voting Intention Correctly |
|---|---|---|
| Conservative | 40 | 38 |
| Labour | 29 | 31 |
| Liberal | 8 | 5 |
| Other | — | 1 |
| Total correct identification | 77 | 75 |
| Incorrect identification | 23 | 25 |
| Total | 100 | 100 |
| N | (376) | (386) |

NOTE: Respondents who expressed no voting intention were excluded.
SOURCE: SRA survey, May 1979.

**Party Appeals.** Many of the stereotypes concerning women are changing as women's position in society changes. Today women in Britain represent 38.6 percent of the work force, and two out of three women workers are married. The little wife at home no longer corresponds to the reality of things. The average woman works at least a third of her life.

The political parties are well aware of these changes, and their campaign propaganda stressed arguments they believed would appeal to women. Not surprisingly, their priorities differed. The Labour party pledged itself to eliminating the remaining inequalities in the social security and tax systems. It promised better job training for

## TABLE 8–7
### SURVEY OF COUPLES: VOTING INTENTIONS OF HUSBANDS AND WIVES

| Voting Intentions | Percentage |
|---|---|
| Husband and wife support the same party | 64 |
| Husband and wife support different parties | 17 |
| Husband undecided, wife expresses voting intention | 6 |
| Wife undecided, husband expresses voting intention | 9 |
| Husband and wife undecided | 4 |
| Total | 100 |
| N | (430 couples) |

SOURCE: SRA survey, May 1979.

women, especially older women who were taking up work again once their children had become self-sufficient, and help for one-parent families—over 90 percent of which are fatherless. At the same time, the Labour party stressed that it had passed an Equal Pay Act, a Sex Discrimination Act, an Employment Protection Act, and a Social Security Act, all aimed at defending the rights of women.

The Conservative manifesto contained virtually no explicit mention of women, save for one reference to immigrants' wives.[12] It did, however, state very firmly that a Conservative Government would "Support family life, by helping people to become home-owners, raising the standards of their children's education, and concentrating welfare services on the effective support of the old, the sick, the disabled and those who are in real need." This is clearly an appeal to women when one knows to what extent in Britain they are the effective child-minders and the staple support of the sick and the old.

If women had voted only as women, and age, class, and other variables had been irrelevant, their choice would seem to have been between voting Labour in order to go out and get a better chance in the world of work, and voting Conservative to have a more cohesive, better-supported family life. In fact the courting of the woman voter is somewhat illusory. The Conservatives set out to make the housewife feel she was not being discriminated against. "We are the party of the family," Mrs. Thatcher announced in 1977. Labour determined to prove how much it had done to give women a fairer deal. But the opinion polls showed that women were in fact in agreement on which issues were of moment and should be discussed—and none of them was a women's issue.[13] In order of importance, the major issues were seen as the cost of living, prices, and inflation (57 percent women, 56 percent men); unemployment (29 percent men, 27 percent women); and trade unions and strikes (26 percent men, 27 percent women). Before the 1970 election women had only figured in the manifestoes as housewives worried over prices. It would be difficult to reinstate such an image, but women's issues in the narrowest sense—legislation on equality of the sexes—are not at present conspicuous vote-winners.

## The Woman Candidate

Women M.P.s have never totaled more than 5 percent of the House of Commons. The most obvious explanation of the small number of

---

12 "We shall introduce a Register of those Commonwealth wives and children entitled to entry for settlement under the 1971 Immigration Act."
13 MORI, *Daily Express.*

## TABLE 8–8

NUMBER OF WOMEN CANDIDATES, BRITISH GENERAL ELECTIONS,
1918–1979

| Election | Conservative | Labour | Liberal | Other | Total |
|----------|-------------|--------|---------|-------|-------|
| 1918 | 1 | 4 | 4 | 8 | 17 |
| 1922 | 5 | 10 | 16 | 2 | 33 |
| 1923 | 7 | 14 | 12 | 1 | 34 |
| 1924 | 12 | 22 | 6 | 1 | 41 |
| 1929 | 10 | 30 | 25 | 4 | 69 |
| 1931 | 17 | 36 | 5 | 4 | 62 |
| 1935 | 19 | 35 | 11 | 2 | 67 |
| 1945 | 14 | 41 | 20 | 12 | 87 |
| 1950 | 28 | 42 | 45 | 11 | 126 |
| 1951 | 25 | 41 | 11 | 0 | 77 |
| 1955 | 33 | 43 | 14 | 2 | 92 |
| 1959 | 28 | 36 | 16 | 1 | 81 |
| 1964 | 24 | 33 | 24 | 9 | 90 |
| 1966 | 21 | 30 | 20 | 10 | 81 |
| 1970 | 26 | 29 | 23 | 21 | 99 |
| 1974 Feb. | 33 | 40 | 40 | 30 | 143 |
| 1974 Oct. | 30 | 50 | 49 | 32 | 161 |
| 1979 | 31 | 52 | 49 | 77 | 209 |

SOURCE: Craig, *British Election Results, 1918–1975*, and the *Times Guide to the House of Commons*.

women M.P.s is the small number of women candidates. From 1918 to 1950 the numbers rose fairly steadily, but they then dropped sharply back and only reached their 1950 level again in 1974. In 1979 the number of women candidates was greater than ever before— twice as high as in 1970. But the figures are deceptive, for the number of women candidates put forward by the two major parties constitutes only 40.7 percent of all women candidates, and it is the minor parties, with virtually no chance of having a candidate elected, that nominate women most easily (see table 8–8).

The number of Conservative women candidates has progressed little over the years—three more women candidates in 1979 than in 1950, two fewer than in February 1974, and at no time more than a paltry thirty-three. Women have thus never made up more than 5.2 percent of all Conservative candidates.

Although the Labour party has consistently fielded more women candidates than the Conservative party, it has little reason to be proud of its record. The twenty-nine Labour women candidates in 1970 were the smallest number the party had fielded at a general election for forty-eight years. As a result the party headquarters made strenuous efforts to secure the election of more women candidates; the number rose to forty in February 1974, fifty in October 1974, and fifty-three in 1979.

**Efforts of the Headquarters.** This absence of candidates may at first seem surprising, for the national headquarters of both major parties reacted favorably toward women once they had become voters. The Conservatives invited women to sit on the executive of the National Unionist Association in the 1920s, and in 1930 the Countess of Iveagh became the first woman vice-chairman of the Conservative Party Organization. When the Labour party's constitution was revised in 1918 to admit individual members, the Women's Labour League, born in 1906, called on its members to join the party in their constituencies. Its branches became the first Women's Section, and Marion Phillips, its secretary, was appointed "chief woman officer of the party." At the same time a special women's section was created on the National Executive Committee (NEC). Five seats were reserved for women, nominated and elected by the whole party conference. The function of this section was to create a national representation for women at the decision-making level within an overwhelmingly masculine party. The very existence of this section was challenged in 1968 when the Simpson Committee on party organization sought to abolish it as "an anachronism" and to divide the seats between the unions (three seats) and the constituency Labour parties (two seats).[14]

Both party headquarters have sought to encourage women candidates, but to little avail. The real problem for both would seem to be a hiatus between the elite at party headquarters and the party activists. The central organizations have no direct say in candidate selection, and although they regularly urge constituency associations not to discriminate against women, they meet with little success. The prejudice in favor of women among the governing elites can be seen if we look at the upper house. Since the Life Peerage Act came into force in 1958, both parties have sought to nominate women—so that today they represent over 13 percent of all life peers. Thus, in a field where the elite has a relatively free hand, women are more fairly treated.

**Reticence of the Selectorate.** Within the constituencies things are otherwise. Not only are women seldom selected but they are very

---

14 "Report of the Committee of Enquiry into Party Organisation, 1968," appendix 11, *Labour Party Annual Conference Report*, 1968, pp. 362-80.

rarely nominated in safe seats.[15] In 1979 of the thirty-one Conservative women candidates, fourteen stood in safe Labour seats which they had not even an outside chance of winning. Only one candidate had what can be termed a safe Conservative seat: Margaret Thatcher in Barnet, Finchley. On the Labour side things were slightly better. There were women candidates in eight of the Labour party's safe seats. However, nineteen of the Labour women candidates stood in seats that were safely in the hands of a rival candidate.[16] Thus, women were selected for only eight (1.9 percent) of the 402 safe seats in Parliament. The Conservative record—one out of 191, or 0.5 percent—is particularly poor. Labour's score—8 out of 209, 3.8 percent—is far from spectacular. Four women incumbents in safe seats did not stand in the 1979 election, one Conservative[17] and three Labour.[18] For none of these four safe seats was a new woman candidate selected.

For the next general election, in the 1980s, things may well be different within the Labour party. In October 1980 the annual conference of the party is due to debate the mandatory inclusion of a woman and a manual worker in all lists of candidates to be interviewed by selection committees. The tying together of the two groups may well make it easier to obtain trade union backing. The Campaign for Labour Party Democracy is also campaigning for the NEC's women's section to be elected by the Labour Party Women's Conference. At present it is the male-dominated national conference that elects the women's section.

Why is it that the party activists who exercise their power in that secret garden of politics, candidate selection, are so wary of choosing women? Investigating selection committees in 1965, Austin Ranney found that it was often their very conception of women that led committees to offer them only unwinnable seats: "We noted the widespread belief that women do not make good candidates. That they are ineffective campaigners, weak association leaders, and unacceptable to the numerous voters who feel that women should tend to their families and stay out of politics and other kinds of men's

---

[15] We have considered "safe" the 402 out of the 635 seats listed as safe seats by the National Committee for Electoral Reform. The list was published in the *Daily Telegraph*, April 23, 1979.

[16] The safe Labour seats nominating women were Barking, Crewe, Eton and Slough, Sheffield, Brightside, Thurrock, West Bromwich West, and Wolverhampton North East. Of the nineteen seats safe for a rival, eighteen were held by a Conservative, one by a Liberal.

[17] Betty Harvis Anderson, Renfrewshire East.

[18] Joyce Butler, Wood Green; Barbara Castle, Blackburn; and Lena Jaeger, Holborn and St. Pancras South.

business."[19] This attitude is all the more surprising when one looks at the effective impact of a woman rather than a man candidate on the voters. In 1953, J.F.S. Ross formulated the women's handicap factor which serves to measure the average woman candidate's prospect of defeat compared with that of the average male candidate.[20] The formula is

$$\text{Woman's handicap} = \frac{\text{Women candidates} \times \text{men members}}{\text{Women members} \times \text{men candidates}}$$

The higher the figure the greater the handicap. When the score equals one there is no handicap; should it drop below one, this would signify a positive advantage for women and a handicap for men. Over the years the handicap factor diminished slowly but surely. In 1918 it was 7.5; in 1950, 2.1; and in 1970, 1.2.

The validity of the handicap factor was verified in 1974 when Michael Steed examined closely the thirty-nine cases where one of the parties put up a woman in February and a man in October or vice versa.[21] This was an ideal test situation because between the two elections there was no change in the election register. Steed showed that there was no sign that the sex of a candidate had any effect on voting except marginally among the Liberals. Liberal women did slightly (0.9 percentage points) worse when they succeeded men candidates than vice versa. Steed claimed that this unwillingness of some Liberal supporters to vote for a woman was also evident in the 1964, 1966, and 1970 elections.

The year 1979 has shown a reversal of the trend. The handicap factor shot up again to 1.8; even when only the major parties were taken into account it remained over 1.7. More detailed studies will be necessary to assess the causes of this new discrimination. The legislative stops and bars may have been removed, but those resulting from female stereotypes transmitted from the cradle, reinforced by family and school, no doubt remain.

### The Woman M.P.

The House of Commons is now under the command of a woman prime minister, but there are fewer women members than there have been at any time since 1951. Altogether only nineteen women were

[19] Austin Ranney, *Pathways to Parliament* (London: Macmillan, 1965), p. 138.

[20] J. F. S. Ross, "Women and Parliamentary Elections," *British Journal of Sociology*, vol. 4 (1953).

[21] In David Butler and Dennis Kavanagh, *The British General Election of 1974* (London: Macmillan, 1975).

returned to Parliament in 1979, eight fewer than in October 1974 (see table 8–9).

No Conservative woman M.P. lost her seat—the tide was running in the party's favor—but both Scottish Nationalist women were defeated,[22] as were five Labour women, headed by the former education secretary, Shirley Williams, in Hertford and Stevenage.[23] The Conservatives brought two new M.P.s into Parliament: Peggy Fenner, of Rochester and Chatham, who regained the seat she had lost in 1974, and Sheila Faith, Belper. Labour brought in one new woman, Sheila Wright, who kept for Labour John Lee's seat at Birmingham, Handsworth. Of the nineteen women M.P.s elected, eleven were Labour, eight Conservative.[24]

**Pathways to Parliament.** There have been three major pathways to Parliament for women: inheritance of a seat, victory at by-election, and victory at a general election. The process of inheritance has been called "male equivalence" since it occurs in a situation in which the woman "is considered to be acting primarily as a substitute for, as the equivalent to, a man."[25] The man in question is usually a husband or more rarely a father who has died or been elevated to the peerage. Lady Astor, Lady Iveagh, Lady Davidson, and Mrs. Hugh Dalton are all cases in point. This phenomenon has virtually disappeared. There is little doubt, however, that a political milieu, a spouse or parent willing to associate wife or daughter with political enterprises, helps a woman to eliminate the disadvantage of her sex. Several examples can be found in the present parliament; Shirley Summerskill is the daughter of a former woman M.P. and Labour minister, Edith Summerskill; and Gwyneth Dunwoody is the daughter of the party's former general secretary, Morgan Phillips.

By-elections between 1918 and October 1974 gave 20.1 percent of all successful women candidates their first victory. The phenomenon

---

[22] Winifred Ewing, Moray and Nairn, and Margaret Bain, Dunbartonshire East.

[23] The four other Labour women defeated were Maureen Colquhoun, Northampton North; Helene Hayman, Welwyn and Hatfield: Margaret Jackson, Lincoln; and Audrey Wise, Coventry South West.

[24] Conservative: Lynda Chalker (Wallasey); Sheila Faith (Belper); Peggy Fenner (Rochester and Chatham); Janet Fookes (Plymouth, Drake); Elaine Kellet-Bowman (Lancaster); Jill Knight (Birmingham, Edgbaston); Sally Oppenheim (Gloucester); Margaret Thatcher (Barnet, Finchley). Labour: Betty Boothroyd (West Bromwich, West); Gwyneth Dunwoody (Crewe); Judith Hart (Lanark); Joan Lestor (Eton and Slough); Joan Maynard (Sheffield, Brightside); Oonagh McDonald (Thurrock); Josephine Richardson (Barking); Shirley Summerskill (Halifax); Renee Short (Wolverhampton North East); Ann Taylor (Bolton West); Sheila Wright (Birmingham, Handsworth).

[25] Melville Currell, *Political Woman* (London: Croom Helm, 1974), p. 167.

## TABLE 8–9

### DISTRIBUTION OF WOMEN IN THE HOUSE OF COMMONS, BY PARTY, 1979

| Party | At Dissolution | | | After 1979 Election | | |
|---|---|---|---|---|---|---|
| | Number of women M.P.s | Total number of M.P.s | Percentage of women | Number of women M.P.s | Total number of M.P.s | Percentage of women |
| Conservative | 7 | 282 | 2.4 | 8 | 339 | 2.3 |
| Labour | 18 | 307 | 5.8 | 11 | 268 | 4.1 |
| Liberal | 0 | 14 | — | 0 | 11 | — |
| Plaid Cymru | 0 | 3 | — | 0 | 2 | — |
| Scottish National | 2 | 11 | 18.1 | 0 | 2 | — |
| Total | 27 | 635 | 4.2 | 19 | 635 | 2.9 |

SOURCE: Compiled by the author.

was more common on the Conservative side of the House: 24.3 percent of Conservative women M.P.s first came into the House at by-elections, as did over half of all third-party women representatives. Five out of the eight third-party women M.P.s in 1974 were first elected at by-elections. In the 1979 election, however, third-party women representatives completely disappeared, and of the nineteen major-party women elected, only two—both Labour M.P.s—had first entered the House at a by-election.[26]

Between 1918 and 1979, 109 different women were elected. Of these, 59 were Labour, 37 Conservative. The two major elections since the war from the women's point of view were the elections of 1945 and 1970. In 1945, 17 new Labour women M.P.s were returned, in 1970, 7 new Conservative M.P.s. Reluctantly we put forward the hypothesis that what the 1945 and 1970 general elections had in common was the unexpectedness of the victory, in 1945 for Labour, in 1970 for the Conservatives. What looked like a special effort in favor of women may simply be accounted for by the size of the swing.

**A Parliamentary Profile.** The nineteen women at present sitting in the House of Commons conform to the pattern set by women M.P.s since they first entered Parliament. They are middle-aged. Their average age on first election was just over forty (41.2 for the Conservatives, 41.0 for Labour). Only one woman—the Labour M.P. Ann Taylor—was elected before she was thirty. She was twenty-seven when she won her seat in Bolton in 1974. In the first fifty years of women's representation only two women under thirty entered Parliament: Jennie Lee at twenty-four and Megan Lloyd George at twenty-seven.[27] The two women elected for the first time in 1979 were both in their fifties (see table 8–10).

It has often been said that the women's group in Parliament is a blue-stocking preserve. The vast majority of the women M.P.s elected in 1979 conform to the image: twelve of the nineteen—63 percent—have been to university, a red-brick university much more frequently than Oxbridge. Two others have enjoyed other forms of further education. Their good educational background has usually given them solid middle-class occupations—teachers, barristers, doctors. Housewives are an exception, as they always have been.

Although it is middle-aged and middle class, the group is not staid or unimaginative. One of the striking things about them is the

[26] Betty Boothroyd in 1973, Oonagh McDonald in 1976.

[27] Jennie Lee was the wife of Labour minister Aneurin Bevan, and Megan Lloyd George was the daughter of the Liberal prime minister David Lloyd George.

TABLE 8–10

AGE DISTRIBUTION OF WOMEN M.P.s, 1959–1979

| Age Group | 1959 | 1964 | 1966 | 1970 | 1974 | 1979 |
|-----------|------|------|------|------|------|------|
| 20–30 | 0 | 0 | 0 | 1 | 3 | 0 |
| 31–40 | 2 | 5 | 4 | 4 | 5 | 2 |
| 41–50 | 7 | 7 | 8 | 8 | 11 | 6 |
| 51–60 | 13 | 9 | 8 | 9 | 6 | 11 |
| 61–70 | 3 | 7 | 4 | 3 | 2 | 0 |
| 71–80 | 0 | 0 | 2 | 1 | 0 | 0 |

SOURCE: Compiled by the author.

manner in which these women have combined multiple activities. On the Conservative side, one is a statistician company executive, another a dental surgeon and at the same time a director of the family fashion business, yet another is both barrister and farmer, and the prime minister herself is a research chemist turned barrister, doubly qualified. On the Labour side there are women who have combined membership in the national and European Parliaments, a village postmistress turned Labour agent, a medical practitioner and one-time manager of a group of London primary schools. The list is not exhaustive. It aims to show that women in the British Parliament are not only exceptions, they tend to be exceptional.

If women find it more difficult than men to enter Parliament, once they are in the House, their chances of promotion are considerably higher than those of men. Even in Mrs. Thatcher's Government, which is less favorable to women than was that of Harold Wilson or Edward Heath,[28] three of the eight Conservative women in the House hold office—Margaret Thatcher herself, Sally Oppenheim as minister of state for consumer affairs, and Lynda Chalker as undersecretary of state to health and social security.

Women have penetrated the inner circle of the cabinet more rarely. Ramsey McDonald gave the important post of minister of labor to Margaret Bondfield in 1929, but this was more of a freak occurrence than a breakthrough. The next woman cabinet member was appointed over fifteen years later in 1945, under another Labour Government. Not until 1953 was a woman given a seat in a Conservative cabinet. Including the present prime minister, only six women have ever had a seat in the cabinet. Until 1979 none of them

---

[28] Seven women were included in the 1964 Government, nine in the 1966 Government; under Edward Heath, five women M.P.s were in the Government.

had ever held a major post—no foreign secretary, no minister of defense, no home secretary, no chancellor of the exchequer. With Margaret Thatcher's accession to the post of prime minister the situation has changed little. She is the only woman in the cabinet.

## A Woman Prime Minister

The fact that Britain's new prime minister was a woman was almost as widely commented on throughout the world as the Conservatives' return to power. As Indira Gandhi noted when she cabled her congratulations, "Glad that Britain has caught up with Asia as regards women at the top."[29] Within Britain, former Prime Minister James Callaghan elegantly congratulated his successor: "It is a great office, a wonderful privilege, and for a woman to occupy that office is, I think, a tremendous moment in the country's history. Therefore, everybody must on behalf of all our people wish her well and wish her success in the great responsibilities that now fall to her."[30] The *Daily Mail* headlined its editorial "The woman who played a man's game . . . and won" and claimed that Thatcher "was blasted by force of popular vote triumphantly through the ultimate political sex barrier."[31]

But who is Margaret Thatcher? What effect, if any, did the fact of her being a woman have on the election campaign and on the results?

**Background.** Ridiculed by Denis Healey as "La Pasionaria of privilege," Hilda Margaret Roberts was in fact born in a two-room flat over her father's grocery store in Grantham, a small town in Lincolnshire. Her father, son and grandson of rural shoemakers, had left school at thirteen, taken a job in the grocery trade, become a manager, and finally bought a grocery business. He was a lay preacher, a magistrate, and a Rotarian, sat on the town council as an independent, and became mayor of Grantham in 1945. Her mother was the daughter of a railway worker, trained as a dressmaker, working from home. Margaret Roberts won a scholarship to the local grammar school, and from there went up to Oxford, where she read chemistry and became an active member of the Oxford University Conservative Association. After graduating from Oxford, Margaret Roberts worked as an industrial chemist for several years. At twenty-six she married

---

[29] *Guardian*, May 5, 1979.
[30] *Daily Telegraph*, May 5, 1979.
[31] *Daily Mail*, May 5, 1979.

Denis Thatcher, owner of a local paint firm, Atlas Preservatives, which he sold to Castrol for a reported £530,000 in 1965.

In 1951, Margaret Thatcher decided to change course and began to read for the bar. She was called at Lincoln's Inn in 1953. In 1957 she was adopted as Conservative candidate for the North London suburb of Finchley and was elected in 1959.

Her ministerial experience prior to her premiership was narrow. She had served as a junior minister under Harold Macmillan at pensions and had been education secretary with a seat in the cabinet for the four years of the Heath administration, from 1970 to 1974. In the autumn of 1974 she formed with Sir Keith Joseph the Centre for Policy Studies with its stress on Adam Smith, the market economy, and monetarism. She was not an agitator in the backbench rebellion against Edward Heath in 1975 and had no truck with the Heath-must-go brigade. However, when he stood for reelection she stood against him—a courageous action which few thought would turn out as it did. On the first ballot for the leadership, Heath obtained 130 votes to her 119, and on the second ballot she topped the poll with 146 votes to William Whitelaw's 79.[32]

**A Conviction Politician.** Her rise to leadership showed independence of judgment, courage, and deep ideological commitment. Margaret Thatcher presents herself as a conviction politician, and she is not by temperament conciliatory. Hostility toward her crystallizes around the rather unfair image of a middle-class suburbanite, wearing silly hats and sporting out-of-date right-wing views. In fact she has strong moral principles she is not afraid to air and a deep commitment to save Britain from becoming a corporate state, to halt what she sees as the ever-increasing encroachment of the public sector. The historian Lord Blake, provost of Queen's College, Oxford, declared shortly before the election, "There is a wind of change in Britain and in much of the democratic world and it comes from the right not the left." It is on that wind of change that Margaret Thatcher swept into Downing Street.

**Images.** During the campaign the Conservatives strove to make their leader better known to the public. At the same time her media director, former television producer Gordon Reece, controlled her delivery and planned her campaign. In terms of publicity, Margaret Thatcher

---

[32] The first ballot took place on February 4; Hugh Fraser polled eleven votes. The second ballot took place on February 11; Sir Geoffrey Howe polled nineteen votes, John Payton eleven.

was an unknown quantity with, some believed, the built-in disadvantage of being a woman.

The result was a two-sided image of the Conservative leader. One side was a softly modulated, carefully prepared, visibly rehearsed leader who did not refuse the odd gimmick in front of the cameras—sitting in a damp field with a calf in her arms, packing chocolates in a factory, or using a sewing machine. All meetings were for ticket holders only, no question and answer sessions were held after speeches, and she maintained her refusal to meet James Callaghan in a television debate. The press undertook a searching examination of the way Thatcher looked and talked. Her hair and clothes were discussed as only a woman's are in the male-dominated world of politics. None commented on amiable Jim's shambling gait, or on his suits and ties. In fact there was no call for the anxiety her campaign team showed. She did not lose her voice despite the grueling it was given, and whenever she was allowed to be herself—as she necessarily was when she toured innumerable precincts on her walk-abouts, answering off-the-cuff questions with great aplomb—a more convincing, more natural Margaret Thatcher came to the fore.

The impact of campaigns is always difficult to gauge, but the NOP and MORI polls both show that as the campaign advanced, although James Callaghan kept clearly ahead of Margaret Thatcher on the question, "Who would make the better Prime Minister?" the gap between them closed. It is therefore a little harsh to suggest as some commentators have that the Conservatives won in spite of their leader rather than because of her.

To a certain extent Margaret Thatcher was protected from her rivals because she was a woman. Misogyny was at best a secret weapon. Attacks might be perceived as sexist rather than political. As Harold Wilson said in an interview published in the *Daily Mail*, "Jim's been absolutely right in forbidding personal attacks. You see, while she might put off some people from voting for her there are others who will vote for her because they just want to see a woman succeed." And he added, "I can see the force of that argument: it's just because she is a woman that my wife would vote for her."[33]

A MORI poll set out to study whether or not there was a sizable misogynist vote.[34] It showed that in fact Margaret Thatcher had overcome a considerable bias against having women in positions of authority. A male prime minister was preferred by 52 percent, a female by 16 percent, and 29 percent said it would make no difference. How-

---

[33] *Daily Mail*, April 27, 1979.
[34] *Economist*, April 28, 1979.

ever, further probing showed that the real reasons why Mrs. Thatcher lagged behind Callaghan were factors such as inexperience and extremism—which owed more to her politics than to her sex.

## Conclusion

The extension of the franchise to women has certainly not resulted in their arriving in droves at Westminster, as some of the opponents of the vote for women believed it would. Likewise the arrival of a woman prime minister has not filled the cabinet or the House with women. The 1979 election saw a woman prime minister elected for the first time, yet the number of women in the House is smaller than in recent years, the handicap is greater, the number of women in the cabinet has not increased, and the women's charter elaborated by the feminists in 1968, with its claim for equal rights, is less likely to be fully implemented than was the case in the 1970s. From the women's point of view, the election can be summed up as a stride forward and several small steps back.

# 9

# Why the Conservatives Won

## Ivor Crewe

A satisfactory explanation of the 1979 election result has to account for four distinct yet slightly contradictory features of the Conservatives' victory.[1] On the one hand, the win was thoroughly decisive. Their lead in votes over Labour was the largest enjoyed by one party over the other since 1935; their lead in the share of the poll, the largest since 1945. The national swing of 5.2 percentage points which produced it was the most emphatic turnaround of party fortunes since the war. Thus the chance and fleeting incidents which sometimes determine close-run contests can hardly be held responsible on this occasion. To account for the exceptional shift in the electorate's allegiance one must look for matching changes in its political outlook.

On the other hand, the Conservatives' triumph was qualified in three ways. First, it owed more to an exceptionally low Labour vote—at 36.9 percent, the party's lowest since their debacle in 1931—than to an unusually high Conservative one. The Conservative share of the vote, although up from 35.9 percent to 43.9 percent, was well below that obtained at their earlier postwar victories in 1970 (46.4 percent) or in the 1950s (49.0 percent, on average). Thus the question to answer is not only Why did the Conservatives win? but also Why

I am grateful to Hugh Berrington, John Buchel, and Peter Pulzer for their useful comments on the original draft of this chapter.

[1] This chapter is based on an analysis of the campaign polls, in particular a Gallup survey designed by the author and conducted on the eve and day of polling (May 2 and 3) for BBC television. The *Economist* of May 12, 1979, carried a summary of the results (pp. 25-26) based on the author's preliminary report, from which one or two passages in this chapter are taken. The Gallup survey should not be confused with the British Election Study's panel survey, which was not available for analysis at the time of writing. Its findings will be reported in *The Conservative Victory of 1979* (Cambridge University Press, forthcoming).

did Labour lose—and lose so badly? Second, by postwar standards the movement to the Conservatives was exceptionally uneven, both between and within regions. The Midlands and the South moved strongly to the Conservatives, especially in the more prosperous working-class suburbs of London and Birmingham, in the new towns, and in other areas of economic expansion.[2] But the North was more cautious, notably in the big cities and in areas of economic decline, where the swing would not have put the Conservatives in office. And in Scotland the swing to the Conservatives was under one percentage point. An adequate explanation of Labour's downfall must be consistent with these variations. Third, the Conservatives won despite the election campaign, not because of it. Their lead over Labour in the polls narrowed from an average of 11.9 points at the start of the campaign (March 28–April 4) to 7.2 points by May 2 and 3. For a complete account of the Conservatives' victory, therefore, one must look beyond the five-week campaign period.

To most observers where to look is patently obvious: the explosion of strikes in January and February 1979. Figure 9–1 charts the devastating impact they had on the Government's electoral standing. In the last quarter of 1978, according to the monthly Gallup polls, the two parties were running neck and neck, but with Labour a nose in front (by an average of 1.7 points). Labour enjoyed the additional advantage of having by far the more popular leader: 54 percent said they were satisfied with Callaghan, whereas only 37 percent said the same of Thatcher. By February 1979 the position had been transformed. The Conservatives had jumped into an 18-point lead and approval of the Government's overall record had plummeted from 41 percent to 23 percent. Satisfaction with Callaghan had tumbled to 33 percent while satisfaction with Thatcher had risen to 48 percent. In its forty years of polling Gallup had never recorded such a sharp reversal of party fortunes in the space of two months. And there could be no doubt about the cause: in the final quarter of 1978 the proportion of respondents mentioning strikes as the single most urgent problem facing the country was a modest 14 percent; by February 1979 it had soared to 51 percent.

Major strikes rarely win the sympathy of the general public and usually result in temporary unpopularity for the party in office, especially when that party has long had close ties with the trade union

---

[2] A detailed analysis of interregional and intraregional variations in the swing can be found in "Two Nations—North and South," *Economist*, May 12, 1979, p. 21, and Ivor Crewe, "The Voting Surveyed," *The Times Guide to the House of Commons May 1979* (London: Times Books, 1979), pp. 249-54; see also pp. 258-69.

FIGURE 9–1

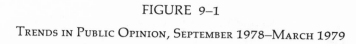

TRENDS IN PUBLIC OPINION, SEPTEMBER 1978–MARCH 1979

Percentage Points

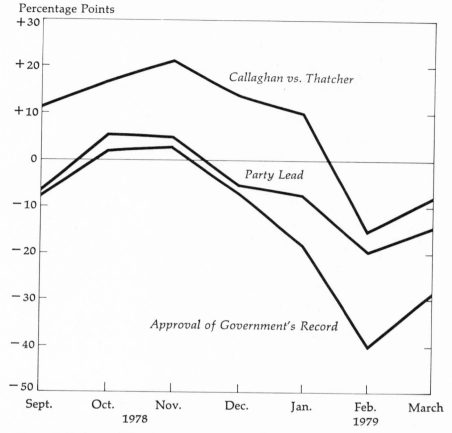

NOTE: *Callaghan vs. Thatcher:* % satisfied with Callaghan *minus* % satisfied with Thatcher.

*Party Lead in Polls:* % intending to vote Labour *minus* % intending to vote Conservative (including "leaners" but excluding "don't knows" from the percentage base).

*Approval of Government's Record:* % approving *minus* % disapproving of "the Government's record to date."

SOURCE: Monthly Gallup polls, as reported in the monthly *Gallup Political Index*, nos. 218-225 (London: Social Surveys [Gallup Poll] Ltd., 1978-1979).

movement, as the Labour party has had. But many strikes have badly inconvenienced the public in the past without the Government, even a Labour one, suffering such an electoral drubbing as a consequence. Why was the damage to Labour's standing so dramatic this time? One reason was that so many strikes coincided: the petrol tank drivers', the lorry drivers', the engine drivers', the various groups of local authority workers', and in some regions like the North West, the bus drivers' and water workers' as well. Another reason was the extent of the disruption of people's day-to-day existence: people had difficulty getting to or from work because petrol was unavailable or the buses or trains were not running; they could not find basic items in the shops because the lorry drivers were not delivering them; their dustbins went unemptied while the refuse collectors were on strike; their children's schools closed down for lack of caretakers.

But these factors are not the whole story. The strikes were also marked by two other unusual features: the vehemence, bordering on violence, of some of the picketing; and, often as a consequence, what appeared to be malicious disregard for the safety and health of the ordinary public. The local authorities' road maintenance men refused to grit the roads, which had been made dangerously icy by an unusually cold spell. More serious, if somebody had an accident there might be no ambulance to take him to hospital because drivers were on strike, in some areas refusing to deal even with emergency calls. If he reached the hospital gates under his own steam he might be turned away by pickets of hospital porters or ambulance men. If he got into the hospital there would be no porters to ferry him to the operating theater, nor laundry staff to clean his bed linen. And if he died, there might be nobody to dig his grave, because the cemetery workers too were on strike. This unusual fierceness and nastiness, moreover, was vividly communicated to the public day after day in the newspapers and on television: the shortages in the supermarkets, the turning away of ambulances, and the unburied dead were "gift" stories for the media. As one moderate Labour M.P., Kenneth Weetch, put it, "one felt the ground slipping from under one's feet." But why was public anger with the strikers, and perhaps the trade unions generally, also aimed at the Government? The fact that Labour happened to be in office and was associated with the trade union movement was not the only reason. Labour had won the two 1974 general elections partly on the claim that it was politically and temperamentally better equipped to obtain the cooperation of trade unions. Until late 1978 there was substance to the claim: industrial relations under Edward Heath's Conservative Government of 1970–1974 had deteriorated badly, culminating in the miners' strike and the February 1974 election itself, whereas between July 1975 and October 1978 the Labour Government's "social contract" with the trade unions had secured a considerable reduction in industrial stoppages and in the size of wage settlements.

But the winter's strikes destroyed the Labour party's slowly accumulated credibility as the only party to handle industrial relations. Despite its much-vaunted special relationship with the trade unions, it could not persuade their leaders to call off the strikes, or even to modify the vigor with which they were being pursued.[3] In the meantime Mrs. Thatcher was proposing legal reforms—including state-financed but compulsory postal ballots for the election of union officials and for decisions on strike calls, the prohibition of secondary picketing, and the taxing of social security benefits paid out to strikers' families—all measures opposed by the Government but, according to the polls, supported by the vast majority of the electorate.[4] The ground appeared to be slipping under the Government's feet too.

The obvious is no less true for being obvious. The "winter of discontent" made it much more difficult for Labour to win the election, certainly more difficult than it would have been had Callaghan chosen to go to the country in the previous October. Although the Conservatives' lead over Labour, and Thatcher's over Callaghan, was already narrowing in the March polls (see figure 9–1), Labour failed to recover all the ground it had lost. Many previously undecided voters must have finally made up their minds to defect from Labour or to the Conservatives as a result of the strikes, although we shall never know the exact number. Callaghan's decision—and it was very much his own—to postpone the election till the spring of 1979 turned out to be a blunder.

However, this does not necessarily mean that Labour would have won an election in October 1978. One Transport House official wryly suggested that Labour's campaign slogan should be "Vote As You Would Have Done in October," but it is by no means certain that this would have ensured Labour's reelection. The evidence points in both directions. On the one hand, in October 1978 Labour was given a four to five percentage-point lead in both the Gallup and NOP polls, and Callaghan was far more popular than Thatcher (or, for that matter, than Wilson in October 1974). On the other hand, Labour never

---

[3] This was not so much because the Government carried little weight with union leaders, but because union leaders in turn appeared to carry little with their own members. The resulting impression of a general loss of control and authority in society also damaged the Government's standing.

[4] See the MORI poll for the *Daily Express*, February 1979. Eighty-nine percent agreed that "no strikes should be called until there is a postal ballot of union members concerned"; 89 percent that there should be "a ban on secondary picketing: that is a ban on picketing a company not directly involved in a strike"; and 65 percent agreed that "social security benefits paid to strikers' families should be subject to income tax." The proportions of trade union members who agreed were almost as overwhelming—91 percent, 86 percent, and 57 percent respectively.

managed to sustain a commanding or consistent lead in the polls. Moreover, by October public confidence in the economic future—for long a reliable barometer of imminent changes in the electoral climate —was clearly slipping. In the first two quarters of 1978 the proportions expecting to see an improvement over the coming year were 44 percent and 36 percent respectively; by the third quarter the figure had fallen to 29 percent and by the fourth to 20 percent. Most important of all, throughout 1978 the by-election results were persistently contradicting the polls. While the monthly Gallup polls were indicating a swing of 2.6 points to the Conservatives since the previous general election (insufficient to guarantee them office), the average by-election swing to the Conservatives (outside Scotland)[5] was 7.2 points, enough to provide them a three-digit parliamentary majority. At the Pontefract and Castleford by-election in October 1978 the swing to the Conservatives was 7.8 points.[6] One can safely conclude, therefore, that Labour had a better chance of winning in October 1978 than in May 1979—but no more than that.

Nor should one assume that the winter's strikes made it impossible for Labour to win in May. To be sure, the Conservatives entered the campaign in late March with an average lead of 11.9 percentage points in the polls, much of it the after-effect of the strikes. But the Conservatives in February 1974 and Labour in June 1970 had enjoyed similar leads during the election campaign, only to lose in the end.[7] Moreover, already by late March strikes had slipped well behind prices as the most important issue for electors, and by late April they had also fallen behind unemployment. Furthermore, it would be simplistic to suggest that Labour lost merely because it was forced to go to the

---

[5] In 1978 Labour did markedly better in the three by-elections in Scotland (where the mean swing to the Conservatives was only 1.6 points) than elsewhere. The major reason was almost certainly the decline of SNP support, to Labour's net benefit. The pattern was repeated at the general election.

[6] It is true that these by-election results will have included an anti-Government protest vote which could be expected to disappear at a general election. But examination of earlier by-elections held only a few months before a general election suggests that, at least since the late 1950s, this protest vote will have accounted for only two to three percentage points in the overall by-election swing. That would still leave a "real" swing to the Conservatives of between 5 and 6 percentage points—very close, in fact, to the 5.2 points that occurred at the election.

[7] A week before the 1970 election Labour's average lead was 7.1 points, but the Conservatives won the election by 2.4 points. A week before the February 1974 election the Conservatives' average lead was 5.4 points; the Conservative lead in the popular vote at that election was 0.8 points (and Labour won more seats). See David Butler and Michael Pinto-Duschinsky, *The British General Election of 1970* (London: Macmillan, 1971), p. 178, and David Butler and Dennis Kavanagh, *The British General Election of February 1974* (London: Macmillan, 1974), p. 95.

country before it had had sufficient time to regain the ground lost in the winter. For that argument to be convincing we would expect a consistent closing of the Conservative lead *throughout* the campaign. But that did not happen. The Conservatives' lead did gradually narrow in the third and fourth weeks of the campaign, dropping to three to four points by the last Friday; but it widened again to seven points in the final week. The abnormally long campaign period, deliberately arranged by Callaghan for the purpose of regaining lost ground, did not prove to be the advantage he assumed; had the election been held a week earlier the Conservative majority would probably have been smaller, perhaps insufficient to secure it office for a full five years. The final week of the campaign was therefore crucial to the Conservatives' victory and, as we shall see later, went the Conservatives' way for reasons other than the winter's strikes.

Without underestimating the undoubted importance of the strikes, therefore, we need to examine the campaign itself to obtain a complete explanation of the Conservative win. Two important possible factors can be eliminated straightaway: the party organization and the party leaders.

## Organization and Publicity

The Conservative party's organization has always been stronger than Labour's. It employs more headquarters and research staff, its constituency associations have a larger and more active membership, and both locally and nationally it is better funded. In close-run elections these advantages can be crucial. They have enabled the Conservatives to win up to a dozen seats at each election simply through more efficient mobilization of the postal vote. In the October 1974 election one reason for Labour's unexpectedly tiny majority (three seats) was the below-average swing to Labour in Conservative-held marginals, part of which has been attributed to superior organization. In 1979 the superior strength of Conservative party organization was particularly apparent. Their full-time constituency agents outnumbered Labour's by 346 to 70; they also had much more money. Reliable figures are not available but they are reputed to have spent at least five times as much as Labour on billboard posters, press advertising, and television broadcasts. Advertising and publicity were handled by Saatchi and Saatchi, a company with a reputation in the public relations world for talent, innovation, and boldness. By contrast Labour not only had less money to spend, but had to rely on the unpaid services of an informal group of party sympathizers drawn from the worlds of advertising and the media. In addition to these traditional

269

## TABLE 9–1

CONSERVATIVE AND LABOUR CAMPAIGNING: SIZE OF IMPACT

(percent)

| Question | Yes, a Conservative One | Yes, a Labour One |
|---|---|---|
| During the past few weeks have you . . . | | |
| . . . seen any party political broadcasts on TV? | 86 | 87 |
| . . . heard any party political broadcasts on radio? | 20 | 19 |
| . . . seen any political advertisements on billboards? | 32 | 29 |
| . . . had any political leaflets put through your letter box? | 88 | 87 |
| . . . been called on by a representative of any political party? | 28 | 23 |

SOURCE: MORI postelection re-call survey for *Sunday Times*, May 4–5, 1979 (N = 833). For the full set of findings, see MORI, *British Public Opinion, General Election 1979*, Final Report, p. 66.

advantages, the Conservative party was more willing to exploit modern advertising techniques. The Conservative Central Office was more prepared than Transport House to relinquish control over matters of design and presentation to the advertising and media experts; and whereas Thatcher was ready to follow the advice of her public relations consultants on such personal details as the style of her hair and pitch of her voice, Callaghan steadfastly refused to do so.

The evidence from the polls, however, suggests that in the end the Conservatives' financial and organizational superiority made little difference. If the impact on the vote was to their advantage, it could only have been by the slightest fraction. Table 9–1 shows that the size of each party's impact on the electorate was very similar. In a MORI panel survey, equal proportions claimed to have watched a Conservative or Labour broadcast on television (86 percent to 87 percent), to have heard a Conservative or Labour radio program (20 percent to 19 percent), and to have read a Conservative or Labour election address (88 percent to 87 percent). The Conservatives' poster blitzkrieg both before and during the campaign appears to have been a poor investment: only a fraction more had noticed a Conservative rather than Labour hoarding. Similarly, the larger membership of the local Conservative parties appears to have paid only a modest dividend: 28 percent remembered being called upon by a Conservative party worker, 23 percent by a Labour party worker (Gallup's figures were 28 percent and 24 percent). Moreover, both surveys found that Labour out-canvassed the Conservatives in its own marginal seats.[8] The fact that the swing to the Conservatives in Labour marginals was below average also suggests that where it was most essential Labour's ground organization was not noticeably weaker than the Conservatives'.[9]

The number of electors reached, however, is only one test of the effectiveness of organization and publicity. A second and more important test is the number who voted differently as a result. The BBC's election-day survey (see table 9–2) suggests that the number was negligible in the case of posters (2 percent) and canvassing (3 percent) and only slightly less so in the case of "party politicals"—the Conservative, Labour, and Liberal party television broadcasts (7, 6, and 4 percent respectively). Even these figures, moreover, exaggerate the number of genuine converts, since a substantial proportion of those claiming to have been influenced in these ways will have been strongly predisposed toward the party they voted for. Thus the *net* advantage to any party must have been minute.

Not surprisingly, the minorities claiming to have decided how to vote only during the campaign (14 percent) or in the last few days (12 percent) were the most likely to cite canvassing or publicity as a factor. Only amongst these voters can one discern the possibility that Conservative party advertising, especially Mrs. Thatcher's final "party political," brought a small net benefit. Two sets of figures provide the clues (see table 9–3). First, amongst the 87 respondents in the BBC survey (4.1 percent of the total) who plumped for the Conservatives in the last few days, 39 claimed to have been attracted by a Conservative broadcast or put off by a Labour broadcast. But amongst the 70 respondents (3.3 percent) plumping for Labour at the last moment, only 13 mentioned either party's television broadcasts as a reason. Second, of the 153 respondents who cited a Conservative party political as an influence on their vote, 59 were Conservative "recruits" and only 7 Conservative "defectors," a net gain of 52. But of the 126

---

[8] By 38 to 35 percent according to the Gallup survey of April 30–May 1; by 43 to 41 percent according to MORI's postelection re-call survey. Gallup data refer to Labour marginals (up to 10 percent majority in October 1974), MORI data to all marginals.

[9] A uniform 5.2 point swing would have transferred sixty-four seats from Labour to Conservative; Labour saved twenty-one of them (although it lost another twelve vulnerable to higher swings).

## TABLE 9–2
### THE CAMPAIGN'S EFFECT ON VOTE CHOICE
(percent)

| Reason for Vote Choice | All Voters | Conservative Voters | Labour Voters | Liberal Voters |
|---|---|---|---|---|
| I was persuaded by a party worker who canvassed me. | 3 | 3 | 3 | 3 |
| Because of a Conservative newspaper advert/poster I saw. | 1 | 2 | — | — |
| Because of a Labour newspaper advert/poster I saw. | 1 | 1 | 1 | — |
| Because of a Conservative broadcast on TV. | 7 | 13 | 3 | 4 |
| Because of a Labour broadcast on TV. | 6 | 3 | 12 | 3 |
| Because of a Liberal broadcast on TV. | 4 | — | 1 | 29 |
| N | (2,117) | (884) | (735) | (261) |

Dash (—): less than 0.5 percent.
SURVEY QUESTION: "When you finally decided which way to vote, was it for one or more of the reasons on this card?"
SOURCE: BBC Gallup survey, May 2-3, 1979 (N = 2,435).

respondents claiming to have been influenced by a Labour party political, the net gain to Labour was only 19 (22 recruits and 3 defectors). The inference to be drawn from these figures, however, should not be exaggerated. On the most unlikely assumption that all the respondents claiming to have been influenced by the party politicals were genuine converts, the net advantage to the Conservatives amounts to less than 1.5 percent of the sample. This is well below the swing required to bring the Conservatives to office, although enough to increase the Conservatives' parliamentary majority from precarious (as it might have been had the election been a week earlier) to comfortable (as it turned out to be). Moreover, there is a final qualification to make. The Liberal party's television broadcasts appear to have had an even greater impact than the Conservatives'. Of the 67 "late Liberals," 36 (53 percent) cited the Liberals' party political; of the 85 who claimed to have been influenced by a Liberal

## TABLE 9–3

### Partisan Impact of the Three Parties' TV Broadcasts

I. *Among voters who decided how to vote in the last few days*

| Final Decision Influenced by: | Voted Conservative | Voted Labour | Voted Liberal |
|---|---|---|---|
| Conservative TV broadcast | 29 | 6 | 5 |
| Labour TV broadcast | 10 | 7 | 2 |
| Liberal TV broadcast | 1 | 0 | 36 |
| Total | 40 | 13 | 43 |
| Percent | 46% | 19% | 64% |
| N | (87) | (70) | (67) |

II. *Among voters who said they had been influenced by a TV broadcast*

| Voter Group [a] | Conservative Broadcast | Labour Broadcast | Liberal Broadcast |
|---|---|---|---|
| Loyalists | 87 | 101 | 40 |
| Recruits | 59 | 22 | 45 |
| Defectors | 7 | 3 | 0 |
| Net gain [b] | 52 | 19 | 45 |
| Percent gain | 34% | 16% | 53% |
| N | (153) | (126) | (85) |

[a] Conservative loyalists, recruits, and defectors in the case of those watching Conservative broadcasts; Labour loyalists, recruits, and defectors in the case of those watching Labour broadcasts; and so on. Respondents fitting none of these categories, such as Labour loyalists who watched a Conservative broadcast, have been excluded from the analysis.

[b] Recruits minus defectors.

SOURCE: BBC Gallup survey, May 2-3, 1979.

party political, none were Liberal defectors and 45 were Liberal recruits. But the impecunious Liberal party could not afford a public relations company. To conclude that the party politicals made a difference is one thing, therefore; to conclude that Saatchi and Saatchi did is quite another.

## The Party Leaders

Had the electorate been asked to choose a prime minister, Callaghan would still be in 10 Downing Street. All the polls reported the same pattern (see figure 9–2). Already at the start of the campaign Cal-

FIGURE 9–2

PREFERENCE FOR PRIME MINISTER, APRIL 6–MAY 3, 1979

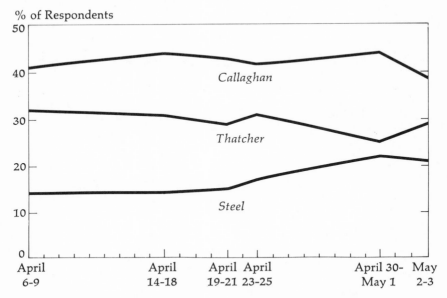

NOTE: Respondents were asked, "Who would make the better prime minister: Mr. Callaghan, Mrs. Thatcher, or Mr. Steel?" Percentages do not total 100 because "don't knows" have been excluded. The phrase "best prime minister" was used in the BBC TV survey on May 2-3.

SOURCE: Gallup surveys for *Daily Telegraph* and BBC TV (May 2-3).

laghan was the more popular choice for prime minister. His lead over Thatcher steadily increased as the campaign progressed, only to be cut back sharply to almost its original level in the last few days. According to Gallup, for example, Callaghan's percentage lead over Thatcher was 41 to 32 on April 6–9, rose to 44 to 25 by April 30–May 1, but fell to 39 to 29 by May 2–3. According to NOP, Callaghan's lead was 41 to 35 on April 2–3, an astonishing 57 to 33 on April 28–30, but only 49 to 40 by May 1–2. Mrs. Thatcher's narrowing of the gap in the final few days parallels the late surge of Conservative support, although whether as cause or consequence is impossible to establish.

How, then, did the Conservatives win in spite of Mrs. Thatcher? The main reason is that, despite television's concentration of coverage on party leaders, British general elections are very different from American presidential primary elections. The purpose of general elections is not primarily to choose a party leader to become prime minister, but to choose a party to form the Government. More important, the British electorate tends to vote according to what a party represents rather than who represents the party. In answer to the question, "When you decide which way to vote, what will influence you more— the parties' leaders or the parties' policies?" 13 percent replied "both equally," 11 percent said "leaders," and 71 percent said "policies" (MORI, April 1979). In contrast to their American counterparts, British voters, if forced to choose between leader and party, tend to abandon the leader, as the well-liked Harold Wilson discovered in 1970 and the overwhelmingly popular Winston Churchill found out in 1945.[10]

But it is also possible that the party leaders' popularity scores give a misleading impression of their respective capacities to win votes. The figures cited above express their *relative* not their *absolute* popularity: the fact that electors preferred Callaghan to Thatcher as a prime minister does not mean that those who chose Callaghan actually disliked Thatcher. An examination of poll questions which did not force respondents to choose between the two party leaders suggests that Thatcher was not particularly unpopular. For example, in March 1979, shortly before the election campaign, in answer to two separate questions, more people said Mrs. Thatcher was "proving a good leader of the Conservative Party" (47 percent) than were "satisfied with Mr. Callaghan as Prime Minister" (39 percent). Moreover, the public thought better of Margaret Thatcher than Ted Heath, contrary to the common assumption in the media, which often bracketed the two together in personality—and unpopularity. When Heath was leader of the Opposition the proportion considering him a "good leader of the Conservative party" averaged out at 33 percent over the period July 1966–December 1969; for Thatcher the figure for July 1975–December 1978 was 40 percent.[11]

One other feature of the public's attitude to Mrs. Thatcher should be mentioned. During the campaign the polls reported that Callaghan was better liked in most respects—but not all. He was

---

[10] In the Gallup survey for the BBC, seventy-two respondents (3.8 percent), in answer to separate questions, preferred Labour leaders but Conservative policies; of these, fifty-three voted Conservative, only six Labour. Eighty-nine (4.4 percent) preferred Labour leaders but thought of the Conservatives as "best for people like themselves"; of these, fifty-six voted Conservative and only eleven Labour.

[11] The contrast is more impressive than it looks, because Heath led a more popular Conservative Opposition, and Wilson a less popular Labour Government, than their successors. According to the monthly Gallup polls from July 1966 to December 1969, Heath was running an average of 7.4 points *behind* his party, whereas from July 1975 to December 1978 Thatcher was running an average of 2.0 points *ahead* of hers.

TABLE 9–4

WHAT OCTOBER 1974 ELECTORS DID IN 1979

(percent)

| Vote, May 1979 | Recalled Vote, October 1974 | | | | | |
| --- | --- | --- | --- | --- | --- | --- |
| | Con. | Lab. | Lib. | Other | Did not vote | Too young |
| Conservative | 87 | 11 | 32 | 11 | 29 | 30 |
| Labour | 4 | 75 | 10 | 13 | 27 | 29 |
| Liberal | 6 | 10 | 52 | 9 | 7 | 11 |
| Other | — | 1 | 1 | 62 | 2 | 5 |
| Did not vote | 3 | 3 | 5 | 4 | 34 | 26 |
| Total | 100 | 100 | 100 | 100 | 100 | 100 |
| N | (772) | (834) | (211) | (50) | (267) | (213) |

NOTE: Columns may not add to totals because of rounding. Votes in October 1974 are reported as recalled in May 1979.
SOURCE: BBC Gallup survey, May 2-3, 1979.

considered to be, *inter alia,* the more honest and trustworthy, the more capable and experienced, the more down to earth and in touch with ordinary people, the more moderate, and better able to lead the country as a whole. But in one respect the polls gave Mrs. Thatcher a clear edge: "strength of personality."[12] Quite what the public understood by this is difficult to know, but it probably included determination and toughness, and these qualities may well have been projected onto the party she led.

### The Flow of the Vote

To explain the 5.2 percentage point swing to the Conservatives a more rewarding approach is to ask, Who swung? Table 9–4 displays the flow of the vote from party to party between October 1974 and 1979. There is one caveat to enter about the table: it is based not on panel data, but on respondents' *recall* of their vote five years earlier in 1974.

[12] An NOP poll on April 21-23 found that Thatcher led Callaghan by five points as a "strong personality" (and by ten points three weeks earlier) even though she trailed him on ten of the other eleven attributes on which respondents were asked to judge. A MORI poll on April 18 reported six points more respondents willing to describe Thatcher than Callaghan as someone who "has got a lot of personality." See NOP, *Political, Social & Economic Review,* vol. 19 (June 1979), p. 16; and MORI, *British Public Opinion, General Election 1979,* Final Report, p. 84.

Recall data are subject to well-known biases, such as the underestimation of previous abstention or Liberal support and the projection of current party preference onto past party preference.

There were five ways in which electors could have changed their vote between the two elections to produce a Conservative victory:

1. *Straight switching*: more defections from Labour to Conservative than vice versa.
2. *The two-way traffic of Liberals*: more former Liberals defecting to the Conservatives than to Labour and/or more Liberal recruits among Labour than Conservative defectors.
3. *Differential abstention*: more former Labour than former Conservative voters deciding to abstain.
4. *Differential turnout*: more October 1974 nonvoters turning out this time for the Conservatives than for Labour.
5. *The physical change of the electorate*: more deaths (or emigration) amongst previous Labour than Conservative voters, or a Conservative majority amongst those entering the electorate for the first time (through coming of age or immgration).

Preliminary analysis[13] of the vote-flow table shows that the crucial components of the swing were straight switching and Liberal traffic (see table 9–4). About half can be attributed to the first: 11 percent of October 1974 Labour voters crossed over directly to the Conservatives, whereas only 4 percent of October 1974 Conservatives moved in the opposite direction. Much of the rest of the swing came from the Liberal two-way traffic. About half the October 1974 Liberals defected, splitting three-to-one in the Conservatives' favor. At the same time the Liberals attracted over twice as many ex-Labour (10 percent) as ex-Conservative voters (6 percent). But apathy amongst Labour supporters—the traditional lament of Labour officials when elections are lost—was not a factor. There was a similar abstention rate amongst former Labour and Conservative voters, and the turnout of previous abstainers only helped the Conservatives by a whisker. It is impossible to put a precise estimate on the partisan impact of the physical turnover in the electorate. However, first-time voters were evenly split between the two parties, whereas there were almost certainly more Conservative than Labour supporters among those

---

[13] The analysis is preliminary because table 9-4 does not incorporate the impact of immigration and emigration or estimate the October 1974 vote of those who have since died. In addition, it does not adjust the cell entries to ensure that both rows and columns sum to the actual distribution of the vote, including abstention, at the two elections. For tables incorporating these refinements, see David Butler and Donald Stokes, *Political Change in Britain*, 2nd ed. (London: Macmillan, 1974), pp. 255-67 and especially p. 255, fn. 2.

who died between the two elections. The net effect of this demographic evolution must have helped Labour. But it will not have done so as much as usual, because in previous elections Labour has enjoyed a clear lead amongst new voters (whereas the Conservative-to-Labour ratio among those dying between elections is fairly stable). The Conservative party's exceptional success amongst first-time voters will therefore have reduced the normal advantage that accrues to Labour from the departure of the Conservative-inclined elderly, and the addition of Labour-inclined young, between elections. In that sense, first-time voters made a significant contribution to the aggregate swing to the Conservatives and, along with Labour-to-Conservative converts and Liberal-to-Conservative defectors, will require closer examination.

Table 9–5 adds flesh to this skeletal analysis by showing how the net swing to the Conservatives varied between different social groups.[14] Three main features emerge:

• *A class factor*: Labour lost the election through a massive hemorrhage of working-class votes. The swing to the Conservatives was 6.5 percentage points among semiskilled and unskilled workers, 7 points among trade unionists (so much for the extra campaign efforts

---

[14] The October 1974-1979 "swing" in a social group is calculated by averaging the Conservatives' percentage point increase and Labour's percentage point decrease in the share of the vote. Figures for 1974 were taken from the merging of three Louis Harris polls (N=4,296; see David Watt, "Long-term Lessons from Election Swings," *Financial Times*, October 25, 1974, p. 23). Confidence in the swing figures reported in this chapter is increased by the very similar findings of two other major surveys, the ORC poll (N=4,328) on May 3 for Independent Television News, and MORI's six campaign polls for the *Daily Express* and *Evening Standard* (merged and weighted to produce an N=6,445). Their swing figures are:

|  | *MORI* | *ORC-ITN* |
|---|---|---|
| Men | +7 | +8 |
| Women | +5.5 | +5 |
| 18–24 | +9.5 | +13 |
| 25–34 | +5 | not reported |
| 35–54 | +9.5 | not reported |
| 55+ | +3.5 | not reported |
| ABC$_1$ | −1 | AB −5 } −3.5 |
|  |  | C$_1$ −2 } |
| C$_2$ | +11.5 | +10 |
| DE | +10 | +9 |
| Trade union members | +7 | +6 |

MORI, *British Public Opinion, General Election 1979*, Final Report, pp. 5-7; and "Labour's Breakdown," *Labour Weekly*, May 18, 1979, pp. 8-9.

of union officials), and an enormous 11 points among skilled workers. The latter gave Labour a mere 1 point lead over the Conservatives, less than in any previous postwar election. And those who had experienced unemployment over the last two years (or whose family had) walloped Labour with a 14.5 point swing. On the other hand the swing was down to 4.5 points among office and clerical workers and actually in Labour's favor in the professional and managerial classes. Thus the growth in the Labour middle class, which has been gradual but persistent since the early 1960s, continued.

- *An age factor*: As usual, the young were more anti-Government and electorally more volatile than the old. But this time the generational differences were particularly marked, with a 9.5 point "swing" between the new voters of 1974 and the new voters of 1979 (mainly through a collapse in Liberal support from its high 1974 level) but almost none among the over sixty-fives.

- *A sex factor*: Men swung to the Conservatives much more heavily than women (by 9.5 points compared with 3 points), so that the traditional sex differences in party support all but disappeared. The last-minute surge of male chauvinism some had predicted never came. The Conservatives won the election by making their greatest inroads in those social sectors which are normally their most difficult territory: manual workers, the young, and men. Indeed, the swing between the eighteen- to twenty-four-year-old male manual workers of 1974 and those of 1979—stereotypical anti-Conservative (and anti-Thatcher) voters—was a staggering twenty-one percentage points; whereas middle-class women over fifty-five, the identikit Conservatives, swung by 3 points—*to Labour*.[15]

What concerns made new Conservative recruits from young working-class men in particular? The poll data fail to reveal any clear or consistent answer. For example, contrary to widespread assumptions, there is no evidence that young, skilled working men migrated to the Conservatives in the hope of tax cuts or a chance to buy their council houses (although some of their wives did). The data do hint at an impatience in this group with the Labour Government's incomes policy—which had narrowed the differential between skilled and non-skilled wage rates—but it is no more than a hint.[16] The one issue of

---

[15] These two swing figures are based on the MORI polls for 1979 and the British Election Study for October 1974 (N=2,365) because four-way breakdowns were not available on the NOP and Gallup data reported in table 9-5.

[16] The BBC Gallup survey asked whether the Government "should set firm guidelines for wages and salaries" or "should leave it to employers and trade unions to negotiate wages and salaries alone." The electorate as a whole split 47 to 53 percent; male manual workers under thirty-five split 39 to 61 percent.

## TABLE 9-5

### 1979 VOTE AND PARTY SWING, OCTOBER 1974–1979, BY CLASS, SEX, AND AGE
(percent and percentage points)

| | Professional & Managerial (AB) | | Office & Clerical (C₁) | | Skilled Manual (C₂) | | Semiskilled, Unskilled, Manual (D) | | Trade Unionists | | Unemployed During 1974–1979 | | Men | | Women | |
|---|---|---|---|---|---|---|---|---|---|---|---|---|---|---|---|---|
| | 1979 | Oct. 1974–1979 | 1979 | Oct. 1974–1979 | 1979 | Oct. 1974–1979 | 1979 | Oct. 1974–1979 | 1979 | Oct. 1974–1979 | 1979 | Oct. 1974–1979 | 1979 | Oct. 1974–1979 | 1979 | Oct. 1974–1979 |
| Conservative | 65 | +2 | 57 | +6 | 44 | +18 | 31 | +9 | 30 | +8 | 38 | +19 | 46 | +14 | 45 | +6 |
| Labour | 17 | +5 | 21 | −3 | 45 | −4 | 53 | −4 | 51 | −6 | 47 | −10 | 38 | −5 | 38 | 0 |
| Liberal | 15 | −7 | 20 | −1 | 10 | −10 | 12 | −4 | 15 | −2 | 11 | −9 | 13 | −5 | 14 | −6 |
| Conservative lead | +48 | | +36 | | −1 | | −22 | | −21 | | −9 | | +8 | | +7 | |
| Swing to Conservatives | −1.5 | | +4.5 | | +11 | | +6.5 | | +7 | | +14.5 | | +9.5 | | +3 | |

280

| | 18–22 | | 23–34 | | 35–44 | | 45–64 | | 65+ | |
|---|---|---|---|---|---|---|---|---|---|---|
| | 1979 | Oct. 1974–1979 | 1979 | Oct. 1974–1979 | 1979 | Oct. 1974–1979 | 1979 | Oct. 1974–1979 | 1979 | Oct. 1974–1979 |
| Conservative | 40 | +16 | 44 | +11 | 45 | +8 | 46 | +12 | 50 | +1 |
| Labour | 39 | –3 | 39 | +1 | 36 | –3 | 39 | –5 | 37 | 0 |
| Liberal | 15 | –12 | 14 | –10 | 16 | –3 | 12 | –7 | 12 | 0 |
| Conservative lead | +1 | | +5 | | +9 | | +7 | | +13 | |
| Swing to Conservatives | | +9.5 | | +5 | | +5.5 | | +8.5 | | +0.5 |

NOTE: NOP's two youngest age categories were 18-24 and 25-34. Columns do not add to 100 percent because they exclude votes for other parties.

SOURCE: October 1974 figures taken from NOP. 1979 figures taken from BBC Gallup survey, May 2-3, 1979.

## TABLE 9–6
### Conservative Voters' Reasons for Their Choice
(percent)

| Reason | All Conservative Voters | Manual Workers ($C_2D$) | Male Manual Workers ($C_2D$) under 35 |
|---|---|---|---|
| Like Conservatives | 48 | 56 | 41 |
| Dislike Labour | 52 | 44 | 59 |
| Total[a] | 100 | 100 | 100 |
| Specific reason | 68 | 67 | 52 |
| Time for a change | 32 | 33 | 48 |
| Total | 100 | 100 | 100 |
| N | (884) | (408) | (74) |

Survey questions: "What would you say is stronger—your *like* of the Conservatives or your *dislike* of Labour?"
"And are you voting Conservative because of something in particular that you like about them, or because you just think it is time for a change?"
[a] Excludes those saying "both equally."
Source: BBC Gallup survey, May 2-3, 1979.

peculiar concern to this group was, not surprisingly, unemployment; but on this issue Labour led the Conservatives, especially among those most concerned about it. Perhaps *specific* issues had little to do with it. The most distinctive feature of young, male, working-class attitudes was the extent to which Conservative votes were cast for reasons that were general rather than specific and negative rather than positive (see table 9–6). Theirs was an anti-Government protest vote which owed far more to general dissatisfaction with Labour's record than to enthusiasm for Conservative policies.

### Issues

It was issues, not organization or personalities, that won the election for the Conservatives. Had it been feasible, the electorate would have voted for a Government of Labour men but Conservative measures (see figure 9–3). Throughout the campaign they preferred Labour to Conservative leaders (not only Callaghan to Thatcher, but also other Labour leaders to other Conservative leaders); but with equal consistency they preferred Conservative to Labour policies. One aspect of this Conservative edge on issues is worth noting. On the issues

## FIGURE 9–3

### Conservative Party's Standing Relative to Labour,
### April 6–May 3, 1973

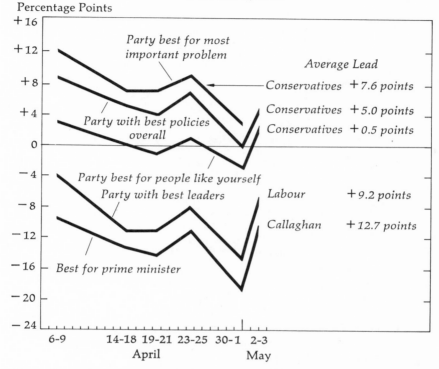

NOTE: Respondents were asked the following questions: "Which party do you think can best handle that problem [the most important problem facing the country]?" (not asked on May 2-3); "Taking everything into account, which party has the best policies?"; "Leaving on one side the question of which party you support, which party is best for people like yourself?"; "Taking everything into account, which party has the best leaders?"; and "Who would make the better (May 2-3: the best) prime minister, Mr. Callaghan, Mrs. Thatcher, or Mr. Steel?"

SOURCE: Gallup surveys for *Daily Telegraph* and BBC TV (May 2-3).

electors regarded as particularly important, the Conservative lead (7.6 percentage points on average) was even larger than it was on policies in general (5.0 points). The Conservatives' success came from saying the right things about the right issues—the ones of most personal concern to the voters.

But which issues were these? The "right" issues for a party are those with the double advantage of being important to the electorate and being ones on which the party's record or proposals are preferred.

283

## TABLE 9–7

### THE CAMPAIGN ISSUES: IMPORTANCE AND PARTY PREFERENCE
(in percent and percentage points)

| Issue | All Respondents | Those Citing Issue as Important (preferred party's lead) |
|---|---|---|
| Prices | 42 | Lab. +13 |
| Unemployment | 27 | Lab. +15 |
| Taxes | 21 | Con. +61 |
| Strikes | 20 | Con. +15 |
| Law and order | 11 | Con. +72 |

SURVEY QUESTION: "Think of all the urgent issues facing the country at the present time. When you decided which way to vote, which *two* issues did you yourself consider most important?"

No prompt card was given to respondents. The five issues above were the most frequently mentioned.

SOURCE: BBC Gallup survey, May 2-3, 1979.

Table 9–7 rank orders the two issues which electors said, on the eve and day of polling, most influenced their vote. For the fourth consecutive time prices topped the list at 42 percent, followed by unemployment (27 percent), strikes (21 percent), taxes (20 percent), and law and order (11 percent).[17] The table also shows the party lead on each issue amongst those mentioning it as decisive; and comparison of the two sets of figures immediately presents a puzzle. For on the two most important issues of all—prices and unemployment—Labour was the preferred party, ahead by thirteen points and fifteen points respectively. How, then, did they still lose on the largest postwar swing?

First, Labour lost because the Conservatives' advantage on their own best issues, taxation (+sixty-one points) and law and order (+seventy-two points), was so much more decisive than Labour's advantage on its best issues. Whereas the Conservatives were still preferred by substantial minorities of those worried about inflation and unemployment, almost nobody concerned about taxes or law and order plumped for Labour. Second, to deliver votes to one party rather than another it is not necessarily sufficient for an issue to be important and for that party to be preferred on it. The issue must also be regarded as soluble and the party's proposals as credible. Here lay the dis-

---

[17] After which came education (8 percent), pensions (7 percent), and immigrants (5 percent). Both pensions and education were higher ranked than law and order amongst Labour voters.

tinctive advantage, for the Conservatives, of two issues: strikes and, above all, taxes. For as table 9–8 shows, although electors were overwhelmingly in favor of Labour's objective of reducing the annual rate of inflation to 5 percent within three years, they were also overwhelmingly skeptical; although emphatically behind Labour's aim of achieving a long-term agreement with the trade unions on wages, after the winter's events they were understandably less than sanguine about the prospects. By contrast, the Conservative party's commitments to reduce supplementary benefits to strikers and bring down the rate of income tax were not only widely supported, but widely believed: believers outnumbered disbelievers by forty-two percentage points and forty-nine percentage points, respectively. The contrast cannot be put down to the pro-Conservative bias in the sample, because on another popular Conservative promise—to reduce violent crime and vandalism—a majority were skeptical. One reason for the doubts about Labour's credibility is that the governing party's promises are always open to the charge, Why didn't they get on with it when they had the chance? But a more plausible explanation lies in the nature of the issues themselves. It is not difficult to understand why electors should be cautious about claims by any party, especially the one in government, to solve the problems of prices or unemployment (or crime). Unemployment steadily rose under the Labour Government, and inflation and crime have been serious problems throughout the 1970s. Moreover, there will be some public awareness that these problems have complex causes of which many are beyond a Government's control. But the tax issue is different: tax rates, as well as welfare benefits, are directly and exclusively within a Government's control (although the consequences of changing them might not be). To promise a reduction in the income tax, as the Conservatives repeatedly did, is as clear, tangible, and accountable a campaign commitment as a party can make. The electorate felt that something ought to be done about prices, jobs, strikes, crime, and taxes, and on the first two it was marginally more inclined to put its trust in Labour; but only on taxes did the voters also believe that something could and would be done—and that it was the Conservatives who would do the doing.

So far, however, our analysis of the impact of issues on the election result has been incomplete, for an election result arises from *changes* in the distribution of votes from one election to another. Such changes cannot be explained by issue data limited to one election. We require parallel data for the October 1974 campaign issues to see how their relative importance, and the electors' party preferences on each, shifted between that election and 1979. An issue

## TABLE 9–8
### CREDIBILITY OF CONSERVATIVE AND LABOUR PROPOSALS

| Objectives | % of Respondents Naming the Issue as One of the Three Most Important | % Saying the Government Should Attempt to Achieve These Objectives Minus % Saying It Should Not | % Saying the Government Would Succeed in Achieving These Objectives Minus % Saying It Would Not |
|---|---|---|---|
| *Conservative* | | | |
| Reduce violent crime and vandalism | 40 | +94 | −20 |
| Reduce supplementary benefit for strikers, on the assumption that they are getting strike pay from their unions | 20 | +63 | +42 |
| Reduce income tax, especially for the higher paid | 18 | +33 | +49 |
| Give council-house tenants the right to buy their homes, with discounts for people who have lived in them for 3 years or more | 12 | +61 | +61 |
| *Labour* | | | |
| Bring the rate of price rises down to 5 percent a year within 3 years | 53 | +92 | −41 |
| Reduce income tax, especially for the lower paid | 48 | +92 | +30 |
| Achieve a long-term working understanding with the trade unions on wages | 32 | +89 | −3 |
| Prevent increases in Common Market farm prices | 16 | +84 | −29 |

SOURCE: RSL survey, April 17-18, 1979 (N = 1,199). See Anthony King, "Labour Voters Give Tories the Nod," *Observer*, April 22, 1979, p. 4.

could have produced a swing to the Conservatives in either or both of two ways: first, if support for the Conservatives on the issue had grown; and second, if, in cases where the Conservatives were already the preferred party, the importance of the issue had grown. Table 9–9 provides the comparison with October 1974[18] and shows how the Conservatives in fact benefited from all five issues.

The importance of law and order and strikes as issues rose only slightly. Nonetheless, the winter's strikes had left their mark, for there was a strong movement of opinion on the issue in the Conservatives' favor. At the previous election Labour had led on the issue by thirty-three percentage points, and as late as October 1978 Labour was nineteen points ahead; by May 3 this had been converted into a small Conservative lead (three points). On unemployment the Conservatives benefited doubly from the narrowing of the Labour lead (from nineteen to three points) and the growth of the issue's importance by fifteen percentage points. But the prices issue provides the best illustration of just how misleading information restricted to one election can be. At both elections Labour was ahead by a similar margin (nineteen and eleven percentage points), and at both, prices was the single most important issue. But in October 1974, when the annual inflation rate was 20 percent and rising, it was mentioned by 82 percent of respondents; whereas in 1979, with the inflation rate down to 10 percent, it was of concern to only half as many (42 percent). Here lies the explanation for Labour's loss of an election in which it was the preferred party on the most important issue: Labour still had the electoral advantage on the issue, but because it had declined in saliency—by half since October 1974—that advantage was no longer worth much. Labour's reward was inversely proportionate to its success in halving the inflation rate.

Once again taxation emerges as the single most helpful issue for the Conservatives. In October 1974 it was so insignificant an issue that Gallup did not even list it—a sign that fewer than 4 percent had mentioned it as important. As late as April 1978 the issue was unlisted; but a year later it was mentioned by 21 percent, and, as we shall see, it gained continually in importance up to polling day itself. Putting the income tax on the campaign agenda was only part of the Conservatives' achievement, however; equally important was their success in establishing themselves as the party that would take

---

[18] Sharp-eyed readers will notice that the 1979 figures on preferred party on an issue differ from those appearing in the righthand column of table 9-7. This is because they are based on all respondents, not just those who mentioned the issue as important. This change was made necessary by the fact that the only comparative data available for October 1974 were based on all respondents.

## TABLE 9–9

### THE CAMPAIGN ISSUES: CHANGE IN IMPORTANCE AND PARTY PREFERENCE, OCTOBER 1974–MAY 1979

(percent; preferred party's lead and swing in percentage points)

| Issue | October 1974 | | May 1979[c] | | Change 1974–1979 | |
| --- | --- | --- | --- | --- | --- | --- |
| | Importance of issue[a] | Party preferred on issue[b] | Importance of issue | Party preferred on issue | Change in issue's importance | Swing on issue[d] |
| Prices, cost of living | 82 | Lab. +11 | 42 | Lab. +9 | −40 | 1 to Con. |
| Unemployment | 12 | Lab. +19 | 27 | Lab. +3 | +15 | 8 to Con. |
| Taxes | less than 4 | not asked 1974 (Con. +2, April 1978)[f] | 21 | Con. +42 | at least +18 | (20 to Con. since April 1978) |
| Trade unions | 15 | Lab. +33 | 20 | Con. +3 | +5 | 18 to Con. |
| Law and order | 8[e] | not asked 1974 (Con. +7, April 1978)[f] | 11 | Con. +37 | +3 | (15 to Con. since April 1978) |

| | | | | | | |
|---|---|---|---|---|---|---|
| Common Market | 11 | Con. +3 | 4 | Con. +4 | −7 | 0.5 to Con. |
| Pensions | 6 | not asked 1974 (Lab. +22, April 1978)[f] | 7 | Lab. +23 | +1 | (0.5 to Lab. since April 1978) |
| N | (8,428) | (1,059) | (2,435) | (2,435) | (2,435) | |

[a] Combined Gallup surveys, September 19–October 3, 1974. The question was "What would you say is the most urgent problem facing the country at the present time? And what is the next most urgent?" There was no prompt card. The figures are percentages of respondents who mentioned the issue as either the most or the second most urgent problem. See *Gallup Political Index*, no. 171, October 1974, p. 10.

[b] Gallup survey, September 11–16, 1974. The question was "Which party do you think can best handle the problem of . . . ?" See *Gallup Political Index*, no. 171, October 1974, p. 6.

[c] BBC Gallup survey, 2–3, 1979. The questions were "Think of all the urgent issues facing the country at the present time. When you decided which way to vote, which *two* issues did you yourself consider most important?" and "Would you tell me which party you think would be best at. . . ."

[d] *Half* the change in the party lead.

[e] From Gallup's September 11–24, 1974 survey. Law and order was not listed in the September 19–October 3 survey results.

[f] Gallup survey, April 19–24, 1978. The question was "Which party do you think is particularly good at . . . ? Any others?" See *Gallup Political Index*, no. 214, May 1978, pp. 7–8.

action. A year before the election the Conservatives' lead over Labour as "the better party to reduce taxation" was a mere two percentage points; by polling day, the Conservatives' lead was forty-two percentage points. On no other issue did public concern and party popularity move so decisively—and swiftly—in the Conservative party's favor.

These general conclusions about the impact of different issues are refined but reinforced by an examination of the high-swing groups identified earlier. Table 9–10 confirms how the carrot of tax cuts attracted Conservative recruits and the stick of unemployment kept Labour supporters in line (and even forced some conversions). But different issues won over different factions into the Conservative ranks. Contrary to the common assumption in the election post-mortems, it was the prospect less of tax cuts than of tougher measures against strikers which captured Labour and Liberal defectors. It was amongst first-time voters, the eighteen- to twenty-two-year-olds, that income-tax cuts proved most decisive—perhaps because this group more than others, and much to its surprise, had been caught by the tax net under the Labour Government.

Finally, a regional analysis of the issues sheds some light on the geographical variation in the swing to which we referred at the start of the chapter. The common assumption is that Scotland and the North largely stuck by Labour because they are regions of industrial decline and social deprivation, for which high public spending in the form of aid to industry and welfare benefits remained attractive; whereas the higher-growth and more prosperous Midlands and South swung heavily to the Conservatives in the hope of tax cuts and easier conditions in general for private industry. Table 9–11 suggests a more complicated story. Fear of unemployment does appear to have been behind Labour's staunching of the Conservative advance in Scotland, where 42 percent mentioned it as a decisive issue, as against 30 percent in England and Wales. This difference cannot be explained by the fact that Scotland is more working class than England and Wales, because within each social class in Britain concern about unemployment was substantially higher north of the border. Scotland's history of unemployment and poverty, and its traditional dependence on state aid, does indeed seem an important factor. But it can only be part of the explanation, for on *every* major issue more preferred Labour and fewer preferred the Conservatives than elsewhere in Britain; the Scottish dimension took the form of a generally more favorable climate for Labour. A similar conclusion emerges in the case of the North. Here the relative importance of issues hardly differed from that in the rest of England (concern about unemploy-

## TABLE 9–10

### ISSUE SALIENCY AMONG STABLE AND CHANGING VOTERS
(percent)

| Issue | All Voters | Con. Loyalists | Con. Recruits | Too Young 1974, Con. 1979 | Lib. 1974, Con. 1979 | Lab. 1974, Con. 1979 | Lab. Defectors | Lab. Loyalists |
|---|---|---|---|---|---|---|---|---|
| Prices | 42 | 38 | 39 | 45 | 37 | 39 | 40 | 49 |
| Unemployment | 27 | 20 | 20 | 31 | 17 | 14 | 21 | 34 |
| Taxes | 21 | 30 | 28 | 43 | 22 | 24 | 23 | 12 |
| Strikes | 20 | 27 | 30 | 13 | 29 | 35 | 39 | 14 |
| Law and order | 11 | 18 | 13 | 9 | 21 | 11 | 10 | 5 |
| N | (2,425) | (607) | (271) | (63) | (59) | (79) | (189) | (563) |

NOTE: Figures are percentages of the respondent group who mentioned the issue as one of the two most important in influencing their vote.

SOURCE: BBC Gallup survey, May 2-3, 1979.

TABLE 9–11

THE CAMPAIGN ISSUES: IMPORTANCE AND PARTY PREFERENCE, BY REGION

(percent; preferred party's lead in percentage points)

| Issue | Scotland | England and Wales | North | Midlands | South |
|---|---|---|---|---|---|
| Prices |  |  |  |  |  |
| Importance | 45 | 41 | 40 | 34 | 44 |
| Party preferred | Lab. +27 | Lab. +11 | Lab. +22 | Lab. +5 | Con. +1 |
| Unemployment |  |  |  |  |  |
| Importance | 42 | 30 | 31 | 22 | 33 |
| Party preferred | Lab. +35 | Lab. +11 | Lab. +16 | Con. +9 | Con. +6 |
| Taxes |  |  |  |  |  |
| Importance | 19 | 21 | 18 | 21 | 24 |
| Party preferred | Con. +8 | Con. +16 | Con. +37 | Con. +46 | Con. +49 |
| Strikes |  |  |  |  |  |
| Importance | 16 | 21 | 19 | 21 | 22 |
| Party preferred | Con. +30 | Con. +64 | Lab. +11 | Con. +17 | Con. +7 |
| Law and order |  |  |  |  |  |
| Importance | 12 | 12 | 9 | 17 | 12 |
| Party preferred | Con. +57 | Con. +73 | Con. +32 | Con. +48 | Con. +42 |
| N | (966)[a] | (1,987) | (656) | (378) | (953) |

NOTE: For Scotland and England and Wales, "party preferred" is determined on the basis of those citing the issue as an important influence on their vote; for the English regions, on the basis of all respondents (because more refined data are not available).

[a] This N is unweighted, unlike those for England and Wales and the English regions.

SOURCE: BBC Gallup survey, May 2–3, 1979.

ment was no higher, although mention of taxes was slightly lower), but again, for each issue Labour's lead was larger, or its deficit smaller, than in the Midlands and South. Ecological and historical factors, one suspects, were at work: in the older-established, more stable, but also more deprived working-class communities of the North and Scotland, traditional partisan loyalties were more resistant to the Conservative party's blandishments.[19]

In one sense concentration on the few most important issues underestimates the votes the Conservatives won on their policies. As in all elections, there were a host of minor issues, each of which will have influenced the vote of a small minority. On these too the Conservatives had the decided advantage. The issue of council house sales is a good example. The Conservatives promised that, if elected, they would guarantee council tenants the right to buy their houses, and on favorable terms. In none of the polls did enough respondents mention the issue to define it as "important." But all polls agreed that the proposal had wide support among council tenants, and it is difficult to believe that at least some were not persuaded to switch to the Conservatives as a result. The exceptionally high swings in many new towns in the South—where there were large numbers of high-wage manual workers renting council property—is strong circumstantial evidence.[20] And on a series of other secondary issues —capital punishment, the grammar schools, defense spending—Conservative policies and emphases were decidedly popular.[21] This is well brought out in table 9–12, which lists most of the specific policy proposals (as opposed to aspirations) contained in the Conservative

---

[19] And especially those of Mrs. Thatcher, who trailed behind Callaghan (as preferred prime minister) by twenty-one points in the North and thirty points in Scotland (where she was behind David Steel also) compared with only one point in the Midlands and South. The class and party composition of the two regions is not the explanation: in every social group Mrs. Thatcher was markedly less popular (and Steel more so) north of the border. Antiwoman prejudice could have played a part. The Scots were more convinced than the English that a woman would make a worse prime minister, or M.P., than a man (although the majority maintained it made no difference). This too held true after controlling for class, party, and sex. But whether sexism was a cause or post-hoc rationalization of the swing to Labour is difficult to disentangle. Another possible factor, but for which no data exist, is that the Scots (and Northerners) also disliked Mrs. Thatcher for her open opposition to Scottish devolution, made more conspicuous by her obvious roots in the South.

[20] For example, Harlow (12.9 point swing), Basildon (11.0 points), Braintree (9.2 points) and Hertford and Stevenage (8.1 points).

[21] Attitudes split 59 to 41 in favor of an "increase in defense spending" (MORI poll for *Daily Express/Evening Standard*, April 17, 1979) and 74 to 26 in favor of "bringing back grammar schools" (NOP survey for *Daily Mail*, April 2-3). On council house sales, see table 9-12.

TABLE 9–12

Support for Conservative and Labour Manifesto Proposals
(percent)

| Proposal | All Voters | Liberal Voters, Oct. 1974 | New Voters | Manual Workers | Conservative Voters | Labour Voters |
|---|---|---|---|---|---|---|
| *Conservative* | | | | | | |
| Ban secondary picketing, that is, the picketing of a company not directly involved in a strike | 91 | 91 | 84 | 90 | 96 | 96 |
| Have a free vote in the House of Commons on the death penalty | 90 | 91 | 81 | 92 | 94 | 88 |
| Sell more council houses to tenants | 80 | 77 | 85 | 79 | 89 | 69 |
| Stop social security payments to the families of strikers | 60 | 65 | 49 | 56 | 81 | 38 |
| Cut top income-tax rate for people with large incomes | 57 | 48 | 62 | 56 | 67 | 49 |
| Put up VAT in order to reduce income tax | 51 | 59 | 49 | 45 | 70 | 30 |
| Average | 71.5 | 71.8 | 68.3 | 69.7 | 82.8 | 61.7 |

and Labour manifestoes. The Conservative proposals had by far the wider appeal: three were overwhelmingly popular (a ban on secondary picketing, a free Commons vote on hanging, and selling council houses) and all were endorsed by a majority of the electorate. Labour only produced two proposals with widespread appeal—a tougher stand against the EEC's agricultural policy, and government subsidies to protect jobs. The other three—a wealth tax, installing trade union representatives on company boards, and reducing the powers of the House of Lords—were actually opposed by the majority of electors.[22]

---

[22] On another Labour proposal, not included in the BBC Gallup survey, the nationalization of the banks, public opinion divided 87 to 13 *against* (NOP survey for *Daily Mail*, April 2-3, 1979).

## TABLE 9–12 (continued)

| Proposal | All Voters | Liberal Voters, Oct. 1974 | New Voters | Manual Workers | Conser-vative Voters | Labour Voters |
|---|---|---|---|---|---|---|
| *Labour* | | | | | | |
| Take tougher stand against the Common Market's agricultural policy | 94 | 93 | 89 | 94 | 94 | 94 |
| Give government subsidies where that is necessary to protect jobs | 79 | 81 | 86 | 82 | 66 | 91 |
| Introduce a wealth tax | 49 | 47 | 48 | 57 | 30 | 73 |
| Give trade unions seats on the boards of major companies | 45 | 48 | 50 | 46 | 33 | 62 |
| Reduce the powers of the House of Lords | 43 | 33 | 43 | 48 | 21 | 66 |
| Average | 62.0 | 60.4 | 63.2 | 65.4 | 48.8 | 78.2 |

SURVEY QUESTION: "I am going to read out some of the proposals that the different parties have put forward in this election. In each case I would like you to say whether you think the proposal is a good idea or bad idea."
NOTE: "Don't knows" were excluded from the percentage base.
SOURCE: BBC Gallup survey, May 2-3, 1979.

Overall, support for Labour's proposals averaged at 62 percent, for Conservative proposals at 72 percent. And amongst two crucial "swing" groups—first-time voters and October 1974 Liberals—Conservative proposals were also the more popular, by 68 percent to 63 percent in the first case and by 72 percent to 60 percent in the second. Indeed, they were also the more popular amongst working-class electors—a matter to which we shall return.

In another sense, however, concentration on the issues can over-estimate their contribution to an election result by giving an exaggerated impression of specificity and clarity in the voters' motives. The fact that survey respondents answer questions about issues does not mean that they enter the polling booth with a particular issue or

TABLE 9–13

CONSERVATIVE VOTERS' REASONS FOR THEIR CHOICE, BY LENGTH
OF ATTACHMENT TO PARTY
(percent)

| Reason | All Conservative Voters | Conservative Loyalists | Conservative Recruits | Decided to Vote Conservative in the Last Few Days |
|---|---|---|---|---|
| Specific reason | 68 | 74 | 57 | 47 |
| Time for a change | 32 | 26 | 43 | 53 |
| Total | 100 | 100 | 100 | 100 |

SURVEY QUESTION: Did you vote Conservative because of something in particular you like about them or because you just think it is time for a change?"
SOURCE: BBC Gallup survey, May 2-3, 1979.

party policy in mind. Many will have been influenced by no more than a diffuse impression of the two parties' records and proposals without it being possible to say which issue, if any, was decisive. It was noticeable that whenever a poll asked respondents to give reasons in their own words for supporting one party rather than another, references to particular issues were rare; much more frequent were broad preferences for or against change, and general expressions of satisfaction or dissatisfaction. Table 9–13 shows how important a factor ennui with the Labour Government was; 43 percent of Conservative recruits—and 53 percent of last-minute Conservatives—gave as the reason for their vote that they "just thought it was time for a change" rather than "because of something in particular they liked about the Conservatives." In any explanation of the Conservative victory one should not underestimate the importance of that most basic of political feelings—that, after five years of a Labour Government, and five years of economic decline, it was time to give "the other lot" a chance again.

## From Explanation to Interpretation

Pinpointing the immediate causes of the election result is always easier than assessing its wider, historical, significance. But two preliminary interpretations seem uncontentious. First, whatever else it signified, the election was an emphatic rejection of the Labour party. Not since its disaster in 1931 had Labour suffered such an adverse swing or seen its share of the vote sink so low. Second, Labour lost not through inferior organization, lack of money, last-minute campaign incidents, or, of course, Callaghan's personal appeal, but for the most obvious and proper of reasons—its objectives and policies. Labour lost the political argument.

Despite earlier predictions that time and demography were on Labour's side,[23] it now appears that Labour is in deep electoral trouble. It is easy to forget that although Labour twice won office (just) in 1974, it did so by electoral default: its share of the vote at both 1974 elections was actually below its 1970 level. And 1979 was the third consecutive election in which the Labour vote fell to below 40 percent, thus completing the party's worst decade since the 1930s (when, moreover, it fielded fewer candidates). The only other European democracies in which the left does as badly are Eire, Switzerland, and Belgium, but in these cases rurality or religious and linguistic cleavages can be cited in explanation. Working-class desertion of the Labour party has been particularly remarkable. With barely more than one in three manual workers (37 percent) bothering to turn out for Labour, and with the majority of working-class *voters* (52 percent) going elsewhere, Labour's claim to be the party of the working class now looks a little thin.

One reason for the steady erosion of Labour support undoubtedly lies in the record of the two full-term Labour Governments of 1966–1970 and 1974–1979. But it cannot be the whole explanation. For one thing, the erosion gathered speed between 1970 and 1974, when Labour was in opposition. For another, on two major aspects of the Labour Government's performance—prices and jobs—the electorate preferred the Labour party and gave it half-hearted applause. The source of Labour's electoral problems lies deeper: not in its record but in its enduring principles.

This is vividly demonstrated if we return to the Conservative and Labour manifesto proposals listed in table 9–12. Manual workers, Labour's natural sympathizers, were on average slightly more in favor of Conservative than Labour proposals. Comparison on individual items is particularly revealing. For example, manual workers were as much in favor of cutting the *top rate* of income tax (the Conservative proposal) as of introducing a wealth tax (the Labour proposal). More

---

[23] See David Butler and Donald Stokes, *Political Change in Britain*, 2nd ed. (London: Macmillan, 1975), chaps. 7, 8, and 10. Labour was believed to be the beneficiary of two demographic processes: (1) the dying out of those who had first entered the electorate before 1918 and thus had been socialized into partisanship before Labour was a serious contender for power; and (2) the greater fertility amongst the working class (especially the Labour working class) and the narrowing of class differences in longevity.

# TABLE 9–14

Labour Identifiers' Attitudes toward Nationalization, Social Spending, and Trade Union Power, 1964–1979
(percent)

| Attitude | 1964 | 1966 | 1970 | 1974 Feb. | 1974 Oct. | 1979 | Change 1975–1979 | Change 1964–1979 |
|---|---|---|---|---|---|---|---|---|
| In favor of nationalizing more industries | 57 | 52 | 39 | 50 | 56 | 32 | −24 | −25 |
|  |  |  |  | 53 | | | | |
| Do not believe that trade unions have "too much power" | 59 | 45 | 40 | 44[a] | 39 | 36 | −3 | −23 |
|  |  |  |  | 42 | | | | |

In favor of spending
more on social services

| | | | | | | | | | |
|---|---|---|---|---|---|---|---|---|---|
| Question 1 | 89 | 66 | NA | 60[b] | 61[a,b] | NA | NA | * | —28 (1964–Feb. 1974) |
| Question 2 | NA | NA | NA | NA | 47 | 39 | 30 | —9 | * |

43

NA = not asked.

* = cannot be estimated.

NOTE: Percentage bases exclude "don't knows."

SURVEY QUESTIONS: "There has been a lot of talk recently about nationalization (that is, the Government owning and running industries like steel and electricity). Which of these statements comes closest to what you yourself feel should be done? 1. A lot more should be nationalized. 2. Only a few more industries (such as steel) should be nationalized. 3. No more industries should be nationalized, but industries that are now nationalized should stay nationalized. 4. Some of the industries that are now nationalized should be denationalized (become private companies)." (Responses 1 and 2 are combined in the above figures.) "Do you think that the trade unions have too much power or not?" Question 1: "Do you feel that the government should spend more on pensions and social services, or do you feel that spending for social services should stay about as it is now?" (Asked in 1964-February 1974.) Question 2: "Now we would like to ask what you think about social services and benefits. Which of these statements do you feel comes closest to your own views? (1) Social services and benefits have gone much too far and should be cut back a lot. (2) Social services and benefits have gone somewhat too far and should be cut back a bit. (3) Social services and benefits should stay much as they are. (4) More social services and benefits are needed." (Asked in 1974–1979).

[a] Taken from 1970–February 1974 panel sample.

[b] Excludes the small numbers who said that only spending on pensions should be increased (coded separately in 1970 and February 1974, but not in 1964 and 1966).

SOURCE: Butler and Stokes's cross-sectional samples, 1964, 1966, and 1970; British Election Study cross-sectional samples, February 1974, October 1974, and 1979.

sided with the House of Lords, whose powers Labour proposed to reduce, than with trade union officials, whom Labour proposed to put on company boards. There is another telling comparison. Not surprisingly, both Conservative and Labour voters were more likely to approve of their own party's proposals than of the other side's. But the pattern of approval was not symmetrical. Whereas the majority of Conservative voters (temporarily swelled in 1979, moreover, by many without deep Conservative commitments) explicitly opposed Labour's proposals, a substantial majority of Labour voters (reduced in 1979 to a loyal core) actually supported the Conservative proposals.

A divergence between the policies of the Labour party and the views of its supporters is not new. As much was discovered in the early 1950s.[24] Over the last fifteen years people have voted Labour despite its policies, Conservative despite its leaders. But there are two crucial differences between the late 1970s and a generation earlier. First, as table 9–14 shows, this divergence between what the Labour party and its supporters stand for has steadily grown wider. Since 1964 support among Labour identifiers (let alone the general public) for further nationalization, for further spending on social services, and for the amount and form of power exercised by trade unions has dramatically declined, such that each only appealed in 1979 to a one-third minority within Labour's ranks. What began as a policy divergence is now an ideological chasm. Second, the importance of policy principles in securing party loyalty has, quite independently, become greater over the same period. Until the mid-1960s class and partisan allegiance sustained Labour supporters' loyalty even when it was under strain through dissent from Labour policy. As, for various reasons, the strength of those class and partisan allegiances has dissolved, that electoral insulation has disappeared. Labour now enters elections with a major handicap: unlike the Conservatives', its basic, traditional principles run against the popular grain. In opposition this ideological disadvantage might be compensated for by the temporary unpopularity of a Conservative administration. But when in government the Labour party enters the electoral arena without the protective clothing of ideological sympathy from its traditional supporters; the result, not unexpectedly, is the kind of mauling it suffered in 1979. Thus when the electorate parted from the Labour party in 1979 it was also parting, at least temporarily, from social democracy.

Its ideological opponents have been quick to claim not only social democracy's demise but their own rebirth. Within Labour's

---

[24] See, for example, R. S. Milne and H. C. McKenzie, *Marginal Seat, 1955* (London: Hansard Society, 1958), pp. 117-21.

ranks, for example, there is a widespread, alternative explanation for the party's defeat: that the Labour Government was insufficiently socialist. There is a trivial sense in which this is true. Had the economic trends of 1974–1979 been different, had the average standard of living rapidly improved, and had unemployment and price levels remained stationary, it would obviously have been more difficult for the Conservatives to win. But rising living standards, full employment, and price stability are the holy grail of all governments, not just socialist; whether the "socialist path" would have led to it, especially within the period of a single parliament, is a different and debatable question. The explanation is also true in a more serious sense, but still a minor one. If, as socialists within the Labour party urge, the Labour cabinet had been obliged to follow the advice of the wider Labour movement, it would not have attempted to impose a 5 percent limit to wage increases. The events culminating in the winter's strikes would not have been set in motion, and the electorate would probably not have deserted the Government in such large numbers.

But there is a third sense in which the explanation flies in the face of all reality. Had the electorate, or even just the working-class electorate, hankered after bold and imaginative socialist policies, only to be thwarted by fainthearts in the Labour leadership, there would be evidence of it. One would expect to find substantial (and growing) support for socialist leaders within the Labour party, for socialist parties outside the Labour party, and, above all, for socialist principles and policies. But not a hint of this is suggested by either the election result or the opinion surveys. For example, Gallup's election-day survey asked about preferences for Callaghan's successor as leader of the Labour party (see table 9–15). Both the old standard-bearer of the left, Michael Foot, and the new, Tony Benn, trailed behind such center-right figures as Shirley Williams, David Owen, and Denis Healey (the front-runner), not only among the electorate as a whole, but among Labour's natural constituency of manual workers and trade union members. Among Labour defectors—who need to be won back if Labour is to regain office—Foot's and Benn's lack of appeal was even more apparent.

The fate of the far-left parties at the election is even more instructive. They did spectacularly badly, even for fringe parties. The thirty-eight Communist candidates, all standing in overwhelmingly working-class areas, averaged 0.9 percent of the constituency vote. Even the hurriedly formed Ecology party did better (1.1 percent), as did the National Front in ten of the twelve seats in which it competed against Communists. The Workers' Revolutionary party

## TABLE 9–15

THE NEXT LABOUR LEADER: PREFERENCE OF VARIOUS GROUPS OF VOTERS
(percent)

| Next Labour Leader | All Voters | Labour Voters | Labour Defectors | Manual Workers | Trade Union Members |
|---|---|---|---|---|---|
| Denis Healey | 25 | 36 | 20 | 27 | 26 |
| Shirley Williams | 17 | 14 | 27 | 15 | 17 |
| David Owen | 15 | 10 | 14 | 15 | 15 |
| Tony Benn | 9 | 15 | 8 | 11 | 12 |
| Michael Foot | 9 | 14 | 5 | 10 | 9 |
| Peter Shore | 8 | 7 | 13 | 7 | 7 |
| Other | 17 | 5 | 13 | 17 | 13 |
| Total | 100 | 100 | 100 | 100 | 100 |
| N | (1,795) | (615) | (159) | (1,143) | (750) |

NOTE: The survey question was, "If Mr. Callaghan retired as leader of the Labour party, who on this list would you like to see take his place as Labour leader?" Columns may not add to totals because of rounding.

SOURCE: BBC Gallup survey, May 2-3, 1979.

did worse still, aways coming bottom of the poll (except where an independent stood). Disillusioned one-time Labour supporters defected to the right, not the left. To ascribe this to a thirsting after true socialism has a certain dialectical charm, but little by way of logic or evidence to commend it.

A radically different but equally ideological interpretation of the election is held by some Conservatives. To them 1979 marked more than a mere alternation of party in office: it made a decisive break with the postwar consensus.[25] It reflected a popular counterrevolution against the welfare state, the mixed economy, price and wage controls, and state intervention in industry, financed by excessive taxes, and managed by a bloated bureaucracy. This view carries some initial plausibility. The election did offer voters an unusually clear choice of direction;[26] the parties' proposals and objectives were, as

---

[25] For a good example of this view, see Ben J. Wattenberg, "Uncle Jim and the Iron Lady," *Public Opinion*, vol. 2, no. 3 (June/July 1979), pp. 47-50.

[26] In the 1979 British Election Study 48 percent said there was "a good deal" of difference between the parties, and another 30 percent "some difference," the largest proportions since Butler and Stokes began the studies in 1964.

this chapter has shown, the main determinants of the vote; and the Conservative party was the clear victor. Many of its specific proposals and objectives—on council house sales, on taxation, on crime and vandalism, on trade union reform—had an appeal that was nationwide, winning the support and sometimes the vote of Labour's natural sympathizers. Moreover, for the first time in a generation, intellectual fashion had turned to the right. Neoconservative ideas, especially on the role of the market and the limits and dangers of big government, were, if not yet in the ascendant, undergoing vigorous revival; whereas social democracy's collectivist trinity of nationalization, social welfare, and trade unionism had been tried and tested—and, it seemed, had failed.

Yet it would be wildly premature to assume that the 1979 election marks a permanent realignment, either electorally or ideologically. This is not only because what makes an election a realigning one is not the decisiveness of the result itself, but the subsequent success of the Government in consolidating its newly won support. There are two additional grounds for caution. First, in absolute terms 1979 was no Conservative landslide. The Conservatives' share of the vote and its share of the electorate fell below those of its earlier postwar victories. Conservative "identifiers" were, at 40 percent of the electorate, no thicker on the ground than in 1970 or 1964, and only a fraction more numerous than Labour identifiers (39 percent). Moreover, in continuation of a ten-year trend, the *strength* of allegiance among Conservative (and Labour) identifiers declined further.[27]

Second, public support for Conservative policies, however overwhelming in certain cases, remains selective. In particular, it does not extend to the central tenet of the free marketeers: the radical reduction of the state's economic role. Table 9–16 demonstrates that May 1979 was not a British version of Proposition 13. When forced to *choose*, survey respondents split 70 to 30 in favor of "keeping up government services such as health, education and welfare" rather than cutting taxes. Every social and political group, including Conservative voters and the middle classes, preferred to forgo tax cuts. The pattern of opinion on state subsidies to protect jobs was similar: electors divided 79 to 21 in support, and the majority in all groups was in favor. It is true that on incomes policy, public opinion tipped

---

[27] Scoring 3 for "very strong," 2 for "fairly strong," and 1 for "not very strong," one discovers that the mean partisan strength of Conservative identifiers has fallen as follows:

| | | | |
|------|------|-----------|------|
| 1964 | 2.37 | Feb. 1974 | 2.10 |
| 1966 | 2.37 | Oct. 1974 | 2.10 |
| 1970 | 2.40 | 1979      | 1.99 |

## TABLE 9-16

### ATTITUDES TO THREE ASPECTS OF THE STATE'S ECONOMIC ROLE
(percent)

| Attitude | All Voters | Con. Voters | Con. Loyalists | Con. Recruits | Lab. Defectors | Managers and Professionals (social class AB) |
|---|---|---|---|---|---|---|
| In favor of "keeping up government services such as health, education and welfare even if it means taxes cannot be cut" | 70 | 55 | 51 | 63 | 75 | 58 |
| "Giving government subsidies where that is necessary to protect jobs" is a "good idea" | 79 | 66 | 65 | 70 | 80 | 67 |
| In favor of the government "leaving it to employees and trade unions to negotiate wages and salaries alone" rather than "setting firm guidelines" | 53 | 58 | 58 | 59 | 53 | 57 |

NOTE: All percentages are based on dichotomous variables. The small proportion of "don't knows" were excluded from the percentage base.

SOURCE: BBC Gallup survey, May 2-3, 1979.

against state intervention, but only by 53 to 47 percent. The fact is that in Britain public attitudes to big government—unlike those in the United States perhaps—are more a matter of pragmatic self-interest than of principle. Where the state is of direct personal benefit—as guarantors of employment or in the form of the National Health Service—people are broadly in favor; where the personal advantage of its involvement is less obvious, as in many cases of nationalization, people are largely hostile. The result is that hostility to big government is neither widely nor deeply felt. The people's flag may not be deepest red, but it is not deepest blue either.

# Appendix A

## Manifestoes, Speeches, and the Doctrine of the Mandate

### Shelley Pinto-Duschinsky

The style and content of British electioneering have been criticized during the last decade. Party leaders are accused of spending most of their time during general election campaigns attacking their opponents. In the election of 1970, 70 percent of the Conservative leader's speeches and 75 percent of the Labour leader's were devoted to attacking the other side. In February 1974, the pattern was similar. As Richard Rose points out in his study *The Problem of Party Government*, "the choice both party leaders stress is negative: reject my opponent."[1]

The party leaders are also accused of putting forward vague images and avoiding reference to partisan symbols. In the campaign of February 1974, Harold Wilson's speeches referred to socialism only twice, and Edward Heath, the Conservative prime minister, referred to free enterprise only five times. "The two leaders differed in their choice of symbols," Rose writes,

> for Heath most often invoked references to "fairness," "strength" and "moderation," whereas Wilson spoke of "families" and, in attacking the Heath government, "crisis" and "conflict." These contrasting references did not reflect differences in policies, for Edward Heath favoured families and was against conflict, just as Harold Wilson accepted Heath's positive evaluation of fair, moderate and strong government. The contrasts in rhetoric reflect the different images that each leader seeks to project, an image devoid, incidently, of specific meaning in policy terms.[2]

---

[1] Richard Rose, *The Problem of Party Government* (Harmondsworth, Middx.: Penguin Books, 1975), p. 304.

[2] Ibid., p. 303. Rose's comments are based on an analysis by the present author

In their main speeches and on television, party leaders avoid making precise statements about their programs. However, detailed commitments are contained in the fine print of the party manifestoes—lengthy documents which the vast majority of the electors never reads. Nevertheless, the party that wins the election claims a democratic mandate for each pledge included in its manifesto. This doctrine of the mandate Samuel Finer has called a "degradation of the democratic dogma."[3]

When party leaders do make pledges during an election, these often involve reckless government spending. Michael Pinto-Duschinsky attributes the poor economic performance of British Governments in the 1950s and 1960s partly to their policy of "bread and circuses"—"the sacrifice of policies desirable for the long-term well-being of a country in favor of over-lenient measures and temporary palliatives bringing an immediate political return."[4] Finer simply condemns the two main parties for "fiddling the economy" and "economic bribery of the electorate."[5]

This appendix examines whether such complaints can justly be made about the general election of 1979. It is based on an analysis of the Labour, Conservative, and Liberal manifestoes, transcripts of their party political broadcasts, and handouts of the party leaders' election speeches. The excerpts of James Callaghan's speeches issued by Transport House between April 9, 1979, and May 2, 1979, contained approximately 13,500 words; extracts of Margaret Thatcher's speeches from April 11 to May 1 issued by the Conservative Central Office, approximately 18,500 words; and extracts of David Steel's speeches from April 9 to May 2 issued by the Liberal Party Organization contained approximately 11,900 words. The leaders' speeches in 1979 are compared with those of Harold Wilson and Edward Heath, the Labour and Conservative leaders, in the campaign of February 1974.

For each party leader, the following questions will be considered: (1) What were the main themes and key words in the speeches? (2) Which policy pledges were most frequently mentioned? (3) To what extent did the leader's speeches reflect the party manifesto?

of leaders' speeches in the February 1974 campaign. See Shelley Pinto-Duschinsky, "A Matter of Words," *New Society*, vol. 27, no. 596 (March 7, 1974), pp. 570-71.

[3] Samuel E. Finer, *The Changing British Party System 1945-1979* (Washington, D.C.: American Enterprise Institute, 1980).

[4] Michael Pinto-Duschinsky, "Bread and Circuses? The Conservatives in Office, 1951-1964," in Vernon Bogdanor and Robert Skidelsky, eds., *The Age of Affluence 1951-1964* (London: Macmillan, 1970), p. 59.

[5] Finer, *Changing British Party System.*

## Attack Ratios

One of the most striking features of political speeches in the elections of 1970 and February 1974 was that the two main party leaders spent less than one-fifth of their time describing their ideas for the future. In 1979, the Liberal leader charged the two principal parties with once again indulging in "Yah-boo politics" and "mindless cat-calling."[6] Table 1 shows that in the 1979 campaign the leaders collectively gave far more emphasis to their future plans and spent less time attacking their opponents. Whereas the Labour and Conservative leaders had devoted an average of less than 19 percent of their words in 1970 and 1974 to future plans, the figure increased to 41 percent in 1979. The Liberal leader devoted one-half of his words to explaining his plans for the future. James Callaghan in 1979 gave far more emphasis to the future (37 percent) than Prime Minister Heath in February 1974 (17 percent) or Prime Minister Wilson in 1970 (5 percent).

Increased attention to the future in 1979 was linked with some decrease in attacks on other parties. In 1970 and 1974, the Conservative and Labour leaders devoted 62 percent of their output to such attacks compared with 44 percent in 1979. In 1979, the two party leaders still spent slightly more time attacking than putting forward their own plans (44 percent compared with 41 percent). In 1974, when Heath was under heavy attack for his handling of the unions and the resulting three-day week, he spent the greatest proportion of his time (47 percent) defending himself. It is clear that in 1979, Thatcher had no personal record to defend and no wish to defend Heath's; she spent 7 percent of her time defending herself. Callaghan, on the other hand, spent 24 percent of his time defending his record as prime minister. It is not surprising that the Liberal party under Steel spent the most time expounding its plans, for on the Liberals' projected reorganization of elections and government would rest their only chance of any real power.

Evidence offered in this paper suggests that these figures reflect a conscious choice made by the party leaders to emphasize their plans for the future—perhaps out of a sense of facing into the 1980s, perhaps in response to the pressure of economic insecurity. Whatever the reasons, Wilson's dictum "a week is a long time in politics" was no formula for success in this election.

The Labour and Conservative parties were each allocated five ten-minute party political broadcasts and the Liberals three, and each broadcast was shown simultaneously on the three television networks.

---

[6] David Steel, April 17, 1979.

## TABLE 1

### STRATEGIC BREAKDOWN OF LEADERS' CAMPAIGN SPEECHES, 1970, FEBRUARY 1974, AND 1979

(in percent)

| Strategic Emphasis | Conservative | | | Labour | | | Liberal |
|---|---|---|---|---|---|---|---|
| | Heath | | Thatcher | Wilson | | Callaghan | Steel |
| | 1970 | 1974 | 1979 | 1970 | 1974 | 1979 | 1979 |
| Attacking other side | 70 | 36 | 49 | 75 | 69 | 39 | 40 |
| Defending record | — | 47 | 7 | 20 | 8 | 24 | 7 |
| Expounding future plans | 30 | 17 | 45 | 5 | 23 | 37 | 53 |

NOTE: The figures are percentages of words in the leaders' campaign speeches devoted to the stated strategic emphasis. For 1974, the percentages include only speeches delivered in the first days of the campaign (February 11-18).
SOURCE: David Robertson, "The Content of Election Addresses and Leaders' Speeches," in David Butler and Michael Pinto-Duschinsky, *The British General Election of 1970* (London: Macmillan, 1971), pp. 443-444; Shelley Pinto-Duschinsky, "A Matter of Words"; and extracts of leaders' speeches issued by the three party headquarters, 1979 (hereafter cited as leader's campaign speeches).

TABLE 2

STRATEGIC BREAKDOWN OF PARTY POLITICAL BROADCASTS, 1979
(percent)

| Strategic Emphasis | Conservative | Labour | Liberal |
|---|---|---|---|
| Attacking other side | 51 | 44 | 59 |
| Defending record | 14 | 34 | 17 |
| Expounding future plans | 35 | 23 | 25 |

SOURCE: Author's analysis of transcripts of the party political broadcasts.

An analysis of the strategic emphasis of these broadcasts is reported in table 2. It shows that for all three parties, the attack ratio was higher for broadcasts than for leaders' speeches—and highest of all for the Liberals, who accused the other parties of conducting "slanging matches." To some extent this may be the result of a media bias: a dole queue makes more impact on television than graphs showing the anticipated effects of future economic policies. Certainly the advice from media professionals would have been to avoid complex ideological argument, to present one message at a time, and that, simply. It also made sense in terms of overall campaign strategy: if the media could be used for attacking, the leaders in their speeches could maintain a more statesmanlike stance. The thrust of the attacks in the broadcasts, which were subject to review by party strategists, was that the country had no future with the other parties.

## The Labour Campaign

The incumbent prime minister, James Callaghan, lost the election. The discrepancy between Callaghan's political strategy and that of other parts of the Labour party will be documented here. Did Callaghan offer the voter a clear ideology or specific policy choices, which both pointed forward and discredited the radical left?

After the general election in May 1979, the Labour party held its annual conference in September. It may be described as having as its theme "sin and retribution"—that is, Callaghan's sin in losing the election, which the left predictably blamed on the party leader's right-wing strategy and on his neglect of traditional socialist themes, and the left-wing attempt at retribution, which was still going on a year later, though Callaghan remained the leader of his party and leader of the Opposition in the House of Commons.

311

The left accused Callaghan of "using a veto" to keep certain items out of the 1979 manifesto. A section of one left-wing discussion document is headed "What got left out." This document states:

> the most glaring omission in the Manifesto, in terms of party policy, concerns the whole area of economic and industrial strategy.... But what was also important was that the Labour government had publicly indicated its rejection of the party's alternative strategy (reflation, import controls, a stronger National Enterprise Board).... And we therefore knew that the words in the Manifesto meant completely different things to ministers on the one hand, to the National Executive Committee and the party on the other.[7]

The left went so far as to state that at the last joint cabinet-National Executive Committee meeting before the May general elecion, Callaghan had given the left the impression that he would resign as leader if they did not tone down their demands on the manifesto's contents.[8] Were the complaints justified? At the party conference, left-wingers identified nine pledges they had wished to include in the manifesto:

1. abolition of the House of Lords
2. a thirty-five hour working week
3. a cut in arms spending
4. selective import controls
5. a clear target for restoring full employment
6. an annual wealth tax on fortunes over £150,000
7. firm planning agreements between government and big companies
8. scrapping of the Common Agricultural Policy and other offensive Common Market regulations
9. a basic election commitment to a "fundamental and irreversible shift in the balance of wealth and power in favour of working people and their families."

Of these demands, all, in fact, had appeared in the manifesto, two of them unmodified and the others in watered-down form. In addition, the manifesto included other left-wing measures, several of which would redistribute wealth, such as the proposal to nationalize the commercial ports or to give government greater proportionate ownership in private companies, or limit personal choice, such as the

---

[7] *Daily Telegraph*, September 29, 1979.

[8] Reports and quotations of left-wing documents taken from the *Daily Telegraph*, September 29, and October 1, 1979. See also John Cole and Adam Raphael, "How Jim won the battle of the manifesto," *Observer*, April 8, 1979.

## TABLE 3

### MAIN LEFT-WING PLEDGES IN THE LABOUR MANIFESTO, 1979

1. "In the next Parliament, we shall introduce an annual wealth tax on . . . people whose total net personal wealth exceeds £150,000."

2. "Labour will end, as soon as possible, the remaining public subsidies and public support to independent schools."

3. "We shall progressively increase the national stake in the North Sea" [that is, North Sea oil].

4. "We reaffirm our policy to bring commercial ports and cargo handling into public ownership."

5. "We shall conclude planning agreements with the major industrial companies, with the necessary back-up statutory powers to do so."

6. "Wherever we give direct aid to a company out of public funds, we shall reserve the right to take a proportionate share of the ownership."

7. "The Labour Government will ensure that imports enter our market only within acceptable limits."

8. "We propose . . . in the next Parliament, to abolish the delaying power and legislative veto of the House of Lords."

9. "We shall continue with our plans to reduce the proportion of the nation's resources devoted to defense."

10. "Labour will . . . encourage the development of building workers' cooperatives."

11. "The National Freight Corporation must be enabled to provide the basis for expanding the public sector in the road haulage industry."

12. "We seek to bring about a fundamental shift in the balance of wealth and power in favour of working people and their families."

SOURCE: The Labour party's 1979 election manifesto, "The Labour Way is the Better Way."

proposal to end the remaining public subsidies to independent schools (including their tax status as nonprofit institutions). The main left-wing measures in the Labour manifesto are listed in table 3.

Clearly Labour's 1979 manifesto contained some radical proposals —but the same cannot be said of Callaghan's election speeches. Although he was obliged to compromise with the left over the manifesto,

## TABLE 4
### KEY WORDS IN THE LABOUR MANIFESTO, 1979

| Category | Number of Mentions |
|---|---|
| Caring society | 125 |
| Ideology | 64 |
|     public ownership, public sector | (17) |
|     democracy | (12) |
|     working people | (11) |
|     free, freedom | (7) |
|     social justice, injustice | (6) |
|     democratic socialist | (2) |
|     socialist | (2) |
|     social criteria determine distribution | (2) |
|     democratic socialist party | (1) |
|     welfare state | (1) |
|     government take greater share ownership | (1) |
| Families | 53 |
| Jobs, employment, unemployment | 42 |
| Industry | 26 |
| EEC | 26 |
| Inflation | 13 |
| Prices | 11 |
| Taxes | 11 |
| Unions | 9 |
| Crime | 9 |
| Race relations | 8 |
| Devolution | 5 |
| Import control | 4 |
| Disarmament | 4 |

SOURCE: Author's analysis of the Labour party's election manifesto.

Callaghan virtually ignored socialist pledges and themes in his personal campaign output. The contrast between the manifesto and the Callaghan speeches emerges from an analysis of the key words and key-word categories shown in table 4.

Although ideological words appear frequently in the manifesto, the key term "nationalization" is not mentioned. Words such as "public ownership" or "planning agreements" replace it. The words "socialist" and "socialism" usually become "democratic socialist" or "social justice." Despite his need to compromise with the Labour left, Callaghan was able to moderate the overall tone of the manifesto. In characteristic language, the Labour manifesto describes its alternative scenario for society this way:

> We believe in a caring and democratic society where social justice prevails, where working people and their families are protected from the ravages of unemployment. We shall use public ownership to create new jobs. Every man is entitled to food, shelter, education, health care and a dignified old age.

Mention of socialism, redistribution of wealth, and the welfare state assume a back seat, and expansion of the public sector is coupled with the idea of job creation, job preservation, or regional development.

Callaghan's speeches give even less attention to socialist doctrine. The words "socialism" and "socialist" do not appear in the excerpts from his speeches issued by Transport House, and staff members at Labour party headquarters could not locate these words in extracts of his speeches. Allowing that he may have used such words *ex tempore*, one staff member added, "I would hazard a guess that he is unlikely to have used those words, as he is not one given to philosophising about political theory. . . ."[9] Like Wilson in 1974, Callaghan stressed instead his concern for families and for the unity of the British people (see table 5).[10]

The press handouts of Callaghan's speeches did not use the words socialist, socialism, social justice, democratic socialist, social criteria determine distribution, nationalization, extend public owner-

---

[9] The speeches handed out by Transport House do not comprise Callaghan's entire output of words during the election campaign. But they do contain the passages which the party managers wished to draw to the attention of the media and the extracts are therefore particularly significant. When the Labour leader's office was asked about the apparent omission of "socialism" and "socialist" from his campaign speeches, the reply was that these words "appeared with great frequency" in the full texts of speeches. But these full texts were not available for analysis. According to Transport House, there was no reference to these words in the advance texts of the leader's speeches, "however it would be dangerous to surmise from that evidence that he never used the words during the election campaign. He might have strayed from his texts, or mentioned socialism on TV/radio interviews—which transcripts we do not have."

[10] Pinto-Duschinsky, "A Matter of Words."

## TABLE 5
### Key Words in Labour Leaders' Campaign Speeches, February 1974 and 1979

| Wilson, 1974 | | Callaghan, 1979 | |
|---|---|---|---|
| Families | 175 | Caring society | 173 |
| families | (79) | pensions, pensioners | (30) |
| housewives | (33) | housing, homes | (29) |
| British people | (63) | fairness | (26) |
| Crisis and conflict | 82 | education, schools | (25) |
| crisis | (46) | food | (13) |
| divisiveness | (23) | Families | 145 |
| confrontation | (7) | families | (48) |
| conflict | (6) | children | (28) |
| Profiteers and property | | mothers | (11) |
| speculators | 44 | fathers | (1) |
| Moderation | 21 | Prices | 111 |
| Fairness | 13 | Unity | 91 |
| Militants | 13 | Britain, one nation | (25) |
| Nationalization | 11 | Jobs, employment, | |
| nationalization | (6) | unemployment | 83 |
| public ownership | (5) | Taxes | 49 |
| Fraudulent election | 8 | Ideology | 45 |
| Social contract | 7 | working people | (23) |
| Socialism | 2 | class division | (14) |
| | | equality | (8) |
| | | Unions | 33 |
| | | Industrial relations | 28 |
| | | Inflation | 24 |
| | | Crime | 23 |
| | | EEC | 20 |
| | | Race | 20 |
| | | North Sea oil | 7 |
| | | Devolution | 4 |
| | | Disarmament | 1 |

Source: Author's analysis of Wilson's and Callaghan's campaign speeches.

ship, or worker cooperatives. They did refer to a just society (once), working people (twenty-three times), equality (eight times), and class division (fourteen times). The Labour manifesto, on the other hand, used socialist (two times), social justice (six times), democratic socialist (two times), and social criteria determine distribution (two times). Instead of using the word "nationalization," the manifesto spoke of "extending public ownership" (eleven times). It mentioned worker cooperatives (four times) but not class division.

Callaghan's omission of the words "socialist" and "nationalization" is especially significant in view of his frequent mention of making Britain "one nation." "One nation" is a characteristically Tory phrase often used by Disraeli;[11] and the One Nation Group of M.P.s is a postwar Conservative group which included Edward Heath. One could claim, then, that the language of Callaghan's election speeches owed less to Karl Marx than to Benjamin Disraeli.

Other favorite Callaghan phrases were those related to the caring society (173 mentions), controlling prices (111 mentions), and unemployment (83 mentions). He seems to have felt it necessary to refer repeatedly to two Conservative topics, crime (23 times) and race relations (20 times). Paradoxically, Thatcher, whose faux pas had made race an important issue before the election, mentioned the word only once in the campaign speeches excerpted for distribution to the press.

Another contrast between the Labour manifesto and the party leader's speeches is evident from a comparison of the themes and the specific pledges that appear in both. The themes that appeared most frequently in Callaghan's speeches are shown in table 6, the pledges in table 7. A topic is considered a theme if it was treated in general terms but a pledge only if a concrete policy was put forward. Table 6 shows that Callaghan concentrated heavily on the themes of cooperation and national unity and restriction of price rises. Price stability would be achieved only by Labour's proposal for a strengthened Price Commission and by its "concordat" with the trade unions, which would lead to moderation in pay bargaining. A third major theme was the need for greater social benefits for special groups in the population, particularly pensioners and young marrieds.

As table 7 shows, Callaghan omitted to mention most of the main left-wing measures in the manifesto. He maintained silence on the proposed wealth tax, the attack on private schools, the extension of public ownership, and the emasculation of the House of Lords. The manifesto's pledge to plan reductions in the proportion of GNP devoted to defense received no more than a passing nod—and even that

---

[11] In his novel *Sybil*, Disraeli condemned the existence in Britain of "two nations," the rich and the poor, between whom there was "no intercourse and no sympathy; who are as ignorant of each other's habits, thoughts and feelings, as if they were dwellers in different zones or inhabitants of different planets." See Robert Blake, *Disraeli* (London: Eyre and Spottiswoode, 1966), p. 201.

## TABLE 6

### THEMES FROM THE LABOUR MANIFESTO MOST OFTEN MENTIONED BY CALLAGHAN

| Theme | Number of Speeches in Which Theme Appeared at Least Once |
|---|---|
| Cooperation instead of confrontation in society | 10 |
| One nation, united | 9 |
| Voluntary agreement between Government and Trades Union Congress to keep down wage demands and inflation | 8 |
| Pensions linked to prices or earnings, whichever higher | 7 |
| Moderation in pay bargaining for price stability | 7 |
| Ensure Price Commission the power to keep prices down | 6 |
| Halve inflation again in next three years | 6 |
| Freeze on EEC food prices where surplus exists | 5 |
| Home loan scheme for first-time buyers | 5 |
| Cooperation, fairness | 5 |

SOURCE: Author's analysis of Labour party manifesto.

was different in emphasis. "Our defense must be strong," Callaghan said. "We have made it possible to dream the dream of . . . swords into plowshares. . . . But we cannot yet relax the [military] effort."[12]

Beside the glaring omission from the speeches of the main left-wing planks in the manifesto, over a hundred other specific pledges went unsung—quite simply because Labour's forty-page manifesto contained a profusion of declarations about a variety of specialized topics that a party leader could not be expected to refer to in speeches geared to the electors at large.[13] Most of the pledges Callaghan did mention involved an increase in public spending. Only one—the promise that a Labour Government would not print more money than the country was earning—involved a measure of economic austerity.

---

[12] Speech at Cardiff, April 19, 1979.

[13] Thus, the manifesto, but not Callaghan, promised that a Labour Government would "actively participate in the UNCTAD 5 and other negotiations," "press for improvements in the Lomé Convention," "accept the recommendations of the Bennett Committee," "review the 1824 Vagrancy Act, with a view to the repeal of Section 4," and so on. Finer states that the 1979 Labour manifesto included no fewer than 133 specific commitments and the Conservative manifesto, 74. See Finer, *Changing British Party System*, chap. 3.

## TABLE 7

### CALLAGHAN'S SPECIFIC PLEDGES

| Pledges Targeted to Special Groups | Broadly National Pledges |
|---|---|
| 1. Provide a job or job training to anyone who has been out of work for twelve months | 1. Continue freeze on Common Market food prices where produce is in surplus |
| 2. Tie increases in pensions to price increases or earnings increases, whichever higher | 2. Give Price Commission the power to cut unjustified price rises |
| 3. Abolish TV license for pensioners during the next parliament | 3. Raise tax threshold for average wage earner |
| 4. Promulgate a tenants' charter extending the rights of families in council housing | 4. Print no more money than the country is earning |
| 5. Create a home loan scheme for first-time buyers | 5. Hold an industrial summit each spring to increase productivity and to reach some agreement on the economic prospects for the following year |
| 6. Retain the Scotland Act and reopen offer of talks with the other parties | |
| 7. Increase budget of Scottish Development Agency from £300 to £800 | |
| 8. Provide nursery education for nearly all four year-olds and nearly half of three year-olds in the next few years | |
| 9. Introduce a new bill similar to the Local Government Grants (Ethnic Groups) Bill | |

SOURCE: Author's analysis of Callaghan's campaign speeches.

The main conclusion to be drawn from this analysis is that, had Labour won the election, it would have had a mandate for stricter price controls, for the voluntary concordat with the trade unions, and for an extension of various social benefits. There would have been no mandate for the left-wing planks or for the large number of particular pledges which were never brought to the public's awareness by either pronouncements or allusions of the Labour party leader.

## The Tory Campaign

Margaret Thatcher won the election with a working majority in the House of Commons. Did she offer the voter a clear ideology? Did she offer the voter specific policy alternatives for the future?

The key words and key-word categories of the Conservative manifesto for 1979 point to several themes (see table 8). Much time was spent criticizing the power of the unions and union encroachment upon individual freedom and expressing concern about social problems (especially the right of home ownership and the need to maintain high educational standards). The view of the economy that emerges emphasizes the private sector's vital role in job generation and, thus, in the prosperity of the nation, as well as the need to relate wage settlements to productivity. According to the manifesto a free society is one where individuals assume responsibility for their actions, in opposition to statism, which destroys invention and incentive. Crime is a reflection of the breakdown of respect for law (no matter how democratically instituted). The supremacy of a Parliament that is democratically elected must be upheld. With regard to the EEC, a Britain with partners is best able to protect British international interests. And in the world at large, the military threat to the West from the Communist bloc has grown steadily, with the result that British defenses must be improved.

The Conservative manifesto uses more ideological words and expressions than the Labour manifesto, and Thatcher's speeches echo it (see table 9). One reason for this, no doubt, is that the Conservative party constitution gives the party leader more power over the manifesto than the Labour constitution gives to the leader of the Labour party. While Callaghan moved away from the ideological—especially socialist—vocabulary contained in his party's manifesto, Thatcher warmed to the ideological expressions in her party's manifesto, even surpassing it in the frequency of her use of them. Her vision of economic freedom and of an ordered society where Parliament reigned supreme, where individual liberty and individual responsibility were two sides of the same coin, served to unify her speeches. In her attacks on Labour, the same ideological tone emerged.

Thatcher's speeches contained more political philosophy than Callaghan's. Callaghan did not mention "socialism"; Thatcher mentioned "freedom," "a free society," "freedom under the law," "a free enterprise economy," "liberties," and "individuals" seventy-five times. In attacking Labour, she used the words "socialism" and "socialist" forty-nine times. Another vital set of words were "rule of law," "law

## TABLE 8
### Key Words in the Conservative Manifesto, 1979

| Category | Number of Mentions |
|---|---|
| Unions | 50 |
| Caring society | 44 |
| Economy | 43 |
|   private sector | (9) |
|   inflation | (8) |
|   free enterprise economy | (3) |
| Freedom | 24 |
|   responsibility | (9) |
|   free society, freedom | (8) |
|   liberty | (3) |
| Taxes | 24 |
| Socialism | 22 |
|   socialist programs | (7) |
|   nationalization | (7) |
|   extremists | (3) |
| EEC | 21 |
| Jobs, employment, unemployment | 16 |
| Industry | 15 |
| Race relations | 14 |
| Crime | 14 |
| Law and order | 12 |
|   supremacy of Parliament | (6) |
|   uphold Parliament and rule of law | (5) |
| Prices | 10 |
| Defense | 10 |
| Families | 3 |

SOURCE: Author's analysis of the Conservative party manifesto.

and order," "uphold Parliament," and "democracy." These appeared fifty-nine times.

Edward Heath mentioned many of the same issues in 1974. But Heath's speeches did not force home a coherent ideological theme. He mentioned "law and order" and "parliamentary government" twenty-five times; Thatcher mentioned them forty-nine times. Heath mentioned

# TABLE 9

## KEY WORDS IN TORY LEADERS' CAMPAIGN SPEECHES, FEBRUARY 1974 AND 1979

| Heath, 1974 | | Thatcher, 1979 | |
|---|---|---|---|
| Fair | 56 | Freedom | 85 |
| Strong | 54 | free society, freedom | (44) |
| firm | (17) | individuals | (15) |
| law and order | (15) | democrat, democracy | (10) |
| strong government | (12) | responsibility | (10) |
| democratic | (9) | liberties | (6) |
| Moderate | 53 | Unions, picketing, secret | |
| moderate | (32) | ballot, concordat, etc. | 80 |
| one nation | (8) | Caring society | 77 |
| unity | (7) | pensions | (18) |
| conciliation | (6) | medical care, NHS | (12) |
| Responsible | 15 | educational standards | (11) |
| Militants | 15 | housing, home ownership | (9) |
| Crisis | 12 | benefits | (8) |
| Nationalization | 11 | References to socialism | 72 |
| Parliamentary government | 10 | socialist, socialism | (49) |
| Conflict, free-for-all | 9 | British tradition, unity | 61 |
| Inflation | 8 | Law and order, uphold | |
| British tradition | 6 | Parliament | 49 |
| Social enterprise | 5 | Jobs, employment, | |
| The individual, free | | unemployment | 49 |
| enterprise | 5 | Taxes | 43 |
| | | Families | 38 |
| | | children | (15) |
| | | support family life | (12) |
| | | old | (11) |
| | | Economy | 30 |
| | | inflation | (11) |
| | | small businesses | (10) |
| | | free enterprise economy | (9) |
| | | Industry, industrial relations | 26 |
| | | Defense of Great Britain | 25 |
| | | Prices | 18 |
| | | National decline | 17 |
| | | EEC | 10 |
| | | Devolution | 4 |
| | | Race relations | 1 |

SOURCE: Author's analysis of Heath's and Thatcher's campaign speeches.

## TABLE 10
### Themes from the Conservative Manifesto Most Often Mentioned by Thatcher

| Theme | Number of Speeches in Which Theme Appeared at Least Once |
|---|---|
| Create genuine jobs | 6 |
| Freedom under the law | 5 |
| Reduce direct taxation | 5 |
| Reform trade union law | 4 |
| Expand small businesses | 3 |
| Reduce crime on the streets | 3 |
| Reduce inflation | 3 |
| Protect economic freedom | 3 |
| Increase pension levels to take account of price rises | 3 |
| Continue Christmas bonus given to pensioners | 3 |
| Increase productivity | 3 |
| Restore incentives | 3 |

SOURCE: Author's analysis of Conservative manifesto and Thatcher's campaign speeches.

"individuals" and "free enterprise" five times, Thatcher fifteen times. While Heath and Thatcher mentioned "democracy" and "responsibility" a similar number of times, Thatcher alone talked about a free society (forty-four mentions). Thatcher drew more frequent contrasts between her vision and the socialist vision. She also struck a patriotic note more often, addressing herself directly and frequently to British tradition and national unity.

Which policy themes from the manifesto were most popular with Thatcher in her speeches, and which of its concrete pledges did she personally make to the electorate? (See tables 10 and 11.) Unlike Callaghan, Thatcher did not stress rising prices. She linked the case for individual liberty and incentive to the practical claim that economic freedom would go hand-in-hand with a reduction in direct taxes and the creation of new and genuine jobs. "Freedom under the law" and "parliamentary sovereignty" she linked to reforming trade union law and combating crime on the streets. The Thatcher speeches

323

## TABLE 11
### THATCHER'S SPECIFIC PLEDGES

| Pledges Targeted to Special Groups | Broadly National Pledges |
|---|---|
| 1. Allow tenants to purchase their council houses | 1. Draw certain legal boundary lines with regard to picketing, the closed shop, and secret union ballots |
| 2. Maintain the pensioners' Christmas bonus | 2. Cut taxes on income, capital taxes, taxes on savings, and impose taxes on spending rather than on earning |
| 3. Increase pensions in step with price rises | |
| 4. Abolish Earnings Rule for pensioners | 3. Spend more on defense |
| 5. Exempt War Widows' pension from taxes | 4. Spend more on law enforcement |
| 6. Give decisions on school organization back to locally elected councilors and parents | 5. Reform the Common Agricultural Policy and make certain that Britain does not pay more than its fair share of the EEC budget |
| 7. Restore Service Pay to the full amount recommended by the Armed Services Pay Review Board | 6. Abolish laws like the Employment Protection Act |
| 8. Start talks with interested parties to see how Scotland can have more say in the management of its own affairs | |
| 9. Support the new Multi-Fiber Agreement of the EEC | |
| 10. Continue regional aid | |

SOURCE: Author's analysis of Thatcher's campaign speeches.

mention only a small proportion of the individual pledges included in the manifesto. Like Callaghan's pledges, most of Thatcher's were directed toward special groups of electors—particularly pensioners and council tenants. The most important national pledges in her speeches were to reduce the income tax and to initiate those reforms of trade union law relating to secret strike ballots, picketing, and the closed shop.

Thatcher projected a strong vision of the future: "I am a conviction politician," she said. "The Old Testament prophets didn't say 'Brothers, I want consensus.' They said: 'This is my faith and vision.

This is what I passionately believe. If you believe it too, then come with me'"[14] A few basic concepts were the keys. Governments, Thatcher believed, had become reactive rather than directive and their philosophies blurred, with a general drift toward statism and social fragmentation resulting. Thus, Thatcher was more concerned to redefine conservatism than to propose specific policies.

It was an advantage in this election not to be the incumbent, who would be held responsible not only for his own deficiencies but also for the cumulative failures of the Heath and Wilson Governments. Thatcher distanced herself from the immediate past but not from the historic roots of the nation. She received from the voters a mandate for a political philosophy—not, with the few exceptions shown in table 11, for specific policies.

## The Liberal Campaign

Throughout the Liberal campaign there was a consistency of emphasis between the party manifesto, entitled *The Real Fight is for Britain*, and the Liberal position put forward by the party leader, David Steel (see tables 12, 13, and 14).

At first glance, there are similarities between some of the key words in the Liberal campaign and those of the two major parties. The Liberals' talk of "cooperation" recalls Callaghan's theme of "one nation" and Thatcher's emphasis on national "unity." Yet the context and meaning of "cooperation" for the Liberals are distinctive, linked with the key Liberal concept "reform." "Reform" and its variants appear forty-five times in the manifesto and thirty-nine times in Steel's speeches. By standing for "reform" of the country's political and economic institutions, the Liberals could differentiate themselves from both the established parties while avoiding any conventional left-wing/right-wing label. Steel wished to harness the votes of those who disapproved of either "left" or "right." Another distinctly Liberal word was "conservation." It appeared (with variants) thirty-two times in the Liberal manifesto and no fewer than sixty-one times in Steel's speeches.

The Liberals wished to change the British parliamentary system in a number of ways. Through the introduction of proportional representation, they would gain more seats in the House of Commons, possibly enabling them to hold the balance of power. They also wished to introduce a freedom of information act, set fixed dates for general elections, establish powerful select committees of Parlia-

---

[14] Speech at Cardiff, April 16, 1979.

# TABLE 12
## Key Words in the Liberal Manifesto, 1979

| Category | Number of Mentions |
|---|---|
| Cooperation | 64 |
| Britain | (36) |
| cooperation | (11) |
| Lib-Lab pact, agreement | (4) |
| Democracy | 54 |
| Caring society | 52 |
| Parliament | 49 |
| Parliament | (24) |
| proportional representation | (7) |
| Reform | 45 |
| reform | (24) |
| change | (19) |
| Taxes | 40 |
| Conservation | 32 |
| Industry | 29 |
| EEC, Europe | 25 |
| Profit sharing, distribution of wealth | 11 |
| Confrontation | 8 |
| Incomes | 8 |
| Jobs, employment, unemployment | 7 |
| Crime | 6 |
| Inflation | 4 |
| Prices | 1 |

Source: Author's analysis of the Liberal party's election manifesto, *The Real Fight Is for Britain.*

ment to assert vigorous control over the executive, and replace the House of Lords with a new, democratically elected, second chamber. They favored a massive decentralization of power from Westminster and Whitehall to Scotland, Wales, and the major regions of England, with the introduction of a federal approach, which would involve giving the United Kingdom a written constitution, a bill of rights, and a supreme court. Besides this battery of institutional reforms, Steel emphasized alternative economic policies; in particular, a tax credit

## TABLE 13
### KEY WORDS IN LIBERAL CAMPAIGN SPEECHES, 1979

| *Steel, 1979* | |
|---|---|
| Conservation | 61 |
|   energy | (19) |
|   conservation | (15) |
|   nuclear power | (14) |
| Parliament | 54 |
|   Parliament | (29) |
|   people's Parliament | (11) |
|   proportional representation | (2) |
| Democracy | 53 |
|   individuals | (15) |
|   democracy, democratic | (10) |
|   liberty, liberties | (7) |
| Reform | 39 |
| Taxes | 37 |
| Cooperation | 31 |
|   Lib-Lab pact, agreement | (9) |
|   partnership | (7) |
|   cooperation | (7) |
| Caring society | 26 |
| Industry | 20 |
| EEC | 15 |
| Inflation | 13 |
| Confrontation | 11 |
| Incomes policy | 11 |
| Families | 8 |
| Profit sharing | 7 |
| Crime | 6 |
| Regions | 6 |
| Prices | 6 |

SOURCE: Author's analysis of Steel's campaign speeches.

system and profit sharing for workers. And he harkened to the call of the new ecological politics with his accent on resources and environment.

Steel's "Queen's Speech for a People's Parliament"—the speech with which the queen would open Parliament under a Steel Govern-

## TABLE 14
### THEMES FROM THE LIBERAL MANIFESTO MOST OFTEN MENTIONED
### BY STEEL

| Theme | Number of Speeches in Which Theme Appeared at Least Once |
|---|---|
| Reform tax system, tax credits | 6 |
| Reform attitude to resources and environment | 5 |
| Introduce profit sharing for workers | 5 |
| Change to government built on cooperation and partnership | 4 |
| Reform electoral system, introduce proportional representation | 4 |
| Make Liberal M.P.s a powerful wedge in next parliament | 3 |
| Adopt a permanent prices and incomes policy | 3 |
| Protect individuals from mass society | 3 |
| Protect minority rights regardless of race, age, nationality, sex | 3 |
| Pass a freedom of information act | 3 |
| Pass a bill of rights | 3 |
| Create a people's Parliament (power back to people) | 3 |
| Liberals can unite country | 3 |

SOURCE: Author's analysis of Liberal manifesto and Steel's campaign speeches.

ment—pledged six measures of constitutional reform, nine measures of economic and industrial reform, four measures of tax reform, and four measures relating to conservation and the environment (see table 15). Certain that they would not have to assume the responsibility of office, the Liberals felt free to commit themselves to an ambitious program. The party could not be accused of being vague about its intentions. Yet it was not the pledges enumerated but the central theme—institutional change—that got through to electors. Although the election results show that the public was not ready to accept the Liberal recipe, it is a fashionable brew in some influential circles and may yet reward the Liberals in the years ahead.

## Conclusion

Does the winning party in an election have a mandate to enact every measure outlined in its manifesto? Samuel Finer thinks not, and the

## TABLE 15
### STEEL'S SPECIFIC PLEDGES

| *Pledges Targeted to Special Groups* | *Broadly National Pledges* |
|---|---|
| 1. Institute consumer representation on public boards | 1. Introduce profit sharing for workers |
| 2. Increase old age pension | 2. Legislate a permanent incomes policy |
| 3. Set up Cooperative Development Bank to assist producer-cooperatives | 3. Remain in EEC |
| 4. Expand national program of industrial training | 4. Propose: <br>—freedom of information act <br>—proportional representation <br>—fixed election dates <br>—elected upper chamber to replace Lords <br>—parliamentary reform including establishment of select committees corresponding to main government departments <br>—constitutional conference to determine methods of devolution of power to regional assemblies <br>—one-tier local government authorities <br>—parish councils <br>—a national efficiency audit of central government |
| 5. Establish Agricultural Land Bank to assist small farmers | |
| 6. Adopt industrial democracy for workers | |
| 7. Encourage worker cooperatives | |
| | 5. Implement a minimum incomes policy |
| | 6. Introduce a tax credit system |
| | 7. Reject the sale of profitable public assets proposed by Labour |
| | 8. Reject the extension of nationalization |
| | 9. Establish a permanent energy Commission |
| | 10. Launch a major research and development drive into alternative energy sources |

*(Table continues on next page)*

## TABLE 15 (continued)

| Pledges Targeted to Special Groups | Broadly National Pledges |
|---|---|
| | 11. Postpone for five years construction of a commercial nuclear reprocessing plan and fast breeder reactor |
| | 12. Institute development planning in the national coal industry |
| | 13. Conserve North Sea oil and gas |

NOTE: This list is not exhaustive. For additional Liberal pledges see "The Queen's Speech for a People's Parliament," May 2, 1979.

SOURCE: Author's analysis of Steel's campaign speeches.

evidence presented here, showing that the leaders' speeches, with the exception of Steel's, mentioned only a fraction of the proposals in their parties' manifestoes, lends support to his view. If Finer is right, the critical question becomes whether a particular proposal has been forcefully presented to the electorate as a basis for future policy. The voter should not be considered as having endorsed policies he knows not of.

If the party leaders spent less time attacking each other in 1979 than they had in 1970 and 1974, it was because they spent more time expounding ideas for the future. And those ideas presented the voter with a clear choice. Margaret Thatcher's "conviction" politics introduced an ideological tone absent not only in her predecessor, Edward Heath, but, more critically, absent also in James Callaghan. Her pure ideological language and her distinctive policies meant that a ballot for Thatcher was an ambiguous endorsement of a radical reduction in the role of government. The voters took the plunge. Will they rue the day?

# Appendix B

## The British Ballot, 1979

The ballot used in the Colchester constituency in the May 1979 general election is shown here, reduced slightly from its actual size (five and one-half by two and three-quarters inches). Before 1970 no party affiliations appeared on the ballot; since then each candidate has been allowed to state his affiliation in up to six words of his own choosing.

| | | PARLIAMENTARY ELECTION<br>YOU MAY VOTE FOR NOT MORE THAN **ONE** CANDIDATE | |
|---|---|---|---|
| **1** | | **BUCK**<br>(Philip Antony Fyson Buck, of<br>Pete Hall, Colchester Road, Peldon, Colchester, Essex)<br>Your Conservative Candidate | |
| **2** | | **GAGE**<br>(Martin Charles Gage, of<br>20A Inglis Road, Colchester, Essex)<br>Liberal | |
| **3** | | **RUSSELL**<br>(Robert (known as Bob) Edward Russell, of<br>35 Catchpool Road, Colchester, Essex)<br>The Labour Party Candidate | |

# Appendix C

## British Election Returns

*Compiled by Richard M. Scammon*

This appendix breaks down the results of the 1979 General Election, in percent of the vote and number of seats won, for the regions within England, Scotland, and Wales.

THE UNITED KINGDOM
Showing regions for which electoral
returns are given in this appendix.

NORTHERN

SCOTLAND

CENTRAL

SOUTH WESTERN

EDINBURGH AND
THE BORDER

GLASGOW

NORTHERN
IRELAND

NORTHERN

YORKSHIRE
AND
HUMBERSIDE

NORTH
WESTERN

EAST
MIDLANDS

WALES    ENGLAND

MIDLANDS

EASTERN

CENTRAL
AND
NORTHERN

SOUTHERN
AND
WESSEX

SOUTH
EASTERN

SOUTHERN

SOUTH
WESTERN

OUTER LONDON

INNER LONDON

## Results of the British General Elections, May 3, 1979

| Region | Total | Conservative | Labour | Liberal | Other[a] |
|---|---|---|---|---|---|
| England | 25,971,994 | 12,255,281 | 9,526,838 | 3,876,576 | 313,379 |
| % | | 47.2 | 36.7 | 14.9 | 1.2 |
| Seats | 516 | 306 | 203 | 7 | — |
| London—Outer | 2,510,909 | 1,227,397 | 406,504 | 325,321 | 51,687 |
| % | | 48.9 | 36.1 | 13.0 | 2.1 |
| Seats | 57 | 40 | 17 | — | — |
| London—Inner | 1,170,049 | 466,247 | 552,581 | 112,772 | 38,449 |
| % | | 39.8 | 47.2 | 9.6 | 3.3 |
| Seats | 35 | 10 | 25 | — | — |
| South Eastern | 2,168,241 | 1,240,520 | 521,043 | 383,291 | 23,387 |
| % | | 57.2 | 24.0 | 17.7 | 1.1 |
| Seats | 40 | 40 | — | — | — |
| Southern and Wessex | 2,467,024 | 1,341,703 | 607,596 | 494,435 | 23,290 |
| % | | 54.4 | 24.6 | 20.0 | .9 |
| Seats | 42 | 38 | 3 | 1 | — |
| South Western | 1,887,374 | 962,449 | 483,076 | 418,206 | 23,643 |
| % | | 51.0 | 25.6 | 22.2 | 1.3 |
| Seats | 34 | 29 | 4 | 1 | — |
| Eastern | 2,711,645 | 1,395,268 | 864,797 | 428,222 | 23,358 |
| % | | 51.5 | 31.9 | 15.8 | .9 |
| Seats | 45 | 39 | 5 | 1 | — |
| East Midlands | 2,213,814 | 1,034,050 | 845,742 | 313,557 | 20,465 |
| % | | 46.7 | 38.2 | 14.2 | .9 |
| Seats | 40 | 24 | 16 | — | — |
| Midlands | 2,830,387 | 1,334,079 | 1,135,803 | 323,961 | 36,544 |
| % | | 47.1 | 40.1 | 11.4 | 1.3 |
| Seats | 56 | 31 | 25 | — | — |
| North Western | 3,603,778 | 1,577,534 | 1,530,862 | 471,953 | 23,429 |
| % | | 43.8 | 42.5 | 13.1 | .7 |
| Seats | 76 | 30 | 44 | 2 | — |
| Yorkshire and Humberside | 2,654,731 | 1,044,167 | 1,195,802 | 391,406 | 23,356 |
| % | | 39.3 | 45.0 | 14.7 | .9 |
| Seats | 54 | 19 | 34 | 1 | — |
| Northern | 1,754,042 | 631,787 | 883,032 | 213,452 | 25,771 |
| % | | 36.0 | 50.3 | 12.2 | 1.5 |
| Seats | 37 | 6 | 30 | 1 | — |
| Scotland | 2,916,637 | 916,155 | 1,211,445 | 262,224 | 526,813 |
| % | | 31.4 | 41.5 | 9.0 | 18.1 |
| Seats | 71 | 22 | 44 | 3 | 2 |

| | | | | | |
|---|---|---|---|---|---|
| South Western | 790,867 | 238,797 | 381,469 | 56,750 | 113,851 |
| % | | 30.2 | 48.2 | 7.2 | 14.4 |
| Seats | 17 | 3 | 14 | — | — |
| Central | 558,518 | 150,736 | 261,667 | 28,169 | 117,946 |
| % | | 27.0 | 46.9 | 5.0 | 21.1 |
| Seats | 11 | 1 | 10 | — | — |
| Edinburgh and the Border | 524,600 | 194,748 | 182,824 | 80,263 | 66,765 |
| % | | 37.1 | 34.9 | 15.3 | 12.7 |
| Seats | 12 | 6 | 5 | 1 | — |
| Glasgow | 377,234 | 97,499 | 218,861 | 15,081 | 45,793 |
| % | | 25.8 | 58.0 | 4.0 | 12.1 |
| Seats | 13 | 1 | 12 | — | — |
| Northern | 665,418 | 234,375 | 166,624 | 81,961 | 182,458 |
| % | | 35.2 | 25.0 | 12.3 | 27.4 |
| Seats | 18 | 11 | 3 | 2 | 2 |
| Wales | 1,636,588 | 526,254 | 795,493 | 173,525 | 141,316 |
| % | | 32.2 | 48.6 | 10.6 | 8.6 |
| Seats | 36 | 11 | 22 | 1 | 2 |
| Central and Northern | 645,590 | 235,664 | 228,048 | 101,415 | 80,463 |
| % | | 36.5 | 35.3 | 15.7 | 12.5 |
| Seats | 14 | 7 | 4 | 1 | 2 |
| Southern | 990,998 | 290,590 | 567,445 | 72,110 | 60,853 |
| % | | 29.3 | 57.3 | 7.3 | 6.1 |
| Seats | 22 | 4 | 18 | — | — |
| Northern Ireland | 695,887 | — | — | — | 695,887 |
| % | | — | — | — | 100.0 |
| Seats | 12 | — | — | — | 12 |
| United Kingdom | 31,221,362 | 13,697,923 | 11,532,218 | 4,313,804 | 1,677,417 |
| % | | 43.9 | 36.9 | 13.8 | 5.4 |
| Seats | 635 | 339 | 269 | 11 | 16 |

a Other vote in Britain includes: 584,259 Scottish National party (2 seats); 132,544 Plaid Cymru (2 seats); 191,719 National Front; 39,918 Ecology party; 16,858 Communist; 12,631 Workers' Revolutionary party; 83,601 other. Other vote in Northern Ireland includes: 254,578 Ulster Unionists (5 seats); 70,975 Democratic Unionist party (3 seats); 36,989 Independent Ulster Unionists (1 seat); 39,856 United Ulster Unionist party (1 seat); 137,110 Social Democratic and Labour party (1 seat); 22,398 Irish Republican (1 seat); 133,981 other.

# Contributors

Monica Charlot holds a chair in British political institutions at the Sorbonne, where she was director of the Institut des pays anglophones from 1973 to 1976. The author of several books on campaigning in France and Britain, she has contributed to *At the Polls* studies of both countries, and is coeditor of the *European Journal of Political Research*.

Ivor Crewe is director of the SSRC Survey Archive and codirector of the British Election Study, both at the University of Essex. He has been editor of the *British Journal of Political Science* since 1977 and is coeditor of *Party Identification and Beyond* and coauthor of *The Conservative Victory of 1979* (forthcoming).

Anthony King, an adjunct scholar at the American Enterprise Institute, is editor of *The New American Political System* and author of *Britain Says Yes: The 1975 Referendum on the Common Market*. He is professor of government at the University of Essex and comments on elections for the British Broadcasting Corporation and the London *Observer*.

Dick Leonard has been assistant editor of the *Economist* since 1977 and will direct its European coverage from 1980 to 1982. He was a Labour M.P. representing Romford from 1970 to 1974 and is the author of *Elections in Britain*, coauthor of *The Backbencher and Parliament*, and a contributor to *Britain at the Polls, 1974*.

William S. Livingston is vice-president and dean of graduate studies at the University of Texas at Austin and a former president of the Southern Political Science Association and the Southwestern Social

Science Association. His publications include *Federalism and Constitutional Change, Federalism in the Commonwealth,* and *The Presidency and Congress.*

MICHAEL PINTO-DUSCHINSKY, lecturer in government at Brunel University, is executive secretary of the International Political Science Association's research committee on political finance and political corruption. He is the author (with David Butler) of *The British General Election of 1970* and of *British Political Finance* (forthcoming), as well as a contributor to *Britain at the Polls, 1974.*

SHELLEY PINTO-DUSCHINSKY is a freelance researcher who has lived in England since 1970. Her work has ranged from studies of race relations for the Runnymeade Trust and of politics for *New Society* to script research for London Weekend Television.

AUSTIN RANNEY, a former professor of political science at the University of Wisconsin-Madison and a former president of the American Political Science Association, is currently codirector of the American Enterprise Institute's Political and Social Processes Center. His recent works include *Participation in American Presidential Nominations, 1976; The Federalization of Presidential Primaries;* and *Referendums.*

JORGEN S. RASMUSSEN is professor of political science at Iowa State University, executive secretary of the British Politics Group, and a member of the editorial board of the *American Political Science Review.* His works include *Retrenchment and Revival: A Study of the Contemporary British Liberal Party* and articles in British and American journals.

RICHARD ROSE is director of the Centre for Public Policy at the University of Strathclyde, Glasgow, secretary of the committee on political sociology of the International Political Science Association, and an adjunct scholar of the American Enterprise Institute. His publications include *Governing Without Consensus: An Irish Perspective, Electoral Behavior,* and *Do Parties Make a Difference?*

RICHARD M. SCAMMON, coauthor of *This U.S.A.* and *The Real Majority,* is director of the Elections Research Center in Washington, D.C. He has edited the biennial series *America Votes* since 1956.

# INDEX

A Note on the Book

The typeface used for the text of this book is
Palatino, designed by Hermann Zapf.
The type was set by
Hendricks-Miller Typographic Company, Washington, D.C.
R.R. Donnelley & Sons Company printed
and bound the book, using Warren's Sebago paper.
The cover and format were designed by Pat Taylor,
and the figures were drawn by Hördur Karlsson.
The manuscript was edited by
Claudia Winkler, of the Political and Social Processes staff,
and Anne Gurian, of the Publications staff,
of the American Enterprise Institute.

# Contents of
# Britain at the Polls:
## The Parliamentary Elections of 1974
### Edited by Howard R. Penniman

*Available from*
American Enterprise Institute for Public Policy Research
1150 Seventeenth Street, N.W., Washington, D.C. 20036

# AEI's *At the Polls* Studies

*Australia at the Polls: The National Elections of 1975,* Howard R. Penniman, ed. (373 pp., $5)

*The Australian National Elections of 1977,* Howard R. Penniman, ed. (367 pp., $8.25)

*Britain at the Polls: The Parliamentary Elections of 1974,* Howard R. Penniman, ed. (256 pp., $3)

*Britain Says Yes: The 1975 Referendum on the Common Market,* Anthony King (153 pp., $3.75)

*Canada at the Polls: The General Elections of 1974,* Howard R. Penniman, ed. (310 pp., $4.50)

*France at the Polls: The Presidential Elections of 1974,* Howard R. Penniman, ed. (324 pp., $4.50)

*The French National Assembly Elections of 1978,* Howard R. Penniman, ed. (255 pp., $7.25)

*Germany at the Polls: The Bundestag Election of 1976,* Karl H. Cerny, ed. (251 pp., $7.25)

*India at the Polls: The Parliamentary Elections of 1977,* Myron Weiner (150 pp., $6.25)

*Ireland at the Polls: The Dáil Elections of 1977,* Howard R. Penniman, ed. (199 pp., $6.25)

*Israel at the Polls: The Knesset Elections of 1977,* Howard R. Penniman, ed. (333 pp., $8.25)

*Italy at the Polls: The Parliamentary Elections of 1976,* Howard R. Penniman, ed. (386 pp., $5.75)

*Japan at the Polls: The House of Councillors Election of 1974,* Michael K. Blaker, ed. (157 pp., $3)

*A Season of Voting: The Japanese Elections of 1976 and 1977,* Herbert Passin, ed. (199 pp., $6.25)

*New Zealand at the Polls: The General Elections of 1978,* Howard R. Penniman, ed. (295 pp., $7.25)

*Scandinavia at the Polls: Recent Political Trends in Denmark, Norway, and Sweden,* Karl H. Cerny, ed. (304 pp., $5.75)

*Venezuela at the Polls: The National Elections of 1978,* Howard R. Penniman, ed. (287 pp., $7.25 paper, $15.25 cloth)

*Democracy at the Polls: A Comparative Study of Competitive National Elections,* David Butler, Howard R. Penniman, and Austin Ranney, eds. (360 pp., $8.25 paper, $16.25 cloth)

*Referendums: A Comparative Study of Practice and Theory,* David Butler and Austin Ranney, eds. (250 pp., $4.75)

Studies are forthcoming on the latest national elections in Belgium, Canada, Colombia, Denmark, Greece, India, Italy, Japan, the Netherlands, Norway, Spain, Sweden, and Switzerland and on the first elections to the European Parliament.

## Selected AEI Publications

## AEI Associates Program

The American Enterprise Institute invites your participation in the competition of ideas through its AEI Associates Program. This program has two objectives:

The first is to broaden the distribution of AEI studies, conferences, forums, and reviews, and thereby to extend public familiarity with the issues. AEI Associates receive regular information on AEI research and programs, and they can order publications and cassettes at a savings.

The second objective is to increase the research activity of the American Enterprise Institute and the dissemination of its published materials to policy makers, the academic community, journalists, and others who help shape public attitudes. Your contribution, which in most cases is partly tax deductible, will help ensure that decision makers have the benefit of scholarly research on the practical options to be considered before programs are formulated. The issues studied by AEI include:

- Defense Policy
- Economic Policy
- Energy Policy
- Foreign Policy
- Government Regulation

- Health Policy
- Legal Policy
- Political and Social Processes
- Social Security and Retirement Policy
- Tax Policy

For more information, write to:

American Enterprise Institute
1150 Seventeenth Street, N.W.
Washington, D.C. 20036